Elias C Whitfield   10/02

A Special Gift

Presented to:

Elies

From:

Elies

Date:

12/19/00

Be of good courage, and He shall strengthen your heart,
all ye that hope in the Lord.
—Ps. 31:24

BOUQUETS of HOPE

The Women's Devotional Series

BOUQUETS *of* HOPE

A Daily Devotional for Women by Women

ARDIS STENBAKKEN, EDITOR

REVIEW AND HERALD® PUBLISHING ASSOCIATION
HAGERSTOWN, MD 21740

The author assumes full responsibility for the accuracy of all facts and quotations as cited in
this book.

This book was
Edited by Jeannette R. Johnson
Copyedited by Delma Miller and James Cavil
Designed by Tina Ivany
Interior designed by Patricia S. Wegh
Cover photo by Barbara Peacock/Getty Images
Electronic makeup by Shirley M. Bolivar
Typeset: Minion 11/13.5

PRINTED IN U.S.A.

06 05 04 03 02   5 4 3 2 1

R&H Cataloging Service
Stenbakken, Ardis Dick, 1939-   ed.
    Bouquets of hope, edited by Ardis Dick Stenbakken.

    1. Devotional calendars—SDA.   2. Devotional calendars—women.
3. Women—religious life.   4. Devotional literature—SDA.   I. Title.

                    242.643

ISBN 0-8280-1648-8

O Lord,

you alone are my hope.

—*Psalm 71:5, NLT*

Living in the Rearview Mirror

Therefore, if anyone is in Christ, he is a new creation; the old has gone, the new has come! 2 Cor. 5:17, NIV.

ONE DAY AS WE were driving, my 6-year-old son asked, "Why do you need that?"

"Need what, sweetie?" I asked, not sure what he was asking about.

"*That!*" A little finger came from the back seat and pointed toward the rearview mirror.

"So I can see what's behind me," I replied. *A nice, concise answer,* I thought, but apparently not completely satisfactory for my young questioner.

"Why do you keep looking in that mirror?" He really sounded confused.

"To see what's behind me," I repeated.

A few moments of silence passed. Then, "But *whyyyy?*" This time there was a little whine in his voice.

"Why what, Brandon?"

"Why do you keep looking in the mirror?"

"What have I said before to you?" I asked.

He repeated the answer I had given, then with the wisdom and simplicity that only a child's words can impart, he said somewhat matter-of-factly, "But you're going *forward.*"

I explained that the rearview mirror, as well as the other mirrors, helped to keep me aware of the other cars around so that I could react correctly should I need to change lanes or should an emergency situation develop. However, his words not only caused me to smile right then and there, they have remained with me. How right you are, son; I *am* going forward.

I have found that no period of time causes one to look in life's rearview mirror of "if only" like the beginning of a new year. There are some things I wish I could undo, and many things I had hoped to accomplish this past year remain little more than a to-do item. But that's all behind me now. I cannot—nor should I—ignore the past; neither can I change it. I must not get stuck gazing backward. Instead, with God's help, I can glance at it, learn from it, and focus on the future by recommitting my life to Christ anew this day, and every day this year. A new year—another opportunity—another chance. Truly blessed! Happy New Year!

MAXINE WILLIAMS ALLEN

January 2

God Loves Ewe

The Lord is my shepherd; I have everything I need. . . . Even when I walk through the dark valley . . . you are close beside me. . . . My cup overflows with blessings. Ps. 23:1-5, NLT.

I SOMETIMES WONDER HOW God puts up with us. Face it. How often has God done something incredible in your life, or answered a prayer in an unbelievable way, then the next day you're faithlessly knotted up with worry? I can remember thinking that I'd never forget God's awesomeness in plucking an unknown nurse with latent writing and editing gifts and placing her at a Christian publishing house to help birth *Women of Spirit* magazine. I don't want to tell you how many times since that I've worried, doubted, or wondered what on earth God was up to in my life.

Good thing God isn't surprised by our behavior. What reassures me about this is that God compares us to sheep. Now, little lambs may be cute, but it's not really flattering to be compared to sheep. You see, sheep are dumb. They're timid, defenseless, and easily influenced.

But the great thing about being compared to sheep is that God says He's our shepherd. He claims us! And He takes His job very seriously. Good shepherds watch over their sheep 24/7/365.

A good shepherd is especially attentive when a sheep is cast down. A cast-down sheep is flat on its back with its feet flailing in the air. Ever felt that way? I surely have. It seems that sheep can get cast down on a rather frequent basis. (Hmmm . . . more similarities.)

When shepherds find a cast-down sheep, they talk gently to it as they begin rolling it onto its side and massaging its legs, which have lost circulation. Caressing its face and talking soothingly, the shepherd straddles the sheep, lifts it to its feet, and holds it steady. Wobble-wobble-fall is the routine—but each time the shepherd lifts the sheep back up and steadies it. Staying with the sheep until strength returns to its legs, the shepherd then leads it gently home. That's what God does for you and me! I'm glad He is my shepherd—I need that kind of caring.

Are you cast down? Are you frightened or worn? Jesus, your good shepherd, is right by your side. In your exasperated condition you may not sense Him, but listen closely—He's talking soothingly to you. He's there to lift you up, to steady you, to restore your soul.

HEIDE FORD

The Amen Corner

But when you pray, go to your room, close the door, and pray to your Father, who is unseen. Matt. 6:6, TEV.

WHAT DO YOU THINK of when you think of a church? Steeples, organs, and stained glass windows? People have different ideas of what the ideal church should look like. Some people thrill to the sight of a cathedral, while others prefer a small, comfortable chapel. The important thing about a church, though, is not what it looks like on the outside, but what's going on inside.

With that in mind, I have come to rely on picking my own spots for private worship. When I was a college student, my dorm featured walk-in closets. So I would literally go into the closet to pray. The closet became my private sanctuary, a place where I could be alone with God and my thoughts. It was a haven for me away from the noises and cares of college life.

Today my favorite place to worship God isn't a real church, but I like to think of it as my private chapel. I didn't create it so much as I discovered it.

My chapel is located in an added-on room that I use mostly for storage. It has cans and newspapers for recycling and old garden tools. I found an easy chair that a neighbor had thrown out. The upholstery wasn't great, but it was on casters, and I rolled it home, threw a blanket over it, and put it in the corner of the storage room.

At first I used the chair to read in. Then I discovered that I could sit in it with a notebook and write my journal. One day when I came home and felt too exhausted to read or write, I sought out the comfort of my corner and just sat there and prayed. I had finally found the perfect use for the chair.

That was when I got into the habit of going to the "amen corner" after dinner every night. Now I keep devotional reading material next to it and a pad of paper to write my own observations. Sometimes I pray aloud, seated in my chair. Sometimes I'm so angry that I complain to God. Other times I feel so miserable that I cry before Him. But I know He's always there to meet me in the amen corner.

GINA LEE

January 4

Birthdays Are Precious Memories

You made my whole being. You formed me in my mother's body. I praise you because you made me in an amazing and wonderful way. What you have. done is wonderful. . . . You saw my bones being formed as I took shape in my mother's body. . . . All the days planned for me were written in your book before I was one day old. Ps. 139:13-16, ICB.

A S I PASSED ANOTHER milestone on my journey through life I did some reflecting on God's goodness toward me. Having a birthday in January helps me start the new year off right. As I reflected, I prayed:

How wonderful, Lord, to be blessed with yet another year of life! Thank You for all Your goodness toward me during these past years. I want to thank You for all my friends who helped celebrate this year with me, and for my family who remembered this was a special year. I am so thankful to be alive and experience good health. I am thankful for my job; my comfortable home; my family; my wonderful husband; my church family. For the peace I have, living in America, I am very grateful. For the privilege of worship—openly, with others—whether it be at home, church, or work. I'm thankful for Your Word, which brings comfort, guidance, direction, and correction.

I am glad You still allow me to sing and praise Your holy name! You are my God, my Maker, and my King. Help me always to serve You fully and completely. May I always put my trust in You as my shield and protector, my sustainer and guide. For You alone are worthy of praise! Please give me a portion of Your grace and mercy for today. Fill me with Your Spirit. May I love You more by the end of each day throughout this new year. Change my heart, O Lord. Make it ever true. May I be like You!

Guide my thoughts, helping me to be more positive each day, to encourage those around me. Help me be Your hands, feet, and lips this year. May my life reflect Yours. May I always see You in everyone with whom I come in contact and be reminded You died for them, as well as me, so we all can have eternal life. I love You, Lord. Amen.

LOUISE DRIVER

Lacemaking

Rejoice in the Lord alway: and again I say, Rejoice. Phil. 4:4.

MY FRIEND LESLIE MAKES lace. Not the ordinary, pretty, want-to-have lace, but delicate bobbin lace and the even more delicate Old Irish carrickmacross lace. With her unusual skill, her fingers spin the thread to form designs of intricate patterns. She also creates her own uncommon lace pattern. One that looks as delicate as frost is an enhancement of carrickmacross, aptly named carrickmafrost. The finished product is uniquely beautiful. Her artistry is made to last as each thread is tied in its fashion. With each tie, strength is formed, belying its fragile appearance.

Leslie's singular work has won her acclaim as an American lacemaker. A few years ago four lacemakers in the United States were chosen to have a postage stamp bearing their design—she was one of this elite group.

She gifted me with a special piece of her artistry. The design is a butterfly made into a lapel pin. It's perfectly feminine. I consider it a treasure.

God gave Leslie a unique ability, one that blends patience with artistry. Her craft takes countless hours to perfect, yet she finds great peace as she produces her work. It is a joyful time for her. Leslie wants the owner of each piece to appreciate its beauty and to care for it gently.

As I feasted my eyes on the gift she gave me the other day, I thought, *God is like that: He takes such care in creating us women as a gentle, delicate sex. Yet He ties us in such a way as to give us unusual inner strength—a strength not always obvious—like lace.*

As I compared lacemaking and the words of Philippians 4:4, I realized, indeed, that God has tied us to His heart. He wants our beauty to last. He desires us to rejoice in Him. "Rejoice in the Lord alway."

The wonderful part of God's lace making is that we can be His lacemakers too. Sharing His love with others is indeed a tying of heart threads.

With whom will you share your spiritual lacemaking today?

BETTY KOSSICK

I Never Knew You

Not everyone who says to me, "Lord, Lord," will enter the kingdom of heaven.
. . . Then I will tell them plainly, "I never knew you. Away from me, you
evildoers!" Matt. 7:21-23, NIV.

AN IRISH PLAYWRIGHT, who was visiting with me, invited me to accompany him to the opening night of a prestigious production in London.

As we talked together in the foyer, a familiar figure came toward us. I beamed in recognition and put out my hand. In that instant I realized that I had made a mistake. I covered it up by introducing my friend, and the two men had a brief conversation about their shared homeland.

When the older man left, my companion turned to me and said, "I didn't know you knew ——— ," naming a well-known television personality.

"I don't," I said. "He just looked so familiar that I thought I did."

We laughed a lot about the incident during the evening, imagining the personality wracking his brains to remember who the mad Irishwoman could have been, but I felt foolish and more than a little embarrassed.

My children, when I told them the story, wondered how I could have made such a mistake, but I explained that I had grown up with this man. He was on television often, and my parents were great fans of his. I made the mistake of thinking that because I knew his face, I knew the man. Of course, I didn't.

As I thought about the incident I was reminded that one day I could face much more than mere embarrassment—I could face annihilation. If I have made the mistake of thinking Jesus knows me, just because I recognize His face, but I do not have a close personal relationship with Him, I may hear those dreadful words, " I never knew you. Away from me."

We don't get to know Jesus by being spectators in church. We get to know Him by talking to Him, reading His Word, and spending time with Him, not just once a week but every day. If we do, we will be able to spend eternity with Him because we will carry out His commission and one day hear the thrilling words "Come, you who are blessed by my Father; take your inheritance, the kingdom prepared for you since the creation of the world" (Matt. 25:34, NIV).

AUDREY BALDERSTONE

My Influence

And whether one member suffer, all the members suffer with it; or one member be honoured, all the members rejoice with it. 1 Cor. 12:26.

I HAD INVITED GUESTS FOR the evening meal, and now it was late afternoon, time to finish preparing it. The curry had been cooked the day before so that the flavor would be right, and the apples were already baked. Before I began preparing the rest of the meal, I decided to send e-mail congratulations to a family member who was celebrating his fiftieth birthday. As I was almost finished, the phone rang. Since I am a novice with the computer, I decided to finish, in case I lost my file. But the phone kept ringing, so I hurried into the other room to answer it. In my haste, I took a step past the phone, pirouetted around, slipped, and crashed down onto my ankle. The pain let me know immediately that my ankle was cracked.

I answered the phone while sitting on the floor. I needed help, but my husband was out visiting in the village, so I rang a few homes with no success. I then prayed that he would come home, and my prayer was answered immediately.

When medical examinations confirmed that I had a broken ankle, my husband alerted the guests to delay their arrival, since I was still at the medical center. Because a friend was leaving for the United States the next day, we did not cancel the meal.

A slow recovery followed that eventful evening. Since I am a senior citizen, other members of my body did not adjust immediately to the extra work they had to perform because of the broken ankle. At first I had to keep my leg elevated; when it was not, my foot ached and my toes turned purple. My left leg objected to the extra burden; my shoulders ached from the crutches; the palm of one hand blistered; my lower back ached; and the tendons in my foot suffered.

My situation illustrated Paul's verse in Corinthians. Other people are influenced by defects in my character and suffer as a result. I would like my influence to bring my friends much joy and happiness, allowing them to be able to rejoice with me as a result. I don't want to be the fractured member causing distress!

JOY DUSTOW

January 8

I Am a Woman God Can Use

I am the Lord's servant. Luke 1:38, NIV.

D EAR GOD, GIVE THE translator the right words so that Your message can be passed on," she prayed. *Oh yes, Lord, do give me the right words. Help me concentrate, and use me. Let me be Your channel of communication.* We were kneeling for the silent prayer, and the whispered prayer of the women's ministries director reflected my desire. Ardis Stenbakken, world women's ministries director, had come from Washington, D.C., to a gathering of women's ministries leaders in Germany, but she would be with us for only a very short time. I had been asked to translate the sermon. She had been assigned two hours to present anything she had to say. I knew it would be hard to keep going for two hours, particularly as I was suffering from exhaustion anyway and having problems concentrating on even easy tasks.

As Ardis started to speak, I shifted into the translation mode. She spoke, and I translated. I seemed to know what she was going to say before she had finished, so I picked up speed and got into the rhythm of her speech. I was astonished at the ease with which the words came to me. I never knew exactly what I would say before I opened my mouth—I didn't even try to think about it. All I did was open my mind and let God use me. It was as if I were standing somewhere at the sidelines, watching what was happening. I knew it was God who was working through me. All through that morning I did not get tired or lose my concentration.

At the close of the meeting the women came to thank me for the good job I had done in translating. All I could say was "Thank you, but it was not my effort—God gave me the words. I was just a communication channel He used."

This experience has been an encouragement to me ever since. It has made it clear to me that I am a woman God can use. For me it was a modern miracle like the one at Pentecost at which God made it possible for people to hear God's message in their own language. Knowing that translation is one of the gifts God has given me, I have done it quite a bit. But this experience was something extraordinary, something special, because I could feel how everything I said came to me as a gift from God. God can, and will, use us if we allow Him to do so.

HANNELE OTTSCHOFSKI

16

A Recipe for Prayer

Therefore confess your sins to one another, and pray for one another, so that you may be healed. The prayer of the righteous is powerful and effective. James 5:16, NRSV.

IT WAS 2:30 A.M., January 7, 1997, and I couldn't sleep. My thoughts wandered to the tartan plaid recipe box with index cards my niece Tiqua gave me for Christmas. I wrote the names of 30 family members and friends on individual cards and placed them inside the box. Beginning the following night, I'd randomly select a card and pray especially for that person. I had read about someone doing this and the blessings they had received. My anticipation at the prospect of a more satisfying and full prayer life cheered me as I fell asleep.

What happened next was inspiring, faith-building, and chilling. The first night I had selected my oldest niece, Yesenia, the daughter of my brother, Kevin. Extending myself in heartfelt prayer for her felt good.

Kevin's card was next; I was actually in tears on January 9, 1997, as I praised, pleaded with, and wrestled with God to continue to spare my brother's life until he gave his heart to Jesus. How merciful and kind the Lord had been to keep Kevin these 33 years, in spite of himself. Although my heart ached for my only brother and youngest sibling, I rejoiced that each day of his life represented another God-given opportunity for salvation.

Then Kevin was violently killed on January 10. After the initial shock, unbelief, and grief, I remembered God's divinity, mercy, and grace in allowing me, just the night before his death, to intercede in prayer on his behalf. Fear and amazement seized me each time I reflected on this.

How comforted our family was—and still is—because of God's omniscience in allowing me a final opportunity for intercessory prayer the night prior to Kevin's death.

"We won't know the result of that prayer until we get to heaven," my mother said.

What I do know is that my prayer life has never been the same as I now pray for more than 55 individuals and organizations. And the list is still growing. An added blessing occurs when I sometimes phone the individual and have prayer *with* them instead of *for* them. For me, this is the perfect recipe for prayer.   LAVERNE HENDERSON

Quick Answer to the Prayer

God has surely listened and heard my voice in prayer. Praise be to God who has not rejected my prayer or withheld his love from me! Ps. 66:19, 20, NIV.

IT WAS CHRISTMAS VACATION of my eighth-grade year. Letters had been sent home from the school saying that all bills for my sister and me must be cleared before we returned to the school.

We planned that on the day we returned to school Daddy would go to the bank and then to the school by bicycle. Mommy, my sister, and I would come later by bus and meet Daddy there.

As planned, Daddy went to the bank and withdrew the money, got on his bicycle, and headed for the school with the bag of money hanging over his shoulder. However, unknown to him, several men had seen him withdraw the money and had followed him. They tried every means possible to get hold of the bag. They even sprayed some dirty white substance from behind. Thinking that it would dirty his shirt, Daddy took the bag down from his shoulder and tied it on the front of the bicycle. As he continued pedaling, it happened—the men punctured his bicycle tire. In the instant it took him to check the tire, the bag disappeared.

Not knowing what to do, Daddy still continued toward the school. When we met, he told us what had happened. We were shocked and didn't know what to do either. Daddy still met the school officers and tried to tell them his problem, but they told him he would have to get the money. Only then could we be permitted to continue in school.

With a sad heart and many tears I returned home. I was very worried because I had to write my tenth-level board exams. I was personally praying. Then we as a family cried and prayed to the Lord to show us the way. The next day Daddy was able to borrow 1,000 rupees and took me to school.

I thank God for helping me financially. Because of Him, I have come this far and am involved in my professional course. I'll soon be finishing, by His mercies.

Lord, we do not always understand why some things happen. But we praise You that we are never rejected, nor do You withhold Your love from us. We praise and thank You.

PHULMAH TUDU

January 11

Only at Home

And when we had taken our leave one of another, we took ship; and they returned home again. Acts 21:6.

I HAVE ALWAYS BEEN fascinated by faraway countries. When I was about 8, I made up my mind that I would go off and visit every single one of them.

But now I was bored; only two hours of the five-hour layover at the Cairo International Airport had gone by. On my way back to Maxwell boarding school in Kenya after a wonderful Christmas break with my family in Cyprus, I was stuck on a hard, yellow plastic chair in the cramped transit lounge. Around me were people who looked just as exhausted as I.

Then I noticed a scruffy, middle-aged man at the door. He carried a well-worn briefcase and a duffel bag, stuffed to the limit. After scanning the room, he headed my direction, sat down near me on one of the slick plastic chairs, and started up a conversation. He had a couple days' stubble on his face, a warm smile, and a funny accent. I learned that he was a jack-of-all-trades on his way to Sudan, but his main profession was that of a sailor. He had started out at 15 as a cabin boy, and from there quickly rose in rank to second in command. He told of visiting many exotic and exciting places—India, Mombasa, and Japan.

Taking a bottle of whiskey and two small glasses from his briefcase, he offered me a drink, but I declined. I don't think he realized he was offering a drink to a 13-year-old. As he drank, he told me about his family. His tongue became loose. He told me he was divorced, and his children shunned him. He had nothing left. He told me how he hated his wife for taking away his children and hurting him. Now all the lightheartedness was gone from his voice. He was a bitter, lonely man. All the years of adventure and seeing the world did not matter anymore.

Two hours later, as my flight was announced, I promised to pray for him. He gave a slight snort; in his eyes I could see hopelessness. As my plane was taking off, I thought about our conversation. I still wanted to go out and see the world, but I had learned that no matter how far I travel or how many exotic places I visit, home and family is where I will find my peace and joy. If I am not at peace and happy there, I will never find peace, joy, or beauty anywhere.

SUSAN JEDA ORILLOSA

January 12

Blizzard

Strait is the gate, and narrow is the way, which leadeth unto life. Matt. 7:1.

THE MORNING WAS CLEAR and cold, but the forecast called for a winter storm to hit later in the day. Sure enough, an hour before we were to
leave for the weekend, the snow began—fast, furious, and with a vengeance.
A few minutes later my daughter-in-law called to warn us they were experiencing the same blizzard, and there was no hope of the snow letting up. This
meant we would be driving right into the storm.

Not wanting to miss our first grandchild's first birthday, my husband and
I said a quick prayer, gathered up a few emergency items, and set out to meet
the storm head-on.

The weather proved to be all that was predicted and more. We soon discovered we would be traveling on an unplowed interstate highway. Ever alert
to our surroundings, we inched our way through the deepening snow and
slush, passing numerous cars in the ditch. We were especially happy to be
owners of a trendy sport utility vehicle. We were also happy that our usual
two-hour trip took only three hours and was rather uneventful.

Expecting our grandson to be asleep when we arrived, we were thrilled to
find not only our son and daughter-in-law waiting expectantly, but our
grandson as well. As he stretched out his infant arms, blue eyes sparkling, I
was the first to receive Trevor's radiant smile, a smile that lighted up his entire face, generating happiness all around him.

Holding that precious baby, did we regret the perhaps foolish decision we
had made to brave the elements to be with family? Not for a moment! And
being snowed in for the next two days gave us more time to play with our
grandson and visit with our family. We quietly praised God and enjoyed the
time together.

Each of us is facing another trip, and we must each decide for ourselves if
we are willing to take the risk involved. The trip may be long and tedious,
filled with obstacles. However, it's a trip I want to take, whatever the cost,
and when at last I reach my heavenly destination, I hope to see the smiling
face of each member of my family and each friend so that we may all rejoice—together forever.

PAULETTA COX JOHNSON

Preparation

Watch therefore; for ye know not what hour your Lord doth come. Matt. 24:42.

AS 1999 DREW TO A close, many people, including my husband and I, were preparing for the millennium bug. Millions of dollars had been spent worldwide as companies worked to make sure their computers were ready. The catchword as the weeks ticked by and the countdown to the year 2000 continued was "Is your company Y2-compliant?"

Commercialism ran riot. The shops had a field day selling millennium safety packs. What did we all do? We bought candles and matches, in case the electricity failed. We bought spare batteries for our flashlights, in case the electricity failed. We had our gas bottles filled so we could still cook, in case the electricity failed. We stocked up on canned food, in case the supermarkets closed. We filled bathtubs and bottles with water, in case the water supply failed. We took extra cash out of the bank, in case the ATMs failed. The banks assured everybody there really was no need to do this, but the element of doubt remained.

And so by New Year's Eve there was the feeling that as much as possible had been done in preparation for the Y2K bug. Then the whole world, it seemed, partied into the new year. Television had universal coverage as the new millennium came to every country. And the dreaded Y2K bug? It was a false alarm. Aircraft didn't drop out of the sky, the lights stayed on, and water came out of the taps.

There is a major event coming to this world of ours that will not be a false alarm. The second coming of Christ is imminent; and I'm sure once more there will be universal TV coverage. But in spite of being given so many warnings in the Bible, the world parties on, "eating and drinking, marrying and giving in marriage" (Matt. 24:38). How much preparation are we making? We don't have to purchase candles, food, and batteries. We don't have to stock up on water, and we don't have to worry about money. There are no safety packs to buy, because God's gift of eternal life is free. I pray God will help us all to make the right preparation. LEONIE DONALD

January 14

Confusion in the Parking Lot

I [the Lord] will instruct you and teach you in the way you should go; I will counsel you with My eye upon you. Ps. 32:8, Amplified.

ONE WINTER EVENING I drove a friend to the airport to catch the last flight to Chicago. Pulling in to the parking lot, I glanced at my watch. We had 15 minutes to spare. He grabbed his duffel bag, and I picked up his briefcase. Together we rushed to the departure gate. Suddenly he stopped short. He had left his ticket in the car.

"Give me the keys," he urged. "I'll race back and get it."

"The car's not locked," I reminded him as he dashed off.

A few minutes later he returned, shaking his head. "It is locked." I knew it wasn't, but there was no time to debate the issue. I handed over the keys. He came back shortly with ticket in hand and a rueful grin on his face. "I was trying to get into the wrong car," he admitted.

There were indeed two black Cherokees, parked side by side. But the differences were obvious—to me. "How could he have made that mistake?" I asked the cold moonlit night. "The other car is brand-new. It has neither the dents nor the rust bubbles that decorate my jeep. Mine has gold-colored running boards; the other one doesn't."

But as I listed the differences, I remembered a similar thing had happened to me several months earlier. I, too, had tried to get into someone else's car, simply because one of the same color and size as the one I had rented was parked in the same area. There are differences, it finally occurred to me, that are obvious only to full-time owners. Especially at first glance.

Sometimes as we rush along on life's journey we become confused by look-alikes. But our Creator and Redeemer will never be confused. He made each one of us, numbering the very hairs on our heads. Then He redeemed us with His blood. He knows the difference!

God, thank You for Your loving watchcare. You know what makes us unique. Turn Your face joyfully upon us and grant us peace. GLENDA-MAE GREENE

The Transformation

And be not conformed to this world: but be ye transformed by the renewing of your mind, that ye may prove what is that good, and acceptable, and perfect, will of God. Rom. 12:2.

IT WAS A VERY BUSY morning with all the household chores I had to do, including windows to wash. The sun was hot, and the wind was blowing. I was worn out when the jobs were done. I needed a boost, something to buoy my spirit. I was long overdue a visit to the hairdresser.

As I waited my turn, I watched the women coming in. Some were young; some older. Some fat; others slender. Most looked tired and worn, others looked depressed. But all came to lift their spirits and beautify their hair. There was also a variety of hair types, but once the shampoo woman had washed their hair and the hairdresser took over—it was wonderful to watch the transformation.

It's strange that some who had curly hair wanted their hair straightened. Those with straight hair asked for curly perms. Some wanted their hair color changed, and a few asked for just a cut or trim.

I have tried to change my hair myself, but I'm useless and hopeless on my own. I need a professional to do the job. We women care passionately about how we look, even putting our health on the line at times to meet an ideal "beautiful me."

The hairdresser's job done, she removed the shoulder sheet and held up the mirror so I could check my hair from all angles. What a transformation! The way I walked and acted as I exited the salon revealed that I felt like a new person.

How much more important is the transformation only God can make in an individual's life. No one can make changes in her own strength. When the Spirit of God takes possession of the heart, it transforms the life. Sinful thoughts are put away, evil deeds are renounced. Love, humility, and peace take the place of anger, envy, and strife. God forgives our sins and transforms our lives.

When He transforms us, the way we walk, talk, and act will show that we are indeed made new. How wonderful to be a daughter, transformed to His likeness.

PRISCILLA ADONIS

January 16

Forgiveness Demonstrated

Forgiving each other, just as in Christ God forgave you. Eph. 4:32, NIV.

SHE WAS NON-CHRISTIAN, illiterate, old, wrinkled, and withered. She was also scantily clad. As we walked to the clothing storage room that nippy January morning, I noticed slashlike scars extending from the tops of her bare feet nearly to her knees. Pointing, I asked, "What happened here?"

The woman looked pensively at the jagged scars. Then, slowly and quietly, she explained. She had been working for the wife of a very wealthy merchant. Although her people adhered to one religion and her mistress to another, she had been well treated and was happy. For some time the difference in religions did not seem to matter. That is, not until unbelievably ugly animosity developed between the two religiopolitical groups.

"Every day homes in our neighborhood were looted and vandalized," she told me. "Some of our neighbors were injured, some slaughtered. Actually, madam, there was blood in the streets." She described how some neighbors had fled across the border. But her mistress didn't want to leave. She had been born in the city. Her husband had a good business. "And my mistress could not take me with her because of religion—that was the whole problem," she sighed. "Day by day my mistress became more and more distressed," the little woman continued. "One morning when rioters were just outside in the street and the shouting and crying were hideous, my mistress seized a big knife and began slashing my feet and legs."

I shuddered as the woman continued. "I crawled away. I was sick a long time." After a lengthy pause, the woman remarked pensively, "My poor mistress. I don't know what happened to her. I never saw her again."

I tried to comfort her. "I'm sorry. I'm so sorry you have had so much trouble and pain." Then I blurted out, "But your mistress! To have slashed you so brutally!"

The woman in front of me was feeble, but her voice was warm and loving. Without one hint of animosity she responded, "Never mind, madam; my mistress didn't know what she was doing. She just didn't know."

It was like an echo that had endured for centuries—"Forgive them; for they know not what they do" (Luke 23:34).

Non-Christian? I had received far more than I had given!

LOIS E. JOHANNES

Trusting God in the Affairs of Life

Commit thy way unto the Lord; trust also in him; and he shall bring it to pass. Ps. 37:5.

HAVING HAD SOME financial difficulties, I was behind in paying a very important bill. I did not know where the money would come from to meet that payment, or the following month's payment.

My sister, who lived in another state, had been very ill, and I had been traveling frequently to be with her and to help put her affairs in order. This was very costly, and before I knew it this bill was in arrears.

One evening while I was talking to a friend on the phone, we were praising God, thanking Him for His power in our lives and for my sister's improved health. I happened to mention the bill.

"Our Father takes care of our needs," she responded emphatically. She suggested that I call my creditor and explain my position. Together we prayed that God would intervene on my behalf, that He would have His person there to receive my call.

Apprehensive, embarrassed, and ashamed to call, I procrastinated, but finally made the call.

God did have a person there to receive my call. The customer service representative was interested in not only the agreement but also the well-being of my sister. We spent a little time talking about God's healing hand on my sister, who had survived a brain aneurysm and was improving daily. Not only was that month's bill deferred, but also that of the upcoming month, with no additional interest. The CSR said to put a little more with my following month's payment—this would get me back on track.

I was reminded once again that we can trust God in all our affairs. He has His person waiting to do His will.

JUNE E. MORGAN

Chasing Shadows

And I have put My words in your mouth; I have covered you with the shadow of My hand, that I may plant the heavens, lay the foundation of the earth, and say to Zion, "You are My people." Isa. 51:16, NKJV.

WE RECENTLY ACQUIRED SUGAR, a mixed Chihuahua-dachshund. Previously, we had had older male dogs, each of whom had developed disabilities: one blindness, one deafness, and one a heart condition. Shortly after we mourned the loss of the last one, the humane society called to say they had a Chihuahua. As she bestowed her little doggie kisses on each of us, we fell in love with this seven-and-a-half-pound miniature and brought her home.

The first week she was glued to my lap, apparently grieving for her previous owners. The second week she decided that maybe it was all right to lie in the sun on our bed. She played with her food before she ate it, and I wondered if she had ever had toys to play with.

It is difficult to describe the difference between three older dogs with disabilities and this little 1-year-old dog. We had forgotten how fast a little dog can run, how sharp their eyesight and hearing can be. We learned very quickly that Sugar had none of the disabilities of our previous dogs. Whenever she heard neighborhood dogs barking, she responded noisily from her spot at the foot of our bed—even if it was 2:00 in the morning. Understanding why she may have been turned in to the shelter by her previous owners, we nevertheless determined to keep her, even with these defects in her personality.

She will chase anything that moves, especially insects, and is very adept at catching them. One day I noticed that she was chasing something on our kitchen floor. It turned out to be the shadows made by the sun hitting the glass on our bird feeder hanging outside the window. No amount of coaxing could deter her from chasing the shadows.

At first I laughed at her determination to catch something that didn't really exist. And then I thought how like Sugar we are, chasing after material things that will not exist after our Lord returns instead of dwelling on the heavenly things that will exist for eternity. I pray that rather than shadows, each of us will focus on that which endures. LORAINE F. SWEETLAND

The Fertile Pastrami

And in thy seed shall all the nations of the earth be blessed; because thou hast obeyed my voice. Gen. 22:18.

THE NEWS STORY ON television caught my attention. A woman had gone to the emergency room because she was not feeling well and thought she may have gotten food poisoning. She attributed it to the pastrami sandwich she'd had for lunch. However, the findings of the emergency room staff were not what she and her husband had expected.

It turned out that the woman was seven months pregnant and delivered a very healthy baby. What a surprise that must have been to the woman and her husband! What makes this story even more interesting was that the woman and her husband of 11 years had been told nine years before that they would never have children. The reporter telling the story jokingly said, "It was the pastrami!"

I believe the pastrami had nothing to do with it and that God had everything to do with it. His timing is always perfect. He knows what is best for us.

I considered that this was not the first surprise birth to happen. There are some similar situations that can be found in the Bible. Luke 1:31 says, "And, behold, thou shalt conceive in thy womb, and bring forth a son, and shalt call his name Jesus." Mary, the mother of Jesus, was probably a bit surprised when she heard she would have a son in a very unconventional way. And Sarah laughed when hearing she would give birth at 90 years of age. "And the Lord said unto Abraham, Wherefore did Sarah laugh, saying, Shall I of a surety bear a child, which am old?" (Gen. 18:13).

I think I would have been surprised, too. I cannot imagine how many times God has blessed me and I may have not recognized that God's hand was involved. It is so easy to get caught up in the hustle and bustle of this world. It is truly amazing what God can do—more than we can ever imagine. His promises are even more special when little surprises happen—such as the surprise for the woman who ate the pastrami. I think of the fertile pastrami often to remind me that all things are possible with God and that He tends to our needs and wants in His time.　　　　　Mary Wagoner Angelin

A Child of God

He also brought me up out of a horrible pit, out of the miry clay, and set my feet upon a rock, and established my steps. Ps. 40:2, NKJV.

A S I WAS TAKING MY early-morning walk one day I picked up a penny that was very old, cracked, and battered. I thought perhaps it had been run over hundreds of times. But as I looked at it, I knew it was still a penny. It was still recognizable in spite of its deplorable condition. I looked at it again intently and said to myself, *This is a real penny; it is a cent that can make 99 cents a full dollar. Certainly, without a penny, 99 cents couldn't be counted a dollar.*

After musing about its condition, I thought of myself. Wasn't I like that penny, battered by the enemy through temptations, trials, and difficulties? Yes, I had succumbed to many complaints. I had made many mistakes. I had disappointed and displeased my heavenly Father again and again. Oh, how could I deny that time and again I had given in to the enemy's wooing? I had absolutely fallen short of God's glory.

Yes, just like that cracked penny, I had been broken. Satan had tried hard to batter me, hoping to separate me completely from my loving God. But "who shall separate [me] from the love of Christ? Shall tribulation, or distress, or persecution, . . . or peril or sword?" (Rom. 8:35). Thank God, "He . . . brought me up out of a horrible pit, out of the miry clay, and set my feet upon a rock" (Ps. 40:2, NKJV). Like the apostle Paul I can say, "I am persuaded, that neither death, nor life, . . . nor principalities, nor the powers, . . . shall be able to separate [me] from the love of God" (Rom. 8:38, 39).

And now He calls to me—His child, His daughter, His very own. How wonderful it is God has restored my identity! I am His own as a brand plucked from the burning. And I am a part of the beautiful royal family of God.

Dear Lord God, You are such an awesome God. You are so forgiving and accepting. You are so loving and merciful. Thank You for calling me from the world of darkness unto this marvelous light of knowing You. Thank You for putting invaluable worth on me in spite of my deplorable condition. Oh, thank You for not giving up on me. Please help me never to wander away from You again. Amen.

OFELIA A. PANGAN

For Want of a Dot!

I tell you the truth, until heaven and earth disappear, not the smallest letter, not the least stroke of a pen, will by any means disappear from the Law until everything is accomplished. Matt. 5:18, NIV.

I TRIED TO SEND A message by E-mail, but it was later returned saying, "Address Error." I was sure I had it right. But when I checked the source again more carefully, there it was—just one little dot that I had left out. What a difference that little speck of a dot made in my effort to correspond. Besides being a loss of time, it was a frustration to trace down the correct address again in my busy work time, so I postponed sending the message.

I thought of the words in the above verse. In His sermon on the mount, when Jesus explained that He came to fulfill the law, not abolish it, He added the words of today's text—that even the tiniest stroke of a pen is important in His law. I felt a twinge of guilt when I remembered little things I have done or left undone that broke God's law, little things that really matter to our Lawmaker, even though I had not thought them so significant at the time.

I read further into the chapter, discovering what is meant by the "least" and the "greatest," and "righteousness" that surpassed some of the misled leaders in the days Jesus was on this earth. Then I began to understand why the makeup of God's law cannot be changed by even one tiny dot or stroke of a pen, whether added or left out. No, not by me or by you or by anyone.

But you and I needed a Savior, so He came to fulfill the law. And He magnified the law by His obedience to even the smallest part of it, proving that through His grace it could be obeyed perfectly. And He showed us how by example.

How important are the details in our Christian lives! Even the way we obey God's law is important; whether we do it spiritually—in His love and grace—or whether we do it legalistically. Jesus showed us the way, the spiritual nature of His law, making it an eternal obligation with far-reaching principles.

Dear Lord, guide me today as I, by Your grace, follow Your example in how to keep the perfect law of God. BESSIE SIEMENS LOBSIEN

God Knows the End From the Beginning

In my distress I cried unto the Lord, and he heard me. Ps. 120:1.

I NOTICED A WHINING sound coming from my car, but I drove home, hoping it would diminish on its own. Unfortunately, on Sabbath morning it was really loud. As I drove off, I attributed the increased volume to the possibility of the car being cold, since I did not allow it to warm up before I drove away. I was really in denial—I did not want any new bills.

When church was over, I stopped by a service station and asked the mechanic if he had any idea what was causing this horrifying noise. I told him I noticed it became worse as I turned corners, and wasn't sure if I was going to make it home. Something was definitely wrong.

The mechanic said it sounded like the power steering pump was going and gave me an estimate of $180. He asked me to bring it in on Monday, and he would check it out further.

That afternoon I prayed about my car. Sunday morning I decided to walk to a supermarket near my home. The weather was beautiful, and this was the perfect time to talk to God about my car, among other things. I reminded God how I try to make the best of what I have financially, and how I hate pity parties. I begged to be able to maintain my financial freedom.

After returning home I talked with my next-door neighbor, who I knew was looking for a part for his van. I mentioned my car problem of the day before.

"Let me check your power steering fluid," he said, opening the hood.

Sure enough, the power steering fluid was low. When he had put fluid into the car, there was no more noise. "That should be good for another six months to a year," he said.

I thank God for listening to and answering my prayers. I thank my God, too, for the help He sent me through my neighbor. Most of all, I thank God for Jesus, who intercedes on my behalf to my Father. I can talk to Him any time, and He is not too busy to hear and answer my prayers.

God knows, and He watches over His children. A can of power steering fluid costs less than $2. It doesn't get any better than that!   CORA A. WALKER

Feelings, Motives, Thoughts, and Desires

The law of the Lord is perfect. . . . Keep your servant also from willful sins; may they not rule over me. Then will I be blameless, innocent of great transgression. Ps.19:7-13, NIV.

HOW IMPORTANT ARE MY feelings, motives, thoughts, desires, and emotions? This is a question I have asked myself often. We are at the dawn of a new century, a time when personal emotions are treated with great importance; more so, in fact, than just a few years ago. Society is constantly encouraging us to express ourselves and show how we really feel.

We humans judge others based on what we see. If someone cries a lot, we call that person emotional. If someone is easily angered, we tag him or her as being volatile. But God has taught us that we cannot draw conclusions in that manner. God's judgment does not take cognizance only of the outward actions but also of the thoughts and intents, the desires and emotions of the heart.

Human laws deal only with the outward actions. A woman may be a transgressor and yet conceal her misdeeds from human eyes. So long as she is not discovered doing wrong, the law cannot condemn her as guilty.

But God's law goes further; it takes note of the jealousy, envy, hatred, malignity, revenge, lust, and ambition that surge through the soul but have not yet found expression in action. In the day when "God shall bring every work into judgment, with every secret thing, whether it be good, or whether it be evil" (Eccl. 12:14), all these sinful emotions will be brought into account.

Even though I am careful with the exterior part of my behavior, what in my heart or in my mind is more important. Often I try to cover my thoughts and negative feelings because I do not want to give a bad impression. But whom am I kidding? Maybe I can fool some people, but I can never fool God. He is the only one who can judge me, because He can see the whole picture—my inside and outside.

God has given us a wonderful promise: "For it is God who works in you to will and to act according to his good purpose" (Phil. 2:13, NIV). He is the only one who can change my feelings, emotions, motives, and desires. I want to ask Him to do just that.

ELLEN E. MAYR

January 24

Cookie Dough and What's Good for You

And we know that in all things God works for the good of those who love him, who have been called according to his purpose. Rom. 8:28, NIV.

I HAVE TO ADMIT IT: I like to eat cookie dough—maybe even better than baked cookies. I know, they say you shouldn't, but I can't resist. There are even ice creams now that are cookie-dough flavor. As long as I'm confessing, I like cake batter, too. Mmmm, good!

Some think it is the baking that makes the ingredients taste good, as in chocolate chip cookies or a good Snickerdoodle. But I think it is the combining of the ingredients. Have you ever tried eating plain flour? Or a nice big tablespoon of shortening? It is revolting to think of it. The sugar or the chocolate may be tolerable in small amounts, but the eggs? No, thanks. And keep the soda or vanilla. But mixed together, it's right tasty, baked or not.

There can be a problem sometimes, however, when an ingredient is left out. I remember the time I forgot the eggs when making egg roll wrappers. Bad news.

The ingredients not only need to be combined, they have to be the right ones, in the right amounts, and even in the right order. I once tried to mix the salt into bread dough after the dough was all mixed and kneaded. Not easy!

There is a text that has bothered many people. It talks about all things working together for good (Rom. 8:28). I may think, *What I am going through right now can't be God's will. How can this be good for me?*

Taken by themselves, many things are not good: death, illness, divorce, betrayal, abuse—the list can go on and on. How can they be good for me? By themselves, they may not be. But when put all together, as part of God's total plan for my life—His molding of my character—they can be beneficial. God may be training, strengthening, and preparing me for greater challenges or ministry in the future. Or He may be supporting me through something from which I can learn that, when put all together with other events in my life, is really for my good.

Thank You, Lord, for mixing the ingredients of my life for my best good. I trust You for today and always.   ARDIS DICK STENBAKKEN

There's No "Left" in Heaven

*Now I know it's true that God doesn't respect one person more than another.
. . . Anyone who loves Him and does what is right, He accepts as part of His
people, no matter what nationality or race he or she belongs to. Acts 10:34, 35,
Clear Word.*

I FIRST USED THE WORDS "left" and "right" when learning to put my
shoes on the correct feet. At first I didn't know which shoe was which, but
I could tell by the feel. If they were comfortable, all was well. Does left and
right matter? Yes, when it comes to fit and comfort!

My next exposure to left and right happened when I went to boarding
school. The boys sat on the right side during chapel and church services, and
the girls sat on the left. Seating arrangements and chaperons were mandatory
for "character insurance"! Does left and right matter? Maybe, when it comes
to making wise decisions or maintaining order.

Twenty years later I had a more disturbing experience with left and right.
Queen Elizabeth and the duke of Edinburgh were scheduled to arrive at a
public park in Yellowknife. They had come to celebrate the centennial of the
Northwest Territories in 1970. I was excited about getting a close-up view of
the royal couple. Yellowknife isn't a big metropolis, as is Montreal, Toronto,
or Vancouver, where one would have to use binoculars to see their smiles.

My friend and I arrived early to get a choice seat. As we waited, I
glanced around at the expectant crowd. Suddenly my eyes focused on a mi-
nority group seated to the left and behind us. I had never experienced segre-
gation before. Why did it happen? How did it happen? I don't know. There
were no posted signs to designate the seating arrangement. For the first time
I experienced a truth. There will be no *left* in heaven. The American Indians
of the Far North had back seats, while we—whoever we were!—had the seats
closest to the roped off area where the royal couple would walk, nod, wave,
and greet us.

Jesus didn't promise Mrs. Zebedee choice positions for her sons, James
and John, when they got to heaven. He has reserved a place on His right for
each one of us. We'll all have equal status in heaven, but we must first learn
to intermingle with one another here. Does position or status matter?
Definitely not in the eyes of Jesus!   EDITH FITCH

January 26

An Answered Prayer

Can a woman forget her sucking child? . . . yea, they may forget, yet will I not forget thee. Isa. 49:15.

I WAS BORN OUT OF WEDLOCK. At the time of my birth my father and mother had already parted, so I was raised by my father and grandmother. I also had a brother (we didn't have the same mothers) whose mother would often come to visit and sometimes even take him with her for weekends or holidays. I remember crying and wondering when my mother would come for me. She never came, and no one ever said anything about her. My childish thoughts told me she didn't want me, so I became very angry and bitter toward my mother.

In spite of all my bitter thoughts and feelings, God was still leading. He gave me several special people who had a positive influence on my life. I will always be grateful to them.

Then it happened! One day I received a letter. I was stunned and shocked. Words cannot adequately describe the rush of emotions I felt. For the first time in my life I had heard from my biological mother. She related her story and apologized for abandoning me. I had mixed feelings: I didn't know whether to be happy or angry. One thing I was sure of—I wanted to see her.

My biological mother came into my life at a time when I had lost my grandmother, who had been a real mother to me. I discussed the matter with my father, who finally explained everything. Now I faced a dilemma. I had to make a choice. I could either forgive my mother or reject her. I prayed earnestly and remembered how God always forgives me. When I finally met my mother, she bore visible signs that life had been tough for her.

I thank and praise God that He never forgot about me. I am praying that God will give me a heart to really love and accept my mother, because He saw my tears and answered my prayers of 25 years. Now I, too, have a chance to be with my mother.

Through this painful experience I learned that because God loved me through my father and grandmother, by their example I can also learn to love my mother. Believe me, it might take days, weeks, months, and even years, but God does answer prayer.

God, You have been faithful. I put my trust in You and, just as You promised, it is good to draw near to You.

DEBRA MATSHAYA

Surgery, Anyone?

Finally, brethren, whatever things are true, whatever things are noble, whatever things are just, whatever things are pure, whatever things are lovely, whatever things are of good report, if there is any virtue and if there is anything praiseworthy—meditate on these things. Phil. 4:8, NKJV.

I ONCE HEARD A STORY of two little boys who were taking part in an experiment. The first boy was placed in a large room filled with all sorts of toys. He picked up one after another, playing with each for only a moment before discarding it for the next. Soon he was hunched against the wall, totally bored. When the researchers came for him, he shared his disgust.

The other boy was placed in a room of the same size. But in this room there was just a huge pile of horse manure and a pair of gloves. The little boy wiggled his nose, put on the gloves, and started digging through the manure. He dug and dug until he was exhausted. But he kept at it. In fact, he was still digging when the researchers opened the door. When they asked what he was doing, he replied, "With all this horse manure, I figured there just had to be a pony in here somewhere!"

Wow! What an attitude. So often I concentrate on the negative, the things that have gone wrong or may go wrong. The mistakes I've made. The hurts and sorrows endured. The things I don't like.

Why can't I think about the positive? All the things that have gone right? The blessings—big and small? the good things I've done? the good things others have done for me? the joys I've known and have yet to know?

Our God is so very good. Let's not throw away the toys He gives for our enjoyment. And when we walk through a valley that's filled with horse manure, let's look for the pony. After all, as Christians we know for certain that we have far more than the very best pony awaiting us. We have life eternal with our Savior, filled with joy beyond our imagination.

It's so easy to be negative. Let's pray continually that God will give us attitude surgery. He can carve away the negative and fill us with the true, the noble, the just, the lovely, the virtuous, and the praiseworthy.

DAWNA BEAUSOLEIL

January 28

What Is This in My Mouth?

For he shall give his angels charge over thee, to keep thee in all thy ways. Ps. 91:11.

AWAKENING UNUSUALLY early one morning, I decided to relax for a change and enjoy a leisurely breakfast before going to work. In order to lose weight, I had begun eating my main meal in the morning, consisting of an entrée, vegetables, salad, and even dessert. In this way, the calories would have all day to burn.

Often too busy to enjoy reading, I sat at the table enjoying an article while soft, beautiful music played in the background. And instead of my usual pattern of rapid eating to get out quickly, I took a different route, chewing slowly and savoring every morsel.

While enjoying this pleasurable atmosphere, I felt something strange in my mouth that was not food. It felt comfortable but unusual. Curious, I reached into my mouth and pulled out a diamond-shaped piece of glass, razor-sharp, with very tapered points on each end. It had lodged itself between a tooth and the gum, with one point extended upward. One more bite would have sent the glass into the gum, splitting it, or possibly becoming embedded inside.

In utter dismay, I looked at the glass. Where had it come from? How did it get on my plate? Then I remembered. The day before, while I was putting away the food after preparing a meal, a heavy glass blender had fallen onto the floor, breaking into a thousand pieces. Evidently a very small piece had popped into the refrigerator and into the bowl holding the green beans that I had for breakfast that morning. How I thanked God for saving me from utter tragedy!

This did not happen by accident. By His divine providence God had allowed me to wake up earlier than usual, to have a leisurely breakfast, to relax so completely, and to chew ever so slowly.

His word is true: "The angel of the Lord encampeth round about them that fear him, and delivereth them" (Ps. 34:7). His promise is sure: "For he shall give his angels charge over thee, to keep thee in all thy ways" (Ps. 91:11).

We can trust Him.   AUDRE B. TAYLOR

Friends Forever

My command is this: Love each other as I have loved you. Greater love has no one than this, that he lay down his life for his friends. John 15:12, 13, NIV.

THE FORMAL VISIT TO the mission school was over, and Sarai and I had to return to Apia, Western Samoa, that evening. Just as the meeting with the staff was over, I was called to the telephone. I immediately recognized the voice on the other end. It was my friend Falesoa. She had specific instructions for both Sarai and me.

She said, "Flo, a taxi will be there at 2:00 p.m. to pick you up from the transit flat. Pack all your bags and come. We will take you to the airport."

"Where do we go from the flat?" I asked.

"The driver knows—just hop on and relax."

We could not imagine what was in store for us, but when we arrived at the Deluxe Café, our friends Falesoa and Emma had purchased food and drinks. We boarded Emma's minibus and drove to a special park, had lunch, and reminisced on what had transpired in our lives since last we were together at Fulton College, Fiji, in the late 1970s.

Because this was my first visit to American Samoa, the women had wanted to show me true island love and care. A combination of all sorts of tours, sightseeing, and visiting with friends followed. We did not get to Western Samoa that evening. Emma and Soa booked us into a hotel and later took us to a special dinner at Emma's residence. At the end of that dinner, we each received a special gift—something that neither of us could have afforded back at our respective missions—a women's devotional book.

As I experienced that special care and love from my wonderful friends, Emma and Falesoa, I was reminded of God's special love for us. He gave me that one best thing He had—His Son. Each time my children sing the song "Love Is the Flag That I Fly From the Castle of My Heart," it affirms that God resides there. I am convinced that love breaks barriers and binds our hearts together. He bids us to love one another because He first loved us and gave Himself for us. And when we love through caring and sharing, we show that God is in us.

FULORI BOLA

January 30

In the Secret Place

He that dwelleth in the secret place of the most High shall abide under the shadow of the Almighty. Ps. 91:1.

THERE ARE TIMES WHEN life overwhelms me. I feel that I can't handle any more. Trials, disappointments, and sorrow seem to come all at once or one after another. How can I cope?

I came across the ninety-first psalm one day as I was reading my Bible. I was so amazed by the words of this psalm that I learned it by heart. Now when days are rough, this psalm gives me comfort in my trials and tribulations, for it speaks of dwelling in the secret place of the Most High. I can't just visit there when I'm caught in a crisis—I must dwell there.

In life we are all going to be tempted at one time or another. We're all going to have days when we feel that we've been tried more than we can bear. But if we dwell in the secret place of the Most High, Satan cannot lead us astray, for this psalm assures us that if we dwell there, God's truth shall be our shield and buckler. We have nothing to fear.

"Thou shalt not be afraid of the terror by night," it says (verse 5). And as we read further we find that God also promises that no evil shall befall us and that angels shall bear us up, "because thou hast made the Lord . . . thy habitation" (verse 9). He does not promise that we shall not know trouble, but He says, "I will be with them in trouble, I will rescue them and honor them. With long life I will satisfy them, and show them my salvation" (verses 15, 16, NRSV).

The precious promises in this psalm are conditional, as is much of Scripture. Still, I've decided that I want to meet the conditions. Not next week, or tomorrow. I want to dwell in the secret place of the Most High today, don't you? I know that's the only way I can dwell with Him forever in heaven. So no matter what life throws at me, I will stay close to Him.

That is why I love the ninety-first psalm—especially when life really gets tough. It keeps reminding me that as long as I dwell in the secret place of the Most High, my Father in heaven will be there for me. And one day I will see Him, face to face. What a precious promise.

Thank You, Father, that in Your secret place I have comfort, rest, and peace. Help me to dwell with You forevermore. Amen.   PAM CARUSO

Waiting Styles

Awaiting eagerly the revelation of our Lord Jesus Christ. 1 Cor. 1:7, NASB.

I WANDERED THROUGH THE nearly deserted airport. Ticket counters, shops, and restaurants were closed. I sat down on a bench at gate A-l to await Ron's arrival.

The plane was 90 minutes late. To pass the time, I began to people watch. Soon I was absorbed in the idea of the different kinds of waiting styles people exhibit in an airport.

A young man to my right studied a book, perhaps cramming for coming exams. A thirtysomething woman to my left relaxed with a paperback novel, oblivious to the rest of us. Another woman was jotting down a list in a small notebook. I wondered if it was her shopping list, a list of invitees for a party, or her to-do list for the next day.

A teenage girl paced the area, went outside, came back in, and went out again. At last she sat down beside me for about 30 seconds, then got up again to pace. Two young women who came together with pop in their hands made themselves comfortable in an unused corner and began to laugh and chat. The wait was a chance for a party. Three men stood at the bank of video screens the whole time, waiting for the announcement to appear that the plane had landed. A woman with gray hair lay down on a bench and closed her eyes for a nap. An older couple sat down beside me and began to criticize the man who was cleaning the floors.

Yet another woman, seemingly more anxious than any of us, went to the rope that separated the waiting area from the expected route of deplaning passengers and stood there, eyes fixed on the far-off gate, waiting for the first sign of her loved one.

It seems to me that I see the same attitudes in those waiting for the second coming of Jesus. Some have their mind on studies, and some on work. Some get impatient, while others sleep. A few become critical, while others party and enjoy the wait. Some stare at the signboards, while others watch. A few keep their eyes fixed on the gate.

So engrossed was I in my people watching that I didn't notice the rope was down. Several passengers walked by before I turned my eyes to the gate, wondering if I had missed my beloved. A moment later I saw him, and my heart felt warm at the sight. It was worth the wait. DOROTHY EATON WATTS

February 1

Fully Covered!

Blessed is he whose transgressions are forgiven, whose sins are covered.
Ps. 32:1, NIV.

A WOMAN ASKED ME if it ever snows where I come from. Just like me a few years ago, snow is something she had read about in books and heard others talk about but had never seen or touched.

The first time I experienced snow was in British Columbia, Canada, on my way to the public library. The softly falling snowflakes were so light and delicate on the palm of my hand. I gazed in awe as these feathery wonders of nature continued to come down, covering the sidewalk and the lawn. I folded my umbrella and whirled around like a little girl who has just received an incredible surprise. I turned my face upward to let the snow touch my face. I was totally oblivious of my surroundings—I was savoring every moment of my new experience. When I noticed that my hands were awfully cold, I came to myself and looked around me. Complete transformation! Gone were the pieces of paper, candy wrappers, pop bottles, dry grasses, brown leaves, and dead twigs. Everything was white! What a different world!

I remembered the song "Covered with His life, whiter than snow." I hummed a few phrases. Then I realized it was no longer a song that I sing because it sounds appropriate. Suddenly it held a new meaning. The trash that littered the lawn was like the sins that cluttered my life. But my Redeemer came to cover me with His own life. What an amazing act of love!

King David must have known how wonderful and exhilarating it feels to be forgiven! He exults, "Blessed is the man [or woman] whose sin the Lord does not count against him [her] and in whose spirit is no deceit" (Ps. 32:2, NIV).

The snow melts when winter is over, and once again the unsightly trash is uncovered. But not so with the life that covers me. It is an eternal covering, because He who covers me is eternal.

I feel so blessed! I could whirl around again like a little girl who has just received an incredible surprise. I have. Praise God! MERCY M. FERRER

I Want to Go Home!

Do not let your hearts be troubled. Trust in God; trust also in me. In my Father's house are many rooms; if it were not so, I would have told you. I am going there to prepare a place for you. And if I go and prepare a place for you, I will come back and take you to be with me that you also may be where I am. John 14:1-3, NIV.

AFTER MORE THAN 50 years of pastoral ministry within the confines of a single conference, my husband and I have made the big move—sold our first retirement house, trekked 500 miles north, put our belongings in storage, and begun the monumental task of building a house in a wholly new area, finding a new church, and making new friends.

God's leading was evident in the sale of our house, the move, and the purchase of a lot in a new location. Our son and his family, who lived near our new home-to-be, have welcomed us into their home as we begin the building process. We are delighted to have time to bond more closely with our grandchildren. Yet a vague sense of displacement and homelessness persists. I long for a place where I belong.

The other day a wave of great longing for my familiar house, church, neighbors, and friends swept over me. I put my head in my hands, and tears welled up behind my closed eyelids. *Lord, I want to go home! I want to go home!* I cried. *I can't bear this, Lord. I need my home.*

Adulthood immediately took over. *How silly to feel like this,* I decided. *Surely I'm mature enough to realize that soon I'll have a home again. Why this great desire for home?*

As I looked up, the cover of my son's CD caught my eye. It pictured five men, backs to the camera, gazing expectantly into the sky. God spoke to me through that picture. I realized that the greatest longing of my heart was not for my old home—or even a new one—but for my eternal home, for Christ's return to earth to take us all home to live with Him forever. I began to see that my longing for home was not an evidence of immaturity, but rather Holy Spirit implanted to help me realize the impermanence of earthly dwellings contrasted with the glorious eternal home Jesus has prepared for me.

My heart cry, along with the apostle John's, is "Even so, come, Lord Jesus!"

CARROL JOHNSON SHEWMAKE

February 3

Finding Peace Within

Little children, . . . sin not. And if any man sin, we have an advocate with the Father, Jesus Christ the righteous: and he is the propitiation for our sins. 1 John 2:1.

IT WAS A BEAUTIFUL day in February. There was not a cloud in the sky. The sun was shining brightly, and a soft breeze was blowing. I felt especially thankful to be alive. I was expressing my gratitude to God that I now resided in Florida, "the Sunshine State." Then my girlfriend called. "My husband and I are going orange picking. Would you like to come along?"

I've always wanted to go orange picking. Since this would be my first experience, I accepted without a second thought. Fifteen minutes later I was picked up, and we were joined by four other friends. We all had a great time picking oranges and filling our bags. The owner was not around but trusted us to leave the money for the number of oranges picked.

As we were leaving, my friends stopped to pick some lemons. I was helping pick lemons when I observed, in the middle of the lemon trees, an orange tree facing the sun, laden with golden oranges. I said to myself, *These oranges must be better than the ones I already have.* So I proceeded to pick them.

My friend's husband called out to me. "No, do not pick from that orange tree! Permission was given only to take freely of the lemons."

Nevertheless, I yielded to the temptation and picked a couple more, in spite of the warning given. *Why was that tree placed in the middle of all those lemon trees facing the sun by the exit road?* I wondered. My mind went back to the Garden of Eden and God's command to Adam and Eve: "Of every tree you may freely eat, but of the tree in the midst of the garden thou shalt not eat thereof." That tree interested Adam and Eve more than all the trees in the garden. We're now living in a sin-sick world because of their disobedience.

All the way home I pondered over the fact that I had yielded to temptation; I was overwhelmed with guilt. I, too, was disobedient, and I asked God to forgive me.

Lord, I am once again so thankful that I have an advocate with the Father, Jesus Christ the righteous, who alone gives peace within. Forgive us of our sins once again.

DOLORES SMITH

42

What a Trust

Those who trust in the Lord are like Mount Zion, which cannot be shaken but endures forever. Ps.125:1, NIV.

I SAT AT THE DEPARTURE control area at the Banjul airport, waiting for my delayed flight that would take me to Accra, Ghana, for a conference.

"*Ça va?*" A woman spoke to me.

I told her that I couldn't speak French. The smile on her face disappeared, but she didn't give up. "I am traveling to Conakry, but I am so afraid. This is my first time flying, and I have never entered any *avion* before."

Even though she was struggling to speak the little English she knew, I was able to assure her that all would be well, and God was in control. Later, she started to smile again and said, "*Mon amie,* will you help me and guide me till I get to Conakry?" I continued to try to reassure her and tell her that I would help her. From our conversation, I learned that she had traveled with friends by road to visit her husband, who was working in Banjul, but he had insisted that she return by air.

This woman followed me wherever I went until we took our seats in the plane. She even followed me to the bathroom. What a trust! When we landed in Conakry, I unfastened her seat belt for her, and before she disembarked she embraced me wholeheartedly. "*Merci beaucoup,*" she said. "God bless you, and I will never forget you." We both wiped away tears as we waved goodbye.

As I watched her go it dawned on me that if a person in distress over her first flight can put all her trust in a stranger like me, then why do I waver in my trust in God? I have known God since I was 4, and He has kept me through thick and thin. Yet I fail to trust Him completely. I realized that day that we need the kind of faith the French woman has that made her trust me without any doubt.

From now on, I will lift up my eyes unto heaven from where my help comes and trust God all the time, just as *mon amie* did, even though she did not know who I was.

MABEL KWEI

February 5

Cataract

Give light to my eyes. Ps. 13:3, NIV.

ABOUT 10 DAYS BEFORE my scheduled cataract operation the pastor called. "Could you serve as organist for the next church service? Our organist is not available."

"You know that I haven't played for years because of my eyesight. I just can't see the notes," I replied.

Because it would be a sad Communion service without music, the pastor promised to try to find somebody else to play, but to no avail. He called me again, and I promised to try.

When the church service was about to start, I went to the organ and pulled out the stops. I put on my glasses and looked at the hymnbook. I could not make out a single note—it was just a gray blank. I put my glasses away; they wouldn't help. Panic seized me. What had I got myself into? What if I wouldn't be able to play? Had I been presumptious? In my panic I prayed, "Lord, if You want me to play the organ today, please help me see the notes."

The first hymn was announced. At that moment the music in the hymnbook was surrounded by a bright glow, and I could distinguish every single note! I played the hymn and sat down to thank God for His help. The same thing happened with every hymn. After the service, when members of the congregation thanked me, I said, "Thank God for His help!"

Two days later I went to the hospital for a preliminary checkup before my cataract operation. As the doctor checked my eyesight I could see only the big letters on the top of the chart. "Can you read anything?" the doctor asked.

"Hardly anything lately," I replied. Had I realized how bad my eyesight really was I would never have tried to play the organ. Only now, after the successful operation, when I see how bright the world can be, do I realize in what darkness I had lived recently.

Jesus took my pitiful possibilities and performed a miracle to bless His children with music. "Apart from me you can do nothing" (John 15:5, NIV). By myself it was impossible, but God gave light to my eyes because I offered Him my little gift in simple faith. I thank Him in awe for showing me again that He is willing to help every day.

HILKKA ROUHE

Pray Without Ceasing

Pray continually. 1 Thess. 5:17, NIV.

PRAY WITHOUT CEASING. Impossible? Yes and no. After we have read a few Bible texts and prayed our usual dear-God-please-bless-and-guide prayer, do we rise from our knees, mentally rubbing our hands together, and saying to ourselves, "Now that the daily devotions are taken care of, let's get to work."

All too often that is our attitude. Like the superstitious person who carries a good luck symbol in their purse or pocket, we tend to feel that we have paid our respects to God, and now it's up to Him to care for us during the remainder of the day.

Brother Lawrence was a sixteenth-century monk who held the lowest position in the monastery hierarchy: he spent his days in the kitchen scouring pots. In those times of cooking over open fires and with no modern cleaning aids, Brother Lawrence's job was dirty, boring, and tiresome. But Brother Lawrence smiled and sang as he worked.

"How do you remain so peaceful and happy when you spend all your days alone at such a task?" visitors to the monastery asked.

"I practice the presence of God," he replied.

What a simple yet profound answer. We know that God is watching over us, but if we practiced becoming aware of His presence every moment of every day, what a difference it would make in our home, workplace, and community. There would be no more complaining, arguing, boasting, hasty words, nasty gossip, cruel jibes, or judgmental innuendos coming from our corner.

With God there right beside us, what a difference it would make in our attitude. There would be no need to pray without ceasing—we would be sharing every moment of our lives with One who knows us best, loves us most, and offers us His overcoming power.

I want to practice Your presence all of this day, enjoying communion with You, whether I'm washing pots and pans or managing a company. With You, I look forward to a good day. GOLDIE DOWN

Lord, Help Me!

He will call upon Me, and I will answer him; I will be with him in trouble; I will rescue him, and honor him. Ps. 91:15, NASB.

I WAS DRIVING HOME FROM work one night on a busy highway when I noticed a slow moving tractor-trailer ahead of me in the fast lane. I increased my speed to overtake him in the slow lane. When I was almost past, the truck began to move into my lane. I tried to gather more speed so that I would not be crushed against the guardrail. When I thought I was clear of the vehicle, I heard a loud bang.

The truck had hit the back of my car and was now propelling me across the road in front of it, over the edge, into the grassy, tree-lined median strip that had a ditch at the bottom. I realized the car was out of control as I went over the bank, and that I was in big trouble. "Lord, help me!" I screamed out in panic. My mind raced—I knew that any moment could be my last, and I committed myself to God. From that moment on, I know for a certainty that the angels guarded me. With much sliding over bushes and crashing against trees, the car eventually came to rest in the ditch. Miraculously, the car had not rolled over. I was conscious, and the engine was still running. I turned it off and managed to get out of the car. The trees had smashed the windows, and the undercarriage was wrecked. To my utter amazement, I did not appear to have any cuts or scratches or broken bones.

When the police saw the wrecked car and determined what had happened, their unanimous comment was "You must have someone looking after you, because you should not be alive." The next day the insurance assessor made the same comment.

I had a medical examination to make sure there were no hidden injuries. The doctor was amazed to find there was no evidence of injury from my accident—not even a mark from my seat belt.

My car was wrecked, but I was untouched. I firmly believe that when I called for help, God sent His angels to preserve my life. Surely He does not forget us when we cry out to Him. I believe He had a purpose in saving my life, and, by His grace, I want to do His will daily.

ANNE TINWORTH

A Second Chance

I will come like a thief, and you will not know at what time I will come to you.
Rev. 3:3, NIV.

AT ABOUT 1:00 IN the morning, in Irkutsk, eastern Siberia, we were awakened by loud banging on the door. We were ordered to leave immediately because the hotel was on fire. As we hurriedly dressed, my husband told me to put on a warm jacket. I grabbed my handbag, containing all our documents, and we ran out to join the throngs of people scurrying down the stairway.

The atmosphere was electric. Outside the hotel it looked like a war zone. The police, firefighters, ambulance drivers, paramedics, and news reporters were galvanized into action, while bewildered hotel guests stood around not knowing what to expect. We could see no flames or smoke. It had been raining earlier in the evening, and it was now freezing cold. We tried to avoid water puddles as the police cordoned off the area and rushed us across the road. I couldn't believe this was happening, but I felt no panic. I found myself studying the people around me.

An elderly woman shivered as she stood in a thin T-shirt. My husband took off his jacket and placed it around her shoulders. Other women were in nightgowns and bedroom slippers. Some cried and begged the police to allow them to go back into the hotel to retrieve documents and valuables. Terror etched some faces, while others overcame their nervousness by talking nonstop. Some stared blankly, as if they had given up hope. With hindsight, I am amazed at the calm I felt. I am sure it was because I had prayed before going to bed and asked for the Lord's protection.

My thoughts drifted to another scene—the second coming of Christ. I imagined a scene fraught with much more emotion, panic, fear—and even rejoicing. There will be no going back to fetch anything; our passports will be our characters, and our clothes will be robes of righteousness. We will either be ready or unprepared—nothing in between. There will be much weeping and panic and terror that words cannot describe. In contrast, there will be joy and relief unlimited.

"Even so, come, Lord Jesus."

FRANCES CHARLES

Idle Words

Put not thine hand with the wicked to be an unrighteous witness. Ex. 23:1.

THOMAS THEODORE WAS one feline in our long succession of many cats. He was very playful, as kittens are. One day he discovered a dried milkweed pod I used in my decorating theme in the living room. It was a new plaything for him, a toy to enjoy. He batted it around the house, up and down, round and round, dragging it in every room. What a wonderful time he was having—until it split open. A milkweed pod can take only so much cuffing, and then the inevitable happens. Those tiny seeds drifted all over the house. The least little gust of wind, the least little hint of air, the tiniest whisper of a breath sent those infinitesimal poufs soaring.

I took the broom after them. I took the dustmop after them. I knelt down on the floor and tried to gather them up, one by one, but only succeeded in setting them afloat again. Thomas Theodore was having a ball, twisting and turning in midair as he jumped and sailed down to earth. He only succeeded in evading those poufs again and again. I put him outdoors, and a few of the poufs went out with him.

I got out the vacuum cleaner, hoping to suck them up. But some even eluded the vacuum cleaner. Then I wondered how to empty the vacuum cleaner safely.

Even though it's been awhile, an occasional stray pouf still dislodges itself from somewhere and floats down through the air, and Thomas Theodore tries to reach it before it settles.

There are several dried milkweed pods I am still using in our decorating theme. It is only a matter of time before that playful kitten discovers them. I am wondering whether to get rid of the milkweed pods—or get rid of Thomas Theodore.

Remember Thomas Theodore and the milkweed pod when you are inclined to spread a morsel of gossip. You can never gather in everything you might have told someone else. Though you might try to squelch a story, there will always be infinitesimal poufs that are never captured, no matter how hard you try.

Lord, please help me to say something nice about a person, or to control completely the desire to say anything at all.   LAURIE DIXON-MCCLANAHAN

God's Plans—My Plans

*Many, O Lord my God, are the wonders you have done. The things you
planned for us no one can recount to you; were I to speak and tell of them,
they would be too many to declare. Ps. 40:5, NIV.*

AS I OFTEN DO, I was taking my mother and my uncle to lunch at one
of our favorite places which is near a Christian bookstore I needed to go
to. As I exited the freeway, I was thinking that right after lunch I would go to
the bookstore, make my purchases, and then take my uncle back to his residence. Suddenly, almost as though someone turned the steering wheel of my
car, I found myself in the outside lane, where I was forced to turn the corner
leading to the bookstore. So I decided to go ahead and run my errand first,
and then we would go to lunch. My mom and uncle agreed that that would
be fine.

As I looked around the store, one of my dear friends, the mother of one
of my former students, came in. As we greeted each other she told me she
hadn't even planned to come into the store either, but was going next door to
one of the offices. When she saw my car, she recognized the license plate and
knew it was me, so decided to come in.

As we visited she asked if I knew anyone who might have an old hymnal
she could buy for her daughter, who now lives in another state. She said she
just couldn't afford a new one, but her daughter had indicated she would love
an old hymnal that had the songs she was familiar with.

In that instant, before I could even think what I was saying, I responded,
"Let's just go buy her a new one." I told her I would buy the hymnal if she
wanted to mail it to Melissa, and that is just what we did. It was so exciting
for both of us.

Melissa was thrilled to receive the hymnal, and I was thrilled that the
Lord directed her mother and me to go to the Christian bookstore at the
same time. That had not been in our plans at all that day, but He knew where
we needed to be to fulfill His plan for Melissa to have that hymnal that has
brought her so much joy.

We can never go wrong when we follow God's leading in our lives.

ANNA MAY RADKE WATERS

February 11

Great and Precious Promises

Great things doeth he, which we cannot comprehend. For he saith to the snow, Be thou on the earth. Job 37:5, 6.

THERE'S SOMETHING ABOUT freshly fallen snow that whispers a message of beauty, purity, and peace. However lovely it may be, though, I can only gaze upon such a glorious sight for a limited number of weeks before wondering if I'll ever see green grass again.

Looking forward to a short trip out of town lifted my spirits as I made travel plans. *What good timing for a change of scenery,* I thought as I headed down the highway to the sound of crunching snow beneath the tires.

When I returned home after my mini vacation, I couldn't believe the transformation. My mind had to adjust to what my eyes were seeing. Almost every bit of snow had disappeared. In a short time, God, through His book of nature, unfolded a comforting lesson.

Although weather may be different in various areas of the world, this planet is subject to its extremes. Each continent has its season of harshness. But there is one thread of commonality everywhere—whatever the weather is at the moment, it's temporary.

I gaze with wonder at my green lawn, replaying memories of past winters. I understand anew that no matter how severe it may seem at the time, one day this winter will pass away and spring will arrive. I'm reminded, too, that present trials weighing heavily on my mind now will one day pass like winter. Then hope, like springtime, will come, melting the problems of yesterday and giving way to new beginnings.

This world seems to be in a constant state of winter anguish, tossed by storms of strife and fear, seemingly frozen in that mode. When I think of it, oh, how I wish Jesus would come! If I find myself becoming impatient, I try to remember God's promises. For as surely as the seasons change, the God who never changes will come. Then the harsh winter of the times in which we live will end. The seeds of hope once planted in our hearts will blossom into a never-ending springtime. His promise, like the promise of spring, is sure.

MARCIA MOLLENKOPF

March Praise

Day after day I was there, with my joyful applause, always enjoying his company, delighted with the world of things and creatures, happily celebrating the human family. Prov. 8:30, 31, Message.

WHAT A DAY TO praise the Lord! God is so full of His love and goodness. How can I not praise the Lord? Out my window I'm seeing the nature and beauty of winter—barren branches sway gracefully as the wind passes through them. The sun is peeking through the clouds, waiting to burst the universe with its rays. The squirrels are jumping from tree to tree, chasing each other, playing tag. They leap out to the edge of the weak, feeble branch, gently bouncing in delight.

Ah, that is what God wants me to do: bounce with praise when I'm in His presence. Bouncing with gladness and joy. *I'm in love with You, heavenly Father.*

At the bird feeder the cardinals, mourning doves, and finches come to feed on Dr. Weiss's feed, the best in the country. That reminds me that Jesus provides the best feed for me in His special love letter to me, the Bible. Oh, how God delights in loving me; in spite of all my blotches, He loves me. Oh, how I praise Him for His loving character!

I read, "He waits with unwearied love to hear the confession of the wayward and to accept their penitence. He watches for some return of gratitude from [me], as the mother watches for the smile of recognition from her beloved child.

"He would have [me] understand how earnestly and tenderly His heart yearns over [me]. He invites [me] to take [my] trials to His sympathy, [my] sorrows to His love, [my] wounds to His healing, [my] weakness to His strength, [my] emptiness to His fullness" (Ellen G. White, *Thoughts From the Mount of Blessing*, pp. 84, 85).

That's what I long for! My heart and soul hunger after You! In Jesus' name, amen.

MARY MAXSON

February 13

Daisies and Roses

The grass withers and the flowers fall, but the word of our God stands forever.
Isa. 40:8, NIV.

IT WAS A VERY special and romantic occasion. Other wives might have received bunches of red roses. My husband, Bernie, however, brought me a bunch of mixed flowers, including some simple yellow-and-white daises. At the time we had very little money as we struggled to pay three sets of school fees, house payments, and the mechanic who tried to keep our cars on the road.

Even at our most economically challenged times, Bernie found the occasional bunch of flowers for me in an old-fashioned flower stall at our local English market. Quite often he will surprise me with a simple bouquet to show his appreciation, and it always thrills my heart.

But on this special occasion, even though the flowers were pretty, something in me still felt a little saddened to have daisies and not roses. I wondered how long we would go on struggling to pay school fees and buying clothes in hand-me-down charity shops. Bernie found a vase (and even that was broken, so we had to be sure not to fill it above the crack line), and I arranged the flowers. They were certainly very pretty, several different kinds of blossoms with a heart decoration in the middle of the bouquet. Still, no matter how I arranged them, they would never be red roses.

I thought about the red roses Bernie had sometimes brought me. They might look beautiful for a day or two, but their heads often drooped, no matter what I did to rescue them, and usually the rosebuds never opened up into full flowers. After a few days I would hang them up-side down to dry, saving the petals for weddings, potpourri, or craft projects. But this simple bunch of daisies lasted for five weeks. I kept the vase filled with water, pinched off the occasional dead flower, and still they looked almost like new. By the time I finally threw out the flowers, I was more than glad to have been given daisies instead of roses!

How often God gives us something that may seem less than ideal or is not what we had in mind, and yet, as time goes by, we grow to appreciate His loving wisdom more and more. The day will come when we can truly say that even though we hoped for roses, God's daisies were even better!

KAREN HOLFORD

Unto One of the Least of These

And the King will answer and say to them, "Truly I say to you, to the extent that you did it to one of these brothers of Mine, even the least of them, you did it to Me." Matt. 25:40, NASB.

IT WAS VALENTINE'S DAY. As soon as I picked up her flowers, I was meeting Mom for lunch. As I fidgeted at the flower shop counter, a frail, thin woman hesitantly stepped beside me. "Excuse me," she said to the overwhelmed clerk. "Do you have just one extra daisy? I'm sorry; I don't have any money," the woman pressed. "I wondered if you had one small daisy. I just wanted one daisy for my daughter," she finished softly.

"Well, they'll be $2.50 each, and we're really very busy now," the clerk snapped.

The woman slowly backed up, then quietly turned and left the flower shop. I watched her leave and impatiently turned to see if my flowers were ready. Then it hit me. *"What was I thinking? Where was my Christian brain? What was $2.50!* I silently prayed for forgiveness and for another chance.

On the way home after a wonderful lunch I stopped for gas. After filling the tank, I went inside to pay. An elderly man stepped up to the cashier and said, "I'm on pump 4."

"That'll be $12," the cashier said.

The man nervously looked around. "I wasn't watching close, and I meant to stop at $10—that's all I have," he said as he handed the clerk a wrinkled $10 bill.

The clerk let out a noisy sigh and said, "I need two more dollars."

Obviously flustered, the elderly gentleman said, "Maybe I could phone my daughter."

By now more people had come in to pay for their purchases. Behind the elderly man stood a teenager with two small gold rings in his left eyebrow. The teen took out $2, laid it on the counter, and said, "Here, man; this help?"

The visibly relieved older man could only say "Thanks!"

"No problem," replied the teen.

Then it hit me again: "Unto one of the least of these . . ."

SUSAN WOOLEY

February 15

One February Morning

A cheerful heart is good medicine, but a crushed spirit dries up the bones.
Prov. 17:22, NIV.

I SNUGGLED INTO MY cocoon of blankets on the couch in my uncle's apartment and stared out at the leafless trees. I didn't want to get up. I couldn't face more decisions. And besides, there was nothing to eat for breakfast. Earlier in the week my sister and I had cleaned out the refrigerator, and yesterday we had finished up what was left of our grocery purchases.

It was a frustrating and sad time. The frustrations had begun several days earlier when my flight between Calgary, Alberta, and Washington, D.C., had been delayed 32 hours. The sadness had begun long before that. Two months earlier, in December, my uncle had checked into the hospital for surgery. He never returned. Now my sister and I had come to attend to his burial and to clean out his apartment.

The frustrations and sadness continued throughout the week. There was a multitude of people to meet and even more decisions to make. What should we do with his shirts, jackets, and ties? Where were the addresses of his friends who were to receive the valuable artwork that decorated his walls? How should we dispose of the furniture that the secondhand store didn't want? Where was the library, so we could return his long-overdue books? When could we fit in an hour with the lawyer? And underlying all our activity was the ache of losing our well-loved uncle, someone whose thoughtfulness had brought us joy as children, and whose sharp humor had brightened our adult lives.

Well, I thought, *I can at least deal with this one carton.* According to the customs' label it contained "two books." It was my unopened Christmas present to my uncle. But I had also enclosed a decorative tin. I couldn't remember what was in it.

As I pried off the lid, my sister, a dietitian, walked out of the bedroom. "I'm really tired," she said with a sigh, "but we've got to keep working." Her face lit up as she saw what I had in my hand. "Caramel corn!" Then her eyes twinkled as she said in her most professional voice, "We can have it for breakfast. You know it's a whole-grain cereal!"

Energized by our laughter, I pushed aside the blankets, and we began to plan our day.

DENISE DICK HERR

54

Hot Cinders

Before they call I will answer; while they are still speaking I will hear.
Isa. 65:24, NIV.

IT WAS WINTER, and our house was situated about halfway up a mountain in a beautiful setting of surrounding forest in southwest Virginia. My four young sons and I were preparing to have evening worship when we noticed that the fire in the fireplace had gone out and the room was getting cold. My husband was out visiting church members, so Greg, then 12, and I decided to clean the ashes out of the fireplace ourselves and restack it with wood. The fireplace had a handy clean-out trap, so we started shoveling the ashes into the trap.

"Greg," I instructed, "go outside, open the trap, and scrape all the ashes out."

He did as instructed, not realizing that some of the ashes we had dumped along the side of the house were still hot. We stacked the fireplace and sat down for family worship. Our two Scottish terriers, Love and Bobo, curled up on the boys' laps as I began reading.

We were reading a story about God's protection, how He sometimes sends angels in disguise. The boys begged me to read another story. In the background we could hear the gentle crackling of the fire in the fireplace. After a while we heard a knock at the door and wondered who would be out there in the dark. I answered the door, the boys clustering behind me.

"Mrs. Cruz, do you know you had flames leaping up the side of the house just outside the chimney?" It was a neighbor's son, home from college to visit his parents. He was passing our house on his way farther up the mountain.

Using the lights from his car, he'd been able to find the garden hose and turn on the water to put the fire out before he even knocked on our door. We all ran outside to see what had happened, but the fire was already out. I offered to pay the young man, but he refused to take money. We thanked him for stopping, and then he went on his way.

We went back inside the house, knelt in a circle, and thanked God for sending someone just when we needed help. Yes, God does answer before we call! Praise the Lord!

CELIA MEJIA CRUZ

February 17

Fear Not, I Am With You

Call upon me in the day of trouble: I will deliver thee, and thou shalt glorify me. Ps. 50:15.

IN FEBRUARY 2000 I was traveling by myself from Botswana to Harare, Zimbabwe, where I had gone to conduct a women's ministries leadership training seminar. Then I had some business to do in Lusaka, Zambia.

One of the highways I was using passes through a game park for more than 60 miles (100 kilometers). And there are many elephants along the way. I must admit that I fear elephants. I had been advised that when I found elephants crossing the road, I should just park the car and wait until they have crossed. If I found them on the side of the road, I should just slow down.

I found many elephants grazing along the side of the highway, and at one place about seven elephants were crossing the road. I parked the car about 160 feet (50 meters) away and waited nearly 20 minutes before they finally crossed. As soon as the road was clear I continued my journey. This made me wonder why I had decided to use the road that goes through the game park with so many elephants.

After driving for about 30 minutes, I saw an elephant that was walking toward me, right on the tarmac. It was a very big elephant, and it was walking majestically. The advice I had been given before I began my journey was about precautions I should take when I met elephants on the side of the road or when I came across elephants crossing the road. No one had told me what to do when I found an elephant walking right on the road toward me.

I prayed earnestly to the Lord, asking Him to deliver me from the elephant. *Lord, no one told me about this. I am frightened; I don't know what to do. Please help!*

I began claiming these promises: "I will be with you when you go out and come in" (Ps. 121:8) and "Call upon me in the day of trouble: I will deliver thee, and thou shalt glorify me" (Ps. 50:15).

When I approached the elephant, it raised its ears and trunk. I held my breath, swerved the car to avoid hitting it, and passed on safely. Indeed, the elephant did not attack me, and I glorified my God for His protection and deliverance. He is the God of mountains—and elephants.

PRISCILLA HANDIA BEN

56

A Free Ticket

Here is a trustworthy saying that deserves full acceptance: Christ Jesus came into the world to save sinners—of whom I am the worst. 1 Tim. 1:15, NIV.

The February weather was unseasonably warm for Vermont. Our daughter was only 2, walking and talking and interested in everything. Our sunporch windows not only let in the welcome sunlight, they also warmed the mud wasps. Soon one was flying around the room. Before I realized it, Kathy had been stung. It hurt for only a while, but I was determined not to let that happen again to our precious little girl.

Later in the week Kathy and I drove to town to buy our groceries. Sidewalk parking meters were new, but I planned ahead to put money in to cover our parking time. Before I could do that, Kathy was excitedly telling me about "that bug" that was flying around our car. It was another horrid mud wasp! I opened the window to let it out, then opened the door of the car and hurriedly pulled her from her seat. In my hurry to keep her from being stung again, I forgot to put the money in the meter.

After purchasing our groceries, we went back to the car and found that the mud wasp was gone. We also found a parking ticket on the windshield. Since we were a young family and had little money, I felt bad that I had been the cause of using money that we really couldn't afford.

We drove down to the police department to pay the fine. When we went in, Kathy began telling them all about the "bug" that had stung her earlier in the week and about the one in the car. When she finished, they asked me questions about it, and then said, "Since that is what happened, you don't need to pay for the ticket." I was very grateful that I didn't have to go home and tell my husband that I had wasted money for my first-ever parking ticket by failing to put money in the meter.

I laugh now when I think of it, but I'm still grateful to that little girl who saved my day. I like to think she was prompted by our heavenly Father, who gave His Son, Jesus, to die for you and me, and who paid my "heavenly ticket" for me.

LORAINE F. SWEETLAND

February 19

Holy Snow and Wind

Though your sins are like scarlet, they shall be as white as snow; though they are red as crimson, they shall be like wool. Isa. 1:18, NIV.

I will lead the blind by ways they have not known, along unfamiliar paths I will guide them; I will turn the darkness into light before them and make the rough places smooth. Isa. 42:16, NIV.

IT IS WINTER, and snowstorm after snowstorm has dumped snow on the bare ground. Last night we got five more inches. Then the wind came, blowing the white powder into drifts and waves until now the ground looks like a frozen sea. All traces of tracks are gone.

Every day I try to go for a walk in nature. This afternoon I had to rebreak my walking path, for I settle for nothing less than spending time in true nature, away from human interference. I love walking and enjoying the beauty of winter, but I do get tired of having to break paths in the snow after each new snowstorm. It is a lot of work! I start to complain, but then it hits me: Humans are like nature in a winter without snow—bare and naked, lacking goodness, love, and kindness toward others and themselves. As the snow covers the bare ground, so the Lord covers us with forgiveness and love. We then become clean and beautiful like the ground when the snow falls. We mar it many times, but just as the snow keeps coming in winter, the Lord keeps forgiving and covering us all over again if we ask Him.

The new snow over the old always covers all traces of people. The wind wipes away further evidence, blowing snow across my path until it cannot be seen. In the same way, the Lord blows our paths over when we give Him full command. He makes my sins as white as snow; then He creates a whole new path for me to follow. It is so unlike the path I have been on; but somehow I know that with His help I can break through it, even though I do not know where He is taking me.

Lord, help me to be as receptive to Your cleansing power as the cold winter ground is receptive to the snow and wind that blows and molds it how it will. Please take my life and let the wind of Your choosing blow me where I need to go; guide me to that unknown path You would have me follow. Thank You. Amen.

RISA STORLIE

58

Much Better Than I Had Hoped For

And I assure you of this: If anyone acknowledges me publicly here on earth, I, the Son of Man will openly acknowledge that person in the presence of God's angels. Luke 12:8, NLT.

IT THRILLS MY SOUL to watch and help Sonny collect the "Lamb's Offering" during worship service on Sabbath. Soon he'll be 14. He still proudly does his job, just as he's done for many years. Only now he towers far above the other little children—physically, but not so mentally.

Sonny loves to go to church. Often he greets the day by asking me, "Church Day?" Even after I tell him "No, not today, Sonny," he sometimes puts on his suit and tries to make it "Church Day" anyway. He'll always need a one-on-one caregiver. My heart breaks, yet I can still smile, because the love of Jesus is in my Sonny.

For all of his life it's been my joy to dress him appropriately for church. Now Sonny, himself, desires to look nice. He holds very still while his daddy shaves him, knowing that in the morning it will be "Church Day!"

Many of Sonny's suits were blessed gifts to him from my sister, his aunt Jan. For the past several years I've been getting Sonny's suits at the Salvation Army thrift shop on Bag Days— everything you can stuff in a bag for a certain price. I so much enjoy shopping with several precious friends on Bag Days. We have fun, and I like the way the Lord recycles.

Sonny once got sick and needed medical attention. My friend, Louise, our doctor's office nurse, handed me a big box when we were ready to leave. She said that it had been in the office for some time. She was just waiting for our next visit to give it to me. Louise said that the box contained craft supplies. Sonny kept pointing at the box, saying, "Clothes!"

Louise said, "Actually, Sonny, there are some clothes in there for you." Sonny gave her a big, long hug. I was silently praying that she wouldn't catch the nasty flu from him.

In the box were three beautiful three-piece suits. They fit Sonny perfectly. This happened on Friday. I had already been anticipating Bag Day on the following Monday, but Jesus gave Louise the joy of providing Sonny with his new blessed Sabbath suits—much better than I had hoped for.

DEBORAH SANDERS

February 21

Trouble!

I have loved you with an everlasting love. Jer. 31:3, NKJV.

MY 4-YEAR-OLD BLUE merle Australian shepherd, Molly, is the kind of hyperactive dog that movies could be made about. She is a brat. She is beautiful—with her black, gray, and white mottled fur and ice-blue eyes—but she is a pain. Anyone who knows her—or has even met her—will tell you that. No reasonable human being would have possibly put up with her as long as I have. Her mischief knows no bounds.

Molly started out normal enough, going through what we hoped was the normal "puppy" stage, but even after she was grown she continued to be a handful. Several friends joke that the "Molly" experience has given me the "bat ears" and "trouble radar" of the most patience-tried mother and I will be well prepared for motherhood. When she was a puppy, she chewed up the leg of a new coffee table. She destroyed the leg of a plant stand. She ate a corner of one of the living room chairs. She even sampled the hem of my brand new curtains. One day we came home to find her, triumphant, over a gaping hole in the middle of my down comforter, feathers strewn about the bedroom. I am absolutely sure she was grinning. She gets in the trash if we leave the bathroom door open and is not above pulling food off of the counter, if she can reach it. Just the other day Molly somehow managed to jump onto the dining room table (like a cat) and was helping herself to a box of chocolates that had been pushed to the middle just so that she couldn't reach them.

But I love Molly. When she climbs up in my lap, just to be close to me, and gives me a "kiss" or that infamous "puppy dog look," my heart melts. And she returns that love unconditionally.

I have caused my Master a lot of trouble and grief too. No "reasonable" God would have put up with me as He has, let alone die for me. I forget to spend time with Him. I snap at those I love, and bark at the people around me. I obsess over silly things and forget what's really important. I ignore the sunsets He paints, and many times don't stop to hear His still small voice telling me that He loves me. I am His child, and He loves me. Unconditionally. In spite of myself.

VICKI L. MACOMBER

A Ride to Beltsville

For I the Lord thy God will hold thy right hand, saying unto thee, Fear not; I will help thee. Isa. 41:13.

THE VOICE ON THE phone was my brother-in-law's. Sounding almost numb, he related the news that his wife, Virginia, had slipped suddenly away. Her damaged heart was simply too tired to continue longer.

My invalid husband was unable to go with me to the funeral, but with encouragement from my son, who secured my ticket, I arranged to go. Knowing I would arrive at the Baltimore-Washington airport very late, I elected not to request anyone to meet me. I'm sure God was guiding, for my connection out of St. Louis was two and a half hours late.

When my plane landed, I took a taxi to a nearby motel. The next morning I searched the telephone book for transportation to Beltsville, Maryland, where I would meet Virginia's family. There were pages of choices. I knelt beside my bed—a hesitant senior citizen, alone in a strange place, wondering whom I could trust. I asked my heavenly Father to indicate His leading; then I picked a listing at random and called. The operator indicated a driver would arrive in 30 minutes.

Right on schedule, an unmarked but impressive black Lincoln Town Car arrived. An amiable Ghanaian gentleman in a black uniform helped me with my luggage. "O, God," I prayed, "please, come with me. I'm not used to being alone like this."

As we drove, I remarked that I recalled the surroundings because my husband and I had lived in the Washington, D.C., area and had worked at our church world headquarters. He asked me what church. When I told him, his face broke into a broad smile. "Oh! I, too, am a member!" he beamed. Then he held up his proof—a Bible study guide that I immediately recognized.

"Thank You, Father! Thank You so very much!" I breathed. "You really did hear me! You really are right here with me!" Tears filled my eyes as I related my answered prayer to the driver, and he, too, was touched.

Many times since I've dropped to my knees and thanked my caring heavenly Father for strengthening my faith by keeping watch over me when I needed Him most.

LORRAINE HUDGINS

February 23

What Lies Ahead

*Thou shalt guide me with thy counsel, and afterward receive me to glory.
Ps. 73:24.*

WHAT LIES AHEAD OF me each day I do not know. Recalling some of
life's unexpected experiences, I find myself comparing them to various
signs as I travel along busy streets and highways.

While driving, I sometimes find I have passed the right exit; I see a sign
saying no U-turn and have to drive farther to find an area in which to turn
around. I think I have made a mistake by not keeping focused. In my
Christian life I also must keep focused on Christ, and He'll guide me straight
to the right exit from Satan's roadblocks.

When I name a few signs to which I have compared my Christian travel,
I think of the detour sign, meaning I must take another route. When Satan
tempts me with impure thoughts and temptations, I know I must not take
this route but must turn around and take the route Christ gives me in His
Word: "Whatsoever things are honest, . . . whatsoever things are of good report; . . . think on these things" (Phil. 4:8).

I think of another sign I've come upon as I travel that says "Danger
ahead." Satan has his Ph.D. in human psychology, and he's out like a roaring
lion, seeking whom he may destroy. I must be vigilant in my travel, realizing
danger is ahead.

"Watch out for falling rocks" is another eye-catcher. Whether little or
big, rocks can harm my spiritual travel, as well as my physical being.

As I travel on life's journey and see all of the signs, I thank God for the
road map He has given me to follow. The road can become tiresome, but His
map, the Bible, tells me, "Come to me, all you who are weary and burdened,
and I will give you rest" (Matt. 11:28, NIV). So when I see the road sign saying "rest area," I know that following God's map will bring me to the end of
the road, to the Savior I love, who will be waiting for me. He will be there
with outstretched arms, welcoming me.   ANNIE B. BEST

Mr. Blackbird

Jesus Christ the same yesterday, and to day, and for ever. Heb. 13:8.

AS THE SNOW MELTED and the days became sunnier, I decided to go out walking more often and wear off some unwanted baggage. Each day my route took me past a pond with cattails that had gone to seed but still waved happily in the breeze. They were huge, fluffy, and white.

One sunny Sabbath day my ears were drawn to an unusual "whit, whit, whit" sound. Very harsh and nonmelodic. Looking in the direction of the strange tune, I saw a blackbird with a tiny yellow stripe on its wings sitting atop the spike of one of the seed clusters. I paused—the contrast of black on a sea of white fluff was eye-catching. The bird seemed agitated that I was there and continued with his "whit, whit, whit" and bobbed his body up and down with each note. My ear was tuned also to other birdsongs, but I could not see the birds that made them.

I stayed to watch this bird of spring longer as his actions were interesting. He would spin around in circles atop his pencil-thin pinnacle, then stop; spin and stop. *I'll never know what you are trying to tell me*, I thought. But in between his three-word sentences, what I had thought was another bird was really him: "Ja Caw, Ja Caw, J-a-C-a-w," in a musical and much sweeter tone. Maybe he wanted me to think he was not alone, that other birds were near, so I would not focus entirely on him. Or perhaps he, like some of us, had a split personality—singing one tune at home in front of spouses, and children, and another in public. Being harsh and loud and going in circles, stressed out. But when we get to church, talk on the phone, or visit others, our tune is sweeter; our voice is calm, complimentary, nonjudgmental—and we even smile.

Am I guilty of two types of song coming from my lips at the same time? Am I two types of person—one for others to see and hear, and one for my loved ones?

My Jesus is not two-sided. "He is the same today, tomorrow, and always" (see Heb.13:8). When I get to heaven, I want to know what Mr. Blackbird was really saying. Perhaps it was not what I think it was after all.

VIDELLA MCCLELLAN

Take Your Pick

I have put my words in your mouth and covered you with the shadow of my hand. Isa. 51:16, NIV.

A S A PREACHER'S KID I had plenty of opportunity to hear Scripture read and quoted, or misquoted. I certainly did my share of misquoting. For example, when I was quite young and was asked to say a memory verse, it was such fun (if I thought I could get away with it) to ponderously repeat Hezekiah 13:13: "Better to be silent and be thought a fool than to open one's mouth and remove all doubt." It sounded so authentic! Later on, of course, I'd die laughing, remembering the puzzled expression on some of the faces in the group. I thought it was hysterical because what sounded like such a wise saying was attributed to someone who was once quite unwise, to say nothing of the fact that the book of Hezekiah does not even exist.

Around 700 B.C., King Hezekiah became very sick and feared for his life. Although he recovered miraculously, ambassadors from Babylon came bearing gifts because they'd heard of his illness. Unfortunately, Hezekiah opened his big mouth and voluntarily showed the visitors everything in his palace and in his kingdom. Years later, all his treasures were stolen in a raid, based on information gleaned during that visit.

It's very easy, as pointed out in Proverbs 6:2, to become trapped by what we say and ensnared by the words of our mouth. And once released to the world, ill-advised words are a bit like Humpty-Dumpty—very difficult to retrieve or to put back together properly. On the other hand, pleasant words are sweet to the soul and healing to the bones (Prov. 16:24).

Becoming "real" means that we avoid sharing personal information inappropriately. We refrain from contributing to the gossip column. We learn from our mistakes without broadcasting them to those who delight in sabotaging our personal and spiritual growth journey.

The quality of our self-talk is equally important. It is critical to our success that we remove from our personal vocabulary all negative personal pejoratives (e.g., words such as messy, clumsy, silly, stupid, ugly). Metaphorically, self-talk can be our Achilles' heel or our Aladdin's lamp. Take your pick!   ARLENE TAYLOR

God's Bright Sign

Jesus did many other miraculous signs. . . . But these are written that you may believe that Jesus is the Christ, the Son of God. John 20:30, 31, NIV.

AS I LAY IN MY bed on the ninth floor of the hospital, I contemplated the past eight months that had brought me here: a diagnosis of colon cancer, then resection surgery, followed by six months of chemotherapy. Now my blood count had fallen dangerously low, and I found myself in the hospital once again with a diagnosis that I might need a second surgery.

Lord, where are You? I cried out. Very weak, barely able to move, and desperately not wanting to undergo another surgery, I asked for a sign that everything was going to be all right.

It was dark outside, and my eyes were closed as I talked with God. Strangely, I was impressed to open my eyes, and through the window, where I could see a small space of sky, I was astounded to see a bright full moon shining down on me. At the same time I felt a warmth and sense of joy that God had indeed given me a sign.

Of course, I assumed it meant that I would not need surgery. But a few days later, when the doctor called my family in and expressed the fear that I might have a cancerous tumor blockage, it seemed surgery would be mandatory. Immediately I questioned God. Had He really answered my first-time-only prayer for a sign? If so, what did it mean?

A few days later, as my family awaited the results of my surgery, they knew the blockage had been only an adhesion and not cancer when they saw the doctor coming toward them with a big smile and two thumbs up!

I spent a total of 24 days in the hospital and came home very weak, but I praise the Lord each day as I continue to regain my strength and become fully involved in my active life.

The interpretation of my special sign, I believe, was that God was simply saying to me, "It is going to be all right! Not necessarily for what you are asking, but for your greater benefit in the end." I do know that in all those February nights in Columbus, Ohio, outside that hospital window, I saw rain, snow, fog, and clouds, but only on that one night did I see the moon in all its glory!

MARJORIE KINKEAD

February 27

Hidden Muck

He brought me up also out of an horrible pit, out of the miry clay, and set my feet upon a rock, and established my goings. Ps. 40:2.

NOT LONG AGO MY husband and I set out to retile the worn floor of our kitchen and breakfast nook. We'd never ventured such a job before, but after talking to a couple experts we felt it would be easy enough once the old floors were stripped and prepared. After all, the new tiles had adhesive backing. After finishing the job in two days, and even working on the molding, we felt rather proud of ourselves. We wouldn't think of hiring ourselves out, but for us our job was acceptable.

A few days later at work I shared with my boss what we had done, and he in turn told me the experience he and his father had had retiling their kitchen floor many years ago when he was only 16. Once they stripped and prepared the old floor, they began putting down the tiles, piece by piece, using a tarlike adhesive substance. After finishing and allowing the floor to dry for a period of time, the family began trafficking as normal. Not long after, they noticed it—black tar oozing up between the tiles. What a mess it made! And what effort was needed to correct the job. Either the adhesive had not dried sufficiently, or too much had been applied and the pressure from the traffic had forced what lay beneath to ooze out.

Hearing my boss's experience with the adhesive reminded me of the "naturally carnal self" and how, under pressure and lacking sufficient prayer and preparation, it at times surfaces and is not a pretty site to behold. It will often make a real mess of circumstances that otherwise would be solved easily and peacefully. Amazingly, as we fully submit ourselves to Christ, day by day, we begin to realize that He carefully and tenderly prepares us for what lies ahead. Sometimes this preparation hurts, but it is never for any reason other than our own good. He knows us individually and would lead us down no other path than that which we would choose for ourselves could we see the end from the beginning.

Thank You, Lord, for Your ability and willingness to clean up the muck in our lives that would destroy us, if left to ourselves.   GLORIA J. STELLA FELDER

Saved by an Angel

The angel of the Lord encampeth round about them that fear him and delivereth them. Ps. 34:7.

WE HAD A HOUSE built on our land, but it is nearly four miles (seven kilometers) away from my workplace. So I have to travel for 20 minutes on a city bus to get there. It is very hard to get the bus in the morning because many schoolchildren travel by bus, and the villagers bring their vegetables and other things to sell in the market, making it very crowded.

One day my son and daughter and I were waiting for the bus. Some buses came but did not stop. At last a bus stopped, but it was very crowded. My son got onto the bus first. My daughter was behind me. As I put my right foot up on the step of the bus, the driver took off. I couldn't catch my balance, and I fell down. Thankfully, I wasn't hurt. I remembered the promise: "He shall give his angels charge over thee, to keep thee in all thy ways" (Ps. 91:11). I thanked my Lord.

Later that same month I was again traveling by bus. When the bus reached my destination, I waited my turn to get off, as many other passengers were ahead of me. As I stepped down, the driver, again thinking that everyone was off, started driving. One of my feet was still on the footboard of the bus, and I was about to fall. I didn't know what to do.

Just then a boy ran to me to keep me from falling. He helped me to stand. I thanked him for helping me, and I thanked my heavenly Father, because I know God sent the boy to save me from falling. I have never seen that boy since.

My heart was full of thanks and gratitude for all the things God had done for me and my family. Such a wonderful God we have! He takes care of us well.

As I remember all these things, I admire the words of the psalmist: "The Lord shall preserve thy going out and thy coming in from this time forth and even for evermore" (Ps. 121:8).

What a wonderful and mighty God we serve! Make Him first and the best in your life. He will guide you throughout your life.

Thank You, Lord, for sending Your angels to deliver us from dangers that surround us each day. May we always look to You and know Your love and peace. Amen.   PACKIALEELA SAM SELVARAJ

March 1

Dora's Dilemma

Is there any wrong on my tongue? Cannot my taste discern calamity?
Job 6:30, NRSV.

I CAME TO FULFILL A promise to you, Doc," Dora sailed into my office to announce. My raised eyebrows begged for clarification. "You said to remind you to invite a group of us for Sabbath lunch each quarter. Now, when's the date?"

I grinned. The young graduate student's patience was eclipsed only by her brilliant smile. "I'm not into cooking at the moment," I explained. "Right now, juicing is the thing. I've uncovered a wonderful recipe for an extraordinary juice—carrots, celery, apples, kale, garlic—"

Her upstretched hands stayed my list before I could invite her to sample a glass. "Oh, please," she implored. "My sister went on that bandwagon last month." Her Haitian-American accent seemed more obvious in her distress. "She bought this book and set to work at the juicer. My mother and I could hardly wait to taste the juice of her labor. But when we took the first sip, we almost died." Her wry smile acknowledged the hyperbole.

"What happened?" I had to ask.

"We don't know. She followed the directions exactly. I checked." She listed the ingredients of the now infamous juice, her hand motions shaping each word as she pronounced it.

It was my turn to interrupt. "Tell me what a clove of garlic is," I asked, not understanding the dome-shaped movement of her elegant fingers when she mentioned the savory herb. Laughter exploded through the office suite when she discovered her sister's gaffe. She had used a large bulb of garlic instead of a tiny clove!

"Somebody should have told us," she exclaimed. "In our home we rarely used a recipe book, so we never needed to know the English meaning of 'clove.'"

Sometimes it is what we learn that is crucial. Always, it is who we know that makes the difference. A difference between the sweet and the bitter; between life and death. Our heavenly Parent is more gracious than our taste buds. When we recoil in distress or disgust at the taste of calamity, He grants us a taste of His goodness and gives us a spiritual kiss to make it all better!

Thank You, precious Lord, for Your long-suffering goodness.

GLENDA-MAE GREENE

Meditations on a Cat

Don't urge me to leave you or to turn back from you. Where you go I will go, and where you stay I will stay. Ruth 1:16, NIV.

I REFUSE TO CALL SASHA and Chloe "grand-cats," but when our daughter and son-in-law asked if we wanted to care for their two cats while they were on a short trip, we did some cat-sitting.

The minute I got up in the morning and went into the bathroom, Sasha showed up to keep me company. But as soon as I tried to scratch her behind the ear, which she loves, she would move. She obviously wanted the attention and love but would move just out of arm's reach and stop—and then complain. Those two cats were always on the move. Other times, when I got one of the cats on my lap to pet it, it would stay for only a moment or two, and then off it went.

Lord, I am beginning to wonder. . . . Do I stop long enough to enjoy the fact that You are trying to show me some love? Or do I keep moving, just out of arm's reach of Your care?

I noticed, too, how much Chloe loves to rub against our legs. The two cats don't rub against each other, so why us? Then I noticed that she rubbed against anything—furniture, door frames, corners—anything that was not moving. I felt like a piece of furniture!

Do I use people like that, Lord? Do I get some help, some use, some gratifying sensation out of the computer, the dishwasher, my secretary, my friend, and move on? People, furniture—making no distinction—using them for my benefit? Do I use You that way, too?

When I opened any can or walked toward the laundry room where their food was served, both cats were right under my feet. But when I dished the food out for them, Chloe would take a look and a smell and wander off—unless it was tuna.

I say I want spiritual food, but when it is offered, do I partake? Communion, personal in-depth Bible study, sermons . . . Do I get the spiritual value offered, or is my mind wandering?

They say that dogs treat people as masters, but a cat treats them as staff.

I have to wonder, are You my master, or my staff, to do my bidding, to answer my prayers; or am I here to love and serve You today?

ARDIS DICK STENBAKKEN

Just in Time

Before they call I will answer; while they are still speaking I will hear.
Isa. 65:24, NIV.

GOD HELPS ME IN practical ways, as well as in spiritual and physical ways. When I reached the age that required me to use my individual retirement account (IRA), I knew it was time to apply for a reliable health insurance plan. I prayed for guidance to find the right one to supplement Medicare.

The banker who handles my IRA knew just the one for me. The insurance was established and working well when I developed a frightful pain in my left side. I needed a good doctor! I prayed for guidance, and a church member gave me a name to call. They accepted new patients with my insurance. I was diagnosed and sent to the hospital for major surgery.

The doctors removed the cancerous tumor, spleen, one node, and part of my diaphragm. They told me I had a type of lymphoma. Many friends prayed for me through the surgery, recovery, and subsequent chemotherapy treatments.

That health insurance paid my way through it all and still pays for the follow-up care. I thank God for His miraculous healing and for the insurance He guided me into just in time. I still thank God for every day He gives me. God still takes care of my finances when I turn them over to Him. My medical needs seem to increase with my age, and God's blessings increase right along with them.

Other wonderful answers to prayer have been seen in my family through the years. I could list many more miracles. Finding the perfect item I need at an affordable price seems to always come just in time. My faith has been tested more than once. But I have been greatly rewarded for my patience and trust in God.

Even though it seems at times that God delays His help, He is never too late. The answer is always just in time. I try to remember that the school of patience and trust graduates exceptional scholars. My Bible lists them in its "hall of fame."

Dear Lord, keep me humble and patient as I wait for Your answers to my prayers that I know will come just in time. BESSIE SIEMENS LOBSIEN

The Scheduled Train

All who are oppressed may come to him. He is a refuge for them in their times of trouble. Ps. 9:9, TLB.

H I, LANNY. I HAVE good news!" It was my friend, Dewi, on the line. Her voice was full of enthusiasm when she continued. "I'm getting married next month—to Anto."

"Congratulations! I'm happy for you, Dewi," I said. We had been good friends since we were in college.

When I asked permission from my boss to take time off for the wedding, he let me go on one condition—I must be back in the office the Monday after the wedding.

The wedding was held in Salatiga, a small town in central Java, where Anto comes from. It took eight hours for a friend and me to get there by train from Jakarta, the capital city of Indonesia. Salatiga is a beautiful small town, and we had a wonderful time until we had to go back on Sunday morning.

The train was scheduled to leave at 9.00 a.m. Anto was ready to take us to the station at 8:00, but my friend was not ready until 8:20. On the way to the station, I found out it was at least a 45-minute drive. We would be late. Anto drove as fast as he could. I knew he was nervous because that was the only train to Jakarta on Sunday. The next train would be on Monday, too late to get me home on time.

I prayed, "Lord, You know how much I need Your help this time. Help me to be able to catch this train."

As I finished my prayer, I heard Anto say, "We are at the station. Just hope the train has not yet left."

We ran as fast as we could, carrying all the luggage. We could see the train, ready to leave. Just as we put the luggage on the train, it slowly began to move.

Thank You, Lord, I breathed. My heart was overjoyed with the help God showed me. God is in control and has a perfect plan, goal, will, and complete foreknowledge of this and all the difficult trials we will ever face.

LANNY LYDIA PONGILATAN

March 5

Bethany's Advice

O, Lord, . . . be thou my helper. Ps. 30:10.

RON PARKED OUR CAR in the driveway of our daughter's home, and we began carrying suitcases inside. After hugs from our granddaughters, 7-year-old Rachel and 5-year-old Bethany, we went to our room to unpack and settle in. The girls followed us to find out what Grandma and Grandpa had brought them from India.

We unpacked suitcases one through four. The tiny brass elephants for the girls were not in them. I tried my keys on the fifth suitcase, but none of them opened the lock. I tried them the second time, and still none of them worked. Agitated now, I emptied my purse and checked the front pockets of all of the suitcases.

"I have to have the key somewhere!" I exclaimed impatiently. "I know I had it when I locked this suitcase. Why can't I find it? It must be one of the keys on my ring, but none of them work."

"Don't get upset, Grandma," Bethany said in a very grown-up tone. "Everything will be OK. Jesus lives in this house. He can help you, so don't get upset."

"OK," I responded, feeling chastened by her words. "I'll not get upset. You are right. Jesus will help us find the key for this lock."

Once again I picked up my ring of keys and chose a key to try. Slowly, I inserted it in the stubborn lock, and it popped open. "Now, why didn't that work before?" I mumbled.

"See, Grandma!" Bethany said. "I told you Jesus would help you."

The elephants were inside, and so were some coloring books and other gifts for the children. They ran to show their treasures to their mother, leaving me to think about Bethany's advice. Her complete assurance that Jesus could set things right was humbling. How often I get frustrated, trying on my own to set things right in my life, only to find it does not work.

Yes, Lord, I prayed silently, *I know You have the key to all the situations I face. Help me to calm down, and look to You instead of to myself for help. Help me to remember the wise words of Bethany the next time I face a frustrating situation I can't handle. "Don't get upset, Grandma. Jesus lives in this house and He will help you."*

DOROTHY EATON WATTS

Lost

In all your ways acknowledge him, and he will make your paths straight.
Prov. 3:6, NIV.

I HAD BEEN ON THAT street many times. The numbers on the buildings were big and obvious. What could be hard about getting there on time? I knew the general directions. I left 20 minutes before my 2:00 appointment. Without traffic I could breeze through in 12 minutes, and if there was heavier traffic I would still be there on time.

Two blocks away from the spot I got distracted and passed the building, traveling northward for 10 extra minutes. I was lost. I turned around. It took me another 10 minutes to finally find the doctor's office.

Going to the same place another time, but coming from a different direction, I again got lost. This time a police officer stopped me, and this gave me the opportunity to ask him to show me the way. He led; I followed.

Once my doctor friend invited me to attend a seminar. I looked forward to the day because not only would I be able to listen to a lecture with a medical perspective and ask questions, I would also be able to socialize with the doctor and her friends.

It was raining that morning, so I left in plenty of time. The directions she gave indicated I should go to Gate 3 at Little Creek. I had been to this base twice. As I entered the gate I asked for directions, and then asked again when I reached the gas station. The next person I asked was a storekeeper in one of the buildings. He directed me to the officers' club. The last stop I made was at the clinic where the officer made telephone contacts to assist me. Still, there was no trace of the meeting place. I went home very disappointed. Somehow I had lost my way again. Surprisingly, even with modern technology and scientific inventions, I get lost.

I've lost touch with God, too, sometimes. The lost sheep, the lost coin, and the lost son, at last, were all found. Like a lost sheep, through carelessness I've traveled down some wrong paths. My only recourse is to have Jesus help me find my way again. I pray that I may never let go of the hand of Him who reaches out for me, leads me, and keeps me from being lost.

ESPERANZA AQUINO MOPERA

A French Guardian Angel

*For he will command his angels concerning you to guard you in all your ways.
. . . When they call to me, I will answer them; I will be with them in trouble.
Ps. 91:11-15, NRSV.*

W E HAD JUST COMPLETED a guided tour of England, Scotland, and
Wales. It had been a perfect trip. We then took the high-speed train
from England to Paris, France, under the English Channel. What an experience! We had never been on such a fast-moving but quiet train. It proved to
be a very enjoyable trip. There were four of us traveling together: my brother-
in-law, Pete; his wife, Ruthe; my husband, Emil; and me. We were on our
own now to tour Europe via the Eurail train.

In Paris, when we asked where to catch our connection, we were informed that the Eurail train was at a different terminal about three blocks
away. We decided that we could load all eight pieces of our luggage into a
cart and walk to the other terminal. It turned out to be the wrong decision.

After a block or so we encountered a rather high curb. This created quite
a challenge. Pete was recovering from back surgery and had a cane. He tried
lifting the front of the cart while my husband steadied the back. *This is not
working,* I worried. *What are we going to do?*

Then walking up the street came a young Frenchman who spoke English.
He took charge of our luggage cart, lifted it up over the curb, and told us to
follow him to the Eurail terminal. At the terminal we found another obstacle:
a flight of stairs to descend. There were several inebriated men wanting to help
carry our luggage, but our young Frenchman shooed them away and carried
our luggage, two pieces at a time, down the stairway.

We had not exchanged any of our money yet, so our new friend paid for
another luggage cart at the bottom of the stairs and directed us to the money
exchange booth in the terminal. We reimbursed him and thanked him profusely. He smiled, bade us goodbye, and disappeared into the crowd.

We'll never forget his kindness, our French guardian angel. We thanked
the Lord for sending him to us when we were desperate for help.

PATRICIA MULRANEY KOVALSKI

A Space Age God

Neither pray I for these alone, but for them also which shall believe on me through their word. John 17:20.

EVER SINCE MY OLDER brother built and designed models from balsa wood, I have always loved airplanes. Though not of a scientific bent, I'm drawn to anything aeronautical. I even learned the four basic aeronautical principles of lift, thrust, drag, and weight. My favorite aircraft is the now-retired SR-71, the Blackbird, the fastest plane in the world. It is a marvelous sight to see.

One Friday evening, soon after seeing this prodigious aircraft in flight, I was studying the lesson in preparation for teaching the adult Bible study class at church. The text was Ezekiel 1, a vision that despite the musical attraction of the old spiritual, had always had a mystical nonmeaning to me. In my mind I could hear the choir's different parts, soaring to the ceiling, faster and faster, competing with each other, a "wheel in the middle of a wheel," with no meaning. Suddenly I saw an idea that Ezekiel could not possibly have had knowledge of. The following morning as I began the lesson, reading those same verses, Art, recently retired from the U.S. Air Force after some 20 years as an aircraft mechanic, interrupted excitedly, "It's a gyroscope!"

What is a gyroscope? It is a space age invention without which there would be no jet or space flight. It is, in actuality, a wheel within a wheel. It is that very property that makes it an essential navigational and balancing fundamental. The average passenger aircraft has about 25 of them, each with different functions.

I shouldn't have been surprised, but I was thrilled. Ezekiel was describing a space age invention in the best words of his ancient experience—no, a space age discovery. For obviously it is not an invention of mankind. Here for all science to see was an ancient biblical description (with a crystal canopy) of a spacecraft—a godly spacecraft.

What an awesome God we serve—"our help in ages past, our hope for years to come"; God of the past, present, and future, a power in my life still to navigate and balance until He comes through the universe to fly me home. Oh, "wheel in the middle of a wheel, . . . 'Way in the middle of the air."

LOIS K. BAILEY

March 9

An Answered Prayer

Now the just shall live by faith: but if any man draw back, my soul shall have no pleasure in him. But we are not of them who draw back unto perdition, but of them that believe to the saving of the soul. Heb. 10:38, 39.

IT ALWAYS AMAZES ME to hear about the ways people have heard God talking to them and how they felt God's presence. I really wondered if God could truly speak to me as He did to others. Then one day I actually experienced God's presence and knew that He had spoken to me.

That day my spirit was in turmoil. I could not make up my mind whether to continue with my decision to be baptized. At the last minute I changed my mind and wanted to postpone the baptism. My two special friends would not be there to witness that memorable event in my life. One had to go to the Philippines to bury her mother-in-law, and the other had gotten the measles. In their absence I felt so alone and abandoned. I spoke to my Bible mentor and to the pastor about my desire to postpone my baptism until both my friends could be there. I took the pastor's advice to go ahead with the baptism, even though deep in my heart I still wanted to postpone it.

That night I prayed so hard. The following morning I asked the Lord to show me that I had made the right decision. Using a Bible guide, I turned in my Bible to Herbews 10:38, 39, the suggested verses for that day. And there I found the answer to my prayers. I felt so overwhelmed by the message. Tears rolled down my cheeks, and I felt the Holy Spirit within me. I was so glad that I hadn't changed my mind about being baptized that Sabbath.

That day the birds sang melodiously, the sky was bright and clear, and the weather was warm and sunny. Everything seemed to tell me that God was really happy in my decision. It was as if He were saying to me, "Eva, My child, I'll never let you go." I knew that He and His angels rejoiced when I was finally dipped in that watery grave to leave my sinful self and rise as a new Christian, born in the Spirit of the Lord. He was pleased to see me accept His saving grace.

My fear of being alone was gone. Though my two special friends were not there with me, physically, I was in their hearts and minds.

Does God answer prayers? Yes, truly He does in the most amazing way.

MINERVA M. ALINAYA

Car Repair

But my God shall supply all your need according to his riches in glory by
Christ Jesus. Phil. 4:19.

THE SNOW WAS COMING. The news media had people checking their
cars and food supplies. I was concerned about the tires on my van because I was having problems with sliding, even in good weather. The day
prior to the snowstorm, I went tire shopping. In my search for tires, I com-
parison-shopped in three stores. At my last stop the mechanic checked the
tires, then had a tire specialist check them. They agreed that the tires still had
as many as 15,000 miles of wear left.

"Then why is my van slipping and sliding, even in good weather?" I asked
the mechanic. "It has been happening for the past two months."

The mechanic said he'd check the alignment, so I waited four hours for
the electronic test to be completed. While sitting in the shop, I saw many people come and go as they got various repairs on their vehicles. Some were
pleased with the results, and some were angry about the services of the shop.

Finally the mechanic told me the tire arms on the front suspension were
broken, putting the van out of alignment. He was amazed that I had been
able to drive the van without experiencing major problems. Two more hours
of waiting, and the problem was solved.

As I was paying for the repairs, the service manager remarked, "Thank
you for being so patient and understanding in reference to the repairs on
your vehicle. You are someone special." He then gave me a coupon for a
complimentary oil change.

The Lord had blessed me not only with the repairs on my van, but with a
bonus oil change. I thought my need was for new tires, but Christ knew better, and He supplied that need. We can all claim God's help for today and always. I had operated my van for two months with poor alignment and the
tire arms broken, thinking I needed tires.

What a mighty God we serve!

SHARON MARSHALL

March 11

Mistaken Identity

Watch out that no one deceives you. For many will come in my name, claiming, "I am the Christ," and will deceive many. Matt. 24:4, 5, NIV.

I WAS DOING THE LAUNDRY and was in a hurry. I had accidentally splashed some tomato juice on the front of a white blouse. On the shelf, partly hidden by another container, was a white plastic bottle with blue lettering. Only the last two letters of the name were visible: "EX." Assuming that it was Javex bleach, I reached for the bottle and proceeded to try to remove the stains from my blouse with the blue liquid. Nothing happened. The stains remained.

"Poor stuff, this Javex bleach," I muttered as I viewed the now miserable results.

As I returned the bottle to the shelf I noticed the rest of the word on the bottle—Windex. I had tried to remove those stains with window cleaner! How could I have used something without fully reading the label? In my hurry I had done just that.

The bottle of Javex bleach was there on the shelf behind the Windex, and they did look a lot alike. But that was no excuse for using the wrong one. I rinsed the blouse and used the Javex. The stains came out, and there was no harm done.

I learned another lesson that day. How easy it is to make mistakes—to read only half the label and make assumptions that are not true. We do it all the time with those we meet. We make assumptions without knowing the whole story, and the results can be disastrous. Sometimes we half-read Scripture when reading the whole chapter would give a different perspective to the verse we quote.

Jesus warned that there would be "false prophets" claiming to be Christ, and they will "deceive many." Only by looking at the whole picture will we be able to make right decisions.

Dear Lord, I pray that I may take care not to judge without hearing both sides of a story, and not to follow theories and ideas without fully investigating them, and not to follow after "false prophets."
RUTH LENNOX

He Picked Me Up

He brought me . . . out of the miry clay, and set my feet upon a rock. Ps. 40:2.

I SAW SOMETHING FALL from the tree in my backyard where three sparrows had made a nest. Sure enough, a baby sparrow had fallen down from its nest and into the garbage bin. With great difficulty I retrieved it. The poor little creature had no feathers on its back—it was a small, helpless mass of flesh, cold and shivering in the falling rain. I wiped it with a soft cloth, then bundled it up in a woolen cloth. After a nap, it started to open its mouth to be fed.

Now there was a problem. We had a tomcat who cast a wicked eye at the sparrow. He obviously saw the potential for supper here. I took a big cane basket that we used for rearing chickens, turned it upside down, covered it, and put the baby bird inside. The basket served as a hedge so that Tom couldn't get at it. We gave Tom his cup of milk and banished him from the house.

The next day the sparrow parents fluttered in the backyard, chirping. I presumed they were anxious about their baby. So I put the basket with the baby bird at the back of the house. Soon they were talking in their sparrow language. I faithfully fed the helpless little bird every day.

As the days went by, the sparrow began to grow feathers on its wings. At times the tomcat walked around the basket, trying to figure out how to get at the baby sparrow. He watched through the slits in the basket and clawed at it. There were times when he mimicked a sparrow. It reminded me of how Satan wants to destroy our soul. He tries all his tricks on us so that we will fall into his trap.

Every day the parent birds came down in the backyard. When the little bird was able to fly, we let it go. How glad I was to see it join its own family.

Jesus has saved me from my sins. He has covered me with His robe. He has given me hope in His promises. He has fed me with His word. He has strengthened me with His Spirit. He is making a mansion for me in heaven, to be ever with Him.

SOOSANNA MATHEW

Partings and Memories

And there shall be no more death . . . nor crying. Rev. 21:4.

WORLD WAR I HAD started, and my maternal grandfather, a Christian in his early 20s, was a conscientious objector who refused to take up arms. So he was jailed and put in solitary confinement with only bread and water for sustenance. Finally he was able to join the medical corps and was posted to Salisbury, England. He promised a mate back home in New Zealand to look up relatives. So with a two-day pass in hand, grandfather traveled to a farming district in Worcestershire. When he got there, however, he knocked at the wrong door. A young woman of 19 answered his knock and, I'm told, it was love at first sight. And so it was that my grandmother (they were married within a year) emigrated to New Zealand with her husband at the end of the war. How difficult that must have been to say goodbye to her family and friends. Such a sad parting.

As a child I spent many happy holidays with my grandparents—until it was time to go home! They lived several hundred miles away, which meant sad partings.

The years came and went, and what would have to be the saddest parting of all occurred when my grandparents passed on. Later, with my parents, we cleaned out their little house, sorting everything. Those of you who have done this for loved ones know how heartbreaking it is. What to keep, what to give away, what to throw away . . . And with every item come the memories.

In the kitchen a shelf of glass jars brought the memory of my grandmother making jam. The cake tins—oh, the anticipation there was when I was waiting for the tins to come down from the top of the cupboard after the evening meal was over! In the bedroom hung my grandmother's best blue coat that she wore each week to church. In the back room/workshop were more memories as I sorted through tins and containers holding a variety of things. Pieces of string, corks and bottle tops, kept just in case. So many memories. In the lounge so many precious personal pictures and photographs, including the wedding pictures taken in England a lifetime ago.

Won't that day be wonderful when Jesus comes and "the dead in Christ shall rise first" (1 Thess. 4:16)? I pray I will be reunited with my grandparents, never to be parted again.

LEONIE DONALD

Not Nigh Thee

A thousand shall fall at thy side, and ten thousand at thy right hand; but it shall not come nigh thee. Ps. 91:7.

THE RIOTING ENDED the day after the National Guard arrived in Los Angeles on April 30, 1992. The next day there were still flare-ups, particularly around Korean-owned businesses. Gladys Lowe, a Chinese woman in her late 70s, knew this but didn't think about it when she took Elder Stanley Bessent, 80 and nearly blind, to the doctor.

On the way home her car stopped in an area that had seen intense rioting the day before. Unable to restart the car, Gladys spotted a telephone halfway up the block. "You wait here," she told her charge "I'll go call the automobile club." She put her quarter in the pay slot. It came back. Desperate, she tried again and again, wondering how she was to get her helpless friend home if she couldn't summon help.

A middle-aged Black man walked up. "What are you doing?" he asked.

"I'm calling AAA roadside service for help. But the telephone won't work," she answered.

"Service to roadside telephones was cut off during the height of the riot," he said. "I can't leave a lady like you alone here on this street where there is still so much anger after the riots. Why don't you come to my apartment and call AAA on my cellular phone?"

There seemed to be no other option. He took her to his apartment and dialed AAA for her. The AAA operator told Gladys that a tow truck could be there in a half hour. She thanked the operator and the gentleman who had helped her, and left.

As she walked down that long block she was surprised to see the AAA tow truck had arrived and was already hooking up the car. As Gladys told this story to her prayer group, the women said, "Don't you realize you could have been mistaken for a Korean by any nearby rioter? That man probably saved your life!"

Several days later Gladys took a small gift to the apartment house from which she had made her call to AAA. The apartment house manager, hearing the knocking, came to investigate.

"No one lives there, lady," the manager said. "That apartment's been empty for months." DARLENEJOAN MCKIBBIN RHINE

The Perfect Gift

Every good and perfect gift is from above, coming down from the Father of the heavenly lights who does not change like shifting shadows. James 1:17, NIV.

I WAS SEVEN MONTHS pregnant and miserable. I wasn't alone—my loving husband and 5-year-old son tried to make things as easy for me as they could. But things were not going well with our family-run business, and it was easy to get depressed. I loved music, but even listening to it could not always lift my spirits. I had expressed a desire several times to my husband for a piano but knew we couldn't afford one. The last time I had expressed the wish, he had jokingly asked where in the world we would find room for it in our small home.

My son was visiting his grandparents for a few days and was due home any time. I was lying on the sofa trying to nap that warm late March afternoon while I awaited their arrival. The doorbell chimed, and I jumped up to run and answer the door. They were here! We hugged and greeted one another enthusiastically, and I chatted with my son about his week at Grandma and Grandpa's house.

As I passed the front window on my way to the kitchen, I noticed a U-Haul behind my parents' car. A U-Haul? I knew I hadn't sent that much stuff with my son. What were they transporting?

When I asked, they grinned. My mouth nearly hit the floor when they told me they had bought a piano for me. My aunt knew an elderly woman who was selling hers for a very reasonable price, and they knew how much I wanted one, so they had purchased it and transported it the 200 miles to my home.

Many years later that piano is still giving me joy when I play it. I think it is one of the best gifts I have ever received. It wasn't my birthday or Christmas or any occasion for gift-giving. I had no reason to expect this perfect gift. My parents gave it to me because they loved me and wanted me to be happy.

God has given me a perfect gift also—the gift of eternal life through Jesus, His Son. He gives this gift to me not because I deserve it, but because He knows it will make me happy forever!   FAUNA RANKIN DEAN

God Takes Care of a Need Ahead of Time!

"O Lord, please send someone else to do it." Then the [Lord] . . . said, "What about your brother, Aaron the Levite? . . . He is already on his way to meet you, and his heart will be glad when he sees you." Ex. 4:13, 14, NIV.

WHEN MOSES ASKED FOR someone to come and help him when he went into Egypt, the Lord told him that his brother was already on his way. The Lord anticipated his need. A close friend told me this experience of how the Lord anticipated her need in advance.

Don and Cindy were on disability income, both in wheelchairs. By close budgeting they managed to meet their expenses with a little left over to share. One day the woman who helped them with housework and shopping confided that she didn't know where she would get $100 to meet some car expenses. "Let's lend her our $100," Don suggested to Cindy.

"No," said Cindy. "It's all the money we have for the next two weeks."

"It will be all right, honey," consoled Don. "God is good to us; we can share."

Cindy saw his point, but her heart wasn't in it. Reluctantly, she got the money and gave it to the woman. She went into the bedroom and bowed her head. "God," she whispered, "I can't handle this. You are going to have to take care of it."

Yet she couldn't help admiring Don for his simple trust in God and for his generosity toward people. He was a new Christian. She was a longtime Christian. Although they had been married only a couple years, she had watched with joy his delight in his newfound faith.

The next day Cindy called the bank. She hoped it wasn't overdrawn— maybe there'd be a dollar or two still there.

When the teller said there was $400 in their account, Cindy exclaimed, "You've made a mistake! There isn't supposed to be that amount in the account."

A check had come in from Social Security that had been credited to their account. When Don applied for Social Security, they issued the amount earlier than he had anticipated.

The explanation was logical. It was the timing that was an answer to their need.

EDNA MAYE GALLINGTON

March 17

Our Protector

Because thou hast made the Lord, which is my refuge, even the most High, thy habitation; there shall no evil befall thee, neither shall any plague come nigh thy dwelling. Ps. 91:9, 10.

MY PLANS WERE CAREFULLY crafted for the day: clean the house, complete a work-related project, and pick up my son, who was due to arrive for a weekend leave from boarding school. With all the cleaning done, I lit candles in the powder room, kitchen, and living room to add a fragrance of wildflowers to the house.

A few hours later I completed the work-related project and realized that the time had come to drive the 20 miles into the next county to pick up my son. Upon arrival at the designated pickup site, I learned that the bus carrying Darien would be three hours late. Despite my initial apprehension, the time did pass quickly, and he arrived starved for dinner, so he said.

During dinner we shared stories about friends, family, and upcoming school events. After dessert I retired to an upstairs room to read and study while Darien washed the dishes.

Within a few minutes of my departure I heard a commotion, "Mom, Mom!" Darien frantically shouted. "Do you know that a candle is burning in the powder room?"

My hands grew clammy and my face flushed. *Candle burning?* I mused. *Did I forget to blow this particular candle out?*

Dropping my book and papers, I rushed down the stairs to check. The previously hardened candle wax, supporting a barely visible wick, was now an all-pink liquid floating in its watermelon-shaped container. Although my son had extinguished the flame, a trail of smoke lingered beneath a pair of engraved hand towels that could have easily ignited during my four-hour absence.

Darien looked at me and steadied my shaking hands. I could only be thankful for a God who, despite my own forgetfulness, did not forget our home. He knew that my best efforts of remembering to blow all the candles out would be met with a moment of forgetfulness.

My prayers of the morning asking for His protection and the protection of those around me had been answered in a mighty way. What a wonderful Father we serve!

YVONNE LEONARD CURRY

At Home in Heaven

What else do I have in heaven but you? Since I have you, what else could I want on earth? Ps. 73:25, TEV.

I'VE ALWAYS DREAMED OF owning my very own home. Even as I moved from one dilapidated rental to another, I kept before me the picture of a beautiful home of my own. As I fought with landlords, trying to get them to make necessary repairs, I knew that somewhere the perfect house was waiting for me—one without a leaky roof, falling plaster, peeling paint, or tempermental plumbing.

Well, I did finally get my own home—sort of. What I got was my own trailer. Unfortunately, the only place I could afford was just as run-down as my previous rentals. So while I'm happy to own something, my home falls hopelessly short of my dreams.

Then I realized that home isn't so much a place as a feeling, a state of mind. For some people, feeling at home may involve a particular place—perhaps the house they grew up in or a favorite vacation retreat. For me, feeling at home involves being with special people, people I feel safe and secure around.

My friend Emiko always makes me feel at home. You see, we've known each other since eighth grade, and by now we have both given up on the idea of making a good impression. I've seen her hysterical. She's seen me throw up. We've watched jobs, houses, and relationships come and go, and we've both changed a lot since those early days. Because of our long friendship, I feel that she is a safe place to take my problems. She makes me feel at home.

I like to think that heaven will be like that—not a strange, ethereal place but a safe place, a place where I can be myself—only better. I believe it will be home for me because my friend Jesus will be there. He heard me utter my first word. He saw me take my first step. I have no secrets from Him. I don't have to try to impress Him with what a fantastic person I am, how smart, how successful. He knows me and loves me as I am. Heaven is my home. I can't wait to get there!

GINA LEE

My Identity

Whatever happens, conduct yourselves in a manner worthy of the gospel of Christ. Phil. 1:27, NIV.

I WAS TRAVELING FROM Hosur to Trissur in Kerala, south India. As the train neared Trissur, I walked toward the door with my luggage so that I could get down as soon as the train stopped. After settling my luggage, I turned back. To my surprise, I saw a sister and a brother, less than 10 years old, looking at me, saying something, and laughing. They continued, unmindful of my looking at them. I strained my ears to hear what they were talking about. They conversed in Malayalam, the language of Kerala. The brother said, "She is a Malayalee."

The sister said, "No."

I understood the conversation because I speak a little Malayalam. The children really wanted to know my identity. The sister urged, "You ask her."

"No," the brother hesitantly returned. "You ask."

Not wanting to leave them in suspense, I spoke in Malayalam. "I am not a Malayalee. I am a Tamilian, but I can speak Malayalam."

I often come across people who mistake me for a Malayalee. Could it be because my native village, now in Tamil Nadu, was part of Kerala when I was born and still borders Kerala?

In reality it does not matter who I am, what language I speak, or to what community and nationality I belong. What really matters is whether I am a Christian in the true sense of the word. If I am, people who come in contact with me will easily identify me as a disciple of Christ.

How is this possible? I will have the mind of Jesus, let Jesus live in my heart, and reflect His character in my words and actions. I will go about doing good as Jesus did, depend on Him fully, allow Him to take control of my life. I will stand true to Him under all circumstances, believe that all things work together for good to those who love Him, and glorify God in suffering. I will rejoice in the Lord always and not be shattered by anything earthly, be brave enough to confess my faith to strangers, and share the blessings the Lord has showered on me.

Lord, help me to live a life that will bring honor and glory to Your name and keep my identity as a true Christian. Make me a blessing to someone today.

HEPZIBAH KORE

Message From a Brook

You will forget your misery; you will remember it as waters that have passed away. Job 11:16, RSV.

A S I WALKED ALONE on a bright, warm afternoon, I found a small bridge over a swiftly running brook. Brooks do really seem to sing. As I watched and listened to the music of the brook, I remembered this promise in Job: "You will forget your misery; you will remember it as waters that have passed away. And your life will be brighter than the noonday; its darkness will be like the morning. And you will have confidence, because there is hope" (Job 11:16-18, RSV).

"As waters that have passed away." What a wonderful promise! I watched as the water moved under the bridge. I would never see that water again; it would evaporate and come back— remade and cleansed as healing rain, but I would never see it again as it was.

I was attending a women's retreat; many women had courageously shared painful histories of abuse and mistreatment. Lives shattered by emotional and physical pain were healed and remade by Jesus. These same women shared how God used their pain, making them wonderful counselors to those who are going through difficult times. These women, juvenile detention program managers, counselors, nurses, loving parents, wives, friends, and helpers, watched as pain was washed away in the sea of forgetfulness. Their misery had been remade and was now as refreshing rain to someone else. Each day was becoming brighter because in Christ there is hope!

A verse of an old Negro spiritual says, "I'm so glad trouble don't last always." Revelation declares that one day God will make all things new. There will be no more sorrow and no more tears. All of our misery will pass away, and we will indeed know the fullness of joy.

In this life I have had a foretaste of that promised joy as I felt God's comfort and peace during my difficult times. My joy has also been renewed as I have seen how He equips me so that I can aid fellow travelers Also, the memory of my misery is forgotten when I remember the cross, that marvelous symbol of God's love, long-suffering, and salvation. And one day soon, when Jesus returns, all our misery will pass away. What a wonderful promise!

WANDA DAVIS

Sunglasses

For now we see through a glass, darkly; but then face to face: now I know in part; but then shall I know even as also I am known. 1 Cor. 13:12.

A S I SAT IN A women's ministries meeting I glanced to my left and saw Anna (names have been changed), sitting with sunglasses on. I had never seen her wear glasses or sunglasses before.

After the meeting we greeted each other. Anna was usually a bubbly, effervescent personality, but this day she could not hide her sadness. She mentioned that her relationship with her husband was at rock bottom. She could not take the physical abuse any longer. Wearing sunglasses was to help hide her swollen eyes.

Then there was Beverley. Her husband had left her for another woman. She also came looking for sisterly love. Her aching heart was sore. She felt she had no more tears to shed but had to be strong for her little daughter. So she wore sunglasses to hide her tear-filled eyes.

I cannot forget Celeste. Her husband had met with a fatal accident. She was a widow with two teenagers to raise. She tried hard to be brave, to hold back those showers of tears, and to be a source of comfort to her children. With sunglasses on, she just stared into space. I hugged her and assured her of my prayers daily.

There are hurting women all around us. You may be a hurting woman, too, trying to keep your problem private as long as you can by wearing sunglasses—another Anna, Beverley, or Celeste, hiding behind sunglasses. It is possible also for us to be women who, like the sun with its heat and bright glare, scorch a fragile soul with criticism instead of spreading rays of warmth and love.

You can give a hug or a smile to show hurting women that you care. You can pray, drop a card or note, or you can call. It is because of sin that we go through painful experiences. Someday it will be different. "Now we see through a glass, darkly, but then face to face." Likewise, "eye hath not seen, nor ear heard, neither have entered into the heart of man [or woman], the things which God hath prepared for them that love him" (1 Cor. 2:9).

PRISCILLA ADONIS

Blood Power

Come now, and let us reason together, saith the Lord: though your sins be as
scarlet, they shall be as white as snow, though they be red like crimson, they
shall be as wool. Isa. 1:18.

THE HOME IN WHICH I grew up was built on more than two acres of
land covered with a variety of fruit trees. It was always my pleasure to sit
in these trees and eat freely of that which was in season. There is one tree that
still stands out in my mind—the genip. This tree had some real cozy spots in
which a person could sit back and eat or even take a nap.

I still enjoy the genip, but the juice stains whatever it comes in contact
with and renders it unfit for any future public appearance. I can still hear my
grandmother warning us not to eat genip when we were wearing clothes
made for church or any other special occasion. Bleach is one chemical that is
often used to remove these stains from the clothes, but if the fabric is too delicate one runs the risk of having it become discolored.

Today as I reflect on this childhood experience I realize that I am in a
similar situation now. I no longer climb genip trees or stain my clothes with
the juice, but I often climb the tree of temptation, sometimes consciously or
unconsciously, and stain the fabric of my soul with the ugly genip juice of sin.
Like my grandmother, my heavenly Father hates the stain, too, and I can hear
His plea to avoid sinning. He also knows my weaknesses and has made provisions for removing those stains of sin. He gives an open offer for me to come
with my stains so He can remove them, leaving me spotless.

The difference, however, is that the fabric of my soul does not have to be
of any particular texture to be cleansed of theses stains; I need only acknowledge that they are present, submit them to Him, and His amazing power re-
moves them without any resulting discolor.

I will praise Him always because even though the stain on the fabric of
my soul may be like scarlet or crimson, it can be comepletely removed. I am
standing at His laundry door right now, waiting to be cleansed and to receive
power to resist the staining juice of sin each day.

Lord, I want to thank You for that day when You looked far beyond my
thoughts and saw my needs. You then provided a fountain where I can, even
today, come for cleansing. Amen. CHRISTINE MAY SMITH-SHAND

March 23

The Windshield

Be generous to one another, tender-hearted, forgiving one another as God in Christ forgave you. Eph. 4:32, NEB.

ONE DAY MY HUSBAND and I went to visit a friend who was having marital problems. She seemed to harbor deep resentment against her husband, so as good and positive friends do, we listened to the sad story she had.

Some time passed. We were not satisfied with the way things were progressing between my friend and her husband, so we decided to visit her again. As our conversation neared an end, my husband said to her, "I've been thinking about what you've told us, and I'm trying to figure out a way for you to fix things from your point of view. It seems to me that you feel very strongly about what has happened between you and your husband."

My friend grew more interested.

"Your car has a big windshield," my husband continued. "This windshield lets you see the road in front of you. But to look behind, you have only a tiny mirror. If a car is coming toward you or from behind you can see it because you have a windshield and a rearview mirror. You need to look at your problem in the same way."

The analogy seemed interesting, but I was wondering how it would apply to her.

"Your life is like a windshield," he said. "Through it you can see everything, but you have only a very small mirror to look at your past. If this is the case, why would you want to drive all the time looking back through this small mirror? Why not enjoy the view through the nice big windshield?"

Quite often we are drawn to the past, and sometimes we remain in it. We have the tendency to look back through the rearview mirror and bring back the times when we have been wronged. It is good to look in the rearview mirror only to learn lessons from our previous experiences or to see how God has helped us in the past.

Let's learn to look forward, through the windshield, so we can see all the marvelous things that God is going to do for us this very day.

ELLEN E. MAYR

Only Believe

Jesus said to him, "If you can believe, all things are possible to him who believes." Immediately the father of the child cried out and said with tears, "Lord, I believe; help my unbelief!" Mark 9:23, 24, NKJV.

MY HUSBAND CAME HOME one day and announced enthusiastically, "Six of us ministers are going to the Philippines to hold evangelistic crusades simultaneously." Then in a sad tone he added, "But I wish you could go."

You see, each minister was responsible for his airfare, food, pocket money, and expenses for the crusade. Each had to raise at least $1,000. With only one income in the family, it would be quite difficult for both of us to go, although we work as a team in his two churches. In the meantime my daughter-in-law, who lives in Dallas, Texas, called and offered to fly me to Texas while my husband was away. It was too good to refuse, but the following day I called her back and thanked her, saying I'd rather take a rain check. I didn't tell my husband that I, too, was wishing I could go along because I wanted to help. Besides, what wife would want to be left behind for three weeks? I thought that if God wanted me to be a part of the team, He'd surely make a way. He'd done it before, providing for a need, and why wouldn't He do it again? Was there anything impossible with Him?

Meanwhile, without my knowledge, my husband sent an e-mail to a friend and mentioned about his upcoming trip and his wish for me to join the team. Two days later our friend and his wife sent $1,100 for me to go, too. Phone calls were made. Air tickets were purchased. My passport was in order. And on the day the ministers left, I was also on my way to join the team.

Looking back on this experience I think of how little faith I had. "O taste and see that the Lord is good!" (Ps. 34:8, RSV). How faithful our heavenly Father is! I'm positive that He'll do much more exceedingly if I won't waver in my faith and trust in Him.

Awesome God, please endow me with that kind of faith that will move mountains of unbelief so that I can trust You in every situation, whatever it may be. Thank You for being so faithful in providing every need—and even many of my wants. Amen. OFELIA A. PANGAN

March 25

Tender Mercies

The Lord is good to all, and His tender mercies are over all His works.
Ps. 145:9, NKJV.

I TOOK A TEMPORARY live-in job working for a university couple and their children while the wife was recovering from surgery. I brought my youngest son, 8-year-old Adam, with me. One day all the children and I walked to the lake on campus to feed the ducks, some geese, and a swan. When it was time to leave, somehow my son was quick enough to catch a duckling out of the water and run with it. The mother duck jumped out of the lake and chased him, quacking desperately, but Adam ran faster.

Once home, predictably, the professor father said no to Adam's pleas to build a cement pond in their basement. Besides, the thoughts of that mother duck's plaintive wails haunted me, so I drove Adam and the duckling back to the lake.

It was starting to rain, and all the ducks and geese were at the extreme end of the lake. Only the swan appeared as Adam carried the baby duck to its destination. The swan recognized the kidnapper and started thrashing its wings and tried to trip him with its huge webbed feet. Adam was so scared he just tossed the little duckling into the water and ran back to me.

The little ball of fluff spun around in the water as if to say with a gulp, "Help! Where am I?"All was quiet on the lake, but as the duckling continued its dimunitive sounds, out of all the flocks of geese and ducks stationed at the far end, one duck swam out. One duck traversed that length of lake. One lone duck recognized her baby's cry. The rest soon joined her, seeming to re-joice with her.

I saw God's gentleness in that innocent creature, that gentle little ball of fluff, and God's tender mercy that He puts even in the hearts of mother ducks. I saw the fierce love of the swan coming to the aid of another's young. I wept at this revelation of God's gentleness and tender mercies for all His creation.

My prayer is that we may become more aware of Your love as shown in much of nature. Help us always to be kind and gentle to Your creatures ourselves, shar-ing this planet and Your concern for even the smallest of creatures.

ALEAH IQBAL

The Ride

"For I know the plans I have for you," declares the Lord, "plans to prosper you and not to harm you, plans to give you hope and a future." Jer. 29:11, NIV.

I SQUEEZED INTO THE tiny back seat with my date. We snapped our seat belts into place and were on our way. I had known his family since grade school. Our families frequently attended the same gospel concerts and social events. Even so, Mother had inquired into all the details, making certain my reputation and person would remain safe.

The self-assured teen in me leaped at the chance to ride in the tiny car. The car jerked into gear with a deafening roar that made conversation all but impossible. However, I was soon to learn that this was no ordinary ride, and talking would not be the main event. In a blur the car suddenly veered to the right and around the corner so fast that only the seat belts held us in place. Everyone was laughing heartily and, in youthful zest, so did I. Los Angeles is not particularly hilly, but we had found a steep one. It seemed that my heart was truly in my throat as the car accelerated downhill. For a moment scenes from my short life began to flash before my eyes.

No one paid any attention to the police officer relaxing in his cruiser. More alarming, he never even looked up at us. We whipped this way and that at speeds that defied common sense. And then, as suddenly as we had started, we stopped. Within seconds my date was helping me out of the back seat, and it felt good to stand on solid ground again. We strolled to a nearby restaurant, but my still nervous stomach did not permit me to eat. The spectacular seaside view was calming after such a harrowing ride.

Eventually my date turned to me with a sparkle in his eyes, asking if I was ready. My insides tensed at the reminder of the maniacal car ride, but still I rose in silent consent.

Why would any sane, rational person agree to such a hazardous ride? Because the car was attached to a track on the Wild Mouse Ride on the boardwalk.

There are days when it seems my life is out of control, roaring perilously toward pain and despair. Because God has provided the track for my life, I know that no matter how sharp the turn, how great the speed or sudden the stop, I am safe and secure.   SHIRLEY KIMBROUGH GREAR

March 27

Soul Windows

The lamp of the body is the eye. Therefore, when your eye is good, your whole body also is full of light. But when your eye is bad, your body also is full of darkness. Luke 11:34, NKJV.

LENS, CORNEA, RETINA, IRIS, and other delicate parts—put them to-gether with the Creator's skill and we have the eye. The eye is a camera that takes perfect pictures and sends them to the brain to be developed. Sin has made some eyes deficient, but technology can often remedy the problem.

The eye is the window to the soul. Whether blue, brown, gray, or green, all eyes form an opening from the world to the heart. All things viewed go in without discretion. If bad or good, the scene's embedded on the soul. Our prayer should be:

Dear Lord, grant that I may see Your handiwork upon the world—
The scenes of beauty, purity, and loveliness,
The scenes of sorrow surrounded by Your grief.
May the streams of light that enter in enrich my soul.

The eye is so much more than just a complexity of intricate parts de-signed for our vision. Our lives are also played out through our eyes—a drama on our personal stage for all the world to see. Most actions of the eye are unrehearsed. The large, open eyes shocked by the bold. The wide, round eyes of fear. The lighted eyes of joy at seeing that exciting thing or special per-son. The sparkle of mischief. The softened eyes melted by the warmth of love or lover. The narrowing eyes of concern. The fiery eyes of anger, shooting daggers. The steel of resistance without a blink. The steadfast eyes of surety that won't turn aside. The lowered eyes of shame or guilt. The indifferent wandering eyes. The perfect eye connection of understanding. The moist eyes of sorrow or hurt. The tear-filled eyes of pain and agony. The wide-eyed wonder of discovery. The questioning raised brows. The manipulation of fluttering lashes. The darting eyes of uncertainty. The faded eyes that have known too much rejection. The cold eyes that wall off pain too great to bear. Closed eyes—in thought, in prayer, in sleep.

Our eyes are the windows of our hearts on the world. What are we saying today?

DAWNA BEAUSOLEIL

Lost Keys

Do not be anxious about anything, but in everything, by prayer and petition, with thanksgiving, present your requests to God. Phil. 4:6, NIV.

ONE SUNDAY MORNING while visiting with my parents in a neighboring state, our sons needed to be home earlier in the afternoon than my husband and I, so the three of them had taken one car, and my husband and I another.

As final preparations for my sons' departure began, the question on everyone's lips was "Where are the keys?" As precious moments passed, blame and accusations were made and tempers began to flare. The search party expanded to include all other relatives close enough to be recruited.

The most obvious place to look for car keys is coat pockets. My oldest son was the last to drive the car, so his were the first pockets to be searched. But all others were also examined and reexamined thoroughly. Questions were asked, activities recounted, footsteps retraced, and still no keys.

Sneaking away into a quiet bedroom for only a few seconds, I offered up a quick, desperate prayer for help from the one member of the family who had not been consulted, our heavenly Father, who knows and cares for all.

With renewed determination and a hopeful heart, I walked from the bedroom into the living room, picked up my oldest son's jacket from the sofa, reached into the pocket, and pulled out the keys—just that quickly and just that matter-of-factly—to the utter astonishment of everyone involved, especially myself!

Realizing this was truly a miracle, I didn't hesitate to explain exactly what had happened, and how. Quieted and humbled, the search party disbanded and our three sons were soon on their way. Once again I sneaked off into that quiet bedroom for a few minutes, this time to offer a prayer of thanks and to remind myself that indeed our Father cares for us, even in the smallest details of our everyday lives.

PAULETTA COX JOHNSON

Watch Bird

Behold the beauty. Ps. 27:4.

"CHEER! CHEER . . . CHEER . . . church . . . church . . . church!" I looked up, trying to trace the source of the trill. There, up on the highest branch of the leafless apricot tree, perched the triller, head lifted, bill parted in song. Swiftly winging down, it lighted atop the bluebird box I had recently put within clear sight of my work area. Through the windowpane, the handsome visitor was in plain view. It wore a suit as blue as the sky and a coordinating reddish-orange vest. Soon one of lesser color flew to sit beside it; the first bird hopped onto the entrance hole of the box. It poked its head in as if inspecting the interior. Then fluttering up, it sat atop the box beside the newcomer. The pair took turns thrusting their heads into the entrance hole. Then the new-comer—obviously the female—disappeared into the box. Emerging, both flitted like butterflies around treetops, celebrating, in a playful mood. The lovebirds repeated their ritual.

Then there they were, building in earnest. The female tirelessly carried in nest materials. The male perched nearby, watching and, on occasion, poking his head in the hole. Then the flurry of building halted. The female went in—to lay eggs, I suspected. Before long she was staying in, the bright-blue one always nearby. He poked his head into the entrance hole soon after his mate flew away. He swooped away squirrels who scampered around the nest, and chased other birds, particularly brown birds who came as a team, feeding on the ground beneath the box.

Now, where's that bluebird? Below, a brown bird strutted and picked food, looking up stealthily . . . picking . . . strutting . . . closer, closer beneath the box. Whir! The brown bird flew up over the entrance hole. Out popped the head of the female bluebird; its body followed, toes planted on the lower edge of the entrance hole, blue wings spread across the front panel, covering the entrance hole. Suddenly, blue-as-the-sky flashed down, swooping in fury, sending the cowbird and its cohorts in flight.

Thank You, Lord, for keeping watch over all Your creatures.

CONSUELO RODA JACKSON

Sonny's Turn to Pray

The Lord looks down from heaven on the entire human race; he looks to see if there is even one with real understanding, one who seeks for God. Ps. 14:2, NLT.

SONNY LOVES TO GO to church, and I'm delighted to be his escort. Recently we received a personal invitation to attend Joy Chapel, a nondenominational organization that hosts a weekly fellowship supper and worship service that ministers to the disabled, their families, and staff. What an awesome and uplifting experience! Sonny and I were indeed blessed.

Students from a nearby Bible institute came to socialize and to help with the worship service. Other volunteers prepared a delicious meal. Everyone was smiling, and the joy felt by simply being there with friends was for real. Stories were read, Bible texts recited, songs sung, and prayers sent up to heaven. During prayer and praise time everyone had the opportunity to speak. Some used sign language. Each prayer request was also written down on a blackboard.

It appeared that Sonny was the youngest person attending this worship service, and perhaps the only one there who still went to school. Many thanked God for their jobs and their friends and for Joy Chapel. The Holy Spirit guided Sonny when it was his turn to pray. I helped him a little with his prayer. No one had to hurry.

Time is the most precious gift that I have to give back to Jesus and to society, and I try to do what is best for people so they may be saved. The adults and students who volunteer and give freely of their time to make Joy Chapel a beautiful and positive experience for the disabled will never regret it. God honors all who serve Him. Everywhere there are mentally and physically disabled people who desire to be embraced and loved by people who genuinely care. Sadly, too often we don't have the time or are uncomfortable with the role of caregiver. We leave the nurturing to someone else, and the blessings that could have been ours go unclaimed.

When you really try to understand and meet the needs of someone else—sharing your time and talents to make their life as pleasant as possible—the Lord is looking down from heaven. And I'm sure He is very pleased.

DEBORAH SANDERS

March 31

Contented in Christ

Let your conversation be without covetousness; and be content with such things as ye have: for he hath said, I will never leave thee, nor forsake thee. Heb. 13:5.

THE CONTINENT OF AFRICA is blessed with many awe-inspiring natural wonders. In South Africa the famous white sand beaches of Cape Town are framed by the majestic Table Mountain. From the top of Mount Kenya, the second-highest mountain in Africa, I watched in solemn reverence as the sun stretched its fingers, peeped out, and then exploded into the lush valley below. In the game parks I witnessed the fragile balance of life in the lion's chase and the antelope's sacrifice. In Zimbabwe tons of water torrent over Victoria Falls, creating a rainbow in the mist before cascading into the raging Zambezi River. All this majesty drew me to praise the Creator of it all.

Yes, Africa is a land of diversity. It has many beautiful places and large cities, but it is from the people of these areas that I learned a very important lesson—the lesson of contentment, *Hakuna Matata*. No problems! No matter how hard life is, they bear it with a smile.

The average rural African family does not have many earthly possessions and has to struggle to survive. Women are often seen carrying a five gallon container of water or a large sack of maize meal on their head. Yet they do so without complaint. While we struggle to abstain from overeating, some of these people struggle to find food. Yet they are happy to be alive. They have so little, yet they have so much. No cars or trucks or bicycles—and sometimes not even shoes, only feet. They eagerly go wherever they can to share Jesus. No churches, no stained-glass windows, no plush pews. Only the open air and shade from a tree. Yet they lift their voices in thanks and show their exuberance on their faces. They have so little, yet they have so much. Their joy is in Christ—in Christ they find happiness. With Christ they are filled. In Christ they are content.

Oh, that we would focus on Jesus. If we would make Him Lord of everything—our hearts, minds, and lives. If we would cast all our cares on Him and then trust. If we would forget the things of this world, which will fade away, and seek Him, our everlasting Lord. If we would allow Jesus to fill us, we would be content, and happiness would flow from Him.

Susan Jeda Orillosa

Water the Thirsty

For I will pour water upon him that is thirsty, and floods upon the dry ground: I will pour my spirit upon thy seed. Isa. 44:3.

THE ARRIVAL OF SPRING brought much transplanting and seed sowing. Because of a mild winter, my pansies had bloomed during the entire season, and now buds opened in a profusion of blossoms. Their favorite smiling faces emerged everywhere—including places I didn't want them to grow. So early one evening I busied myself and quickly transplanted those healthy pansy shoots into carefully chosen spots. Darkness soon forced me to cease my efforts, and some of my work remained unfinished.

The next morning, to my dismay, I discovered that I had overlooked putting one favorite-color, healthy plant into its selected spot the previous evening. There it sat with wilted leaves beside the hole I had dug for it. Since the stems appeared fresh and there was a lot of soil around the roots, I decided to plant it anyway. I watered it well but doubted it would survive.

That evening I made my rounds to see how my transplants were doing. To my delight, I found that the wilted pansy had come to life. The leaves, instead of drooping, stood upright and vibrant. Amazed at how it had revived, I watered it profusely and hoped it would continue to grow and bloom.

"What a difference a good water soaking and an application of B Start mixture made in the response of that wilted pansy," I mused.

Like my neglected pansy, hectic days wilt me, too! That's when I find that moments of quiet time, reading God's precious Word, refresh my spirits. The precious promises I can claim as my very own revive me like a fresh drink of cool water on a blistering hot day.

Thank You, loving Father in heaven, for pouring the waters of Your precious promises into my wilting soul today. Please water my soul with Your Holy Spirit that I may not wilt under the many cares and demands life hurls at me. Yes, I need You to fill me with Your Spirit so that I may not wither under the end-time trials of aging or from stressful happenings around me from day to day.

NATHALIE LADNER-BISCHOFF

April 2

I'm Grateful

Giving thanks always for all things unto God and the Father in the name of our Lord Jesus Christ. Eph. 5:20.

EVEN THOUGH I'M HEARING-impaired, I'm thankful for my keen senses of smell, taste, and touch. I'm most thankful for glasses that improve my sense of sight and help me in lipreading and anticipating sounds.

I've never heard a robin announcing "Spring is here," nor have I heard the "cheer-up" messages of any songbirds. But I'm thankful I can see the birds and the many beauties in nature. I don't have to hear the rustle of leaves to enjoy their vibrant fall colors or their vivid springtime shades of green. I don't have to hear the ocean roar (does it really?) to feel the mighty power of each wave cresting and breaking. I don't have to hear syrup boiling on the stove to savor the taste of candy in the making.

When I started school I acted the part, pretending to enjoy giggling and whispering secrets with my friends. All my life I strove to act like one with acute hearing, without revealing I was a sham. In spite of my deception, I'm thankful for being accepted by a host of friends.

I have difficulty participating in group conversations, but I'm thankful for those who keep me tuned in by repeating what I miss. And I'm thankful to those who give me a facial view and speak slowly rather than embarrassingly louder.

I can't watch TV and do needlework or prepare a meal at the same time. Neither can I enjoy the chatter in group activities and work efficiently at the same time. But I'm thankful for 24 hours in a day in which to accomplish the priorities in my life—one thing at a time. And I'm thankful I can work and live an independent life.

It's easy to be thankful to those who have been tolerant, kind, and helpful in my hearing loss. Although distasteful at the time, I'm now most grateful to those who were firm with me when I wanted to be spared the stress encountered in hearing situations. These disciplinarians can be credited for pushing me beyond what I might have attained.

Thank You, Lord, for blessings too numerous to mention. EDITH FITCH

A Bag of Noodles

And this gospel of the kingdom shall be preached in all the world for a witness unto all nations; and then shall the end come. Matt. 24:14.

THE SUN SEEMED TO crawl right into my bedroom very early each morning in China, bringing an end to my night's sleep. This Friday I reached over to my nightstand for a book to read. I always kept a pile of books close at hand for reading to replenish my spirit and knowledge. I was in my fifth month of teaching both classes and private students and found it both exciting and challenging. They were so eager to learn.

At 6:15 the telephone rang, breaking the stillness of the early morning. I jumped out of bed and ran to the front room. I picked up the phone and heard the gentle voice of one of my students, Mei.

She asked, "Are you awake?"

Laughing, I replied, "Yes, I was reading."

"I know you always like to get your work and cooking done early on Friday, your preparation day, and I have a bag of noodles for you, so I want to bring them over early." The Chinese by now knew I loved noodles, and they liked to give their teachers gifts.

As her dormitory was just across from my yard, two minutes later she was at my front door with a huge bag of different kinds of Chinese noodles. I smiled and thanked her profusely. Mei was one of the most diligent students. She came at different times for her classes and often helped me with my housework. She therefore witnessed my lifestyle and could see how cluttered my apartment became by the end of the week because of all my different activities and teaching load. And then on Friday, my preparation day, it would take on a new, clean, shiny appearance for my Sabbath. Things and books found their places back on the shelves. And flowers appeared, if I found time to get to the Plant and Pet Market.

Mei quickly took up witnessing in her life. She is a nurse in China, busy smiling and sharing joy with her patients, family, and all with whom she comes in contact. She can't bring me noodles anymore—I still like them and now buy them at the supermarket—but I am often reminded of the importance of the lesson of the bag of noodles. Our life is a book that others are constantly reading. What words are they reading in your life and mine?

DESSA WEISZ HARDIN

April 4

He Is My Help and My Deliverer

Yet I am poor and needy; may the Lord think of me. You are my help and my deliverer. Ps. 40:17, NIV.

WITH MY HUSBAND, Carlos, I had the privilege of working several years on the Amazon River on the *Lightbearer* or *Luzeiro* launches. We used these boats as our home, navigating the long river, meeting the physical and spiritual necessities of those who lived along the riverbanks.

On one occasion we arrived at a location suffering from a malaria epidemic. We began to care for the people, distributing medication. Finally, our medicines ran out, but with the help of the medication and the Lord Jesus, we were able to see the health of all those individuals improve enough that we continued on our trip down the river.

A few days later I began to feel as if I were getting the flu. The fever made me terribly weak, but there was no more medication onboard. I remained quietly in bed while my daughter jumped and played around me. One afternoon when Carlos came to check on me, he found our daughter, praying, and me unconscious.

What should be done? He could only turn to the heavenly Father. Before long Carlos heard the noise of a boat. Incredible! Boats only passed by every two or three weeks. Carlos grabbed a white cloth and signaled the other boat. It approached immediately and left an IV nutrient solution and intravenous medication for malaria. My husband had never applied an IV before, but with courage and trust in the Lord, he applied both the IV and the medication. Within a few minutes I began to improve but still had no strength, not even enough to lift any of my fingers.

During this time we had not been able to communicate with the mission by radio, so Carlos took our radio apart and got it fixed by Friday afternoon. Normally, there is no one at the mission office on Friday afternoon, but that day the treasurer returned unexpectedly and picked up Carlos's call. The next morning a plane arrived and took me for treatment.

Would it be a coincidence that the boat passed by when it did, that the radio worked, and that the treasurer stopped by the mission office on Friday afternoon? There is no doubt, Jehovah thought of me, and He was my helper and the one who delivered me. Praise the Lord!

GRACIELA NOEMI HELLVIG DE HEIN

What's the Question?

Surely I spoke of things I did not understand. Job 42:3, NIV.

WHEN I WAS A little girl one of our neighbors had a favorite saying: "There's more than one way to skin a cat." I heard it so often it must have taken up permanent residence in my memory bank. Decades later I caught myself throwing out that same line during a stimulating but rather tense discussion with a group of brain researchers. Without so much as a pause one of them retorted, "If you have a cat to be skinned." I chuckled with pleasure at the unexpected response and only realized in retrospect its value.

We need to ask the right questions. Indeed, the appropriate question may not be "How do I skin a cat?" but rather "Is this a cat, and does it need to be skinned?"

All progress, all personal growth begins with a question. Sometimes we delay our start or plateau for a time on our journey because we're not asking helpful questions. Or we waste energy searching for answers to questions that don't really matter.

This concept of asking the right question is especially critical in the area of family-of-origin work when we're trying to identify the script we were handed at birth. We can only invent a healthier future for ourselves when we know what our script says. With that "dialogue" in hand, we can then ask if our script matches who we are innately, or if it reflects unrealistic expectations or even unfinished business from the past. We can ask what portions need to be rewritten or perhaps deleted. We can ask what needs to be added in order to enable our script to function as a useful personal map.

Job's wife asked unhelpful questions of her husband after he had been afflicted with painful sores (Job 2:9). In fact, one of the most intriguing stories of all time is filled with questions. God asks Job, "Would you discredit my justice?" (Job 40:8, NIV). And Job asks, "How can I reply to you? I put my hand over my mouth" (verse 4, NIV). In some situations, putting a hand over our mouth is good advice. Especially when we are tempted to speak of things we do not understand!

Ah, yes. "Is this a cat, and, if so, does it need to be skinned?"

ARLENE TAYLOR

Junk Food and Principles

But thou, son of man, hear what I say unto thee; Be not thou rebellious like that rebellious house; open thy mouth, and eat that I give thee. Eze. 2:8.

J UNK FOOD. HOW MANY times I've heard those words! During my childhood years (and they were not yesterday), I recall my mother stressing daily the importance of eating foods that were nutritious so that my brother, sister, and I would grow to be healthy children.

If there were foods we didn't like, she would explain their nutritional value and why it was important to eat them. It just happened that the foods we liked best were not the ones Mother desired for us, because they had no nutritional value. In spite of Mother's counseling there were times, especially after school, when I would use my allowance to buy the junk foods I liked best.

Many years have passed, and having children of my own, I've found myself stressing to Alex, Jr., and Cynthia, and then to their children, the same principles my mother taught me.

Junk foods have not changed their nutritional value even today; now there are only more varieties, colors, and flavors to get one's attention and to arouse one's taste buds. On television, on shelves in grocery stores, junk foods are ever before me. What can I do—what can we do? I ask. Again, as I reminisce about my childhood years and about eating junk food against Mother's principles, my thoughts quickly become focused on 1 Corinthians 13:11: "When I was a child, . . . I understood as a child, I thought as a child: but when I became a man [woman], I put away childish things."

Now as an adult I pray that foods that are tempting will be only those that will help me, physically and mentally. I know that if my body is not functioning well, then my spiritual growth is impaired also.

Lord, I'm thankful for Mother's advice on junk food and Your advice given not only to me but to all Your children through principles laid down in Your written word. May they always be a priority in helping my relationship with You to grow daily, knowing fully that Your way is always the best way, even though at times Satan would have me think otherwise. ANNIE B. BEST

Beneath Angel's Wings

For he has charged his angels to guard you wherever you go. Ps. 91:11, NEB.

FOR A FEW YEARS I owned an old caravan and spent two days each month writing and sketching in the beautiful countryside of Somerset. I chose a different site each year so as to cover the area more closely in my ancient Morris Minor, now 35 years old. Of course, my little Yorkshire terrier always came with me.

Unfortunately, on one visit I fell and twisted my ankle, fractured three ribs, and ended up with a painful neck. After two uncomfortable days I decided to return home to see my doctor. I decided to take the scenic route as it was much more pleasant and had less traffic. I left quietly with prayers for safety. About halfway home I approached a sharp bend and knew there was a steep hill I must climb around the corner. I accelerated to give my little car some power to climb the hill. To my horror, there was a huge furniture removal van parked across the top. They signaled to me to reverse. I struggled but found that because of my injuries I couldn't look back far enough to maneuver down and around the corner.

I got out to tell them I was unable to move when a young man appeared suddenly. "Would you like me to reverse down the hill for you?" he offered.

I never hesitated, and gave him the keys. He whizzed around the corner so easily. I walked down the hill to where he had parked the car to thank him. The keys were in the car, but he was gone. There was only one house nearby, and a couple were standing at their gate.

"Did you see the young man who drove my car down here?" I asked.

They hadn't seen anyone. My dog seemed quite happy and not anxious that a stranger had been there without me.

I sat in the sunshine feeling cared for and protected. A wonderful sense of gratitude stayed with me as I waited for the van to pass so I could continue my journey home.

My dear Father, how can I thank You enough for sending my guardian angel to come to my aid? Not only as I drive my car but wherever I am, I know You care and are watching over me.   PHILIPPA MARSHALL

April 8

Just an Old Boot

Thou preparest a table before me in the presence of mine enemies: thou anointest my head with oil; my cup runneth over. Ps. 23:5.

I RECEIVE MANY INSPIRATIONAL thoughts while out on my walks. For many days I had walked past an old boot lying beside the road in an upright position, as if someone had just stepped out of it. Just an old boot, hardly worth a second glance—and many did ignore it. Cars whizzed by; other folks jogged past, and day by day the boot just sat there.

But one day I did glance its way; something actually possessed me to go over to it. I could see the toes were worn and battered right down to the protective steel toe. I picked it up and discovered that the heel was broken open at the sole. But the laces were of a sturdy nature and fairly new. I looked inside. (Why, I do not know. Sometimes people do strange things.) There, tucked down in the toe, was a brand-new pair of sunglasses. This boot now became more personal and lifelike. I observed that it had been kept clean, even oiled for leather preservation. Why would anyone spend money on oil for such a battered and worn boot? I thought about the owner, probably a hardworking man who had cared for it and was getting the last bit of use out of his boots. He was perhaps sad to have lost it and his glasses.

Just an old boot I am. I have worn toes from the kicks and stumbles of life. My heels are cracked from recollections of unkind words and insinuations from others. Some of my laces are still strong, and most of the time I can pull myself up and carry on with my daily duties. I will never be a new boot again here on this earth. But I know that one day I will be, when Christ makes me over. Until then I will keep this old boot oiled with His Spirit that I receive from the daily study of His Word and from prayer communion time.

I know He has looked inside of me and found a treasure of more worth than my exterior may indicate. And with His layering of heavenly oil—"thou anointist my head with oil"—I can weather the trials, disappointments, and heartaches and get this old boot through this life until I am made into a brand-new one.

VIDELLA MCCLELLAN

Under the Shadow of His Wings

The Lord will be a shelter for His people. Joel 3:16, NKJV.

THE RAIN HAD FALLEN for several days, creating several small puddles on the walks on either side of the road. Taking a midmorning stroll, I saw a family of ducks—a mother duck and seven ducklings. In fascination I stood to watch the little family.

Mother Duck stood at the curb, paused, looked across the street at a glistening puddle, and headed toward it. As she made the first step, the ducklings swiftly formed a straight line behind her as though a secret signal had been given. They all made their way across the road and waded into inviting water. They splashed and paddled in the water gleefully, as only baby ducks can.

Once again the secret signal was sounded, and Mother Duck trotted off with her battalion behind her. This time they headed for a clump of grass, where they settled and watched a pecking session demonstration.

"This is how to do it," I imagined her telling them.

Each little beak pecked in unison, following Mother Duck's example. The pecking session ended, and Mother Duck settled down to take a snooze in the warm morning sun. In between short naps she called a few of them and dressed their ruffled feathers.

At the sound of an oncoming vehicle she sensed the threat and summoned her little brood to shelter. They scurried to hide under her wings. There was enough room for each to be totally hidden. Not one duckling disobeyed. They all stayed protected until the danger was past.

I stood, captivated and amazed. How much like Mother Duck is our heavenly Father! The ducklings were safe while her feathers covered them. When they obeyed her commands, they were shielded from danger. We are His children. He invites us to shelter under His wings. He promises to buoy us up on eagles' wings. When there is danger of our straying, He signals us with messages from His Word, comments from friends, a song, lessons from nature—whatever it takes for us to be reminded of His protection and love.

When there is danger, "he shall cover you with his feathers, and under his wings shalt thou trust" (Ps. 91:4). We must trust and obey Him. His promises are true.

GLORIA GREGORY

Midair Miracle

The Lord is good, a strong hold in the day of trouble; and he knoweth them that trust in him. Nahum 1:7.

MY DAUGHTER, DANA, and her husband, Dani, live a little more than an hour's drive from me, but I don't see the grandkids as often as I like. When Dana arrived with her family for the weekend, I was extremely pleased.

Saturday afternoon, when all of them were going various places, 5-year-old Keila clung to my hand. "Grand, can I stay here?"

"You have to ask your mom," I instructed.

The moment Dana gave permission, Keila squeezed my hand and squealed.

"Remember; be nice," her mother cautioned on the way out. "Have a good time."

We always did. With Keila there was never a dull moment. A doting grandparent, I enjoyed having my granddaughters around. And believe me, I took my grandparent role very seriously. I slipped the girls extra dessert and allowed antics their mother never got away with as a child. Most of all, I prayed every morning for my granddaughters' safety—all six of them. Including Keila, my little chatterbox.

After playing some guessing games, we laughed and waltzed around the floor. Keila loved catching my long dress as it flared above my ankles. We went upstairs to get a barrette, then back down the hall we pranced, Keila giggling and running to catch my dress. As we neared the steep stairs Keila again grabbed but missed, sending her flying over the edge. There was nothing I could do. As I watched in horror, the thought shot through my mind, *I've killed my daughter's child.* I just knew her small body would drop to the bottom of 13 steps in a broken heap.

To my amazement, Keila rolled over gently in midair while still falling, as if turned by an unseen hand that lowered her to a slow stomach-slide. She caught a carpeted step and hung on, fear in her eyes.

I gathered her in my arms. I knew God had performed a miracle—answered a prayer prayed early that morning. And this grandmother offered another prayer. One of thanks.   ETHEL FOOTMAN SMOTHERS

When Tragedy Strikes, God Knows Best

But my God shall supply all your need according to his riches in glory by Christ Jesus. Phil. 4:19.

IT WAS SPRING BREAK, so our family decided to take the week off, first to visit with some friends in Arlington, Texas, and then to visit St. Louis, Missouri. The trip went well until we returned to the parking lot one evening and realized that our car had been broken into. Someone had broken the left rear window, unlocked the trunk, and taken out my brown handbag and my husband's brown briefcase. Most of our precious possessions were gone: my wedding ring, my gold watch inherited from my husband's grandmother's fiftieth wedding anniversary, my cellular phone, a blue purse, a brown change purse with $175 in cash, a pair of walkie-talkie radios, and many other personal items.

We lost more than $5,000 worth of things, none of which we were able to retrieve. Our trip was ruined, so we decided to head home. Although our hearts were broken, we were comforted by the text "Lay not up for yourselves treasures upon earth, where moth and rust doth corrupt, and where thieves break through and steal: but lay up for yourselves treasures in heaven, . . . for where your treasure is, there will your heart be also" (Matt. 6:19-21). The Lord allows things to happen for a reason: sometimes to teach us a lesson, and sometimes to help us to grow and become stronger.

My wedding band, which was so sentimental to me, was gone; however, my love for my husband grows even stronger. After all, we are enjoying each other's company in good health. Things could have been even worse—God does know best. Driving back home, we felt more closely knit and bonded as a family as we struggled to recover from our loss. We remembered vividly that God does not give anyone more than they can bear. As we worked through our loss, we learned to trust God more and to lean on His promises, which never fail. The more you call upon Him, the more blessings He will send your way. Through every trial there is growth and great triumph.

Remember, if He can clothe the lilies of the field that toil not, how much more will He take care of us, His children. Let's turn all of our downfalls into stepping-stones to progress, and keep trusting in Him.   QUTIE DEWAR

April 12

Leaving Gifts

I will ask the Father, and he will give you another Counselor to be with you forever. . . . I will not leave you as orphans; I will come to you. John 14:16-18, NIV.

WE WALKED ALONG THE banks of the Grand Union Canal in central London, then headed back to church through the side streets, close to a redevelopment site. As we wandered along, looking for rare glimpses of nature, I noticed a scrap of paper on the ground. Normally, I wouldn't have given it a second glance, but there was something about the bold and striking handwriting that attracted my attention. It wasn't a scrap of paper at all—it was an envelope, torn open and discarded. The message on the outside read: "Darling, I'll be back soon; but in the meantime, have yourself some retail therapy, and enjoy these gift vouchers. I love you. xxx." The envelope was plain and white, so there was no way of knowing what gift vouchers had once been folded inside.

This being London, I wondered if they may have been from Harrods, Selfridges, or Liberty. I imagined the delight and fun of being given hundreds of pounds of gift vouchers to spend. I had pictures of a twentysomething young woman meeting up with a friend for a shopping spree, and then taking afternoon tea in Covent Garden. Or lunch in an art gallery.

Or maybe the gift wasn't so lavish. The street where I found the envelope wasn't particularly special. It was a dead-end road with an industrial area down one side. Maybe the vouchers were for just a few pounds to spend in a bookstore, or Marks and Spencer. I'll never know. What I do know is that someone was very much in love but had to go away for a while, and left behind a gift to delight the one he loved most in the whole world.

I thought of Jesus, very much in love with us, but knowing He'd have to go away. I think in some ways He may have liked to stay here, to encourage us, to heal us, to hug us, and to teach us, but He knew it was best for Him to go. He wanted to leave us something to show His continuing love and care, and to show that He'd thought about our deepest needs and desires.

"My darlings, I'll be back soon; but in the meantime I'm leaving you the best present I can think of: My Holy Spirit, to comfort you, to inspire you, to guide you, and to remind you of Me and My love for you. Enjoy the experience. I love you so much. Jesus."

KAREN HOLFORD

How to Judge

For in the same way you judge others, you will be judged, and with the measure you use, it will be measured to you. Matt. 7:2, NIV.

HE WAS A LITTLE old man with long hair and a scraggly beard. His clothes were old, ill fitting, and not too clean. His only companion was a black dog, not much more than a pup on a leash. When I first saw him in front of the supermarket, he was trying to fasten the leash to a trash can nearby.

"You wait right here, and I'll soon be back," he seemed to be saying.

His looks were very unimpressive, and as he pushed his cart around in the store the other shoppers didn't pay much attention to him.

When I finished and left with my purchases, I noticed that the little dog was still securely fastened outside the market. I watched the scene for a few minutes. Each time the door opened, eager eyes searched to see if her master was coming back. The eager look would change to one of disappointment, then resignation, as the right person had not yet come.

That little dog, even though she was only a pup, taught me a lesson. I had judged the old man by his unkempt looks, by the way he was dressed. I'm sure others had done the same. But the little dog knew her master for what he really was on the inside—a kind, caring person, in spite of being old and poor.

Just as I was too quick to judge that old man, others could misjudge me, and it would be my due. Why is it so easy for me to judge others without knowing them or their circumstances? After all, they are children of God as much as I am. God loves them as much as He loves me. He knows what is in each of our hearts, not just on the outside.

Help me, Lord, today and every day, to judge others as I would want to be judged. Help me to pray for them and their needs instead of judging them by their looks. Soon we will all be together in Your kingdom because You have looked on our hearts.
BETTY J. ADAMS

April 14

The Handiwork of God

*The flowers appear on the earth; the time of the singing of birds is come.
Song of Sol. 2:12.*

THE TINY YELLOW FLOWER, no larger than a dime, caught my eye one day as I sat on the bank of beautiful Lake Huron in northern Michigan. An array of colorful wildflowers whose seeds had blown in on the rocky shore when the water was low had taken root and were now blooming. I recognized some of them: white and yellow daisies, Queen Anne's lace, and black-eyed Susans nestled among the assorted wild ferns and varied thistles and grasses. But the little yellow one that was growing apart from all the rest was new to me.

I stopped to examine the blossom more closely. Each petal was perfect, though almost hidden and undisturbed beneath the creeping vines. *How was it possible,* I wondered, *to survive so much backyard activity of the past summer months?* I picked some of the flowers and pressed them between the pages of a book. But I left the tiny yellow one intact as a reminder of the beauty of the earth and of God's loving watchcare to even the least of His wonderful creation.

During my stay in Michigan there were many occasions to view God's handiwork. How magnificent is the brilliant sunrise as it peeks over the horizon when only a hint of a ripple is on the water, so calm and quiet there's barely a separating line between lake and sky. Then the following day the white caps come rolling in, washing the stones along the shore.

Many times the simple pleasures of life are the best, for they can arrive without pretense and when we least expect them. Who of us dare dispute the beauty of fleecy white clouds floating in a blanket of blue, or the bright beacon from the lighthouse on the distant shore.

I watched the goldfinches as they came to dine at the bird feeder in the side yard, and I always enjoyed the haunting cry of the mourning dove somewhere off in the distance. It's a great rush of emotions to witness the glow of a crimson sunset on a warm summer evening with a cool breeze caressing your cheek and threatening to lull you to sleep.

Whether it's a tiny yellow wildflower or a magnificent sunrise or sunset, unless you've seen God's handiwork you may not have really known the simple yet profound pleasures of life after all.   CLAREEN COLCLESSER

Spill the Perfume

Then took Mary a pound of ointment of spikenard, very costly, and anointed the feet of Jesus, and wiped his feet with her hair: and the house was filled with the odour of the ointment. John 12:3.

IN MY FAMILY I'M the one who usually wakes up first. If someone needs a wake-up call in the morning, I'm the one they contact. I'm also like a "snooze button" for my husband. He wakes up when I do, but while I get ready, he turns over and tries to catch a few more winks. Sometimes when he falls back into a deeper sleep than anticipated, I have to wake him up. One of the fun ways I do this is by taking a small bottle of perfume and holding it close to his nose. Just watching his nostrils twitch before the sudden opening of his eyes causes me to break out in laughter. He good-naturedly joins in, and that starts the day off on a great note.

I'm reminded of the story in the Bible in which Mary unobtrusively entered the room at Simon's house while Jesus was eating dinner. Driven by love and devotion to her Savior, she quietly broke the alabaster box of spikenard perfume and poured out its expensive contents over the Master's feet. The strong fragrance quickly permeated the room, jolting the olfactory senses of everyone present. They were awakened to the realization that something out of the ordinary had taken place. Judas was the first one to react, disturbed over this obvious "waste" of money. Jesus, however, was pleased and commended Mary for her unselfish deed. The memory of this act of kindness shown to Him while He could still enjoy it was an encouragement as He went through the excruciating suffering in the final hours of His earthly life.

Any "perfume" we can pour on the lives of others is like pouring it on Jesus' feet. So let's break the alabaster box each morning and try to spread the fragrance, beginning with those in our own home. My favorite author says, "Many there are who bring their precious gifts for the dead. As they stand about the cold, silent form, words of love are freely spoken. Tenderness, appreciation, devotion, all are lavished upon one who sees not nor hears. Had these words been spoken when the weary spirit needed them so much, when the ear could hear and the heart could feel, how precious would have been their fragrance!" (Ellen G. White, *The Desire of Ages*, p. 560).

NANCY CACHERO VASQUEZ

Humor Is a Choice?

A joyful heart is good medicine, but a broken spirit dries up the bones.
Prov. 17:22, NASB.

THERE IS ONE GIFT the Lord gave me for which I have always been very thankful—a sense of humor. I enjoy nothing more than a good laugh, even at my own expense. There have been times when I was at the point of despair, when I thought to myself how totally funny and ridiculous the situation was, and decided I might as well find the humor in it.

One of those times was a Friday afternoon when I had just cleaned the house thoroughly, even to washing and ironing the kitchen curtains. I then proceeded to make a batch of bread, an old family favorite, for which I liquefy corn to replace the water in the recipe.

The newly cooked corn was extremely hot when I poured in into the blender. I was thinking I should let it cool a bit before proceeding, but I was in a hurry. When I turned the blender on, the force of that hot corn blew the lid right off, and sticky corn went everywhere. As I stood there, all alone in the kitchen, it was almost overwhelming to think what a mess there was. But then it looked so awful I just stood there and laughed.

I rewashed, dried, and ironed the curtains, completely scrubbed the ceiling, windows, deck tops, floor, and myself. That evening as we enjoyed the fresh bread for supper, I shared with the family what had happened that afternoon. They looked horrified, but then I started laughing, and they did too—eventually.

Another time as I rushed into my boss's office at school to answer his phone, the pocket of my dress caught on the doorknob and ripped the seam out for about eight inches. After I gathered my senses and answered the phone, I could hear the boss returning from lunch. Fortunately, he had some safety pins in his desk drawer, so I told him he could not come in for a few minutes and did a quick repair job. I walked out, laughing, as I shared what had happened. His only response was a hearty chuckle and the wish that he could have been there to see it happen.

These are two of many situations in which I have found myself. We've all had them, and I grant you there are times when there is no humor to be found. But when there is, it's much better for us to laugh than to be upset.

ANNA MAY RADKE WATERS

Shaken, but Not Forsaken

For he hath said, I will never leave thee, nor forsake thee. Heb. 13:5.

TWENTY-FIRST BIRTHDAYS are special in my country. For me, how-ever, April 17, 1994, was not very special. In fact, it was a very, very sad day. My brother had been killed in an accident and was to be buried on my twenty-first birthday.

While I was sleeping at a friend's house a strange dream about my brother woke me up. I can't remember exactly what the dream was all about, but I do remember that I was so alarmed by it that I jumped out of bed and began to pray. I had always prayed for my brother, but that particular night I hadn't prayed for him. Now, restless and uneasy, I couldn't go back to sleep.

Early in the morning I left for home, where I found many cars and peo-ple. I knew something was wrong. I asked about Siyabulela, but no one an-swered me. I ran frantically from room to room. Eventually I was told about the accident and that Siyabulela had died.

I felt as though my world had come to an abrupt end and that God no longer cared about me. Memories of our growing-up years flashed through my mind as I tried to come to grips with the meaning of my loss. I had not been very serious about religion, and now I was quite angry at God.

It wasn't long after this tragedy that God reminded me through so many blessings that He is still there. I received my teaching diploma and immedi-ately got a teaching job.

As I look back I realize that God has been with me all along, even in those dark days of my life. Being single, I had no intention of working at a church school, but that is where God has directed me, and I am still there. Life is still full of challenges, but I'm learning to have a personal relationship with my God. He has brought great blessings out of what seemed at first like a sad, hopeless situation.

My friend, if you are going through a similar experience, remember this verse: "Weeping may endure for a night, but joy cometh in the morn-ing" (Ps. 30:5).

Thank You, Lord, for changing me both spiritually and emotionally. Because You did it for me, I know You can do it for many others. Please use me to fulfill Your plan for my life.   DEBRA MATSHAYA

Patches

The Lord is faithful to all his promises and loving toward all he has made.
Ps. 145:13, NIV.

WHERE IS PATCHES? Do you know where she is?" my husband, Sergie, asked the questions in quick succession as he came back from his early-morning walk.

Patches, named because of the four or more patchlike places on her white body, is a constant presence around the house and in the compound where we live. There is nothing special about her appearance, but she behaves like any trained guard dog.

One evening when Sergie and I left the house for our walk, I brought out Patches' plate and called her to come eat. But she wouldn't come. Instead, she wagged her tail as if to say, "You're going for a walk; I'd like to go with you." And that was it—we all went for our walk. She waited for us whenever we lagged behind. "Such a faithful dog," I told my husband.

Sometimes I wondered how Patches had come to accept us as her new family in such a short time. She had belonged to the man who lived in the house where we are now. And, we were told, another had owned her before that. The fact is that Patches had become our faithful companion and protector.

Now Patches has disappeared. It's been three days. As I go into the laundry room I see her plate, and I remember her. Whenever I walk out the door, she isn't there to nuzzle her nose on my legs. The nights we go for walks without her seem incomplete. Her presence is terribly missed.

Is it the same with my Lord and me when I shun His presence? I believe He's not only missing my presence but that He intercedes for me as I pray for Patches. I know that He loves me and looks for me whenever I go astray.

I'm not sure whether Patches will ever come back or be found, but she has given me a great lesson in faithfulness. There is Someone who is faithful in everything that He promises and in all that He does. Such a wonderful hope in the midst of all the uncertainties that surround us every day!

MERCY M. FERRER

Want to Live Long?

For as the days of a tree are the days of my people, and mine elect shall long enjoy the work of their hands. Isa. 65:22.

HAVING ONLY A SMALL plot of land for gardening, my husband and I got a bit too greedy and planted as many fruit trees as possible. When the trees grew big, we realized our mistake. One fine day my husband decided to cut down some of the less productive trees. We discovered it wasn't easy to destroy those trees. In no time new shoots appeared around the stump. I took a knife and chopped off these shoots and even peeled the bark. In a few days more shoots replaced them. I even removed the stump of one of the trees, yet shoots grew from a root left behind. I actually felt sorry for these trees that refused to die. I then realized the truthfulness of today's text.

In India the largest known tree is the banyan tree. Its branches spread out in all directions. Though the trunk is huge, it is unable to support all the limbs. In order to hold these branches up, the tree sends out roots from the underside of the branches that go directly to the ground. These roots provide support and nourishment to the tree. Arcades are formed all around under the canopy of these branches that keep spreading for many acres. One banyan tree even accommodates a huge market under its canopy. These trees can live for many centuries.

The redwood and the giant sequoia in California rank among the largest and oldest living things on earth. These trees grow to a height of almost 300 feet, and several of them are about 100 feet around the base. Their life span is several thousand years. One of the oldest and largest trees was chopped down before the law was passed protecting these trees. By counting the rings, scientists were able to calculate its age. It dated back to 1305 B.C. These trees have no known enemy. None have been known to die from old age, disease, or insect attack. However, lightning has destroyed the tops of most of the largest of them.

It is fitting, then, that the redeemed will know of no more enemies in the new earth. No more diseases or danger will attack them. They will live long like these trees; in fact, they will live forever. It is hard for us whose life span is less than 100 to imagine this, but, praise the Lord, we shall live forever in His presence.   BIRDIE PODDAR

Hidden Treasure

The kingdom of heaven is like unto treasure hid in a field. Matt. 13:44.

FOR YEARS OUR GARDENING was spring planting only. Then I decided to add fall greens to extend the season. Kale, collards, mustard, and turnip greens flourished as the days grew shorter and cooler. One fall day I went out to pick turnip greens and was startled to find not only greens, but turnips poking out of the ground—dozens and dozens of them! Now, turnips may not be a favorite vegetable, but they really are good, as well as good for you, and we enjoyed them for many weeks.

Last Christmas we gave our younger son a metal detector so he can probe the ground for hidden treasure. The house he and his family bought had been owned by a rather eccentric woman, who was reputed to have buried money here and there in the yard or under the house. After her death her daughter had found a large sum hidden in a piece of furniture. It's doubtful that Tim will be so fortunate, but he will have fun trying and will most likely at least find some small change.

There are any different kinds of buried treasure. Blackbeard, the notorious pirate who ruled the waters off the coasts of North Carolina and Virginia in the early 1700s, may have stowed away chests of his ill-gotten gain where they have never been discovered. There is vast treasure in shipwrecks in the depths of the sea, awaiting those who are willing to go to great expense and take tremendous risks to salvage it, sometimes losing their fortunes or even their lives in the process. Prospectors dig in the earth for precious metals.

The best treasure of all, though, is available to those who are willing to take the time and make the effort to dig deep and search out the riches between its covers. From Genesis to Revelation, the Bible has gems worth more than all the treasures this world has to offer. During the Reformation there were countless faithful followers of Christ who took great risks to make that treasure available to all who would accept it, and many of them also paid with their fortunes or their lives. "They loved not their lives unto the death" (Rev. 12:11). It is my desire to seek that treasure more faithfully. How about you?

By the way, we do have turnips again this year. This time I planted them on purpose.

MARY JANE GRAVES

April 21

My Biggest Spanking

For whom the Lord loves He corrects, just as a father the son in whom he delights. Prov. 3:12, NKJV.

D ID YOU EVER COVET something so much that you were willing to steal it? I have.

I was probably 5 or 6 years old when our family went to visit my grandparents in another city. While there, we made a visit to one of my aunts. While the older folks were talking, I was enthralled with all of my cousin's toys. She had so many. The one item that fascinated me most was a little toy watch, probably made of some cardboard and a little tin and painted a golden color. When no one was looking, I slipped that watch into my pocket. I still remember the scene, even though I am now retired.

All went well until we reached my grandmother's home, where we were staying. I did not want to lose that watch, so I kept my hand in that pocket. That was my downfall. Mother became suspicious.

"What are you holding in your pocket?" My wise mother asked.

How horrified my mother must have been to discover her daughter had actually stolen something. At any rate, punishment was immediate. She gave me the hardest spanking I can remember.

Since it was late at night, I was put to bed and told that first thing in the morning I would have to walk back to my cousin's house and return the watch. Mother went with me, of course. I can still remember giving back that watch while several adults watched.

Even though it was a spanking that really hurt, I am so thankful for it, because I have never since been tempted to steal anything. It was a sure cure. Why did she spank me? Because she loved me.

God is our heavenly Father, and at times He needs to "spank" us. The Bible records several spankings that God administered to King David. In spite of this, David says in Psalm 34:8, "Oh, taste and see that the Lord is good; blessed is the man who trusts in Him!" (NKJV).　　　　ROWENA R. RICK

April 22

Moths and Butterflies

I will praise thee; for I am fearfully and wonderfully made: marvelous are thy works; and that my soul knoweth right well. Ps. 139:14.

YESTERDAY WE VISITED A butterfly farm. Inside a huge enclosure the butterflies flitted about enjoying the sunshine. One lovely orange-and-black monarch settled on a nearby branch.

That will make a lovely photograph, I thought as I reached for my camera. When I looked up, the butterfly had disappeared.

"Did you see where that orange-colored butterfly went?" I asked the person standing next to me.

"If it's the same one that I was watching, it's still there," she said, pointing to the branch.

I looked more closely. Yes, the butterfly was there. With its wings closed and edge on, it was nearly invisible to me. The muted colors on the underside of the wings blended in with the surroundings and hid it from predators.

As we later toured the showcases of mounted butterflies, our guide pointed out that one of the features distinguishing moths from butterflies was that the former rested with wings spread flat, and the latter rested with wings elevated and touching.

"Their feelers are different also, and—"

Our guide gave us a lot of interesting information about butterflies and moths and concluded his remarks by observing, "Nature is wonderful in the way it has programmed all these tiny creatures and provided for their individual needs."

"Nature," I echoed indignantly. "Why not give God the credit? God's handiwork revealed in nature is one of His great lesson books." I was at the back of the group, and the guide didn't hear me.

How sad that humankind has failed to recognize its Creator. Human ingenuity could not devise moths or butterflies and imbue them with the complex propensity to fulfill their humble part in our world. We too are fearfully and wonderfully made. Praise God and give Him the credit and the praise.

GOLDIE DOWN

Miracle Flower

And if God cares so wonderfully for flowers that are here today and gone tomorrow, won't he more surely care for you, O men of little faith? Matt. 6:30, TLB.

IT WAS PROFESSIONAL SECRETARY'S Day, my first working in a new job. We had a nice get-together in our department, and at the end of the program all the secretaries got a flowering plant. I kept my hydrangea in the office, but after several days I found that my plant was dying. All the flowers were dried. I was ready to throw it away when my friend Faith saw my plant.

"Well, I don't think this plant will survive," she said, "but try putting a lot of water on it. I hope it will survive."

I followed her instruction and watered the plant. I watered it twice that day—once in the morning, and once in the evening—before I left my office. My plant still looked dried.

"Well, it won't survive," I observed, talking to myself.

The next morning when I came to the office I was so surprised to see my plant was looking wonderfully fresh. All the flowers were blooming so pretty. I was so happy that I called, "Faith, you have to see my plant. All the flowers are coming back! They all are so nice and fresh. I can't believe this—this is a miracle."

When she saw it, she was surprised too. "I agree; it does look like a miracle!"

Then I thought, *If God took good care of a very small thing like my flower, how much more will He take care of me!*

God is so good. I feel so blessed and happy to have such a caring and loving Father who is able to help us in whatever situation or problem we have. It might be a small thing such as my flower—or it might be a big thing. One thing is for sure: God is able to help and carry all of our burdens.

Lord, help me to be able to acknowledge Your power in my life, and to put all my trust and everything in Your hand. Let me feel Your help and Your love in my life, I pray. LANNY LYDIA PONGILATAN

April 24

Oberammergau

But he was pierced for our transgressions, he was crushed for our iniquities; the punishment that brought us peace was upon him, and by his wounds we are healed. Isa. 53:5, NIV.

I HADN'T BEEN TOO INTERESTED in seeing the *Passion Play* in Oberammergau, Germany, so I had done nothing to procure tickets. But then, a few months before the start of the season, my mother inquired if it would still be possible to get tickets, as she would like to see it.

The *Passion Play* is performed by the villagers of Oberammergau every tenth year to fulfill a vow made by the inhabitants back in 1633 when the village was ravaged by the plague. The *Passion Play* 2000 was to be a new production with new costumes and sets. The ticket office informed me that the tickets had been sold out for a year. No way to get them there. Then we heard that sometimes one can get tickets at the box office on the morning of the performance. We decided to drive over and hope for the best.

In the morning my mother prayed, "Dear God, if You want us to see the *Passion Play,* please help us to get tickets." I had also breathed a prayer before we drove to Oberammergau. Nearly 100 people were standing in line already, although the box office would not open for another 30 minutes. Our hearts sank. Another woman joined the queue about a minute after me. A minute later a woman came up to us. "How many tickets do you need?" she asked.

"One," the first woman replied. But the woman wanted to sell two tickets.

"I need two!" I said, and bought both tickets on the spot.

She was a tour guide who had two tickets too many, not a black-market dealer. The tickets were in a good section.

Radiantly, I went to my mother and waved the tickets. "Look what I've got!" When I told her what had just happened, we just hugged each other for joy.

Thank You, dear God, that You helped us get the tickets! You didn't even want us to wait in uncertainty—You gave them to us right away. How good You are to us! The last week in the life of Christ became so real to us as we watched the play. Touching. Inspiring. It hit us that He had really suffered and died for us. We were there, watching Him hang on the cross, suffering. Our hearts were heavy, but gratitude for Christ's sacrifice filled our souls.

HANNELE OTTSCHOFSKI

Giving Blood

In Him we have redemption through His blood, the forgiveness of sins,
according to the riches of His grace. Eph.1:7, NKJV.

WHEN THE PHONE RANG, the person on the other end indicated
that it was time for the local Red Cross blood drive again. Giving
blood is not my favorite hobby. Many times I have encouraged my husband
to donate his blood, since he is O negative and a universal donor. This means
that his blood can be given to anyone who needs blood, but if he needs
blood, he can be given only O negative. My blood type, O positive, is very
common, and I fully intended to donate, but had been rejected for low
hemoglobin. Sometimes I have been rejected because the nurse couldn't raise
a vein to get the needle in. I always felt so guilty, because I had encouraged
others to give and then was denied the privilege myself.

Finally, after many years, I was able to donate my own blood. And then
came the problems. Sometimes the technician needed to stick me several
times because my veins are deep, and they roll. Other times, when the needle
was removed, I ended up with a large bruise over most of my arm where the
blood bled into the tissues from lack of pressure to stop the bleeding. I finally
learned to state the problems I had previously and learned how to avoid
them. In fact, the last time I gave blood, it was a piece of cake!

The little brochures that are given to encourage you to give blood state
that one pint can help three people. Giving blood is a gift of life. It is beautiful to realize that you may be helping to save three lives by giving about 45
minutes of your time and, of course, your blood.

While we may help to save three people, Christ gave His blood, His life,
to save a world of people. In fact, He can—and will—save everyone who
wishes to be saved and follow Him. What if, when He had arrived at the
cross, they had said, "You're rejected; Your iron count is too low." Or they
might have said, "We can't find a vein on You, so You might as well go
home." I am so glad that Christ was willing to give His blood and His life that
I might live eternally. LORAINE F. SWEETLAND

April 26

Traveling Mercies

All praise to . . . God. . . . He is the source of every mercy and the God who comforts us. . . . When others are troubled, we will be able to give them the same comfort God has given us. 2 Cor. 1:3, 4, NLT.

ON A RECENT TRIP to London with my family I made a bad decision. I need to tell you up front that I'm an impetuous person. So when I saw a train at the station heading into London, I boarded—never mind that the rest of the family wasn't there yet. I encouraged them to hurry, but as they approached the entrance to the train, they stopped.

My sister said, "This isn't the correct train."

"Of course it is. Get on," I responded.

She wouldn't. As I tried to convince her, the door automatically closed. The family was on the platform, and I on the train. As I was whisked away, my heart sank. *How could I be so stupid to get separated from my family? Why didn't I just get off when there was a discrepancy? Where am I going on this train? Can I make contact with them before the day is over?*

The day had started out pleasantly, with no inkling there was going to be a problem—and that I would be the cause of it! What to do? I got off at the next platform, hoping the family would simply get on the next train and follow me. However, when the next train zoomed by two tracks over from my platform, I realized it wasn't going to be solved that easily.

Maybe I should walk across to the other side and take a train back to the original station. I searched each train that went by for my family and finally saw them on the third train. But none of the trains had stopped at my platform. I asked a woman for help. She suggested that I take the next train and get off at the third stop. That would take me to the first stop for the train my family was on.

Although my train had been going to London, my sister had been correct when she said it wasn't the same one we had ridden the night before. You can imagine the relief and joy we felt when we were finally reunited, not to mention the thankfulness I felt when no one scolded or shamed me. They weren't even mad. Praise the Lord! I felt my family's grace and mercy toward me and was reminded how priceless that is.   LOUISE DRIVER

The Cruel Crown

They also hit the crown of thorns with their sticks, driving the thorns deep into Jesus' head. Mark 15:19, Clear Word.

TODAY I PICKED PONDEROSA lemons off the tree just outside our porch door in central Florida. For those who have never picked citrus, I must tell you that all the limbs on the trees are decorated with thorns. Some are smaller thorns, but the Ponderosa lemon has some of the longest and sharpest thorns. I had hardly started picking today when I screamed with pain as the soft skin of my arm was pierced with a sharp barb. It not only hurts going in but also coming out.

Last week my husband and I were in Israel. We climbed the Mount of Olives and saw the olive trees in the Garden of Gethsemane, where Jesus bowed beneath the load of the sins of the world (including mine), where "His sweat was as it were great drops of blood falling down to the ground" (Luke 22:44). We walked the stony streets of old Jerusalem, called the Via Dolorosa, where they led Him to the judgment hall. We visited the site called Golgotha. It was all fresh in my mind.

I also recalled reading that "Jesus was taken, faint with weariness and covered with wounds, and scourged in the sight of the multitude. 'And the soldiers led Him away into the hall, called Praetorium; and they call together the whole band. And they clothed Him with purple, and platted a crown of thorns, and put it about His head, and began to salute Him, Hail, King of the Jews! And they . . . did spit upon Him, and bowing their knees worshiped Him.' Occasionally some wicked hand snatched the reed that had been placed in His hand, and struck the crown upon His brow, forcing the thorns into His temples, and sending the blood trickling down His face and beard" (Ellen White, *The Desire of Ages*, p. 734).

Today I felt the pain of one thorn. How many made up His crown? Why did He endure it? He had the power to end the punishment, to come down from the cruel cross. It is indeed a mystery we can look forward to studying throughout the ceaseless ages of eternity. God's love is unfathomable.

But we can praise Him for it. And every time I encounter a thorn on the citrus trees I can remember what Jesus did for me and share with others that He did it for them, too. RUBYE SUE

April 28

Duckling in Distress

For you know that God paid a ransom to save you from the empty life you inherited from your ancestors. . . . He paid for you with the precious lifeblood of Christ, the sinless, spotless Lamb of God. 1 Peter 1:18, 19, NLT.

I SAUNTERED ALONG THE expansive green lawns of Edwards Gardens in Toronto one sunny Sabbath afternoon. The stately trees and brilliant blossoms reminded me I was reading from God's second book, nature. I came upon a bridge that spanned a stream. I noticed idly that the brook flowed over a series of four small steps. As I leaned over to look for the giant goldfish for which the beautiful park was famous, a duck and some fluffy ducklings came into view.

The mother duck sailed down the steps, quacking directions to her little ones. The first one made it over the steps. So did the second and the third. But the fourth duckling seemed petrified. It swam around in frenzied circles, clucking woefully. The mother duck turned around. Unable to brave the current and move back up the steps, she quacked even louder. With a final call—one of farewell, perhaps—the mother and her other babes began swimming away.

And then I heard a splash. A towheaded little boy had jumped into the shallow stream to rescue the frightened bird. Gently, he returned it to the flock. The onlookers cheered, and the 6-year-old, his pants and sandals soaking wet, bowed. That little boy was the duckling's messiah.

I reflected on that remarkable scene for days, obvious comparisons swirling in my head. For the young lad, the rescue was relatively risk-free; it brought nothing but good to the duckling and a sense of altruistic satisfaction to himself. For our Jesus, His mission brought everything glorious to us and everything painful to Him—God-separated, soul-wrenching agony.

While the boy's clothes were simply splashed with water, our Lord's robes were streaked with the jagged stains of His own blood as He bore the soldiers' angry scourging in quiet anguish. But the saddest of all comparisons is this: while the youngster's mission was greeted with cheers, jeers bade the Messiah farewell.

Oh, dear Lord, thank You for rescuing me. I am blessed by Your sacrifice. Help me to bring You nothing but good. GLENDA-MAE GREENE

He Answers My Prayers

If you believe, you will receive whatever you ask for in prayer. Matt. 21:22, NLT.

I HAD OFTEN HEARD of people's answered prayers and wondered if I, too, could have such experiences in my own life. Then I came to the realization that I didn't have enough faith in the Lord. How, then, could I have such close communion with the Lord?

As I started to work in the vineyard of the Lord, I found myself in many dangerous situations and experiencing great difficulties, and I prayed, "Lord, help me." The Lord has never failed me. He rescued me; He removed my difficulties. Many times the Lord saw my plight and helped me even before I asked Him for any help. For He is our Lord and Maker, our Redeemer and Sustainer.

Recently my friend and I were returning from college. After we got off the bus we had to cross the road to go to the bank. A white van approached at a speed that my friend and I didn't expect. My friend, who was walking ahead of me, was hit by the van and fell down on top of me, causing me to also fall. For a moment my heart stopped beating, and I didn't know what to do. I prayed, "Lord, help me."

Immediately, people gathered around us and asked, "Are you hurt?"

My friend got up and said, "No, I'm OK."

Oh, I was so happy! *She is safe, and it's a miracle!* I thought. Everyone gathered around was so surprised that she wasn't hurt. I wasn't surprised because I remembered the promise: "The Lord watches over you—the Lord is your shade at your right hand; . . . the Lord will keep you from all harm—he will watch over your life; the Lord will watch over your coming and going both now and forevermore" (Ps. 121:5-8, NIV).

Yes, indeed, the Lord hears our prayers and He is always watching over us, so what have we to fear?

Prayers are still being answered and miracles are happening even today—when we ask and when we believe.   BETTY LYNGDOH

April 30

Patterns

Together follow my example and observe those who live after the pattern we have set for you. Phil. 3:17, Amplified.

WHEN I WAS IN seventh grade I enrolled in a sewing class. I even bought a sewing machine with money I'd saved from my first after-school job. I was eager to make my own clothes and show them off. I would flip through catalogs of patterns for hours. It was fun. I never gave much thought to the designers' skills, or to the fact that they had to make clothing that flattered people of all shapes and sizes or with differing tastes. I never even considered how closely I would need to follow the pattern to have my creation look like the one in the catalog.

With an easy-to-sew pattern selected, I would rummage through bolts of fabric for the right piece. After purchasing the pattern, material, and sewing notions, I'd head home to lay each pattern piece onto the fabric, carefully pin them, and cut the pieces out.

My first garment turned out OK. The second and third ones looked nicer, and I was thrilled at my new seamstress status. After I took my second sewing class I graduated to more advanced patterns, ones that were more challenging. But sometimes I simply laid the pattern down on the fabric so it would fit in what I thought was a better spot. That way I thought I'd save some fabric to make a matching hat or scarf. More times than not, however, I realized that the stripes didn't match up as they should, or the garment didn't hang right. Disgruntled, I'd go back to the fabric store to purchase more material (if they even had any left) so I could finish my sewing project correctly. And all because I didn't follow the pattern!

Isn't that just like us? Christians who don't follow the pattern—despite the great deal of time and effort expended by the Creator many years ago to provide us with the very best Pattern. We often decide to do our own thing—skimp on the essentials, choose a more creative approach, readjust the pattern, or disregard it totally because we think we know enough. Then day after day, when things turn out wrong, we wonder why.

Heavenly Father, help me today to live after the Jesus pattern, knowing that only by following Him can I truly be made perfect. IRIS L. STOVALL

128

Trying to Count My Blessings

In every thing give thanks: for this is the will of God in Christ Jesus concerning you. 1 Thess. 5:18.

WE AWOKE JUST BEFORE 6:00 that morning to the sound of pouring rain. A flash of lightning lighted the room for an instant, followed by a loud clap of thunder and a shower of hail. My husband had just said, "It's strange there's no wind." Then *bang!* He jumped out of bed just as the windowpanes shattered across the bed.

We went immediately to the lounge to kneel and pray and to thank the Lord for sparing our lives. A calmness came over me as Psalm 56:3 flashed through my mind: "What time I am afraid, I will trust in thee."

As we looked around, we saw destruction everywhere. All the neighbors' roofs were badly damaged, windows blown in, walls collapsed, garage doors blown away, cars damaged in their garages, trees stripped of their branches, and top stories of buildings blown off. People living in three-story apartments were left homeless when their apartments crumbled to the ground. Telephones and electricity were out, but word got around fast: A tornado had struck—the first ever to hit the Cape of South Africa.

First Thessalonians 5:18 reads: "In every thing give thanks." What was left to be thankful for? Our bedroom was unusable, but we still had a single bed in the small back room to sleep on. There was a huge hole in the kitchen ceiling, so one could see the sky. Our carport was ruined, but our car was safe in the garage.

Relatives and friends from our congregation came to help. The men covered the open rafters. The women organized soup and sandwiches. Even a neighbor and three sisters from the nearby mosque brought food. This reminded me of Isaiah 41:6: "They helped every one his neighbour and every one said to his [brother and sister], Be of good courage."

My thank-You list is long.

You told us to give thanks in everything. I am reminded once again of Your care—and I give You the thanks.

PRISCILLA ADONIS

God Has His Own Timetable

There is a time for everything, and a season for every activity under heaven:
a time to be born and a time to die, a time to plant and a time to uproot.
Eccl. 3:1, 2, NIV.

I RECENTLY RETURNED FROM the Philippines where we had held evan-gelistic meetings. In one of the villages to which we were assigned, there were no markets at all. A couple days after we arrived I asked the local pastor and his wife if we could explore the possibility of buying some bananas. I had seen banana plantations as we drove through the town. It was an exploration I won't forget. We walked for three hours on dusty, rugged roads under the blistering heat of the sun. We had to ask several people before finally finding the kind owners of the plantation.

I was elated and excited—we were taking back two huge bunches of reg-ular bananas and a big sack of cooking bananas. And we paid only $2.50 for the lot. I could already imagine the feast I was going to have. But the bananas were not yet ripe. The people said it would take only two or three days to ripen them, so every day I peeped to see if there were any ripe ones. I was dis-appointed. Not even one ripe banana. It was on our last day that I saw one ripe cooking banana.

Those bananas were mature, but three days wasn't enough time for them to ripen. They too had a timetable. King Solomon says in Ecclesiastes 3:1, 2 that everything has its time. We see this phenomenon, this principle, in na-ture—animals, plants, flowers—for God made them so. At springtime some of the first flowers to bloom are daffodils, irises, tulips, cherries, and almonds. And yes, a lot of baby animals come at springtime, too. Later other flowers such as petunias and marigolds bloom. Then there are perennials that bloom throughout the year. They follow the instinct and the timetable God has set for them.

How about us? Do we follow our Maker's timetable?

Dear God, You've set timetables for mankind and nature. You know the com-ing in and going out of all the plants and animals. Please help me to see Your hand in everything. Help me to be patient and willing to wait upon You. If nature coop-erates with You, help me to do so for Your glory and honor. Amen.

OFELIA A. PANGAN

Birding Buddy

I have loved you with an everlasting love. Jer. 31:3, NKJV.

"I THINK I'LL GO BIRDING," I announced to my family when Sabbath lunch was finished. I was spending some time with my daughter and her family and didn't expect any of them to want to accompany me. None of them were bird-watchers. They had other plans.

"I'll go with you, Grandma," 7-year-old Rachel volunteered.

Surprised, I asked, "Are you sure you want to come? You'll have to be very quiet."

"I know," she said, running to her room to get her binoculars. "I'll be quiet."

Rachel turned out to be an excellent little birding buddy. The first bird we saw was a catbird, a new one for her, and she wanted me to show her the picture in the book and explain how I knew it was that bird. After admiring cardinals, blue jays, chickadees, and mockingbirds, we came to a dead tree where I had seen a pair of red-bellied woodpeckers on other outings. We sat down to await their appearance. At last Rachel snuggled up to me and said, "I love you, Grandma. I like watching the birds with you."

"I love you, too," I replied. "I'm glad you came."

"Do you know why I came?" Rachel whispered. "I came because I didn't want you to be all alone on your walk. I wanted to keep you company because I love you."

How warm and special I felt. My granddaughter loved me enough to give up her plans to come with me because she loved me and didn't want me to be lonely. *Wow! What a loving, sweet, thoughtful granddaughter I have!* I mused. *How fortunate I am!*

Later, in my quiet time, I thought about the many times in life I have headed out on my own, expecting to be alone, only to discover Someone wanted to come along, Someone who whispered to me, "Dorothy, I love you so much that I don't want you to have to walk this path alone. I want to keep you company because I love you."

Rachel can't go on many walks with me because we live so far apart, but how thankful I am for One who is always there, loving me no matter where I am. With Him no walk, regardless of how difficult it may be, need ever be taken alone. How fortunate I am! DOROTHY EATON WATTS

Look-alikes

My sheep listen to my voice; I know them, and they follow me. John 10:27, NIV.

I GLANCED UP FROM MY desk just in time to see a familiar figure go by my office door. Recognizing him as a former coworker at my church's Media Center in California, I hastened down the hall to greet him. "Dr. P, it's good to see you!" I beamed.

The man I addressed looked back at me with a blank expression.

"You remember me," I coaxed. "I used to work at the Media Center." Then, failing to understand his lack of recognition, I added, "I'm Lorraine!"

A smile crossed his face and his eyes twinkled. "I know you think I am Milton. I am not. I am Tulio, his twin brother."

I was too amused to be embarrassed, and we had a good laugh.

Some months later I was standing in the lobby of another department when the door opened and in walked Dr. P. I would not be fooled again and gave a detached smile from across the lobby. This time, however, he came straight toward me, extended his hand, and with a broad grin said, "I am who you think I am—I am Milton!" The word of my blunder had gotten back to the Media Center, and he was quick to put me at ease.

A few years earlier my husband and I had been guests near Anchorage, Alaska, for a lecture series, where I met two 15-year-old look-alikes. Even their T-shirts were alike—except for the messages. One read, "I'm John—he's Jim." The other read, "I'm Jim—he's John." The next day one shirt read "I'm Jim—he's John." The other shirt had no message. A day later "I'm John—he's Jim" came toward me. The other shirt was a colorful print. The following day the shirts were no help at all.

Then I realized I could not depend on outward appearances alone for identity. Personal relationship and shared experiences are much more reliable. I've discovered it is the same way in my connection with Jesus. Many voices are audible; similar messages beckon. But I must base my relationship not on appearance but experience.

I must spend time with the Shepherd, get to know His voice, learn His character. Then when other look-alikes entice me, I will be safe. I will know the difference.   LORRAINE HUDGINS

True Beauty

So shall the king greatly desire thy beauty: for he is thy Lord; and worship thou him. Ps. 45:11.

THE PHONE CALL WE had been waiting for came at 9:00 in the evening. Mrs. Merritt, as promised, called to tell us that her cereus was beginning to open. The night-blooming cereus—how I longed to see one in full bloom. I had prayed for that opportunity, and that opportunity had come at last, and tonight it would bloom. My daughter, Gail, and I drove the few short miles to Mrs. Merritt's house, and our excitement grew with each mile.

As we entered the house a most delicious fragrance greeted us. Before the cereus had scarcely begun to blossom, it was sending out its beautiful fragrance, which penetrated every corner of the house.

Rather than disturb its progress, we waited in another room, giving the plant time to grow in the darkness of the room. We waited for the blossom to reach the full maturity of its limited life, checking in from time to time to note its progress. Close to midnight the bloom reached the apex of development. It was the most beautiful flower we had ever seen. We were able to look into the throat to note its pure white condition, minus shadows of any kind. Its beauty was breathtaking, its fragrance exquisite.

It reached its climax in full majestic beauty, and slowly began to fade. The aroma disappeared and left our presence. By morning the once-beautiful blossom hung suspended and spent from its mother leaf on the cereus plant. There was nothing left to indicate its once-magnificent bloom. It was dead and gone.

I have another desire, too, that my spiritual life in Jesus will continue to blossom to maturity. God forbid that it should wither and die after a short, fruitful season, but rather that it might be faithful and growing to the end, culminating at Christ's appearance in the clouds of heaven.

I longed to see a night-blooming cereus, and God answered my prayer, providing the opportunity. I long to see Jesus. God grant that I may see Him come in the clouds of glory, surrounded by heavenly beings. His love will blossom forever in the earth made new, attended with joy and peace and heavenly fragrance.   LAURIE DIXON-MCCLANAHAN

May 6

Jesus' Second Coming

"Yes, I am coming soon." Amen. Come, Lord Jesus. Rev. 22:20, NIV.

WITHIN A PERIOD OF 10 days I had two dreams, exactly the same, but at the end of the second one there was an added message.

In my dream I was taken to a hill that overlooked the area of Silver Spring, Maryland. It was a beautiful, sunny spring day, quite windy, making it absolutely pleasant.

People below were so busy: school buses running children to their schools; workers with frowns on their foreheads driving to their jobs; house-wives busy completing their never-ending chores; revolving doors at banks moving fast as men and women did their daily transactions; workers at construction sites giving orders. People were so preoccupied. With no exceptions, they all had a look of anxiety in their eyes; worry and mental distress seemed to torment their souls.

Their physical agitation gave me such a sad feeling. Deep in thought, I looked up to the sky, almost hoping for an answer to all this. Beautiful clouds were forming in different tones of pinks and blues, changing shapes rapidly as the wind picked up. A sudden stroke of thick lightning coming from the left side of the sky landed on my right, transforming itself in the form of a bright angel whose face was not really clear because he shone so strongly. He said, "Look far in the sky. Do you see a little cloud?"

Straining to see it, I asked, "You mean, like the little cloud that will appear when the Son of Man is coming?"

"Yes," he answered.

After a few minutes, frustrated, I told him that I could not see anything. His response was "Keep looking. You won't have time to take your eyes from the sky, for He is coming very soon."

With those words the angel disappeared. I focused my eyes back on the sky, trying to find the shape of such great events. Then I woke up. It had been such a sweet, beautiful dream.

A few days later, during camp meeting, the same dream was repeated, but at the end of it the angel said, "Now go; tell others."   GLADYS RIOS

A Matter of Patience

Delight thyself also in the Lord; and he shall give thee the desires of thine heart. . . . Rest in the Lord, and wait patiently for him. Ps. 37:4-7.

I WAS TERRIFIED. SITTING IN my ophthalmologist's chair as he did his yearly examination, I suddenly realized that I could not see out of my left eye—I could not even see the eye chart. A huge black spot was all that was visible to me. What had happened? When had all this happened? Why hadn't I recognized a difference in my vision during the year? A dozen questions flooded my frantic brain.

Scared, I tried to listen as the doctor made an appointment with a retina specialist right away. "But there's good news." His smile was consoling as he walked to my chair. "Laser surgery often takes care of problems like yours, though it is expensive."

Money seemed immaterial then as I clung to that single glimmer of hope. Two days later I went to the specialist, who gave his diagnosis: macular degeneration. I had the operation the following week, even though it meant I could not attend my younger son's doctoral graduation. For five days I had to stay out of the sunlight, but I gladly followed the doctor's orders.

On my next visit, there was no sign of improvement in my vision. Nor on the next. *Dear God*, I prayed, *is this Your will for me?* Disappointment weighed heavily on my heart, but today's text gave me strength and courage. And I waited.

At the third visit my doctor could see improvement. So could I. "You had patience," he said happily. "Your sight will improve." In the following weeks I was overjoyed when I could see that he was correct. My eyesight was just as good as it had been the year before, and my spiritual vision had become even clearer.

My husband often quotes a line from King George VI's 1946 Christmas message: "Go out into the darkness and put your hand into the hand of God. That shall be to you better than light and safer than a known way."

Thank You, dear Lord. You helped me learn to shun the darkness of doubt and put my hand in Yours. You taught me patience, and You gave me the desires of my heart.   CAROL JOY GREENE

My Regrets

I will hope continually, and will praise You yet more and more. My mouth shall tell of Your righteousness and Your salvation all the day, for I do not know their limits. Ps. 71:14, 15, NKJV.

REGRETS. WE SIGH WHEN we say this word. We wish we could do it all over again. We wish we had known better. We wish we had been more understanding. Many wishes, but it's too late.

I met Victoria in Cyprus when I was volunteering in a nursing home. She was a beautiful woman, but something was wrong with her—she didn't talk. I learned that she had lost both her children in a plane crash one Christmas Day. And her husband had divorced her. From that time on, Victoria had never wanted to say a word.

I made it a point to visit Victoria every afternoon. I just talked to her, even if she didn't respond. But one day while I was feeding her, she reached out for my hand and squeezed it hard. I knew that she counted me as her friend; she knew that I cared.

One Sunday I felt I should go see Victoria early in the morning. But I reasoned, *I'll see her this afternoon as usual. I have things to do this morning.* However, the prompting was so strong that I left what I was doing and went to the nursing home. When I got there, they were just wheeling Victoria's body out of the room. She died early that Sunday morning. I had regrets. I wished I had been there to hold her hands as she breathed her last breath. You see, Victoria did not have any family or relatives left—I could have been there for her.

Gertrude (not her real name) had asked me if we could talk sometime. I kept telling her, "I'll call you; maybe we can have lunch or even a cup of tea." But I never did. One day I learned that Gertrude had left town. I felt bad, but it was too late. I felt more remorse, though, when I learned Gertrude had lost her three children in a fire. "Had I known," I said to myself, "I would have taken time to spend with her."

Lord, help me to listen to the prompting of the Holy Spirit. Lead me and guide me to someone who is in need. Help me to be quick to notice the needs of others. Help me to be more like Jesus.   JEMIMA D. ORILLOSA

God's Gift on
My Wedding Anniversary Day

In this was manifested the love of God toward us, because that God sent his only begotten Son into the world, that we might live through him. Herein is love, not that we loved God, but that he loved us, and sent his Son to be the propitiation for our sins. 1 John 4:9, 10.

MAY 9 IS OUR WEDDING anniversary. I got up in the morning and thanked my Father for His marvelous and wonderful guidance in the past. It was vacation time, and guests were at our home. I started cooking breakfast for them.

Somebody rang the doorbell, and I opened the door to the neighbor boy. "Your dog Brownie has fallen into the little well nearby and is whining for help," he said.

My husband had gone to the store, but immediately my sister and my sister-in-law took a bucket and rope and rushed to the well. "O Lord, I love my Brownie so much. Please help them get him out of the well. Please don't let him die. Save my Brownie," I prayed earnestly as I paced back and forth.

A few minutes later my husband came home. "Oh, please!" I cried. "Brownie has fallen in the well, and they are trying to get him out!"

Off he rushed to see what he could do. By this time some of our neighbors had gathered. They all tried hard and finally got Brownie out. They brought the dog home, but he was in shock. He didn't bark. We gave him a good bath, cleaned his wounds, and gave him some warm milk. For the whole day he kept quiet. We all patted him, and by evening Brownie was back to normal.

God had saved my Brownie. That was the greatest gift I got from my heavenly Father on my wedding anniversary.

This experience taught me a good lesson. I too had fallen down in the pit of sin because of traps set by Satan. God sent His only begotten Son to save me. He took me out of the pit of sin, cleaned and healed me. He touches me and says, "I love you, and I gave Myself for you."

He is the only one who can deliver us from the pit of sin. With His priceless and precious blood we all are washed. God loves each and every one of us. Let us love Him and be a witness for Him. PACKIALEELA SAM SELVARAJ

May 10

Jesus, Lover of My Soul

[He] made himself of no reputation, and took upon him the form of a servant, and was made in the likeness of men: And being found in fashion as a man, he humbled himself, and became obedient unto death, even the death of the cross. Phil. 2:7, 8.

ON A GREEK OVERNIGHT ferry, my son, his wife, and I spread our blankets on the upper deck to sleep under the stars on what we were calling a short "Mediterranean cruise." It left from Nicosia, Cyprus, going to Haifa (Mount Carmel), Israel. Arriving at daybreak, we disembarked, passed customs, and rented a small Fiat car. It was an inexpensive way to visit the Holy Land!

Beside the Sea of Galilee we slept under the old olive trees and picnicked on the hillside by the sea. We spent Sabbath reading Christ's sermon on the mount and drove around the sea to visit Capernaum.

Driving through Nazareth, we visited famous sites where the boy Jesus grew up. We imagined how He looked as we watched small boys playing in the dusty streets.

In Jerusalem we visited the streets, tombs, hills, and gardens where it is said that Jesus walked, prayed, and died. Even in its modern setting we could sense the holiness that lingered in each place. We took day trips to other famous sites such as Bethany, Bethlehem, Jericho, and the Dead Sea.

For me the most impressive place of all was the dark little cave, the humble stable in Bethlehem, the manger such as the one in which it is thought Jesus was born among the animals boarding there. It seemed that the presence of the Lord surrounded me as I knelt with the others in reverence. "How could You, my dear Lord? How could You have left the glories of heaven for this?" I lifted my tear-filled eyes to a new awareness of our Lord's unspeakable sacrifice to become one of us. In that place I rededicated my life to knowing Him better.

Since then I've had a closer walk with my brother, Jesus, still in human form, and God and man in one! Only in heaven will I truly sense it when I see Him face to face.

Dear Lord, as that glorious day approaches, keep my heart in tune with Yours today and each day as I await to see You in person, my Lord and King.

BESSIE SIEMENS LOBSIEN

Children Are a Gift of God

Children are a gift from God; they are his reward. Ps. 127:3, TLB.

I WAS TALKING TO ONE of our three adult sons. He inferred that because of a certain act of motherly love I showed toward one of his siblings, surely I must love that son most. I tried to assure him that his mother has no favorites. I tried to help him understand that I love each son equally. I told him that there are many ways each of them is dear to my heart.

When I receive a phone call, hearing one of their voices is special. It touches my heart to know I'm thought of that day.

One day one of my sons called me for no apparent reason other than to wish me a happy Sabbath. I knew that the phone call was being paid for out of his meager wages. Another day I received a thoughtful call from another of our sons. "Hi, Mom! I knew you'd be home alone this weekend, since Dad's traveling overseas, so I called because I thought you might be lonely." A phone call from the third son surprised me. "My girlfriend and I donated plasma today, so you won't need to send money to cover that bill I owe."

A couple years ago one son gave me a special present on Mother's Day, special because I knew that neither he nor his brothers had the finances to bestow any gift of monetary value. One was working his way through school, another paying off his school loans, and their brother was trying to cover his basic monthly necessities and bills. I expected no gifts. That gift is treasured highly because of the great sacrifice made just for me.

I often smile and know the blessing of being remembered. How blessed we are that God thought about us long ago in His master plan. He gave each of us our own personal angel. He made the Sabbath for our rest and for time to spend with Him. God sent us the gift of His Son, who gave His blood to cover our debts. He sends the Holy Spirit to guide and comfort us. He has promised to be with us when we are alone. He is only a prayer away at any moment.

Which of us does He love best? He loves each of us in different ways, for different reasons, but He loves us equally! He loves us very much—just as I love Rob, Hans, and Rolf—all the same, only different.   JUDY HOLBROOK

Under His Wings

O Lord, you preserve both man and beast. . . . Both high and low among men find refuge in the shadow of your wings. Ps. 36:6, 7, NIV.

I RECEIVED ANOTHER LITTLE lesson in nature one night. My husband and I were at the lake on our houseboat when suddenly a dark cloud appeared overhead. Within minutes a severe wind came up, creating huge waves across the water. What once had been tranquil green water was now a churning mass of waves pounding against the docks. We were sheltered under the covered dock, but even our large boat was receiving a steady rocking.

As I stood peering out the window of the stern, I noticed a lone duck bouncing back and forth out in the water. As I watched, it seemed as if the waves would totally engulf her at any moment. Her small body was tossed from side to side. There seemed to be something wrong with her; her body looked all uneven and distorted. Her feathers were fanned out to one side. It looked to us as though she had been injured and was not able to fly to seek shelter from the storm. We continued to watch her as she continued to be tossed to and fro. Unfortunately, I knew there was nothing I could do to help her.

About 30 minutes later the wind subsided, and the water again became calm. The little duck tipped her body to one side, and two little heads came out from under her wing. Then, to our amazement, six more little bodies emerged from beneath her, and her distorted body once again took on its normal shape. She was not injured but had furled her wings wide to protect eight small ducklings from the raging storm.

Such protection is promised to each of us in Psalm 36:6, 7: "O Lord, you preserve both man and beast. How priceless is your unfailing love! Both high and low among men find refuge in the shadow of your wings" (NIV). Whatever it is in our lives that may be creating a storm, tossing us around, making us fearful of being alone to face the trials of life, we can know the protection of being under His wings.

"Under His wings I am safely abiding; though the night deepens and tempests are wild. . . . Sheltered, protected, no evil can harm me; resting in Jesus I'm safe evermore."

BARBARA SMITH MORRIS

Diapers and God's Love

And whatsoever ye shall ask in my name, that will I do, that the Father may be glorified in the Son. John 14:13.

I WAS A YOUNG 24-YEAR-OLD mother of two little boys, ages 2 and 4, living in Miami, Florida, when we became foster parents to four young children. Of the six children, four were under the age of 3 and still in diapers. Disposable diapers had not been invented yet, and we didn't have a clothes dryer. One of my many chores was washing diapers and hanging them out to dry on the clotheslines.

One morning I loaded the washing machine with diapers, knowing that my supply of clean diapers was finished. By the time the washing machine cycle finished, the sky suddenly filled with ominous black clouds and the wind had begun to blow. I hurried to take the clothes basket and the children out into the fenced backyard so I could hang the diapers out to dry. No sooner had I begun hanging the diapers on the clothesline than it began to thunder, and the wind picked up speed. I took the children inside and told them to stay by the sliding glass doors so I could see them while I finished hanging the diapers out.

As I hung the diapers out to dry, I talked to God: *Please hold back the rain until these diapers can dry. You know I need dry diapers!*

When I finished hanging the last diaper, all four clotheslines were full. The wind was so strong it blew my empty laundry basket across the yard and into the fence and whipped the diapers till they snapped. I decided to see if the first ones were dry yet, and to my amazement they were! I prayed a prayer of thanksgiving and kept asking God to continue to hold back the rain until I could get them all off the lines. I worked as fast as I could removing the diapers. Just when I was getting the last ones off, the raindrops started falling, hitting my face and arms. I ran into the house with the basket full of fresh-smelling, clean, dry diapers and shut the sliding glass doors behind me as the rain came down in torrents.

It rained and thundered for several hours. God had once again shown me that He cares about a mother's prayer and children's needs. Praise the Lord, He honors those who honor Him.   CELIA MEJIA CRUZ

Trying God

Ask, and it shall be given you; seek, and ye shall find; knock, and it shall be opened unto you. Matt. 7:7.

I HAD BEEN BAPTIZED ONLY six weeks when I asked God to use me in doing His work. *I am Your humble servant and I will follow where You lead,* I told Him. I had to wait a year before I realized how He was leading me.

I was ushering a 2-year-old child to beginner's class one Sabbath morning. As I stood in the back of the class observing what was going on, the leader asked me to assist her in giving the Bible lesson because the person assigned was absent. I agreed to do it, but I was terrified. I am an extremely shy person, and all of this was new to me. Telling a story to a group of 2- and 3-year-olds so they could understand and be attentive was not me. Besides, most of the children's parents were present, and I was not prepared.

There was no time for story helps or felts. I picked up the lesson guide and turned to lesson five: "Daniel in the Lions' Den." OK, it was a well-known story, but instead of telling the story, I nervously began to read the story, very fast. I immediately learned that little people have short attention spans, and I was quickly losing them. *Lord, what to do?* In despair, a thought came to my mind: *"Unless you become like one of these little ones . . ."*

At that moment I began to change my voice for each character, and roared like a lion in the appropriate places. They all came to life, wide-eyed and smiling. At the end of the story we sang "Daniel in the Lions' Den." As I looked at the children's happy little faces, I knew that the Lord was working.

Now as a leader in the beginner's room myself, I realize my prayer was answered. This is what the Lord wants me to do. I enjoy doing the Lord's will, helping to nurture these little seeds as they blossom into big plants in the gospel of Jesus.

Prayer is a powerful thing. If you have the desire to work for the Lord, ask Him what He wants you to do, then wait patiently. The answer will come in His time. Trust Him—He has a plan for everyone. You will be excited when He leads you into His plan for you!   VELNA WRIGHT

Fifteen Seconds of Fame

For this is what the Lord Almighty says: . . . whoever touches you touches the apple of his eye. Zech. 2:8, NIV.

I HAD PLANNED TO TAKE a different aerobics class at the gym and was running a bit late. What seemed to be the usual attendees were milling around in groups of two or three when I entered the room. Apparently the instructor was running a little later than I, and for this I was thankful.

As I entered the room a few women moved together excitedly. One went to another group, and someone ran from that group to another cluster nearby. Each group, in turn, turned to look at me. Immediately I looked down to see if I had put on my exercise clothes inside out, or something even worse. My eyes scanned those watching me, looking for a friendly response from someone, anyone. A nervous smile froze on my lips. *What is wrong?* I thought.

Questions flooded my mind as I tried to come up with some reason for the whispering back and forth that was going on, obviously about me. I moved to a less conspicuous spot. As I passed by one of the groups, one of the women came over, somewhat embarrassed.

"Excuse me," she began, stuttering with obvious excitement. "Are you—are you ———?" She mentioned the name of one of the star players on our local WNBA team.

Now I understood. "No," I told her. Her disappointment was obvious.

The buzzing quickly died down, and everyone went back to talking in their various groups. A few smiled sheepishly whenever our eyes met. No one paid much attention to me now. I smiled to myself—for a whole 15 seconds I had been rich and famous, even if mistakenly so. Since I wasn't the local "star," I had lost importance to my classmates, and their interest had waned.

I am important, though, you know. You see, I am a child of the King, which makes me royalty. I am the apple of His eye—and so are you.

Lord, help me always to realize how important I am to You and to value myself as Your child, an heir to Your kingdom. MAXINE WILLIAMS ALLEN

Old-time Camp Meeting

Truly I am full of power by the spirit of the Lord. Micah 3:8.

FOR YEARS WE HAVE heard amazing stories about how my husband's family traveled to camp meeting in the 1930s. Their home was a log cabin back in the woods of northern Minnesota, a part of the Chippewa National Forest. During those depression years money was scarce, and so were jobs. It was difficult just to exist, but they always found a way to attend camp meeting with their family of eight. Their old Essex car was packed full of provisions to last two or three weeks, because Dad Burgeson usually went a week early to help set up the camp.

In those days there were rows and rows of tents—a city of tents—plus several larger tents where the meetings were held. Items packed into the old Essex and on top of it included a small oil stove for cooking, enough home-canned goods and other foods to feed everyone, and even a large can of eggs packed in salt to preserve them. Carefully packed into the car were many jars of maple syrup and maple candy from the more than 100 maple trees that grew on their land. These were to be sold to cover their expenses. Of course, bedding and clothing had to be packed for the whole family. The women had been busy getting everything ready!

Often the car was so full that a couple family members had to ride on the running board. One year a neighbor came along and sat on the space between the fender and the hood. The trip from Remer to Anoka, Minnesota, was 150 plus miles, at least half of which was dirt-and-gravel roads. It was necessary to stop now and then, because the tires frequently went flat. And every few miles they had to stop and buy used oil—new was too costly.

We admire the spirit of determination and courage that godly parents displayed in pursuing the values they cherished. Church camp was only one of them. They never doubted that God would provide the ability to accomplish whatever was necessary. Many of us today would be stopped in our tracks by such obstacles.

Father God, when the road looks long and rough ahead, with difficult miles to go, help us to remember that You will give us strength and power.

DARLENE YTREDAL BURGESON

Wake-up Call

Be joyful always; pray continually; give thanks in all circumstances, for this is God's will for you in Christ Jesus. 1 Thess. 5:16-18.

L AST MONTH IT WAS my turn to prepare the weekly bulletin for my church. When Shereen, our church clerk, called me a couple weeks ago with some bulletin information, she asked me about the songwriting seminar I had attended. It was nice of her to ask, but she was referring to the one I had gone to the previous August, not the recent February concert.

After we hung up I remembered how I'd asked my Bible study class, of which Shereen is a member, to pray for me before I left for the songwriting seminar. However, I'd never given a report to the class on how things had turned out.

I had entered two original songs in the songwriting competition, but to my great disappointment neither of them made it into the finalist round. And even though I'd learned a lot at the various classes offered at the seminar, and had gotten to take a songwriting class from Fernando Ortega and talk with him afterward, I still came home discouraged by the reality that even if my friends and family back home were ready for me to get discovered and become a star, the Christian music industry wasn't. I felt as though I had let their faith in me down somehow, so I didn't talk about it unless somebody asked.

But I was wrong. I hadn't let them down by not coming home with a recording contract or a publishing deal. I'd let them down by not talking about it after I'd asked them to pray for me. I realized that while I was willing to share my hopes with the people who cared about me, I wasn't as willing to share my disappointments.

Strangely enough, I often take the opposite approach with God. I can spend a lot of time on my knees, pouring out my concerns and requests, but rarely do I come dancing for joy in His presence.

So from now on I'm going to try, with God's help, to bring some balance into my life. I want to learn to be as willing to share my heartache as I am my delight and to ask God to dance a little more often, too.

Thanks, Shereen, for the wake-up call. TOYA MARIE KOCH

Neck-deep

The eyes of the Lord are on the righteous and his ears are attentive to their cry.
Ps. 34:15, NIV.

ON A BEAUTIFUL SPRING day in southern Mississippi, my friend Traci and I took my dog Molly for a walk in the park. After hiking for several hours, we were hot and tired. Molly especially seemed to feel the heat, and her tongue lolled out one side of her panting mouth.

Walking along the road beside the lake, I decided to take Molly down the slight incline and let her get a drink, since she was looking so pathetic and hot. Traci waited on the road. The rocks lining the shore weren't very stable, and I wobbled a bit, bumping Molly. Having nowhere else to go, she hurled herself into the water, landing with a belly-flopping *slap!* Since her leash was around my wrist, she jerked me in, too. The cement bottom of the lake was slimy, so what started out as a step into the water for my sandaled feet ended up with a shoulder-deep immersion! Molly, by this time thoroughly drenched, headed for the only dry spot within reach—my head. She literally climbed onto my shoulders with her front legs on my head. Every step forward I tried to take made me slide backward two steps. I didn't want to swim because we had no towels in the car. I wanted to stay as dry as possible, but I was stuck. I couldn't get out on my own.

Finally Traci, who had been observing (and laughing) from the road, composed herself enough to come to the edge of the water. She was able to catch Molly's leash in between fits of giggles and reel her in. She then some-how managed to fish me out. Since we didn't have anything to dry off with, we walked until Molly and I were dry enough to get back in the car.

Sin is like that lake. It looks so cool and inviting. I wanted to get close—but not too close. Just close enough to let a friend enjoy it. But my friend ended up dragging me in with her. Once in, it was a slippery, embarrassing slope downhill and, before I knew it, I was stuck, unable to make it out on my own. The harder I tried to get out, the deeper I went. I needed help!

God may smile at some of the predicaments we get ourselves into, but He is always willing to rush to our aid as soon as we ask. He can fish us out of the slimiest, deepest lakes of sin. All we have to do is ask.

VICKI L. MACOMBER

The Anticipation

Determine to live totally for Him. Begin each day with a commitment to live for Christ. This is what it means to put on the new self, to be a new person in Christ, one who has been re-created in uprightness and holiness. Eph. 4:23, 24, Clear Word.

ONE DAY WHILE OUT walking I found the ugliest, creepiest-looking creatures I'd ever seen. Covering the leaves of a bush were blotchy, brownish-gray caterpillars. I couldn't help wondering what they would become. Not beautiful butterflies, I was sure, but my curiosity got the better of me, so I decided to take one home. I picked a stem from the bush with three good-sized leaves on it.

My pet seemed quite content in its new quart-jar home. However, within a day and a half, it had finished off the three leaves, so I needed to get more of the same food. Fortunately, I had made a mental note of approximately where I had found the caterpillar—or so I thought.

After 20 minutes of trying to find the bush, I thought, *This is silly. Here I am wasting valuable time looking for special leaves to feed a caterpillar. What's a caterpillar's life worth anyway?*

At last I spotted the bush, grabbed some leaves, and headed home. The next day I noticed the caterpillar had hardly touched its food, and it was attaching itself to the side of the jar. Over the next few days it turned into what looked like a dry, curled-up leaf.

Days and weeks passed; I took the caterpillar to work with me and checked it constantly so I wouldn't miss any changes. After a month I removed the lid, only to discover the chrysalis had dried up completely. I felt sad and couldn't believe it was over after all the effort I had put into it.

I left the jar with the caterpillar's remains still attached on my kitchen counter for five months before I finally cleaned it out. Every time I looked at it, I was reminded of the effort that God went through to save all of us who are ugly with sin. Just as I had waited in anticipation for what the caterpillar would become, God waits for us to cooperate with Him so we will become all that He knows we can be. If a caterpillar's failed metamorphosis could disappoint me, how God must grieve over us when we fail to live for Him!

DONNA MEYER VOTH

May 20

Racing By

Let the beauty of the Lord our God be upon us. Ps. 90:17.

H E FLITTED PAST ME one early morning, a flash of bright red. I was heading off to the subway, part of the tedium of my everyday life. I am no bird-watcher, but even as a neophyte who has a hard time identifying the distinctly Canadian loon, I recognized the brightness of the cardinal. He stopped for a quick break on the nearby branch, nestled among the heavy foliage. What was he doing in the middle of the city in the middle of summer? This was not the typical season nor the place for him to be.

People walked by, eyeing me suspiciously as I gazed with a smile on my face and a distant look in my eyes. I did not care. I watched him as he chirped heartily on the branch. Then he too eyed me suspiciously and flew off to another branch, a bit farther from this strange creature known as a woman, who was watching him for who knows what reason. That one minute that I spent cost only a small part of my orchestrated life, but it gave me a lighter step for the remainder of the day.

I thought of all the people who walked by, how they had missed so much—the beauty of one of God's creatures. Then I realized how often I myself forget to stop and smell the roses along the way. How can we stop running so fast? We're always in a hurry to get on with life. We don't realize that what we are actually running toward is death. That is what is at the finish line of life.

However, life isn't about reaching the finish line but about the obstacles—or diversions and scenery—along the way. Will you be sorry you ran the race straight to the finish line, placing first, second, or third, and then stand on a pedestal for all to recognize your success? Or will you be glad that you took the time to stop along the way and refuel with the nourishment provided at God's refreshment stands along the way? We need to imbibe those refreshments, the nectar that our heavenly Father has provided to give us a boost of energy and a clearer view of worthwhile goals in life.

Lord, I want to take time to enjoy the beauty You have for me this very day—in people, in nature, in Your Word and life. Bless us each with Your special refreshment, I pray.   Christine Hwang

148

An Image of Jesus

I will betroth thee unto me for ever; yea, I will betroth thee unto me in righteousness, and in judgment, and in lovingkindness, and in mercies. I will even betroth thee unto me in faithfulness: and thou shalt know the Lord. Hosea 2:19, 20.

IT WAS SUCH A discouraging, mournful time of my life—a time filled with disappointments, loss, and frustration. I couldn't understand why these circumstances had come. I thought I was a good Christian, and I expected my life to go a certain way. I never expected God to allow these things to happen to me.

Then one night I had a dream. I was standing in a park with tall trees and green grass all around. In front of me stood an easel, and on the easel was a picture of Jesus. The picture was made of pieces of glass that were put together like a puzzle. I was very proud of my picture of Jesus, and I kept calling people over to look at it. But someone came too close and knocked the picture out of the easel. The pieces were strewn everywhere, and some of them broke to bits. Frantic, I tried to put the picture back together the way it was before, but it was impossible. My picture of Jesus was destroyed. I began to cry and turned to walk away. A man who was standing nearby stopped me. He put his hand on my shoulder and turned me around to face him. I lifted my eyes to see Jesus—the real Jesus—standing before me. He cupped my face in His hands and looked into my eyes with a love that I had never experienced before. At that moment I knew that I had never really known Jesus before—I only thought I did. And the Man who stood before me now was someone I wanted to get to know much, much better.

How reminiscent that dream was of my life. I grew up understanding God in a certain way. But when my experiences shook my faith down to its very foundation, I found that my thinking and understanding were in error. What a pleasure it is now to get to know my Jesus more and more each day! I'm so glad my original picture of Him was destroyed.

Dear Father, I thank You that You allowed circumstances to come into my life that caused me to closely examine my beliefs about You. Please help me to sort out the truth from the lies, and cause me each day to know You more. Amen.

LYNDA MAE RICHARDSON

Prayer and Popcorn

Because he hath inclined his ear unto me, therefore will I call upon him as long as I live. Ps. 116:2.

IT WAS THE LAST official week of classes, and I desperately wanted to do something special for my anatomy and physiology class students. The plan was to surprise them with freshly popped popcorn as they came by my office to submit their final papers.

All was set, and I went about preparing the first bowl of munchables, but the kernels burned without popping. I quickly dashed to the store to get a new batch of corn, fearing that my dilemma had been caused by old kernels.

On my return, students were teeming outside my office, and I was most eager to make my surprise work. When the first batch hadn't gone well, I had breathed a prayer: *Lord, please make it work. I need to do this for my students.* The second batch went well, and I happily distributed it to the waiting students. I was proud of my efforts and more so of the students' response as I put in the third batch. To my great dismay, it was worse than the first batch. It was only then that I remembered my prayer, so I prayed again, the same little prayer. The fourth batch was even better than the second, but this time I knew it was the prayer and not the quality of the grains. All the batches that followed were preceded by a prayer.

As I watched the fluffy puffs of corn spilling over the bowl, I thought how similar to my dreams and aspirations this popcorn project was. As long as I keep praying and trusting, the lousy kernels in my life can become fluffy realities. The key is in the prayers.

So many times we lose the excitement of living because our previous successes have turned our focus in the wrong direction—inward! We blame our circumstances, our families, our spouses, our children—even ourselves—for everything that does not turn out the way we expected. The answer, however, lies in our continuous dependence upon and communication with God. The excitement and true joy is longer lasting when we recognize that our success comes from above.

Father, help me to remember that Your power and strength are only one prayer away.

PATRICE WILLIAMS-GORDON

The Pheasants and the Peas

He turned, and said unto Peter, Get thee behind me, Satan: thou art an offence unto me: for thou savourest not the things that be of God, but those that be of men. Matt. 16:23.

IN MAY I PLANTED three rows of peas. Soon they were poking their tiny heads through the soil. I could almost taste the freshness of them.

A few days later there was not one little shoot to be seen. To be sure, I dug about for a few feet. No peas. My employer said it was the pheasants, and if it were he, he would have pheasant for supper. But it was early in the season, and I could reseed the peas.

Again I counted the days until they would be up. My employer had said that the pheasants would not walk on netting, so I put some down. However, upon viewing my pea patch, I was angry to discover that scattered about were sprouted peas, unsprouted peas, half peas, and decapitated peas. I momentarily felt that if there had been a pheasant within reach I would have wrung its neck.

I faithfully covered up the peas that looked as though they would grow and decided to plan a better defense. I built a wall of netting around the peas with a tarp covering them, just in case the pheasants outsmarted me and flew down into the middle of the patch. Gotcha!

The next morning my husband saw pheasants happily pushing their necks through the holes in the netting, stretching in to reach every pea they could. Not one to give up, I pulled all the net and stakes a foot farther away from the rows.

A week later, when the peas were well up, there were only hit-and-miss patches of greenery. I will chalk this year up as the year the pheasants feasted. After all, I still have some peas from last year in my freezer.

The devil can get his long neck into our life and find a way to feast upon our soul and peck away at our eternal happiness. Only when we hedge our mind and heart with the netting of the Word of God, reinforced with daily prayer and covered with His blood, can we be sure of a successful harvest when the Reaper comes to harvest His fruits. VIDELLA McCLELLAN

May 24

Convocation and Hope

I pray that God, who gives you hope, will keep you happy and full of peace as you believe in him. May you overflow with hope through the power of the Holy Spirit. Rom. 15:13, NLT.

I SAW THE WOMAN WATCHING us as we shopped in the canned-food warehouse in my hometown of Hermiston, Oregon. Sonny, our special son, was around 3 years old. Cautiously, she approached my sister, Janet, and me. "I've never seen a child like him, except for my own son." She began to share bits of her life. Her precious son was 17 and living in a group home. He had a job filling vending machines—that gave me hope. "My son wasn't toilet-trained until he was 12," she said. "Please don't give up."

Those words of wisdom became engraved upon my heart. Only the Lord and I know how many times I would have given up if it weren't for this precious, concerned sister giving me hope.

When Sonny's sister, Andrea, graduated from the University of Lethbridge, Sonny was almost 10 years old. My husband, Ron, Sonny, and I watched the ceremonies from the lowest level of the gym bleachers so that we could exit fast if Sonny misbehaved. We'd been concentrating on Sonny's toileting skills for several years, and he had only recently shown success. Then, as the graduation ceremonies proceeded, Sonny said, "Pee-pee," so I took him to the washroom.

I knew I would miss Andrea's big moment as she walked across the stage to receive her degrees in music and education. It was to have been a Kodak moment. Yet I knew that Sonny had also graduated in a way as well, and it was a promising light at his sister's graduation.

So as Andrea graduated with distinction, Sonny sat on the throne doing a "good job," and even applauded himself. I joined him. Sonny was completely toilet-trained at age 12. Oh, how the Lord has shown me both ends of the rainbow through my precious and blessed children!

The woman in the grocery store motivated me to have hope when others might have offered words of discouragement or scorn. I will strive to have that blessed hope from God. He alone keeps me happy and full of peace. I'm thankful that He sometimes sends others to help in that process. May you experience that happiness and peace today.   DEBORAH SANDERS

The Car That Would Not Stop

God is our refuge and strength, a very present help in trouble. Ps. 46:1.

IT FELT LIKE SUMMER that Sunday morning in May. The day was so
humid—the temperature was already 90° F. It was my third week in
Maryland, having just transferred from Virginia Beach, Virginia.

The place I now live is located on a hill. I had parked my car in front of
the house, headed downhill. That morning my car wouldn't start. I tried
again—still no spark, but the car did start to move downward. I panicked. I
stepped on the brake. But the more I did, the more it gained speed going
downhill. It was like a bad dream. I tried to pull the hand brake, but it didn't
work. Nothing was stopping that car.

"God, please help me!" I cried. My heart was pounding. It scared me
knowing how dangerous it would be if someone were to cross the road while
my car was moving. "O Lord, don't let me hit someone or another vehicle," I
continued to pray.

I was thinking, *Where will the car stop? Will it end up against a tree?* I
thought it would have to hit a tree in order to stop.

The car had coasted about a half mile. I had already passed several stop
signs when I saw another road on my left. I decided to make a left turn.
When I felt the car stop by itself, I realized this road was ascending instead
of descending.

Although my car had stopped, my heart was still racing. I was shocked by
this experience. I realized how God had helped me. He saw to it that the road
was empty—neither cars nor people crossed the road while I couldn't control
my car. I was safe and unharmed because God answered my prayer instantly.
When His children are in trouble and call to Him, He is there.

*Lord, how reassuring it is to remember that You, our prayer-answering God,
are a very present—and instant—help in trouble. Again, thank You, Lord. May I
be aware of Your presence with me all day, in all I do, but especially when I am in
trouble.*   LANNY LYDIA PONGILATAN

Silly Birds

I have told you all this so that you will have peace of heart and mind. Here on earth you will have many trials and sorrows; but cheer up, for I have overcome the world. John 16:33, TLB.

IN THE DARKNESS I heard them, birds sounding off their early-morning herald of spring. I don't believe I've ever heard birds start their morning songs as early as these birds in Germany do. We love the songs of birds, outside or inside our home. We bought our first caged birds in 1971 at a Sunday market in Thailand. The colorful lovebirds kept us entertained with their gymnastics. They would climb to the top of their cylinder cage, hang upside down, and drop, always landing on their feet. This activity would go on all day: climb, hang, drop; climb, hang, drop.

Years later, when we were in a pastorate in Georgia, we picked out a butter-yellow canary and named him Fred. He sang trills and rolls and bird arias for hours on end. We even took Fred along on the long drive from Georgia to our first military assignment at Fort Sill, Oklahoma. I still remember the seating arrangement for our trip across country. Fred was in his bird cage on one side of the car, and our schnauzer, Fritzy, was on the other side in his kennel. A pillow between made a makeshift barrier to keep the two from squabbling in the back seat like naughty children.

One day after we were settled in our new home, however, Fred's song ended. In my absentmindedness, I left a pan on a stove burner, and the fumes from the Teflon stilled Fred's song. I tried to give Fred mouth-to-beak resuscitation, but no attempt at breathing into his little beak could bring him back to consciousness. I cried a lot for my little friend Fred that day.

This morning as I heard the birds sing I thought of Fred. I noted the hour, the darkness, and my desire to sleep and thought, *Silly birds; they sing in the dark!*

It is my prayer today that you, too, may be like those silly birds. When you feel the dark clouds encircle your life, speak up before you feel it and sing praises to God, even before the dawn. After all, if birds can do it, so can we! Sing praises to Him, speak words of power and faith, and watch how miraculously the dawn comes!   NANCY ANN NEUHARTH TROYER

Of Mansions and Flowers

In my Father's house are many mansions: . . . I go to prepare a place for you. And if I go and prepare a place for you, I will come again, and receive you unto myself. John 14:2, 3.

WHILE HAVING DINNER with friends in a Chinese restaurant a few years ago, each of us began reading aloud the fortunes inside our cookies. I found mine to be rather amusing when I first read it silently. The reaction of my husband and friends was somewhat less subtle.

" 'You will live in a mansion and have many beautiful flowers,' " I read. Without really thinking first, I blurted out, "Well, it must mean heaven."

Now, everyone who knows me also knows my number one hobby is my home, whether decorating, remodeling, or just cleaning. I majored in interior design in college and worked as a designer for several years. Because my husband is a contractor, our house is an ever-evolving work in process. Comments from my husband such as "You can dream up more things you think need to be done than anyone I've ever seen" and "I haven't even finished this project yet and you already have the next one planned" are daily conversation in our household. So much for the mansion portion of my fortune.

The flower portion is a newer and less perfected passion, but one I am striving to conquer. Having always been more of an indoor person, in the 10 years we have lived in our current home my lawn grows greener with each new spring, and my flower beds are bursting with color.

With this background information, you can understand why reading this particular fortune aloud caused several chuckles around the dinner table that evening.

I still carry that small piece of paper with me in my wallet. I take it out occasionally and use it as a reference when something in my house isn't quite perfect or some of my flowers aren't doing quite as well as I had hoped.

Lord, this helps me keep things in perspective and also serves to remind me that yes, in heaven I will live in a mansion. In heaven I will have many beautiful flowers; gifts will last an eternity! But best of all, You will be there, too. You are the one who has prepared for me a place.   PAULETTA COX JOHNSON

May 28

God Answers Computer Problems

Is anything too hard for the Lord? Gen. 18:14, TEV.

"NOT AGAIN!" I GROANED and watched helplessly as the file folders on my computer ran helter-skelter, disarranging themselves. It wasn't the first time, either.

Lord, I'd like to finish writing this book. If it's Your will that I continue with it, please repair Macintosh Plus. You know I have promised the proceeds of this book to help fund my alma mater, which needs it so badly. Lord, this is in Your hands. I claimed "Ask and receive" and "Is anything too hard for the Lord?" and thanked Him for honoring my faith.

I dared not take my Macintosh back to the Apple center. The last time I had taken it there the young technician had inadvertently erased all materials in memory. So, carefully, painstakingly, I slowly dragged each file folder to a 3.5 disk in their correct sequential order. *Thank You, Lord,* I sighed, *for the insight on what to do and for the patience and persistence the task fostered in me. Now the file folders are beyond Macintosh's senile acts.*

Several months later my Macintosh Plus burned. The MaCapitol people said Apple no longer made parts for this decade-old version and offered to transfer the file folders to their latest Apple version. I wasn't ready to spend more than $1,000 for a new computer and needed to think it over. I knew the book I was working on and other file folders were safe in memory, in the MacBottom storage, but I needed a Macintosh Plus to retrieve them.

I went back on my knees. "Lord, let me find someone who has a Macintosh Plus. I hand this problem over to You." Soon God provided an answer.

My son gave me a Compaq Presario (IBM-compatible) to do the revision for the course I had developed. The school would offer it in their curriculum and asked me to resubmit it in an IBM compatible 3.5. I had accepted the challenge.

After a long-distance chat with our older son, my husband said, "Sonny has a Macintosh Plus just sitting boxed in his dental office. He'll ship it to you, along with an SE/30 for a spare."

Lord, my heart overflows to praise You each time I use Macintosh Plus and Compaq. Thank You for these reminders—there is nothing impossible with You.

CONSUELO RODA JACKSON

Scrubbed

The Lord is good to all: and his tender mercies are over all his works. Ps. 145:9.

A WOMEN'S MINISTRIES PRAYER breakfast in my home left me with the job of cleaning up some of the utensils that contained the delectable contributions that had been brought in.

Among the utensils was a small saucepan, big enough to hold a pint of gravy. From the expression of those who had tasted it, the gravy was delicious. But the pan? Its real color was not readily observable. Should I throw it out? But it wasn't mine—I had to give it back to the owner.

As I washed it carefully, I noticed it was covered with baked-on residue from previous cooking. I scrubbed it with a detergent, but the residue didn't budge. I tried bleach. No luck. I soaked it overnight with bleach again. Still no luck.

Finally, I tried vinegar. When nothing changed, I tried scraping the pan with a sharp, smooth-edge knife. Now I began to observe some success. Again, I soaked the pan overnight, this time with a milder detergent. Then I scraped some more.

Gradually, very gradually, the stubborn scum disappeared. I felt a degree of success, but I was not completely satisfied. So I scrubbed some more and soaked some more and scraped some more and washed it until finally the white porcelain of the saucepan was visible.

I returned the saucepan to the owner—and wondered if she would recognize it.

When I first noticed the pan, I thought, *This is fit for the dump.* But as I kept scrubbing, I imagined how attractive it must have been when it was new, and how that original beauty could possibly be restored.

God uses a similar procedure to cleanse, polish, refine, and produce spotless characters in the lives of His children. And what a surprise when the change is observed!

The pan yielded; human beings are so stubborn! We rebel at the harsh experiences, the disappointments, the trials, the reverses in health, in business, in relationships. But God does not stop in His attempt to polish and to cleanse. He knows our potential; He is not satisfied to see us submerged in sin, the scum of life. His desire is to make us clean, to see us scrubbed, renewed in His spotless beauty.

QUILVIE MILLS

May 30

A Visit to a Cemetery

The Lord himself shall descend from heaven with a shout . . . and the dead in Christ shall rise first. 1 Thess. 4:16.

THE HENDERSON-BILLS-HERNDON family gathering in honor of the families of my mother and father took place in Memphis, Tennessee, after a year and a half of planning, chiefly by my niece, Brenda. Our first stop, however, took my sister and me to a small cemetery in Collierville, an adjoining former country town that's now becoming a thriving and burgeoning city. My parents and a sister, Mae Sue, who had died long before I was born, had been buried there years before.

When my mother was buried there, the plot was located behind a small wooden-framed church that was overgrown with grass and weeds. We were pleasantly surprised to find that the wooden structure had been replaced by a beautiful modern brick edifice, and the cemetery with its old and modern headstones was well groomed and grass-lined.

We walked around respectfully, viewing headstones, as we searched for and (to our surprise) easily found our family's resting place. We had our pictures taken beside our parents' and our sister's graves and were comforted to leave them resting there.

I was reminded of the time of the Savior's promised return when the tombs of buried saints will burst asunder. Scripture tells us that "the Lord himself will come down from heaven, with a loud command, with the voice of the archangel and with the trumpet call of God, and the dead in Christ will rise first. After that, we who are still alive and are left will be caught up together with them in the clouds to meet the Lord in the air" (1 Thess. 4:16, 17, NIV).

As we await this divine culmination of earth's history, it behooves each of us to pray daily that our lives, our actions, our influence will prepare us to be among those of the first resurrection. Let us be a witness in our homes, on our jobs, in our communities. As surely as Jesus came in the First Advent, He will as surely burst the tombs at His second coming, releasing His sleeping saints.

As we await the coming of our Lord, may we find peace in 1 Thessalonians 4:18: "Wherefore comfort one another with these words."

MARTHA J. WALKER

Lifetime Assurance

So do not fear, for I am with you; do not be dismayed, for I am your God. I will strengthen you and help you; I will uphold you with my righteous right hand. Isa. 41:10, NIV.

IT WAS CONTRARY TO local custom, but I didn't want him to see me dabbing at my eyes. So I asked the man carrying my luggage to walk up the path ahead of me instead of behind. As I stumbled among boulders and de-nuded tree roots I had questions. *How can I leave my children here, so far from home? What will home be like without their chatter and laughter? What will happen if these two countries engage in another physical dispute over territory?* Then I consoled myself, *Well, the children will be healthier in this clean, cool air. The teachers are well qualified. They treat the children as if they were their own. Surely, God does care for us.*

I boarded an ancient vehicle at the bus station. Only days before, I had ascended into these mountains on this same bus with this same driver. The road was steep and the ascent had been slow and tedious. Now we were descending. As we whirled around one curve after another, it seemed to me we were flying. I clutched my seat. Then I recalled that the same God who would care for the children during our separation would care for me on my journey.

At the base of the mountains the driver skillfully maneuvered the bus into a parking lot filled with a mass of swirling humanity, waving their arms and shouting political slogans. I understood the crowd's slogans but not the purpose of their excitement. Could this noisy crowd turn violent? I was uncomfortable, afraid to remain in the bus, afraid to get out. But God's promise was still effective, and He would care for things here, too.

At a small airport in a nearby city I boarded an old DC3 freight hauler. I again utilized my belief in God's concern as that plane rattled and shook as we skimmed over jungle treetops.

To that point in my life, God's love, care, and concern for me were rather loosely defined and unconnected attributes in my simple philosophy. It all crystallized, though, when my husband died suddenly and prematurely. As I searched Scripture for assurance and guidance, I came to Isaiah 41:10: "Do not fear. . . . I am with you. . . . I am your God. . . . I will strengthen you and help you." That's God's infallible and everlasting assurance to me!

LOIS E. JOHANNES

Joyous Occasions

Whom having not seen, ye love; in whom, though now ye see him not, yet believing, ye rejoice with joy unspeakable and full of glory. 1 Peter 1:8.

MOM, MY GRADUATION class is marching in June. I'd like for you to come," my son said.

Eight weeks passed. Several carloads of people were en route to Maryland for Andre's graduate school graduation. For various reasons we were running late leaving for the ceremonies. The closer we came to the university, the longer the line of cars became. And they were barely moving. Our hearts raced as we crept along.

As we entered the campus we could hear the band playing. Andre ran toward the building while we parked the cars. The crowd was enormous. Standing near the bandstand was a no-no; security asked us to move on. We moved through the crowd to another spot, only to be told we couldn't stand there, either. There weren't any vacant seats for family members or friends of the graduates. I was desperate, and had a pretty good idea how Zacchaeus felt trying to see Jesus in the crowd. Undergraduates were marching, so those with chairs nearby were standing. I asked a woman standing next to me if I could stand on her chair. She consented.

When the woman to whom the chair belonged wanted to sit, I asked the gentleman standing next to her if I could stand on his chair. He said, "Yes."

Finally the graduates were marching, and I saw Andre coming down the aisle with his shades on, waving a long-stemmed rose in the air as he had said he would. Talk about adrenaline! I jumped up and down on the chair, yelling out his name for all to hear. I was ecstatic. Andre and I made eye contact as soon as he heard my voice; he smiled as he continued marching.

This was a joyful occasion; however, I am looking forward to a more joyous occasion. The joy that filled my heart that day won't compare with the joy I look forward to having when I meet my Lord and Savior in the air. Oh, what a day that will be!

Father, please help us to be prepared to go home with You when You come for Your children. I pray in the name of Jesus. Amen.   CORA A. WALKER

Message in Ivy Leaves

See, I have inscribed you on the palms of my hands; your walls are continually before me. Isa. 49:16, NRSV.

IN THE THROES OF completing the final chapters of my dissertation some years ago, I encountered a metaphorical logjam. The thoughts that flooded my brain were jumbled. The words seemed meaningless. Taking a break, I did what most of my girlfriends do in similar circumstances—I cleaned my kitchen. I mopped the floor, scrubbed the stove, cleaned the oven, and washed the curtains. Convinced I had breached the impasse, I returned to my computer; but my thoughts were still confused. I resorted to doing more laundry, focusing on linen this time.

Lifting a pot of trailing ivy from the lace covering of a small round table, I noticed that the delicate cloth was attached to the earthen jar. Tugging gently at the cloth I intended to launder, I saw that two ivy fronds had worked their way into the spaces of the crocheted material and grown healthy leaves. Reluctant to break off the tender young shoots, I lowered the vase back to the table.

Staring down at the plant, sprawled as gracefully as cursive on the tiny table, I searched for the spiritual metaphor I am sure is embedded in each of our life experiences. At first I could make no connection with the green and ivory of the lustrous leaves curled in elegant disarray across the table. Then I saw the link. God had written me an elegant note in ivy leaves.

Isaiah's words sprang to mind: "See, I have written your name on my hand. Ever before me is a picture of Jerusalem's walls in ruins" (Isa. 49:16, NLT). It was as if my heavenly Friend had sent me a message in ivy-leafed script. The walls of my disjointed literary style were able to come down.

Infused with the wonder of our God's glory, I returned to my keyboard. In the hours that sped by on angels' wings, I noted that my thoughts flowed freely, the transitions were clear, and the analysis creatively cogent. The wall—my stylistic logjam—was literally in ruins.

I was reminded again that everything that happens, even the writing of a paltry research paper, is part of our Father's concern. Praise God! He never forgets us for a moment.

GLENDA-MAE GREENE

June 3

Saving Homeless Kittens

A righteous man regardeth the life of his beast: but the tender mercies of the wicked are cruel. Prov. 12:10.

IT IS TRAGIC THAT so many animals, especially pets, are unloved and abused. How a person treats animals is a pretty accurate index to his or her character. People who are unkind to animals often don't have much regard for their fellow humans, either. Because of at least one such person, my phone rang.

"Bonnie, do you want a kitten?" The voice on the other end of the line was that of Nancy, my next-door neighbor. "I can bring him over for you to look at."

He was mostly skin stretched over bones, long fur, and two of the biggest, bluest eyes I'd ever seen. He was Himalayan with some tabby thrown in. "How old is he?" I asked.

"I'm not sure, " she replied. "I found him wandering on the grounds of the nursing home where I work. He was so hungry! I fed him scraps from the kitchen and brought him home with me. Would you like to hold him?"

I took the wee mite. He nestled into the crook of my arm and looked up at me as if to say, "Won't you please love me and give me a home?" I fell in love with him on the spot.

Most of the next day was spent at the vet's and the groomer's, for our kitty had fleas. He weighed one and a half pounds.

The vet told me, "This kitten's about 4½ months old. He's stunted be-cause he's been without proper nourishment for so long. Don't expect him to get very big."

Since his markings were the color of dark Hershey's chocolate, we named him Chocolati, and shortened it to Chocky. After a year, Chocky weighed seven pounds.

One summer later we acquired Catie (pronounced Katie), an 8-week-old orange-and-yellow tiger-striped tabby, as a companion for Chocky. Our brother-in-law had brought her, along with her mother and seven siblings, to his house after a coworker had threatened to kill them.

My prayer is that God will help us as Christians to be good stewards and to encourage others to take better care of the animals God has put here on earth.

BONNIE MOYERS

Why Didn't I Ask Sooner?

Thus saith the Lord, thy Redeemer, the Holy One of Israel; I am the Lord thy God which teacheth thee to profit, which leadeth thee by the way that thou shouldest go. O that thou hadst hearkened to my commandments! then had thy peace been as a river. Isa. 48:17, 18.

A CHILDHOOD FRIEND recently told me this story:
"I have never told it to anyone before, but now I need an ear to hear, one I know will understand. I wish I could say I had a happy childhood. I didn't have many close friends. My parents were churchgoing people, but I didn't believe much they told me about God and Jesus.

"My elementary education I received in public school. The next four years were in private school. If there was an ugly duckling in the school, I was it. Not till my junior year in college did any of the boys take an interest in me. When one did notice me, there were no shooting stars in my sky for him as it seemed there were for other girls. He was just a casual acquaintance as far as I was concerned. Eventually my woman's intuition told me he was getting serious. I was not ready to marry, and the idea put me in a panic.

"My prayers up to that time had been 'said,' but this time I was in real earnest. I opened my heart totally to God in a way I had not known was possible. To my surprise, I got the distinct impression that I should not marry this man. I knew of no human friend to talk to, so on the day he proposed, I said yes.

"We were married for 25 years, but his work was his life. I had guilt, as I was sure I was a big disappointment to him. Nothing I did or said or cooked brought any approval. My husband died suddenly while our three boys were young. Then life became one long struggle. I went back to God with my misery—my final resort.

"Why did I wait so long? I talked and listened. I seemed to hear, 'You paid dearly, didn't you? But now I want you to know you are forgiven. Why didn't you ask?'

"How wonderful it has been to have the burden of guilt lifted. I am so grateful to God for understanding my weakness and waiting for me. I now have that peace that passes understanding."   GRACE STREIFLING

The Lord Grants Wisdom

Tune your ears to wisdom, and concentrate on understanding. . . . Then you will . . . gain knowledge of God. For the Lord grants wisdom! From his mouth come knowledge and understanding. He grants a treasure of good sense to the godly. Prov. 2:2-7, NLT.

IT WAS A YEAR of celebration. My oldest son, Greg, completed college; my youngest son, J.T., graduated from high school; and my daughter, Jhovonnah, was entering her senior year. I was the proud mom who had counseled, guided, prompted, listened, advised, suggested, and insisted. Not all at the same time, of course. And let's not forget wept. I'd had a share of that, too. It had been an uphill struggle at times. Thankfully, that was behind me now, I thought. It was time for bigger and better things for everyone!

Greg had spent tedious hours on the Internet researching sites and collecting information, countless weeks without pay on an internship, and hundreds of quarters feeding campus parking meters. Now his search for a job in radiobroadcast would begin.

J.T. considered taking a break from the world of academia, but eventually began browsing through college catalogs. No doubt he would make the right decision when to begin.

Voni was contemplating her last year of high school. Would she sign up for drama again, or be a member of the traveling choir for a third year? What career did she want?

So many choices, I thought. What roads would they choose now? Would their choices be good ones? They realized the value of a good education, and each one had striven for the best. Yet I knew that education wasn't enough. And it wasn't everything. Did they have a knowledge of God? Had my husband and I taught them love for God during their early years? Had we set the right priorities? Would they choose the knowledge and understanding that only the Lord could give? I could not yet "retire" from motherhood. Perhaps the hardest years were just ahead.

Heavenly Father, I entrust my children to You, grown though they be. You know them, Lord, better than I. Help tune their ears to Your wisdom and understanding so they can truly know You and serve You as they seek to serve mankind. And grant me wisdom, too, to know how and when to remind them of how much You love them. Amen.   IRIS L. STOVALL

How Beautiful Heaven Must Be!

I am making all things new! Rev. 21:5, NIV. Nothing impure will ever enter it. Verse 27, NIV. [She] who overcomes shall inherit these things, and I will be [her] God and [she] will be My [daughter]. Verse 7, NASB.

IT WAS THE END of a busy week. My friend and work colleague, Sarai, and I had been visiting schools in the Samoa Mission in Central Pacific all week. Both of us desperately needed relaxation and recuperation. I had to leave for my home country, Fiji, on Monday, and the only time we had free was Sunday. Sarai spoke to a church friend, Fa'afetai, about our need and immediately a plan was developed. We would drive out to the eastern side of the island for a picnic lunch and swim by the beautiful white sandy beaches.

The drive to the beach fales took a little more than two hours. As we drove I admired the great God of creation. This was a perfect day to go out and absorb the beauty and majestic views of nature that are unique to the South Pacific Islands. The deep-blue sky reflected in the clear blue waters; the green foliage and rolling hills were so pleasant; and the sweet smell of Pacific Island wildflowering trees filled the air. *Yes,* I said to myself, *if this is beautiful, even where sin reigns, how beautiful heaven must be! The sweet home of the happy and free. That is exactly where I, a Pacific Islander, really long to be.*

That day as I sat and fully took in the beauty and simplicity of life on Samoa, the happy nature of the people, and even the friendly dogs that frequented our rest house, I also wondered how simple life was going to be with my God.

As we prepared to eat lunch a car backed up toward our beach fale and delivered a dishful of baked bananas, palusami, fish, and taro in coconut cream. The simple picnic turned out to be a feast spread on the mat. There was fresh fruit drink and coconut juice. As I saw the spirit of giving, the sharing of food by everyone around, I began to imagine how plentiful heaven must be, a satisfying home for the hungry, thirsty, and all the lonely.

That day heaven was brought home to me. The experience made me realize how often I forget heaven is here in me. When I share, smile, make life pleasant for someone, or notice the beauty around me, heaven becomes real for me and for others.

FULORI BOLA

A Song to a Spider

And ye shall teach them your children, speaking of them when thou sittest in thine house, and when thou walkest by the way, when thou liest down, and when thou risest up. And thou shalt write them . . . that your days may be . . . as the days of heaven upon the earth. Deut. 11:19-21.

WAIT; BE STILL. Quietness—an avenue of the soul's communication with our heavenly Father.

Children are close to nature, yet we may rob them of even this quality with our nonstop schedules. My week had been hectic. When the weekend came I was tempted to do my tired bedtime ritual, all one-sided, with me reading stories, praying, putting-in-the-crib, saying good night, closing the door. No time to listen to my 2-year-old Hannah. How being rushed can harden our hearts toward one another!

Instead, I brought my daughter to another bed under a window so we could hear the birds going to roost during this peaceful time of a summer day coming to a close. I told Hannah the mommy birds were calling their baby birds to bedtime in their nests in the trees. She leaned on the windowsill and listened. We thought of all the little animals who must be getting ready for bed, just as she was doing. We were quiet together.

Suddenly Hannah said, "What's this?" She pointed to a spider in the corner of the windowsill, its thick, furry legs curled up. She asked questions about it. I said if it were alive it would be moving, but it was not. I hoped she didn't really know what dead meant, but her heart was touched by the spider not being able to move. Perhaps she thought it was sick.

She looked at me sadly. "I want to sing a song to the spider." Then she gave the sweetest rendition of "Twinkle, Twinkle Little Star" I ever heard, her baby voice in a melodious baby tune comforting the little spider. I was reminded of a poem, a child's prayer for God to "hear and bless . . . small things that have no words."

Sometimes people care when a sparrow falls to the ground, but who besides God cares when a little spider breathes its last? Could Hannah's little song be any less an act of worship than the singing of the birds? The bedroom seemed transformed into a cathedral, heaven upon earth. ALEAH IQBAL

June 8

Homecoming

And if I go and prepare a place for you, I will come again and receive you to Myself; that where I am, there you may be also. John 14:3, NKJV.

EVER SINCE I CAN remember, the historic Middlecreek Zion Church in Roselym, Ohio, has held its homecoming celebration the first Sunday in June. It's family reunion time when we praise God, fellowship, potluck, and visit the graves of our loved ones who are buried across the gravel road. In the early 1900s the quaint church and land were given to the African-Americans surrounding the small community of Paulding County. However, it was stipulated that church services must be held there at least once a year if the church and land were to remain the property of their descendants.

For years the older generation had diligently followed the established tradition, but now the promise had been committed to a new generation. I would be facilitating the program for the first time in my life. This year would be more momentous, too, because I had buried my mother's ashes in that country cemetery the previous year. Knowing how my mother loved her garden, I had planned to plant some flowers in memory of her and place a special stone that said "Juanita's Garden" at her burial site.

I prayed for a safe journey and directed my car westbound for the long seven-hour trip to Ohio. Usually, when I travel home alone, I get caught up with communing with God. But this time the Lord told me to slow down. As I pondered the homecoming event I noticed the beautiful wildflowers alongside the highway. I thought, *How beautiful are Your flowers, Lord. Not made by people, but by Your own divine hands. How appropriate it will be to take these flowers to Mother's grave.* So I stopped my car, got out my gardening tools, and dug up some gorgeous wild daisies. When I looked up, approximately 50 yards in front of me was the sign "Welcome to Ohio." I smiled and thought of another promised "homecoming."

O Lord, one day there will be a homecoming more glorious than anyone has ever seen. You, in Your majesty, will be standing there to welcome us home. You will give us flowers that will never die. Never again will we have to visit the graves of our loved ones. Your own hands will wipe away our tears, and we will rejoice in Your presence forever. Hallelujah! EVELYN GREENWADE BOLTWOOD

167

The Dream Home

Eye hath not seen, nor ear heard, neither have entered into the heart of man, the things which God hath prepared for them that love him. 1 Cor. 2:9.

MY HUSBAND AND I began thinking about buying our dream home after we had been married for three years. We dreamed about the type we wanted and began looking for homes. We never liked what we saw.

In our apartment we would discuss and visualize what we wanted our dream home to be like. My husband was reared in a two-story home, and I in a single-story home, called a bungalow. Therefore, he wanted our dream home to be two stories, and I wanted a one-story.

Once we agreed that our dream home would be a single story, we let God guide and decided to purchase land and have our dream home built. We hired an architect to draw the blueprint; then came much discussion as we decided what we wanted and didn't want.

The day came when we began looking for a building contractor. After talking to several, we finalized on one. We were in our 20s and never doubted God's leading, but the contractor doubted us and didn't believe we were serious. What he didn't know was that God was leading. Within a few weeks the huge hole was dug, and the work began. Each day we watched the progress with thanksgiving and praise.

After we had lived in the house a year or two I began to find fault. I found myself saying to my husband, "We should have had a light put down here," or "We should have had the side porch a little wider," or "Maybe the kitchen window should have been a little larger."

Nevertheless, I'm enjoying God's blessing in my dream home here on earth while preparing for my dream home in heaven that Jesus is preparing—so grand that "eye hath not seen, nor ear heard." I rejoice knowing there'll be no "should haves" or "should have puts," because this dream home—a mansion with Jesus as the architect and contractor—will be perfect.   ANNIE B. BEST

Sixty-seven Roses

I am the rose of Sharon, and the lily of the valleys. Song of Sol. 2:1, NKJV.

A S I WAS GETTING ready for church one morning, the telephone rang. "Could you use some roses for your church service this morning?" my neighbor and friend, Pauline, asked. "I have some extra and will bring them over. You can arrange them as you wish."

Of course I said "Yes." How nice it was for her to share a few roses to grace our sanctuary! I thought about the greenery I had and how I could arrange possibly even as many as six roses into an attractive bouquet.

A few minutes later the doorbell rang, and Pauline stood there with a container of roses in her hand. I gasped. There were far more than a few roses. I questioned her if she was certain she wanted to give them all to me. She assured me they were for us and our church.

As I began to arrange the roses, I counted them—67 roses! What a fragrant gift. All during the morning service I was blessed as I looked at them and thought of the beauty God had provided. He not only was the source of life for the roses, but was the source of the goodness of my friend.

Following the service we parceled out the roses so that those of our congregation who were not able to attend that morning received some roses and a visit. It was my privilege to visit an elderly couple who live down the street from the church. I have come to love these people, and it thrilled my soul to see the joy two roses brought them. The wife was sitting in her wheelchair, and the husband quickly got out a vase and made sure they were trimmed to the proper height to display them to their best advantage. Others shared similar experiences of joy and appreciation expressed by the recipients.

I want my life to testify of You, Lord. May I always spread abroad the sweet perfume of the Rose of Sharon so others will see the love of Jesus. Thank You for sharing Your love in the beauty You have created for us to enjoy. EVELYN GLASS

Debating With God

Commit your way to the Lord, trust also in Him, and He shall bring it to pass. Ps. 37:5, NKJV.

I WAS IN A RUSH to leave because I was late leaving for work. However, a friend stopped me in the hall; I could sense she needed to talk to someone. So I forgot the time and attentively listened to what she had to tell me. It was all about family problems—she didn't think her husband loved her anymore. I tried to assure her that her husband still loved her and the children, but he was not thinking right. Satan had darkened his vision and clogged his thinking with self. Isn't this how Satan traps us?

We talked for almost an hour. A friend reminded me, "Hey, you're late to work."

"I know, but it's OK," I responded. I knew God wanted me to stop and listen.

Then I rushed to my car. I realized I was really late. I put the key into the ignition and fairly flew. A few minutes later I was stopped by—you guessed it—the highway patrol. I handed over my license and my registration. The consequence? A fine of $135.

As I drove on, I debated with God. *Lord, if I hadn't stayed to talk to one of Your children who needed someone to listen to her, I would not have driven so fast and would not have gotten this ticket. Why did You allow it, Lord? Next time maybe I shouldn't mind Your "on-the-spot" voice.*

Then for a moment I kept silent and gave God a chance to respond. He spoke to me through my mind and heart saying, "But, Jem, don't you see? Satan has clouded your mind. He wants you to believe that you can do good at one time and be excused from your wrong doings another time. You're trapped in Satan's device—self. Just think of those who would be hurt if you don't follow the rules. Next time take time to ask Me, and in doing so you will block Satan's effort to becloud your mind."

As our verse reminds us: "Commit your way to the Lord, trust also in Him, and He shall bring it to pass."

That is my prayer for today. Bless those with whom I come in contact and help my mind to remain clear for Your guidance in all circumstances.

JEMIMA D. ORILLOSA

My Chosen Love

He brought me to the banqueting house, and his banner over me was love.
S. of Sol. 2:4.

W HEN I WAS 6 years old and in the first grade, I loved my teacher, a
sweet, patient, silver-haired spinster, who first opened to me the joys
of reading. That summer when I received an invitation to her wedding to her
college sweetheart, I was excited. It was held in the old frame chapel on the
Andrews University campus in Michigan. My parents and I sat high in the
side balcony, looking down. When Miss Webber started down the aisle I
nudged my mom. "She's not wearing a wedding dress. How come?"

"Well," whispered my mother quickly, "maybe it's because she's older."

"But it's her first wedding. And where's her bouquet?" I knew all these
things because only a year before I had been a flower girl at my youngest
aunt's wedding.

"I think she's a bit shy because she is a second wife. Dr. Schoonover
was married before, you know. He started seeing Miss Webber after his first
wife died."

I did know the highlights of the story, but even at 6 I was a romantic and
was a bit disappointed that my lovely teacher was not the center of attention
at her own wedding. Carrying small flowers on a Bible, she was dressed in a
conservative bluish-gray suit, as if playing down her role as bride. Her tiny
white summer hat had a short half veil. *Older, and second choice,* I thought.
It's not fair.

She reached the rostrum, and the bridegroom offered a hand to help her
up the few stairs. The service was read. The witnessing congregation rustled
when it was time for the kiss. Embarrassed, she lifted a soft cheek to her new
husband. But he, without hesitation, wrapped his arms around her, bent her
over backward, and gave her a thorough and lingering Hollywood-style kiss.
No, his actions said, she was not second choice; she was his chosen love, no
matter when in life it had happened. He was ready to tell the whole world just
what she meant to him.

All my life I have measured wedding kisses by that one. I have never seen
one as definite, as romantic, as revealing of intent as that one was. I learned
that day what it means to be a special chosen love, one in whom the
Bridegroom delights. Lois K. Bailey

June 13

Where Is Your Focus?

Thou wilt keep him in perfect peace, whose mind is stayed on thee: because he trusteth in thee. Isa. 26:3.

NEVER HAD I BEEN in so much turmoil! Things were not going well with our business. My husband felt he had made the right choices, but they had gone sour, and now we faced some pretty awful consequences. I was angry with him and with God for letting it happen, and angry with myself that I had not been firmer about refusing to sign some papers that had gotten us to this point. But there was absolutely nothing I could do.

Now I was trying to go to sleep, and sleep would not come. I tossed and turned. The more I thought of all that could happen to us, the more upset I became, and the more sleep evaded me. I was actually ill, and I am sure that my normally low blood pressure had gone sky-high.

I kept praying as I lay there that the Lord would bring a resolution to our financial problems, and that in His time and in His way we would come through it all without losing our home, which was also my mother's home.

It seemed that the more I prayed and focused on the problem, the more agitated I became. Finally, I prayed a simple prayer that the Lord would help me to quit focusing on the problem and focus on Him instead.

I could not believe how quickly the peace came. Suddenly my mind was flooded with promises that God would never leave us or forsake us, and that He would give us a peace, not as the world does, but His peace. No matter what the future held, He would be there to see us through. I began to relax and soon drifted off the sleep. In the morning when I woke I felt a true peace in trusting that God truly would lead us through this terrible time.

I wish I could tell you that from then on I had no more anxiety or worries about the situation. I can tell you that every time I started to get upset I would pray this little prayer: *Lord, keep me focused on You, and not the problem.* And every time He would fill my mind with beautiful promises of His love and guidance. I cannot thank Him enough for that wonderful peace of mind that only He can give when we focus on Him.

ANNA MAY RADKE WATERS

Lord, Save Me!

But when he saw the wind boisterous, he was afraid; and beginning to sink, he cried, saying, Lord, save me. Matt. 14:30.

MY PRAYER WAS "Lord, teach me to walk on water." So He sent us to Portland, Oregon, where it rains all the time and one literally walks on water. One writer said it is so wet in the Northwest that moss grows on the north side of his dog. When I had prayed that prayer, I had meant for a nice, calm lake—not too deep—right near home in Memphis, Tennessee. Instead He sent me on a faith-building adventure.

Walking on water meant living by faith, not by sight. Our family income dropped dramatically as the expenses for our necessities rose beyond our ability to meet them. Like Peter struggling toward Jesus among the waves, I saw myself sinking. *Lord, save me!*

At the time of this writing we have lived in Oregon for nearly six years. During this time we have sold a house, bought a house, kept three children in parochial school, bought a new van, and never missed a payment on anything. Incredibly, we have never had the money to do any of these things.

I don't get a sense from the Bible story that Jesus made a mad dash to Peter to rescue him from the watery deep when he prayed "Lord, save me." He simply gave Him a hand. Jesus was close by with His eyes on Peter all the time.

Though much of my learning to walk on water was spent splashing about in doubt, fear, anxiety, and tears, Jesus was always close by. When I look back on this faith adventure, it is clear that He has brought us out of the deep even when I felt there was absolutely no way of escape. What is more, I still face the same financial challenges, but I am not as anxious, fearful, or fretful. I am calmly expecting His help, His blessing, just as He has provided in the past. I am learning that "sometimes God calms the storm; sometimes He lets it rage and calms His child."

Thank You, Lord, for taking such excellent care of me and my family. Thank You for patiently teaching me that You are reliable, faithful to Your promises, and always careful of all our needs. I love You. Amen.

WANDA DAVIS

A Little Bit of Information

Do not judge, or you too will be judged. For in the same way you judge others, you will be judged, and with the measure you use, it will be measured to you. Matt. 7:1, 2, NIV.

WHEN MY HUSBAND and I lived in Russia for four years, I was an unenthusiastic student of the Russian language. I had a private tutor for some time but finally gave up and put my textbooks on the shelf to gather dust. After all, I could speak enough Russian to shop and ask directions; what could be more important than that?

One time when my husband and I were riding the metro, we saw a sign that was advertising cigarettes. A sentence printed at the very bottom of the colorful ad was separated from the rest of the text. I tried to read what it said, but could understand only the last three words: "for your health." I had no idea what the first few words said, but I assumed that they were similar to the warning we find on cigarette ads in America.

I playfully told my husband, who doesn't read Russian at all, that the poster proclaimed that cigarettes are good for your health. "Really?" he asked with disbelief. However, when he saw the twinkle in my eyes, he knew that I was trying to pull his leg.

"Look for yourself," I teased. "The sign honestly says, 'For your health.'" Then I hastened to tell him that that was only part of the information.

Partial information can be deadly! Partial information can be more dangerous than out-and-out lies. A reliable journalist interviews many people to get a balanced picture, but even eyewitnesses give different views of the same story.

When we don't have all the information about a situation, it's easy to draw conclusions that are entirely wrong. Things are not always as they appear. A person's character can be defamed because the accuser has only a little bit of information. Please be sure to get the whole story before you make an important decision today or before you judge what other people are doing.

Remember, no matter how thin a piece of paper is, it always has two sides. Investigate and listen before you speak and act. Never be satisfied with only a little bit of information. BARBARA HUFF

Looking Through Dark Glasses

For now we see through a glass, darkly; but then face to face. 1 Cor. 13:12.

IT WAS A BEAUTIFUL Sunday morning in June, and the weather was just fine—a perfect day for the wedding of my friend's daughter. Karen and I had traveled from Mandeville down to Montego Bay the night before. At daybreak we had worship, enjoyed a sumptuous breakfast, and got dressed. Karen, who was one of the participants in the wedding, wanted to be at her post of duty early, so she hurried off with another friend. I followed not long after.

On arriving at my destination, I took what I thought were my glasses from the car seat and put them on my face. Then, quite lightheartedly, I walked toward the entrance to the chapel. The bride and I exchanged a cordial smile. I noted, however, that my friend, who was one of the ushers, kept looking at me in a questioning manner, but she handed me a program and escorted me to a seat beside some other friends.

It was now time for the procession, so I glanced at the program, but the print seemed blurred. When I mentioned this to my friend seated beside me, he said, "Take off your glasses."

"Why?" I asked. "They are only slightly tinted."

He said nothing more. However, every now and again as I glanced toward the door, I could see my friend looking and smiling with me. She seemed unusually friendly, but of course we were good friends, so I made nothing of the attention I was receiving.

The bridal party took up their positions. It was time for the opening hymn, but I couldn't see a word on the page. I wondered, *Is the light too dim? What's the matter?* I felt uncomfortable, because I like to sing. By this time anxiety began to set in.

The proceedings ended, and the couple was introduced. I automatically removed the glasses from my face. Light flooded in; I could see! The problem? I was wearing my friend's dark glasses.

I reflected on 1 Corinthians 13:12: "For now we see through a glass, darkly; but then face to face." It is wonderful to think that when we get to heaven all our senses will be perfect. There will be no blurring of our vision, and Jesus will be there to answer all our questions.   IRIS HENRY

Creatures Great and Small

Come and see what God has done, how awesome his works in man's behalf.
Ps. 66:5, NIV.

IN THEIR YOUNGER DAYS my twin daughters delighted in bringing me any lost or wounded animals they could find to nurture or, hopefully, to keep. My enthusiasm, I'll admit, did not always match theirs. This was especially true when they found a skunk. The poor animal, caught in a trap, had managed to pull the trap from what was holding it to the ground but could not free its foot. I wisely decided to delegate that rescue to the Fish and Wildlife Department.

Although the girls loved animals, some were not as welcome as others. I thought I understood this until the day they came running to me, screaming, "Mommy, Mommy, there's a moth in the house!" From the sound of their voices I knew I had been given one of those rare opportunities to protect and defend my offspring.

I grabbed my assault flyswatter and ran toward the intruder. With true Olympian marksmanship I annihilated it with one blow. I turned triumphantly to my daughters standing beside me, expecting to see smiles of gratitude. One look at their faces, however, told me that I had just broken the sixth commandment. I wished I could quickly evaporate. Since this wasn't an option, I stammered, "You—you didn't want me to kill it?"

"No," they said. "We just wanted to show it to you. You killed a perfectly good moth!"

Caught up in the business of living, it's sometimes easy for me to forget that people aren't the only creatures the Lord personally placed on this planet. Every life, from a tiny human being, fashioned in God's image, down to the lowly moth, is truly a miracle and is a precious creation.

It's true that the Lord gave people dominion over the earth and the animals. However, we don't own either; He does. We are only tenants and caretakers.

So when I spot a fish swimming in a river or see a deer running through a forest, or even watch a little moth fly around and around a streetlight, I will try to remember that this is really my Father's world. He wants all His creatures to enjoy it. I would like to thank Him for the opportunity and privilege He gives me to do just that.

MARCIA MOLLENKOPF

Why Sweat the Small Stuff?

He giveth power to the faint; and to them that have no might he increaseth strength. Isa. 40:29.

I'VE BEEN KNOWN TO be a bit strong-willed. Bullheaded, my husband used to call it. Coming from a large family, I had to learn early on to fend for myself, so I grew up thinking I could do almost anything I set my mind to.

I was put to the test the spring after Harold's death when I decided it was time to renovate the two upstairs bedrooms. Since the home originally belonged to my in-laws, there were still several boxes of their books stashed away that I needed to dispose of. But the first thing that demanded my attention was the floors. The old, faded blue carpet and horsehair padding that had been down for years had to go.

My trash company will accept anything, as long as it's all in plastic bags. Knowing I couldn't fold two room-sized rugs and pads small enough for that, I faced my first hurdle. I had to rethink my options.

One day I got out an old serrated steak knife and started slashing the carpet into narrow strips small enough to fit in the bags. When I finished with the carpet, I started on the padding. Many hours of cutting and a very sore wrist later, I finally finished the job. I breathed a sigh of relief when I set the final 10 bags out to be hauled away. But I was only half done.

The next challenge was to move approximately 700 hardcover and paperback books and pamphlets from the boxes upstairs to the dining room without lugging them down the steps. So I spread a blanket out on the landing at the top of the stairs where I placed the books, a few at a time, then bumped them carefully down the steps. It took quite a few bumpy trips before I had them all downstairs to be sorted and stacked in piles.

Looking back, I wonder how I did it all by myself, but I've never been one to give up on a chore. I could almost always figure out a solution to some difficult situation.

Being a determined person can't be all bad as long as we use some of that enthusiasm for spiritual activities, as well as the mundane things of life.

Lord, help me to find that happy balance in You.　　　CLAREEN COLCLESSER

A Love Story

See how great a love the Father has bestowed upon us, that we should be called the children of God; and such we are. 1 John 3:1, NASB.

THIS IS A LOVE story. It was a sparkling blue Sunday in early June, and the water was calling us. Boating has always been one of our favorite things to do, and this day was perfect. We loaded our Hydrostream with knee board, inner tube, snacks, and cold drinks and headed for Trimble Lake Park. Our plan was to alternate knee boarding with flinging each other off the inner tube. Steve is the unsurpassed champion in height and distance flinging, and Travis, 7, and Austin, 5, were determined to not get flung off today.

By late afternoon both boys had achieved new records, and we were all needing to rest our sore arms and bodies. We decided this would be the perfect time to cruise up the Dora Canal. It's about 10 miles across Trimble Lake and Lake Dora to the mouth of the Dora Canal, where we had to pause and switch gas tanks.

Contentedly munching on boiled peanuts and hot fries, we leisurely cruised up the mile-long canal, watching raccoons, otters, ospreys, and alligators. The sun was close to the horizon when Steve casually asked, "How's the gas doing?" We suddenly realized our second gas tank was less than half full. We were about 18 miles from our boat ramp, and the only gas pump on this chain of lakes had closed an hour ago. Knowing our gas tank would go 20 miles when full, we decided to get as close to our ramp as possible. Quickly turning around, carefully cutting corners and maneuvering wakes, Steve tried to get as much mileage out of the gas as possible.

Halfway through the Dora Canal the engine sputtered. I tilted the hollow-sounding gas tank on its side to get the last bit of gas into the fuel line. For the next 11 miles Steve and I kept nervously looking at each other, then at the gas tank, and back to each other. As we finally pulled up to the boat ramp, the engine didn't sputter—it quit. We all sat looking at one another, mumbling, "I can't believe that" and "That's amazing."

Then, with the total innocence of childhood, Travis said, "That's what was supposed to happen—I asked Jesus to get us back to the ramp."

"See how great a love the Father has bestowed upon us, that we should be called the children of God; and such we are."

SUSAN WOOLEY

And a Little Child Shall Lead Them

The wolf also shall dwell with the lamb; and the leopard shall lie down with the kid; and the calf and the young lion and the fatling together; and a little child shall lead them. Isa. 11:6.

SEVERAL YEARS AGO WE purchased a large piece of property about five miles from a small town. My idealistic thinking started to run wild as I envisioned an atmosphere of peaceful tranquillity and harmony of nature. What a great chance to have such a unique situation! We could enjoy the wildlife in its many forms, undisturbed by intrusions, and each showing total respect for the others. All sorts of land, air, and water creatures would flourish and thrive peacefully. None would become greedy or obnoxious. They would, as is stated in the Bible, "not hurt nor destroy in all my holy mountain" (Isa. 11:9).

To be totally truthful and realistic about it, spiders, flies, and mosquitoes were not promised the same consideration. Four or five rattlesnakes also became the exception to the "do not destroy" rule. Our friendly, curious dog would come back from exploring the woods and be covered with ticks. One day she got too curious about the cute skunk family that lived in a valley.

Two boys, about 12 years old, were seen shooting at birds and squirrels with a slingshot. Sadly, there were some casualties. Strangers came onto the property and inconsiderately assumed it would be permissible to hunt and fish.

One day we discovered that a very uncaring person had shot a deer and left it to die. That incident and many others brought about the termination of my dream. It was obvious my idealistic plan was crushed and had to be abandoned. As difficult as it was to admit, I had been very presumptuous to even imagine it could ever happen.

Only in the new earth will my dream be possible, and then only because everything will be made new. Not just the animals, but every person who is there will be lovingly changed and transformed into a caring, unselfish being who would not even consider harming another person or creature.

"And a little child shall lead them." How special and honored will be the child who accomplishes such an awesome task!   LILLIAN MUSGRAVE

June 21

A New Bride's Dilemma

For I will be merciful to their unrighteousness, and their sins and their iniquities will I remember no more. Heb. 8:12.

A S A NEW BRIDE I tried to please my husband—especially as a cook. At his request I eagerly fixed his favorite dishes. One such request was that every Sunday morning we have waffles with strawberries, raspberries, or blueberries, topped with whipped cream. This breakfast became a ritual during our married life.

One Sunday shortly after our marriage is "burned" into my memory. The woman who introduced us to each other gave us a shiny waffle iron as a wedding gift. However, the grids did not have a nonstick surface as do today's waffle irons. It was necessary to oil the surface before each batch of batter. I tried seasoning this waffle apparatus, sprayed it, spooned on the batter, and allowed it to bake the recommended time. The first waffle came out fine. But alas, I failed to spray the grids before hastily pouring on the second batch. You can imagine the mess I had trying to remove the waffles that came out in chunks and pieces. Embarrassed and in tears, I complained, "This will take me the rest of the morning to clean these crusted grids!" The remainder of the batter ended up as pancakes instead of waffles.

My patient groom did not scold or criticize. After the waffle pan had cooled, he took a fork and gently picked away at the "stuck-on" grids until they were nearly clean. After soaking, the remaining crusts brushed off easily.

My husband's calm, helpful gesture reminds me of my heavenly Father's loving mercies toward my shortcomings and failures. Even though I become frustrated and unhappy with situations that occur in my life, my heavenly Father is always ready and willing to clean up and forgive the messes I create.

How do I know He is willing and ready to do this? Because of the many promises He has given me in His Word, such as the text for today. Another promise I discovered in Isaiah 43:25: "I, even I, am he that blotteth out thy transgressions for mine own sake, and will not remember thy sins."

Thank You again, Father.   NATHALIE LADNER-BISCHOFF

A Safe Journey

Do not worry about tomorrow, for tomorrow will worry about its own things.
Matt. 6:34, NKJV.

I HAD PLANNED TO take a short trip to Singapore alone. It was the very first time for me to have a holiday on my own; I usually went with friends. Being single, I tagged along with my friends and their families for vacations. I became so used to being with them that I did not worry about anything because I was with a group of people who cared. But one winter break I decided to spend a three-day holiday tour alone.

Though I was afraid, I took the challenge. How I wished God would let me meet and befriend people during the tour. My friends gave me moral support. They also prayed that my fear would be gone. As the day of my departure approached, my worry grew stronger. There were nights I could not sleep for thinking about how I would cope alone. I am not a talker and, being an introvert, am too shy to initiate a conversation. I almost decided to cancel the trip and fly straight home to the Philippines. But through my friends' persuasions, I went on with the trip. Never did I stop praying that I would meet friendly people during the tour.

God is a prayer-answering God. On my very first day I met a Filipino who was staying at the same hotel as I. And I knew at that moment that God really had not left me alone. On the same day during the tour to Sentosa Island I met a Filipino couple who were kind enough to keep me company the whole afternoon. And wonder of wonders, that night during the Midnight Safari Tour, I met a former high school student whom I had not seen for many years. She was on tour with her husband. These incidents showed me that God answers prayers and that I should not doubt the power of prayers.

The experience of the first day gave me the courage to face the challenges during the remainder of the trip. My fear disappeared. During the last two days I met more people, talked with them, and enjoyed their company. The trip made me assertive and friendly. It was a wonderful and exciting trip, and I had a safe journey home. I realized that there was no need for me to worry as long as I prayed and put my trust in Jesus.

Will I be afraid to take another trip alone? No, because I know God will never leave me.

MINERVA M. ALINAYA

Bird Lice

Wash and make yourselves clean. Isa. 1:16, NIV.

W E HAD MOVED ACROSS the Tasman Sea from New Zealand to Australia. The leaving of family, friends, and the country of my birth had been rather traumatic. However, we settled and purchased a home after a few months of renting. The house was older than I would have liked but in a lovely position on a steep hill with a magnificent 180-degree view over Moreton Bay, Brisbane.

I had to get used to lizards in the backyard, cane toads (there were dozens on the road when it rained), cockroaches bigger than I could ever imagine, and a very hot climate. Oh yes, and the odd snake or two.

One day our neighbor came over and spoke to my husband. "I see you have starlings nesting in the roof of your house. Be very careful—they have bird lice. I'd get rid of them if I were you."

My husband replied, "Because they are nesting, Leonie doesn't want to upset the birds." The neighbor warned once more, "Well, if it were my house, I'd soon get rid of them."

Several weeks went by, and then one day I started to scratch. With every day that passed my skin got itchier and itchier and I could feel "something" on me. Red welts began to appear on my arms and on my back. So I visited the doctor. Yes, I was covered from head to toe with bird lice.

How I wished I had heeded the neighbor's warning. The lice had traveled down a wall and infested our bedroom. Then they infested me! Such tiny insects—it was almost impossible to believe the infection they caused. I had to apply a ghastly white lotion to my entire body, starting with my hair. Plus, it took so many hours of work to get rid of the lice. Sadly, the birds had to go, and then every item in the bedroom had to be cleaned again and again. I vacuumed and I washed and I painted the lotion onto my skin time after time.

Sometimes it is such *tiny* sins that can creep into our lives when warnings go unheeded. But thanks be to Jesus we can be cleansed from sin, and He covers us with His robe of righteousness. LEONIE DONALD

The Lord Leads

I do believe; help me overcome my unbelief! Mark 9:24, NIV.

WE WERE FACING A problem. Our daughter, Hannah, had reached marriageable age, and in our culture it was up to my husband and me to find a suitable husband for her. Hannah had just finished her master's degree and was moving away to her first job. I prayed every day for her bright future. We felt pressure to find a God-fearing husband for her.

Another pastor had written a letter to us concerning a boy who was working in Paris. His parents had requested that he help them find a suitable wife for their son. But we didn't know them personally, so we soon forgot the matter.

About a year later my husband had to go to that state to attend to some work. There he happened to meet the same pastor who had written about the young man the previous year. At his request my husband made a casual visit to their home and found them to be a loving, Christian family. They offered a picture of their son to my husband and asked him to help them find Anniel a good wife. (They did not know we had a daughter.)

When my husband came home, he showed the picture to Hannah. We asked her to correspond with Anniel to find out if she would like to spend the rest of her life with him.

Late one night the phone rang. When I picked it up I recognized the sweet voice of my daughter. She said, "I am going to promise to marry the man in Paris."

It struck me like a thunderbolt. Sensing my anxiety, she assured me, "Don't worry, Mother; he is a God-fearing man."

Many questions surrounded and crept like serpents over my soul. I couldn't eat or sleep. Was she making a hasty decision? Did she know him well enough? Was he the right one for her? I pleaded with God to let me know in some way that he was the right one.

Then one day we received some cassettes with a few Christian songs Anniel had sung. When I heard them, peace came into my heart. I thought, *No one can sing with such feeling unless he has God in his heart.*

"Lord, forgive my unbelief," I cried. I had asked for a good husband for my daughter; God responded. I had not believed. I, too, say for each day, "Help me overcome my unbelief!"

SOOSANNA MATHEW

Wubba Wubba

Therefore I tell you, do not worry about your life. Matt. 6:25, NIV.

IF YOUR MIRROR HAS a monster in it, do not shout. This kind of situation does not call for freaking out. . . . Singing, wubba, wubba, wubba, wubba, woo, woo, woo. Wubba, wubba, wubba, and a doodly do. Wubba, wubba, wubba, you can join in too."*

And join in we did. My husband, Rick, our then 3-year-old son, Eric, and I had just arrived at Madison's Westside Sam's Club. Grover's solo on *Sesame Street Platinum All-time Favorites* had not finished when we arrived, so we sat in the car and waited for it to end. But we didn't just sit there—that would be boring. We joined right in and sang at the top of our lungs. I'm thankful there was no one in the parking lot to watch or hear—I can only imagine what they might have thought.

I don't remember going to school and majoring in parenting. I do, however, remember majoring in education. After graduation I planned to teach until I turned 65 and then enjoy the rest of my life having fun traveling around the world. But then I met Rick, fell in love, got married, and my plans changed. After two years of teaching, I quit to start a family.

My life hasn't always gone the way I planned. OK, it's rarely gone as planned. Sometimes I haven't been happy with the direction of my life. Other times I have been delighted. But one thing for sure, I have yet to be sorry for the direction. I didn't plan to spend time sitting in our car at Sam's Club, singing in a quartet with Grover, but God knew that one day it would happen. He also knows the next time it will happen—and everything else that will happen to me. That's one of the great things about God. I don't have to worry what will happen next, because I have Him to trust.

Matthew 6:25 says, "Therefore I tell you, do not worry about your life." So if you will please excuse me for a few minutes, instead of worrying about my future I need to pop in the tape for Eric. Maybe we will join Bob, Oscar, and Ernie and decide who is in our neighborhood. Or maybe we will join Elmo in "One Fine Face" and try to figure out just why we have a chin.

In any case, with God leading my life, I do not have to worry. Neither do you.

MARSHA CLAUS

---

* "Monster in the Mirror," *Sesame Street Platinum All-time Favorites,* No. 9, (Sony), Aug. 22, 1995.

He Couldn't Forget His Bible

Delight yourself in the Lord and he will give you the desires of your heart.
Ps. 37:4, NIV.

I WISH I COULD FIND my Bible," Gary said plaintively. He and Laura were settled in for evening worship. Almost four months had gone by, and the old red leather *New English Bible* had not been located. Laura had called all the churches she and Gary had attended during those months, but no one had turned it in. Every few weeks Gary would ask at the lost-and-found window of his own church, but it wasn't there. Time passed, yet Gary couldn't forget his Bible. He had marked it with his favorite passages. It was his favorite version. Even the new Bible Laura gave him for his birthday couldn't take its place.

This particular evening when Gary said "I wish I could find my Bible," Laura answered, "Then why don't we pray about it?" There was just a hint of exasperation in her voice—she didn't really believe at this late date that the Bible would be found. The couple knelt by their chair, held hands, and prayed that somehow Gary would find his long-lost Bible.

That Monday when Laura went to work, a coworker, who was a member of her church, met her. "Gary's Bible is at the church," Marilyn said.

"It is?" replied a shocked Laura. "But we have been asking at the lost-and-found window if it has been turned in."

"It isn't *at* lost and found," returned Marilyn. "It is in a table drawer outside the pastor's study. The strange thing is that I put some papers in that drawer just last week. It wasn't there then. I'll go by the church on my lunch hour and get it for you."

Laura could hardly wait for evening to come. She wanted to see the amazed expression on Gary's face when she walked in the door and handed Gary the red leather *New English Bible*, with his name printed in gold on the cover.

"Where did you find it?" He had the amazed expression on his face.

"An angel found it for you," Laura said with a sly little smile.

EDNA MAYE GALLINGTON

June 27

The Gift of Crochet

A friend loves at all times. Prov. 17:17, NIV.

IAWOKE WITH THE SUN that June 27 and trembled as my last thought before slumber slammed through me again: *For the rest of your life, when you wake up every morning your mother will be dead.*

I eased out of bed, pulled on the shorts and top I'd taken off the night before, and slipped quietly through my parents' house. I had to get outside. I had to walk. Walking was good. It made no demands beyond putting one foot in front of the other. I enjoyed the zinnias and marigolds blooming in neat beds, and the early-day Texas heat. But with every step the mantra beat in my mind: *Every morning . . . for the rest of your life . . .* It didn't seem possible to live through the day. How would we get through a lifetime?

Friends came, and called, shocked with the death of one yet young. In the first weeks they often filled the living room, holding us up by just being there.

One afternoon a longtime friend of our mother's dropped by. Maryanne had been with us often, encouraging, bringing food, but this time she carried two large cartons. She sat down and said to my sister and me, "I'm going to teach you to crochet. I brought yarn and crochet hooks. It will be good to have something useful to do with your hands. You'll be surprised how it will help." Neither Judye nor I was a stellar student, but practice made passable. We learned.

Summer burned into fall. I crocheted doll-baby blankets and mufflers for all three girls.

School started. I made hats for them and their new baby brother. Fall wept into winter.

Graduating to granny squares, I made a vest for Robyn and began an afghan.

A long, winding thread, if you'll pardon the expression, weaves through that first year, and beyond. It links people and prayers, dark days and springtime, and yes, practical, down-to-earth friendship back in Texas, in a lonely house, when our friend Maryanne gave us the gift of crochet.

God, please give me the gift of discernment for friends in need. Help me be specific in the help I offer, and make me steadfast, continuing to encourage as long as the need remains.   PENNY ESTES WHEELER

The Move

By faith Abraham, when he was called to go out into a place which he should after receive for an inheritance, obeyed; and he went out, not knowing whither he went. Heb. 11:8.

IT WAS ALMOST A year ago when my husband, Randy, called me at work. He sounded more serious than usual. He said he wanted to apply for a position in Tennessee at his company's main plant. At the time I did not completely understand the implications of that statement, but my response was that if the Lord was impressing him to do it, then follow that.

Sometime later Randy informed me he had an interview scheduled within a month. I knew he was exceptionally talented at his work, so the reality of my husband possibly getting hired and all of us needing to move was beginning to sink in. I wished him well and reminded him that if it was in God's plan, it would happen. I think I needed to hear that more than he did.

Randy called me at work to tell me about his interview. He began telling me what he was asked in the interview in its entirety. I thought I was going to burst. I waited patiently, then blurted out, "Did you get the position?" It seemed an eternity had passed before he finally said, "Yes." I knew I needed to put things into perspective fast.

I have to admit I was both scared and excited about moving. I didn't want to leave my family, friends, and job in Kingman, Arizona. I knew I would miss the beauty of Arizona. As I reflected over my potential losses I remembered when I had moved to Arizona from California. I thought I would never leave California, but I was convicted to move. I did not have any friends, family, or job in Kingman. It occurred to me that I had made it and was extremely blessed. Immediately I was at ease. Although I did not know the specifics of our future, I knew the Lord would bless our family.

He did exactly that. The blessings began flowing immediately. I love the family, friends, and job that I have here. And I found that Tennessee has its own beauty for me to enjoy.

As I carry Kingman in my heart and mind, I thank You, Lord, for showing me Your "track record." Please continue to help my faith grow so I do not hesitate when You ask me to do something or to go somewhere.

MARY WAGONER ANGELIN

June 29

Garbage Soup

The rich and the poor have this in common: the Lord made them both.
Prov. 22:2, TEV.

A T THE END OF the month when both groceries and funds are running low, I make a tasty concoction I call "garbage soup." I open up a cheap can of vegetable soup and dump it in a pot with whatever leftovers or canned vegetables I have on hand. Although the result is warm and filling, I used to feel sorry for myself whenever I made it. Wouldn't it be wonderful to just run to the grocery store and pick up whatever I was in the mood for eating? No lists, no price comparisons, and, best of all, no double coupons?

Sometimes reality forces us to live less abundantly than we'd like. The choices may be unimportant—do I buy the sweater I really want, or the one on sale? Other times we have to make compromises, such as do I pay the gas bill this month, or visit the dentist?

Although I realize there are people starving in this world who would love a chance at my leftovers, it's hard not to want more when you can see people all around you who have more expensive stuff—fancy houses, fancy cars, fancy clothes. But when you look more closely, you see that money doesn't really equal happiness. So many people who have lots of money aren't happy with their lives. Some people with low incomes are satisfied with their lives. It makes me wonder if I've named my soup right.

When I sit down to my soup, I know that I've done an honest day's work. I know I haven't cheated anybody to pay for it. I know I've treated my customers and coworkers with respect. I know I haven't neglected my God, my family, or my friends in order to get that meal. Maybe happiness has more to do with what's in your soul than what's in your bowl.

I still dine on "garbage soup" more often than I like, but I have now changed its name. I now call it "super soup." Maybe I've learned to be grateful for what I've got.

Thank You, heavenly Father and provider.   GINA LEE

All Are Invited

Let us be glad and rejoice, and give honour to him: for the marriage of the Lamb is come, and his wife hath made herself ready. . . . Blessed are they which are called unto the marriage supper of the Lamb. Rev. 19:7-9.

I LOVE TO WATCH A bridal party. I always try to sit next to the aisle to get close to the bride as she marches down the aisle to the altar. The bridesmaids, the cute little flower girls, and the Bible boy all add to the beauty of the show. I look forward to enjoying the reception prepared for the guests. I do not always get invited to weddings, but when I do, I see that I do not miss them.

In October 2000 our daughter got married. It was fun to get all her clothes done. It was also a very busy time making sure all the details were taken care of. Because of our love for her, we didn't mind working hard to make it the best wedding we could.

Invitations were sent, even to those who live abroad, for the joy of letting them know about the wedding. A large group would be there from the groom's family—I was getting nervous whether we would have enough food for everyone. So I prayed that Jesus would be present, as He was at the wedding of Cana. The Lord heard my prayer, and all went well.

The food was more than enough and was very tasty, too, as expressed by many. We had a lot of sweets left over, so I thought it would be nice to take some home to give to those who did not come, especially three friends from my office.

Luke 14 tells of three guests who made excuses for not accepting the invitation to the great supper. Sad to say, my three friends did the same thing. I advised them that it was all right to make excuses to me but that they should not refuse the invitation to the Lamb's marriage. One said that he did not even open and read the wedding card. I told him at least not to fail to open the Bible and read God's invitation to the marriage supper of the Lamb. Then one of them asked, "Why, then, have you brought sweets for us?" I said, "Because probation has not yet been closed." They had a good laugh, but I do hope they took my advice seriously.

Yes, friends, while probation is still open, let us accept the invitation and allow the Lord to prepare us as His bride. It will be the grandest of all weddings.

BIRDIE PODDAR

July 1

Help Me, Lord!

Lord, Son of David, have mercy on me! My daughter is suffering terribly from demon-possession. . . . Lord, help me! Matt. 15:22-25, NIV.

DURING THE MORNING OUR Bible study had centered on Matthew 15, the story of the Canaanite woman whose daughter was demon-possessed. She had come to Jesus: "My daughter is suffering terribly from demon-possession." No plea as to what she wanted Jesus to do or how she thought He should solve the problem, simply, "Lord, help me!"

That afternoon I took a walk during a rare break. My mind whirled with the endless list of projects that waited for me back at the office. *How am I ever going to get them done, Lord?* I asked as I tried to think of new plans of attack. *And we need to sell more devotional books so we have more money for scholarships, and . . .*

Whoa! I suddenly thought. *Why are you telling God how to solve the problems? Just tell Him the problem, and let Him solve it.*

I started again. *OK, God, I have too much to do. And we need scholarship money. How are You going to solve the problem?*

As I rounded a corner, I viewed a gorgeous Rocky Mountain scene— jagged Indian Peak and massive Sawtooth stood front and center. It made me think of the Flood—I always think of the Flood when I see craggy mountains. I suppose there were people then who talked to God about the wickedness of the world, and maybe even suggested how God should solve the problem.

But who would have thought of a flood!

Later, the people of Israel had swung from idol worship and other detestable practices to the extreme of a rule for everything, even to tithing the mint, dill, and cumin (Matt. 23:23). I know sincere people talked to God. And maybe they, too, suggested how He could solve the problem.

But who would have thought of a Messiah who would come as a baby, live a life of simplicity, and die as a sin substitute on the cross?

Once again our lives, our world, is full of problems. Only You have the perfect solution. Lord, help us!   ARDIS DICK STENBAKKEN

Prayer Versus Pride

Pride goeth before destruction, and an haughty spirit before a fall. Prov. 16:18.

D URING THE UNITED STATES' tryouts in track and field for the Olympic Games held in Sydney, Australia, there were pole vaults, long jumps, shot puts, and one of the most exciting foot races in history—the showdown between Michael Johnson and Maurice Greene. They were competing against each other to see who was the fastest man.

Before the race people interviewed Maurice and Michael. "I think I have better running legs than him," one bragged. The other said he had better speed. One said the other was scared, and the other said this was no competition. They kept going on and on about how good they were, and how they would beat each other.

Meanwhile, John Capel, also a runner in the 200-meter race, was on his knees, busy praying to his Father. He hoped only to succeed in his race and glorify God.

All the runners lined up. The starting gun sounded. Before Michael could get to the turn, he pulled a muscle in his leg. He lay down on the track in pain. Maurice kept going like a cannon. Then he was hurt, too, and limped off the track. Both top contenders were disqualified from running the 200 meters in Sydney. John Capel won the race.

I like to look at myself in the mirror and take pictures. It used to make me sad when my mom would say someone else was pretty or cute but didn't say it about me. She would remind me that the Bible says, "Favour is deceitful, and beauty is vain: but a woman that feareth the Lord, she shall be praised" (Prov. 31:30). Just like Maurice and Michael, I can be so busy bragging about myself and looking at myself that I can miss hearing the Lord. Or I might even be jealous because someone else is prettier. I don't want to lose the race that Jesus has me running because of pride, either.

"In the mouth of the foolish is a rod of pride: but the lips of the wise shall preserve them" (Prov. 14:3). God doesn't like it when people brag about themselves. Overdoing it can result in some unexpected endings.

Dear Jesus, help me to brag about You and not about myself. Amen.

ARIELLE DAVIS

July 3

Hold On—But Not to Anger

Get rid of all bitterness, rage and anger, brawling and slander, along with every form of malice. Be kind and compassionate to one another, forgiving each other, just as in Christ God forgave you. Eph. 4:31, 32, NIV.

WE RECENTLY GOT A second cat. She arrived in our home just before the Fourth of July, so our children named her Spangle. Our first cat, Noel, had come to us at Christmastime. She was doted upon by the entire family and had proven to be an extremely affectionate and sociable animal. However, upon the arrival of Spangle, we saw a rather striking personality change in Noel. It became clear that Noel was angry! She quit purring or jumping up to sit beside us. When we tried to pet her, she stalked away. We hadn't changed our feelings about Noel, but because of her resentment of the new cat, she had removed herself from our circle of affection. For many months Noel's angry behavior continued. As I watched the cranky cat, I realized that it is the one who chooses to harbor anger and resentment who suffers the most.

Have you been hurt? There have been times in my life when the words or actions of other people have deeply hurt me. Sometimes people have done things unintentionally, never realizing the hurt they caused. At other times people have said or done things that were deliberately meant to be hurtful. I have been left with feelings of bitterness, resentment, or anger against those who have been so hurtful, particularly when that person was someone I trusted or respected. It has been a very real struggle for me to keep from harboring resentment and bitterness.

There have been times I have realized that I am holding on so tightly to my feelings of hurt and anger that I have let go of God's answers for those feelings. Certainly the answer is to hold on—but not to the angry, bitter feelings. Holding on to God's hand, holding on to His promises and accepting His forgiveness so freely given to me is the only way I have found to let Him begin putting His forgiveness in my heart toward those who have been hurtful.

I pray today, Lord, that You will give me the strength to keep holding on— holding on to Your word, Your promises, and Your way for me so that I might be filled with Your love, forgiveness, kindness, and compassion in place of bitterness and resentment. SANDRA SIMANTON

Stuck on the Roof

He delivereth and rescueth. Dan. 6:27.

WE HAD SPENT A steamy, hot Fourth of July with our daughter and granddaughter at the old fishing hole, and we spent part of the afternoon sipping iced lemonade to cool off. Our granddaughter, Andrea, eagerly awaited the evening's fireworks, which we could sometimes see from our upstairs window.

As it began to grow dark, our neighbor said we could climb on their roof because the view up there was terrific. This sounded like great adventure, so armed with mosquito lotion, we all ascended to the roof. They were right; the view from up there was outstanding.

After the fireworks display, however, it was time to go down the ladder. With grim realization, I knew I could not do it! So everyone—five adults and five children—climbed down the ladder, leaving me, Grandma, up on the roof. Of course, the little ones laughed, and so did our daughter. They thought this was great fun. They all tried to encourage me by saying, "Just go slowly," but I couldn't do it. Finally the owner of the house came up the ladder and firmly held on to me so I could climb down. Even then I was scared and felt pretty foolish. It dawned on me then that I should've been smart enough not to have gone up there in the first place.

Ten years before that, in another town, I had painted the siding of our house and convinced myself that I could get on the roof long enough to paint the gable over the back doorway. All went well. Gable painted, it was time to get down. You guessed it—I couldn't do it. Now I was in trouble. No one was home, and there I was on the roof—maybe for the day. I started calling "Help, help!" as loudly as I could. After several hours, our neighbor, a policeman who was off duty for the afternoon, came outside, heard me, and came to my rescue. I felt pretty foolish then, too. So what did I do but climb the roof again that July 4!

How foolish we children of God are! We repeat the same mistakes, even when we know they bring trouble. And even then, with a strong arm, He will help us out of our difficulty, coming to our salvation.

Thanks be to God, who always comes to our rescue.

DARLENE YTREDAL BURGESON

July 5

Yellow Car

O Lord my God, I will give you thanks forever. Ps. 30:12, NIV.

IN HARARE, ZIMBABWE, where I lived for eight years, concrete walls and big gates enclosed properties. Opening and closing the heavy gates can be a chore and a nuisance.

It was to be a quick stop, so I parked my yellow Datsun 210 outside the gate. "I'll have the gardener open the gates. Have dinner with us; I cooked your favorite Ethiopian dish," my friend Kidisty invited.

"Just unlock the little gate. I'll leave my car outside," I hollered through the peephole. I didn't bother to put on the steering wheel lock.

Two weeks before, we had buried Kidisty's husband (my boss) in their home country of Eritrea. The grief was raw, and the loss seemed to be beyond comfort. She needed someone around to talk to and be there for her. She reminisced about the happy times with her husband and how much she missed him. Tears flowed intermittently.

When it was time to leave, the gates were opened—and my car was not there! I was frantic and distressed. Kidisty put her arms around me and calmly said, "Linda, your loss can be replaced. My husband is dead, and I can't have him back." I felt reproached.

I filed a report at the closest police station. It was late when I got home. Sleep eluded me. Anger gripped me. I hated those people who took my car. I was disappointed with God. "Why did You allow this to happen, God?" Hot tears wet my pillow. Suddenly I was engulfed by God's protecting love, and I gave Him praise. I fell asleep peacefully.

That Friday after work I asked one of the men in the office to take me to the main police station. I gave a description of my car. There were hundreds of abandoned and stolen cars, but my heart leaped as I spotted the yellow car. The license plate had been changed, three tires were flat, and there were nine bullet holes, one of them missing the back windshield by a hair. The seats and the carpeting were bloodstained. None of my personal things were recovered.

That night, however, I knelt by my bed, once more overwhelmed by God's protecting love. My God is awesome. My God has limitless abilities.

LINDA ALINSOD

Messages of Remembrance

A scroll of remembrance was written in his presence concerning those who feared the Lord and honored his name. "They will be mine," says the Lord Almighty, "in the day when I make up my treasured possession." Mal. 3:16, 17, NIV.

MY SON RECENTLY TOLD me a story of one of his employees whose wife has cancer. She had been told by doctors that she had only about a year left to live. She was a young woman, 35, with small children, ages 3, 9, and 11. Despite the seriousness of her tragic illness, she always managed to be cheerful and exhibited peace and acceptance of her fate. Were it not for the fact that she had completely lost all her hair, you would think, *There is an average happy young housewife and mother.*

She shared that she was writing a daily book for her children, telling them she knew that as they grew they would encounter all kinds of problems and questions about life. Therefore, she was taking each situation they might have to face and was writing them counsel on how to cope with it. This included situations of trouble in school, self-esteem, disappointments with friends, dating, getting married, relationships with their peers, and how to place their trust in God.

In all this writing she told them that though she would be leaving them, they could read these messages and be reassured of her unending love for them. She wanted them to be able not only to remember her but to know her personally through these messages. So if they needed comfort, if they needed guidance or strength, if they needed to be reassured of her love, they should read these letters from her.

The concerns of this dying mother for her children really touched me. I realized she was following Christ's example. He knew He would die on the cross, and He promised He would remember each one of His children. Though He would physically leave this world, Jesus Christ left us messages of love in the Bible. In His letters of love, He has given us guidance for every situation in life that we might have to face. He left us messages of counsel, messages of comfort, and guidance as to how we should live victoriously. We have only to open our Bible to read those messages of God's continuing love for each of us from our heavenly Parent.   BARBARA SMITH MORRIS

God Found in the Trash

Ask, and it shall be given you; seek, and ye shall find; knock, and it shall be opened unto you. Matt. 7:7.

SUSAN, A 30-YEAR-OLD lawyer, was involved in a bad car accident, was severely injured, and had to be on bed rest. She was very depressed and dejected over her unfortunate situation. Her boyfriend, who was a painter, got a contract to paint an old mansion a mile away from her house. Before he started on his painting job, he noticed a pile of old things in a corner of the room that were to be trashed. He walked over to the trash, and immediately his eyes fell on a book. He picked it up and asked the owner of the mansion if he could have it. The woman gladly gave it to him.

He took the book and gave it to Susan. "Since you are on bed rest, this book might keep your mind and time occupied," he told her.

Out of sheer curiosity and boredom, she started reading it. She got so engrossed that she read it in a few days. As she read the book, her outlook on life began to change. She felt that there was meaning and purpose in her life. She seemed happier and more cheerful and started to feel good mentally and physically. She even started praying to God and reading her Bible. The book she read was about the great controversy between Christ and Satan and the entire plan of salvation.

Susan wanted to know more about the God who loved her and died for her. She looked up the address of the nearest church and found one very close to her house. She visited the church and was warmly welcomed with a big bear hug from a little elderly lady. She regularly attended church meetings, and after having Bible studies for more than a year, she was baptized.

God works in mysterious ways. What seemed to be an unfortunate incident turned out to be the greatest blessing in her life. What seemed like trash turned out to be treasure. She found Jesus and happiness for eternity!

In God's Word we read, "Ask, and it shall be given you; seek, and ye shall find; knock, and it shall be opened unto you." Let us ask for His treasure this day.

STELLA THOMAS

The Handkerchief

But God commendeth his love toward us, in that, while we were yet sinners, Christ died for us. Rom. 5:8.

I HAVE A HANDKERCHIEF that I treasure. If you were to look at it you wouldn't think it that wonderful. It was hand-stitched by a 75-year-old woman who was totally blind in one eye and had only 10 percent vision in the other. The stitching is nearly perfect, and one would never think it was made by a nearly blind woman. I don't use it now for fear of losing it.

Every so often I take it out, lovingly feel its soft texture, and appreciate the fine stitching. Why is the handkerchief so precious to me? It is treasured because it was stitched and presented to me by my mother. She had been diagnosed as having cancer of the pancreas. Her illness was terminal. Through her pain and suffering she wanted me to have a token of her love.

My mother died 11 years ago, but her love lives on in my heart. The handkerchief is a constant reminder of that love. Each time I look at the 10" x 10" piece of cloth with its embroidered bunch of purple flowers in one corner, I think of the painstaking labor she put into that handkerchief—stitch by stitch, day by day.

She never let me see her working on it so she could give me her gift of love as a surprise—a dying mother's love for her child, who is a grandmother herself. I had the joy of looking after Mother for the last few years of her life. Often we sat on the steps of the veranda and recalled the joys and sorrows we had shared through the years.

My mother's gift, that precious handkerchief, reminds me of God's special love for me and for all His children, a love that never ends, a love that endures to the end. If earthly mothers can love their children so much, God's love is so much greater, so great that "while we were yet sinners, Christ died for us." In that sacrificial death we catch a glimpse of His Father's love.

Do I enjoy talking with my heavenly Friend as I did with my mother? Do I share my joys and my sorrows with Him? He loves me so much that one day He is returning to take me to His home, where He will welcome both my mother and me. What wondrous love!   Birol C. Christo

July 9

Grapes

On each side of the river are trees that grow a different kind of fruit each month of the year. The fruit gives life, and the leaves are used as medicine to heal the nations. Rev. 22:2, CEV.

I WAS FORTUNATE TO know both my maternal (Mama and Papa) and paternal (Grandma and Granddaddy) grandparents. As the oldest grandchild of both sets, I feel blessed because I lived in the same city with them, and I was grown before any of them died. My grandmothers outlived my grandfathers by many years. Grandma was 91 when she died, and Mama was 101 when she died.

As far back as I can remember, Mama lived with us. Grandma and Granddaddy lived within walking distance of us. During the school year my visits were on the weekends. The visits were more frequent during the summer. Sometimes I rode my bicycle, and sometimes I walked.

I looked forward to the visits with Grandma. There are very few fruits that I dislike; however, grapes are my favorites, and Grandma knew this. I never told her when I was coming, but she was always prepared. Each time I visited, there would be a big bowl of huge black grapes, all washed and ready for me to eat. What a treat! The delight on her face as she saw how much I enjoyed them helped me to realize that the grapes were a gift of love.

When I went away to school and came home for vacation, I always visited Grandma. The grapes would be there. As an adult, when I visited her, there were no grapes. Weakened by the debilitating disease of diabetes, she was unable to have them for me, but I knew she would have had them for me if she had been able to do so. Having grapes was not my reason for visiting Grandma. I visited her because I loved her and enjoyed spending time with her. She chose this way of showing how much she loved me.

There is another Person who loves me so much that He wants to spend eternity with me. He knows just what I like and is preparing it for me. In the new earth, Jesus will have grapes and all the other fruits I like. I think grapes are beautiful and delicious here, but I have not tasted any that will compare with the taste of those that will be on the trees and vines in heaven. First Corinthians 2:9 tells us that we haven't seen, nor has it entered our minds, the things God has prepared for us. It is worth preparing for heaven.

MARIE H. SEARD

Oh, Such Love!

I will betroth you to me forever, . . . in love and compassion. Hosea 2:19, NIV.

I THINK OF THE LORD longing after us as a lover after his love, for to be-troth—to be engaged to marry—assures us of a deep love relationship, a love relationship even beyond what we can experience in this lifetime. How little we consider His great love and longing for us!

As Hosea sold all to purchase Gomer back from a life of degradation in her prostitution that he might take her back as his beloved wife, so also the Lord seeks us in the degradation of our sinful waywardness. He gave all to ransom us back to be His own beloved. This is the relationship of the Lord to His own.

O Lord, I want to respond with a life of love. It is my intent to put You first in my thoughts when I awake; and all day long I delight to read, think, sing, or hear of You whom I love. You fill my life.

When I am prone to complain that He is slow to answer some of my prayers, when it seems He is doing nothing to bring about righteousness in the world, then I can say as did Habakkuk, "Although [all fail], yet I will re-joice in the Lord. . . . The Lord is my strength, and he will make my feet like hinds' feet, and he will make me to walk upon . . . high places" (Hab. 3:17-19). His love is steady and unfailing.

I must remind myself how much my Lord Jesus loved the world— loved me, loved you—that He willingly gave His life in the most horrible way, stripped of His clothing and laid on a cross like a criminal and nailed to it. And even then He said, "Father, forgive them; for they know not what they do."

The church is His bride, and He the loving bridegroom. What a wonder-ful thought, what a wonderful truth.

Lord, never let me forget it.   PAM CARUSO

July 11

Wait, I Say, on the Lord

Rest in the Lord, and wait patiently for him. Ps. 37:7.

I THOUGHT PATIENCE WAS one of my virtues until I read an article on the subject recently and discovered I was grossly lacking in that quality. On a scale of one to 10 I may be able to squeeze into a five slot, if I really tried.

For starters, I don't enjoy waiting too long for a doctor's appointment when I may already be stressed out. And I certainly don't like waiting for a freight train to pass, especially if I have to go somewhere and I'm caught on the wrong side of the tracks. I guess my least favorite thing is to have to wait on road construction jobs, and it seemed we had our share of those in our travels. But I do manage quite well in checkout lanes, and I don't get ruffled in 5:00 traffic.

What's confusing about waiting is that time seems to creep by if I'm anticipating a trip or vacation, but a prescheduled dental appointment or some other unpleasant task usually comes around before I'm ready for it.

We're all acquainted with people who show their impatience by cracking their knuckles or tapping their fingers on the tabletop. Each has her own way of biding time, whether it be an outward display of some sort or merely rolling of the eyes and sighing. We're all primed for the fast lane, fast food, fast cars, and faster everything. There are diet aids on the market now that will supposedly melt fat while you sleep. It's strange. It's taken perhaps years to put on the extra pounds, and we want to take them off in time for our high school reunion next month.

After a long, hard winter I'm waiting for the first signs of spring, when the purple crocuses will push their tiny heads up through the ground in my side yard, and I'm counting the days until the robins will once again stop by to dine in my garden patch. I can hardly wait for the green grass to appear and hide the dirty snow along the driveway, and I'll be happy to see the skies of blue again after weeks of clouds of gray.

I like what David had to say in Psalm 37:7: "Rest in the Lord, and wait patiently for him." I need to learn to wait on Him, and He'll direct my path.

It's one thing to be able to "wait," but quite another to learn to wait patiently.   CLAREEN COLCLESSER

She Felt My Legs

By this all will know that you are My disciples, if you have love for one another. John 13:35, NKJV.

MY PLANE STOPPED AT a remote airport in a foreign tropical country. It was necessary for me to change planes, and I had a rather long wait before the arrival of my next plane. The airport was small, hot, and humid. I was dressed in a skirt and blouse and tried to keep cool. There were not very many seats in the airport, but I was fortunate to find an empty one. I passed the time watching the people, many of whom were in their native costumes.

Another plane arrived and unloaded, and now the airport was filled with people. There were people milling continually through the waiting area, as there weren't enough seats for everyone. My eyes seemed drawn to one corner of the room, where a group of women seemed to be looking at me and laughing. This didn't bother me, since I long ago got used to being a foreigner, having worked overseas for many years.

I was surprised, however, when one of these women walked deliberately over to where I was sitting. She knelt before me, and taking one of my ankles in each of her hands, she slowly began feeling my legs and going slowly up my legs with her hands. I sat still until her hands reached my knees. When it appeared she was not going to stop at my knees, I quickly stood up. She also stood up and with one hand pushed me aside, plopping herself down in my seat. There was an immediate roar of laughter from the onlooking ladies.

I walked away, chuckling to myself about how I had been outwitted; however, I also thought about how selfish is our world. Sometimes we feel that we must have all that we want, even though it may inconvenience or embarrass others. How many times do we "jump the queue" at the grocery store or the bank? How many times do we cut in front of someone when we are driving? I cannot picture Jesus cutting in front of anyone else. Nor can I see Him suffering from road rage. If we have Christ in our hearts we will not be putting ourselves first, rather we will have compassion for those around us.

ROWENA R. RICK

July 13

Waiting and Watching

What I say unto you I say unto all, Watch. Mark 13:37.

WAITING. IT WAS A glorious morning. Arriving early for my train to work, I stood on the platform reading one of my favorite books, *Steps to Christ*, engrossed and oblivious to what was happening around me. Suddenly I looked up. There was the train! Its doors were closing! I rushed forward, only to find it was too late. As quietly as it had come, it left, with me still standing on the platform, waiting.

Evidently I should have been watching as well as waiting. Almost stealthily it had come. But I was early, not late, engrossed in reading that drew me closer to the Lord, thinking and enjoying spiritual things. How good it felt! Yet I was unaware that the long-awaited train had come, and it passed me by while I was standing there, waiting.

Later I thought, *Could it be that Jesus' coming might be just like that?* Might I be so busy waiting and enjoying other spiritual activities that I am unaware of what is going on around me? Oblivious to the signs that are fast fulfilling to warn me of Christ's soon return and the necessity of looking up? Perhaps I am looking in the wrong direction, even though doing a good thing.

I must consciously watch for His soon return and be sure I am actively mindful of the end result, not just the means. I must be actively looking in order to be in a state of readiness. I need to watch lest the train of angels coming from glory passes me by because I am out of tune with the Holy Spirit and God's Word. The scripture that says "Therefore be ye also ready: for in such an hour as ye think not the Son of man cometh" (Matt. 24:44) applies to me.

I need to remember and not forget what He told His disciples: "What I say unto you I say unto all, Watch."

May God find us both waiting and watching when He comes for us.

AUDRE B. TAYLOR

The Miraculous Hands of Our Lord

Sun, stand still over Gibeon; and Moon, in the Valley of Aijalon.
Joshua 10:12, NKJV.

WE WANTED TO MAKE bricks to build a school building on our campus. We knew the workers could make two stacks of unbaked bricks, and we could bake them in the brick kiln. We would make the bricks on our campus to reduce the cost of the school building. We paid a small amount of rupees to some workers, and altogether 30 people worked for a month. Even though we didn't pay much, we had a hard time paying the wages to these workers. Luckily, it was not the rainy season, so we weren't worried that the bricks would be ruined.

However, before the bricks were baked, dark clouds appeared in the sky at about 4:00 one afternoon. There was darkness everywhere. Along with the workers who had made the bricks, five or six non-Christian men, who stayed nearby, tried to console us. They were ready to help us, knowing the unbaked bricks piled up for baking would be damaged if it rained.

All of a sudden it started to drizzle. Immediately my husband and I knelt down on the ground in front of the workers and started praying. We prayed earnestly, with tearful eyes. The men and women standing around us were questioning whether our prayers would be heard and the rain would be stopped. We were praying without stopping, pleading with the Lord to stop the rain so that through this miracle the non-Christians would know about His power and understand that He was the true and powerful God, who has power over everything.

Our loving Lord, the Lord of redemption and salvation, the Lord of miracles, heard our prayers. He stretched forth His powerful hands and removed the dark clouds, stopping the rain.

Relieved, we were able to bake all the bricks. After all the bricks were baked, we prayed for rain to dismantle the kiln. It did rain, and it was a great help to us.

All the non-Christians who had stood there and witnessed the miracle that day accepted our Lord Jesus Christ as their personal Savior. Later on, they all were baptized and are now faithful Christians. Praise the Lord! What a wonderful, miraculous God He is.   GIRIJA DANIEL

July 15

I Felt His Touch

And he said unto her, Daughter, be of good comfort: thy faith hath made thee whole; go in peace. Luke 8:48.

A WEEK BEFORE MY daughter's wedding I called to tell her that I would not be able to attend. Weeks before, as I was getting out of the car, I had felt a sharp, excruciating pain in my abdomen. I literally crawled out of the car and into the house, reached for the phone, and called my doctor. He told me to come immediately to his office. I was diagnosed with a bad attack of diverticulitis. He referred me to a surgeon, who scheduled me for surgery after taking several X-rays.

With the wedding a week away, and all the preparations set to fly from the United States to India, I had to tell my daughter that I would not be able to make it for her wedding and that she would have to have just her dad and two sisters.

Joyce broke into tears and said, "Mom, I will call Vijay [her fiancé] and postpone the wedding."

Although I did not agree with her, she was adamant about not going on without me. A few days later I was admitted to the hospital. With only three hours prior to being taken to the operating room, I pleaded with the Lord to heal me, if it was His will, so that I would be able to attend my daughter's wedding.

As I lay there, I suddenly felt a touch on my abdomen and was instantly relieved of the pain. At that very moment the surgeon walked into the room to explain the surgical procedure and to examine me once again. I told him that the pain had completely gone. He then ordered more X-rays. A few hours later he came back to tell me that the surgery was not needed. I knew right away that the hand of God, the Great Physician, had touched me, and I was instantly healed.

For the past 21 years I have been praising God for His miracle in my life. I was able to go to India and attend my daughter's wedding. And she is still happily married to Vijay.

What an incredible, awesome God we have! There isn't a day goes by that I am not reminded of His wondrous and miraculous healing.

JOSEPHINE T. FRANCIS

"Keep the Red Side Up!"

Train children in the right way, and when old, they will not stray.
Prov. 22:6, NRSV.

"KEEP THE RED SIDE up," our parents called to us as we grabbed the red-and-blue rafts and ran toward the water. When we were young, Mom and Dad had carefully chosen a beach for our summer vacation. They could relax under the shade of a beach umbrella, while my sisters and I swam in the shallow water or conducted "battles" where we would happily push each other off air-filled rafts. The water was usually peaceful, and the lifeguards were vigilant; however, Mom and Dad wanted to be able to spot us easily in the water, so they repeatedly told us to keep the bright side of the rafts visible. Year after year we'd begin our battles on the red side of the rafts, and if the rafts flipped over to show their blue sides, we'd automatically turn them over.

When we were teenagers, we went to a beach that had exciting waves to challenge us. We were still admonished to "keep the red side up" as we paddled into deep water, attempting to catch a wave before it broke. Although the waves would often upset us and wrench the rafts from our control, we'd grab them and flip them over so the red side was up, and wave to our parents.

The summer our dad turned 80, we returned for a week at the beach. Knowing that our parents were frail and that we needed to take control of many details, we took our teenage children with us to buy new red-and-blue rafts. After our parents were comfortably ensconced in their folding chairs, my sisters and I ran to the surf and tried riding the waves again. Our children bobbed around, trying to master the skill. I looked at the six of us and laughed: the three teenagers were lying on their rafts with the blue side up; my two sisters and I had the red side up.

When I pointed this out, our children got a puzzled look on their faces, so we explained. "We were taught to keep the red side up so Daddy could rescue us if necessary."

"But now you're much better swimmers than he is," countered one of the children.

"I know," I replied, "but we just have to keep the red side up!"

DENISE DICK HERR

July 17

Big Brother

Then [Jesus] added, "Anyone who obeys my Father in heaven is my brother, sister and mother!" Matt. 12:50, TLB.

IT'S WONDERFUL HAVING SISTERS, but there have been times when I have envied those of my friends who have brothers with whom they have a really good relationship. I actually do have a big brother, but he has a disability, which means that even though he's an adult, he requires care much as a child does. However, I was fortunate, courtesy of my sister's marriage, to acquire a delightful brother-in-law. Although I don't see him often, as he and my sister live in another state, it's great when we do get to visit, or at least chat on the phone. I can talk to him about almost anything. He's thoughtful and considerate, and he has a terrific sense of humor. He's very practical and knows what to do with anything from a blown fuse to a broken-down lawn mower. Better still, he even knows how to use a tea towel and an iron. He's big and strong, with very large but gentle hands. As my sister says, you can go anywhere with him and feel safe.

His arrangements, whether for business, travel, or pleasure, usually seem to work out well, owing, I think, to a combination of pleasant manner, careful planning, and exceptional good fortune. In fact, after hearing yet another example of my brother-in-law's luck in obtaining accommodations where it seemed that none were to be had, I suggested to the family that he should always be delegated to make the arrangements for whatever trip or event was coming up, and each of us could simply tell people, "I'm with him!"

How reassuring it is to know that whatever our actual family circumstances, each of us has the ideal Big Brother. Someone who's always there for us; Someone we can talk to about absolutely anything; Someone who is kind, thoughtful, and protective. In fact, more than just protective, Someone who can save us. Ellen White assures us that "the Elder Brother of our race is by the eternal throne. . . . He is watching over you, trembling child of God. Are you tempted? He will deliver. Are you weak? He will strengthen. Are you ignorant? He will enlighten. Are you wounded? He will heal" (*The Desire of Ages*, p. 329). When anyone asks me about my Elder Brother, Jesus, I'm always happy to say, "I'm with Him!"

JENNIFER M. BALDWIN

Purifier

But if we walk in the light, as he is in the light, we have fellowship with one another, and the blood of Jesus, his Son, purifies us from all sin. . . . [He] will purify us from all unrighteousness. 1 John 1:7-9, NIV.

I ONCE LIVED IN AN area where people were very health-conscious. Almost every family had a water-purifying jug. It was my first time to see one. I asked my colleague to explain what it was and how it worked and why almost all families on the campus had them. She told me that the water we drank was from the dam, and they were not sure whether it was purified properly. I also discovered that some families even boiled the water before pouring it into the water-purifying jug. It was a great lesson to me.

One day a friend and I went shopping. She bought me a beautiful water-purifying jug and a filter. I will ever be grateful for that gift. One of my adopted children said that she wanted to drink "clean water," meaning water from the purifier, not straight from the tap.

On one occasion we didn't have water for almost two weeks, and we had to fetch rainwater from the reservoir. Some of the water was not very clean, but because of the purifying jugs and filters, we managed to drink clean water, and none of us became sick.

One evening while pouring water into the jug, I was reminded of the blood of Jesus Christ, which purifies us from all our sins. He purifies us from all unrighteousness. Fortunately, we do not have to buy this purifier; we just have to believe and have unwavering faith in Him. We must believe that it is only His blood that can change our lives, our wild lives, into humble and pleasant lives. It is only Jesus' blood that can change our insensitive attitudes to more sensitive attitudes, especially toward the needs of others. Yes, it is the blood of Jesus that can purify us from doubt and unbelief and bring us to total dependence upon God and into the upper chamber of hope and faith.

Lord, purify us with Your blood and remove every trace of sin in our lives. Please make us as white as snow, because there is power in Your blood. Thank You so much for Your purifying blood. Amen.

NTOMBIZODWA ZIPHORA KUNENE

July 19

Failing the Samaritan Test

All the ways of a man are pure in his own eyes, but the Lord weighs the spirits. Prov. 16:2, NKJV.

I WAS AMONG THE FEW invited to see my college art history professor knighted by the government of Italy for his restoration of great artworks. I was running late and feared I was going to miss the only knighting I was ever likely to witness. I parked the car and rushed toward the house where a half dozen well-dressed people stood in groups on the lawn. Just as I reached the driveway, a tall, elderly man in a tuxedo stepped away from the group and, ashen-faced, reached out to me with his hand. Startled, I pulled back. The man collapsed at my feet.

Conversation stopped, and everyone stood still, staring at the man and me. I looked down the driveway to the decorated backyard where the knighting was to take place, thinking, *I will miss the ceremony if I stop to help this man!* I turned and walked into the backyard, barely conscious of the sudden activity behind me. The program had not begun as I took my seat. The ambulance arrived and carried the stricken man away long before the knighting ceremony began.

Although I saw the knighting, I didn't enjoy it. I kept thinking about the good Samaritan. If the men who passed by the injured man in that story had touched him, they would have been disqualified for a month from serving in the Temple; their livelihood depended upon their fulfilling their religious duties. That was a much better reason for abandoning someone in need than my curiosity about the knighting ceremony. The parallel between the parable and what had just happened that morning weighed heavily on me. Suddenly the story of the good Samaritan was part of my life, and I realized that my priorities were askew.

I have never forgotten that man. I have prayed for forgiveness for not being more sympathetic to his need, and for my wrong choice. I know God has forgiven me for my sin, but the guilt I still feel is a reminder to put the needs of those God puts in my path before anything else that I might consider important.

Lord, help me always to choose Your values over my own. Amen.

Darlenejoan McKibbin Rhine

A Picnic's Coming!

Ho, every one that thirsteth, come ye to the waters, and he that hath no money; come ye, buy, and eat. Isa. 55:1.

WITH NO REST AREA close by and many miles and hours to go before stopping for the night, we were eating our lunch in a secluded area of a mall parking lot. Noticing what we were doing, a little boy came over and asked for something to eat. I put some goodies into his grubby little hand, then was startled and amused when he called out to some of his buddies, "Hey, they're having a picnic, and the food's free!"

It's quite normal to like good things that are free. I'm a coupon clipper and really like it when I find one that isn't just cents off, but *free*. We have a nice young neighbor who works with suppliers for grocery stores and, as a result, gets cases of various products. One day he called to see if we would like to pick out some of the extras. We did, and what fun we had! We were like kids in a candy store. We didn't want to be greedy, but he and his wife encouraged us to help ourselves. We picked out cans of nuts, boxes of pasta dinners, trail mix, different kinds of candy, ice-cream toppings, an expensive brand of chocolate chips, mints, sauces, cleaning supplies, even socks. We brought home two or three boxes of assorted treasures, some of which we are still enjoying while remembering and appreciating his generosity.

We have another Friend who is eager to share with us. He offers something that no other friend or neighbor can give. It's not just food, although He promises that we can eat fruit from the tree of life. It's not just clothing, although He promises to cover us with His robe of righteousness. It's not just a home, although He promises mansions prepared for us. It's not just health, although He promises there will be no sickness. It's not just life, although He promises that there will be no death. It's not just happiness, although He promises that God will wipe away our tears. The best of all will be finally to see our Lord and Savior, face to face, and to spend eternity with Him. He invites the thirsty to come to the waters, and those with no money to buy and eat. Like the little boy who wanted to share our picnic with his friends, why not tell others, "Hey, there's going to be a picnic, and the food's free!"

MARY JANE GRAVES

Look Up!

Look up, and lift up your heads; for your redemption draweth nigh. Luke 21:28.

M OMMY! MOMMY! I CAN'T see! There's shampoo in my eyes, and it hurts!" screamed my 3-year-old daughter as I washed her hair one evening. Every time I tried to rinse her hair, she would look down at the water in the tub, and all of the shampoo and water would run into her eyes. She began to cry and scream louder.

"Emily," I said, "look up! Look up at the ceiling! You won't get shampoo in your eyes if you look up."

She tilted her head back, and the shampoo and water ran down her back and into the tub, not her eyes. At that moment I heard a voice in my mind telling me, "Marla, look up! Look up! You will be able to see clearly if you look up."

During the past several months I had been discouraged, and my faith seemed to be wavering. I felt that I had let down my fellow Christians in leadership positions, and it had upset me a great deal. I was looking down, letting human frailties and mistakes cloud my vision. The Holy Spirit was telling me to "Look up! Look to the Lord!"

When we take our eyes off of the Lord and look at other human beings, we sometimes get disappointed by their human failings. Our vision gets cloudy and our faith may waver. We may not feel like going to church anymore. We may not want to spend personal time with our Jesus. We may want even to scream and cry, as Emily did.

When we look up to Christ and keep our eyes on Him, our vision becomes clear and our faith becomes stronger. We may still be disappointed by the mistakes and human faults of others and ourselves, but they won't cloud our vision.

"Look up, and lift up your heads; for your redemption draweth nigh."

Lord, please help me to keep my eyes on You. You are the only one who never fails.

MARLA JOHNSON

Bats in Our Attic

Lest Satan should take advantage of us; for we are not ignorant of his devices.
2 Cor. 2:11, NKJV.

ARRIVING HOME FROM VACATION, I noticed some dark streaks down the side of the house. I thought, *Oh, no! We may have bats in the attic.* I was almost right. There were louvers and screening at the top of the house. A family of approximately 20 bats had taken residence between the louvers and the screening. I called some pest-control companies and found that bats are federally protected; only someone licensed by the federal government could relocate them. Bats help control harmful garden insects, and I liked that idea.

We discovered that bats do not like water. My husband decided to wash down the droppings on the side of the house. Some of the water accidentally touched the bats, and they flew out of their quarters. Since bats migrate in the winter, we decided to put screening over the outside of the louvers after they migrated and before they came back in the spring. Our intentions were good, but we soon forgot about the bats once they migrated.

One evening I went into our bedroom and turned on the light. I found company—one lone bat was flying around the room. Apparently it came in via our sliding-glass door in the den. I like bats, but not in my bedroom. I didn't want to harm the bat, but I wanted it out of my house.

I opened the bedroom window, took the lamp shade to which the poor, frightened, teeth-chattering creature was clinging for dear life, and shook the bat gently out the window. That took care of that problem, but I decided I'd better check the attic. Sure enough, our family of bats was back. And one was now in the attic. The next morning with screening and water hose ready, I proceeded to rid our house of bats. The bat that was inside the attic was taken outside onto the lawn. It took it about 20 minutes to recover from its fright and gather enough energy to fly away. Our veterinarian later told me that bats have a very high metabolism and can easily die when frightened so badly.

Sometimes Satan takes up residence in our home, and it takes persistence to rid our lives of him. I hope that we make the effort in our spiritual lives that we do in our physical lives.   LORAINE F. SWEETLAND

July 23

Little Things

And even the very hairs of your head are all numbered. So don't be afraid; you are worth more than many sparrows. Matt. 10:30, 31, NIV.

SOME THINGS YOU PUT off doing—like surgeries. The doctors said I needed to have hand and wrist surgery done, and the sooner the better. I knew it would be uncomfortable for a while, although I didn't know just how painful it would actually be, so I wasn't in any hurry. I knew, too, that I would have to take time off from work. So it took from January until September before I set up the appointment.

When I came home from the hospital after the surgery I was still pretty much out of it. Friends sent flowers, cards, and food. One even helped with the ironing. My neighbor took me to the doctor for my follow-up visit. My husband pitched right in with the household chores. All this help was very much welcomed.

I went back to work two weeks later (another area in which I miscued on the healing time). I did find many things I could do with one hand; however, I'm so grateful to work in a place where my boss and coworkers are understanding and helpful. It's always good to be reminded God uses people, too, in our time of need. Praise the Lord!

One challenge I had was folding and mailing the monthly newsletter our department puts out. Before surgery I would fan the newsletters out a bit before putting them into the folding machine, but during the three months that my hand was healing, I had to drop the newsletters in the folding machine a few at a time. Every newsletter folded correctly; not one jammed! But when my hand was healed I tried to place a few newsletters in the folding machine at a time without fanning them. Some didn't fold correctly, and the machine jammed. I had to fan the newsletters so they would fold correctly—something I could not have done during the healing process.

Placing the labels on the newsletters was another challenge; however, the Lord helped me cope there, too, and the newsletters were always mailed on time. I'm so thankful the Lord promises to always be with us and help us through each day.

LOUISE DRIVER

Making Do

*So why do you worry about clothing? . . . Now if God so clothes the grass . . .
will He not much more clothe you, O you of little faith? Therefore do not
worry. Matt. 6:28-31, NKJV.*

I PACKED VERY CAREFULLY, not taking anything that was not absolutely
necessary. A black skirt for dressing up, sandals to match, my Swiss army
knife for making a snack, a pair of shorts for hot weather in Spain, underwear
for a week, and laundry detergent. Worship-book pages copied for daily devotionals and a pair of black dress pants. Socks and hose. Yes, everything fit!
We were off for a three-week trip to Europe.

Arriving in Munich, I was told that my suitcase hadn't made it, but it
would be delivered to my hotel the next day. Fine! I had a change of underwear, a clean pair of socks, and my pills in my overnight bag.

After three days and no suitcase, though, I began to wonder what was
going on. I gave the suitcase to the Lord in prayer and enjoyed the sights and
concerts in Prague. We left the next day for Vienna, and still no suitcase.
Then Saltzburg and the *Passion Play* in Oberammergau, where we stayed in a
lovely hotel in Bad Kohlgrub. We called about the suitcase and prayed about
it and asked at the desk for it. When we left for Rome, we asked again. By this
time I had resigned myself to having to wear the same clothes I had been
wearing and washing for more than a week. The airlines promised that the
suitcase would be delivered to the hotel in Rome.

We left Rome without the suitcase. Florence I saw in the same clothes.
Then on to Spain, Zurich, and back to Munich. The agent there was shocked
that I had not gotten the suitcase. After three weeks with what I had in the
overnight bag, I was nearly used to making do with little.

After we got home the airline called and said they had located my suitcase in the Rome airport, and it was returned to me three days later.

It became sort of a challenge to see how little I needed to survive.
Although in every picture taken on the trip I look surprisingly the same, I
have good memories of many beautiful sights seen on my European vacation,
and God took care of me and all the contents of that suitcase.

JEAN S. MURPHY

July 25

What Would You Have Me Do, Daddy?

"For I know the plans I have for you," declares the Lord. Jer. 29:11, NIV.

SOME DOGS CHASE CARS, but one day my car chased me. Praise the Lord, I'm still alive!

Most of my town's streets slope. About 1:30 that fateful afternoon, I parked on a side street, near the post office. I put the car in gear, pulled up the emergency brake, and went to buy stamps.

When I returned to the car, unlocked and opened the door, it began to roll slowly back, down the grade. Somehow, I couldn't get out of the way, and the open car door knocked me to the pavement in the middle of the street. The car finally rolled into a tree.

I suffered a concussion, several hematomas, two broken bones (not serious), and a six-stitch wound on the right side of my forehead. Strangely, I don't recall unlocking the car door, the police officer coming, the rescue squad taking me to the local hospital, being "derobed" and dressed in a hospital gown, or all the X-rays and the CAT scan. I vaguely recall the emergency room doctor saying, "We'll have to stitch up your forehead," but I don't remember the procedure.

I was so grateful for the loving care, help, and prayers of the hospital staff, family, friends, and for my very busy angel.

Once home, I was shocked! The police report said the car had been in neutral, not in park, as I'd thought! Although my 1986 car was considered a total wreck, I brought it back and fixed it up.

That car didn't scare me! I drove it one month after the accident and couldn't help marveling: God still had need of me here, in spite of my 70-plus years! I asked, "What would You have me do, Daddy?"

The thought that came to me was simple: "Keep doing what you have been doing, My precious daughter."

And what is that? I'm a listener. When people tell me about their health or other problems, I let them know I'll pray for them, and later I ask for updates.

Praise You, Daddy, for my angel, for healing, and for the gifts of listening and intercessory prayer! PATSY MURDOCH MEEKER

Trapped!

O Lord, you have searched me and you know me. You know when I sit and when I rise. You are familiar with all my ways. Ps. 139:1-3, NIV.

I F ENCLOSED SPACES AREN'T a problem to you, the following episode won't seem at all as it did to me. But if you are claustrophobic, it's one of the things you fervently hope will never happen to you.

I was at the airport, going down in an elevator. I had entered it at the fifth floor and was the sole occupant. Being alone in there didn't bother me, since my mind was busy with thoughts of the plane I was soon to board and the journey I was about to make and the joyful family reunion at the other end of it.

Then, suddenly the elevator stopped, and the comfortable humming noise ceased. What had seemed quite a friendly space up to that moment had now assumed the nature of a tomb, and I did not like it.

A prayer from the heart (my lips being quite immobilized) drew my eyes to the little red button on the instrument panel with the word "alarm" on it. Making a fuss is not something I enjoy doing, but I was alarmed, so I pushed it and waited.

"Don't worry! We'll be right with you," a voice assured me.

Then silence again, the peculiar silence of being all along in a box suspended in space.

Finally, joy of joys, a gentle throbbing of machinery, a little jolt, and the doors slid back as if on cue, and I stepped out into the lively bustling world of Heathrow Airport, feeling as if I'd been given a second chance at life.

Afterward, seated comfortably on the plane heading out over the Atlantic (another "box," but the hum of the engines reassured me), my thoughts turned to Psalm 139—very good news for all claustrophobics, as well as those who don't care for heights, depths, or the dark. Wherever we are, God is there with us. And what crowns it all is that our loving heavenly Father doesn't wait for us to push the alarm button.

"Before they call, I will answer," He says. What a God we serve!

PEGGY MASON

God Met My Needs

And my God will meet all your needs according to his glorious riches in Christ Jesus. Phil. 4:19, NIV.

IT HAD BEEN ONLY a few days since I had buried my mother after caring for her through a short but final illness. This had been a great blow, because she had been there for me through 56 years, and I would miss her weekly letters, filled with her love for me and my family. Now my mother-in-law, who had been blind in one eye for many years, was losing the sight in her other eye. I knew it would not be long before she would need my help in meeting her daily needs.

My husband, realizing the strain I had been under, suggested that I spend some time with our youngest daughter in another part of the state. There I could also enjoy our 6-month-old granddaughter.

When the phone rang a few days after my arrival, we had no idea how our lives would be changed. We got the news that our son had been seriously injured in the collapse of a building under construction in southern Mexico where he was teaching. He had been transported over winding mountain roads to the nearest hospital in a city 100 miles from the accident site. Within a few days we were able to arrange for him to come to Loma Linda Medical Center with his wife and 18-month-old son, where we knew he would receive the best of care. An examination by a top neurosurgeon determined that his neck was broken, and he would be a quadriplegic for the rest of his life. How could this have happened to our only son, who was doing a good work for the Lord? He had always enjoyed hiking, being the first one to the top of the mountain, and using his hands in building houses and crafting furniture. Now these things would be impossible for him to do.

At that time of my greatest need God was there for me, giving me strength and comfort. He was also there for our son, who never lost faith in God. I was able to help him and his family, as well as care for my husband's parents in their later years.

Thank You, Lord, for the promise that through the glorious riches in Jesus Christ, someday soon all pain will be stamped out, and our son will be able to walk again. Thank You for meeting our needs. BETTY J. ADAMS

Beautiful People

Make friends with nobodies; don't be the great somebody. . . . Discover beauty in everyone. Rom. 12:16, 17, Message.

IT WAS MY FIRST job as a newly qualified occupational therapist. I worked with those who had severe behavior problems. I enjoyed the challenge of continually being one step ahead of the moment, trying to identify problems before they arose, defusing disruptive behavior through lots of fun, activity, and quiet times of relaxation.

My colleagues worked at the other end of the building with the severely multiple-handicapped residents. I had seen their clients, twisted and grotesque, in cumbersome wheelchairs, specially made to accommodate their distorted bodies. Most of them were unable to talk and showed little sign of being aware of their surroundings. I hoped and prayed that I would never have to go down there to work.

Then a colleague had to leave, and I was asked to split my time between the two units. I stepped into the unknown, full of irrational fears and feelings of insecurity. But soon I learned their names. I knew the music that Shelley liked to rock to. I knew how to feed Tommy, slowly, watching for him to swallow properly. And I met Cheska and Pete. Cheska's eyes flashed with understanding, and her arms twisted up in delight when she laughed. She was in love with Pete, who, though quieter and unable to move, was responsive in other ways.

All too soon I had to leave, as I was getting married. I was so sad to go. The people who had once seemed frightening and repulsive were now my friends. I had taken the time to get to know them, to share in their lives, and to find out what made them laugh. As I looked around the room, my eyes filled with tears. I would miss each one of them. Somehow they were no longer twisted and grotesque. I knew each one of them personally, and I knew they were all beautiful.

I've met many people since then. Some of them have seemed strange, and almost scary. But whenever I have taken the time to get to know them, sharing in their lives and discovering what makes them laugh, the strange and scary things that are based on my irrational fears always dissolve away to show the beauty of the real person underneath.   KAREN HOLFORD

July 29

True Commitment or the Riches of Poverty

But godliness with contentment is great gain. 1 Tim. 6:6.

WE FIRST MET HER more than 20 years ago, an elderly woman living alone in a rented room perched on a steep hillside, overlooking the city of Kavála. Her living faith has never been forgotten, though she herself has long since gone to rest.

When we visited her, the first thing she did after extending a warm welcome was to pull from under her mattress a beautifully embroidered little bag containing her tithes and offerings. This was then presented to my husband with such joy that we were always reminded that "it is more blessed to give than to receive." The amount never ceased to amaze us, as she had no regular income and no pension. Occasionally she gave an English lesson for a few drachmas, or translated something into one of the five languages she knew, but mostly she was dependent on the kindness of friends and neighbors to supplement her meager earnings. However, she tithed faithfully. When a friend brought her a plate of food and a slice of bread, she would accept it gratefully, thank the donor warmly, estimate its monetary worth, and set aside her tithe and offering before eating it.

Although her worldly possessions were minimal, she was always sensitive to the needs of others. One day she found some money that had been pushed under her door and went out to buy some much-needed groceries. Then she found a poor man begging, so she gave him the money and returned home empty-handed. As she opened her door, the same amount of money was lying on the floor!

"I keep trying to give it away," she said, "but God keeps giving it back to me."

One day we took her up into the hills behind Kavála on a brief outing. As she looked out over the vineyards and olive groves to the sparkling Mediterranean and the blue horizon, her face lit up in excitement and she cried out, "Oh, I am so rich!" Then, seeing the puzzled look on our faces, she added, "All this belongs to my Father. I am His daughter, so all this beauty is mine." She was truly rich.

May God grant us, who have so much more of this world's bounties than she ever had, a double portion of her gratitude and praise.

REVEL PAPAIOANNOU

Danger in Ventures

If ye shall ask any thing in my name, I will do it. John 14:14.

THRILLING EXPERIENCES INSPIRE; lively activities keep me alert. I can't focus my attention unless the work I am doing is really interesting. I have to have some form of stimulant in order to keep me awake. Reading is usually dull, unless it is something I am intently interested in. Many times I use reading materials to make me fall asleep.

The most risky activity I have ever done was driving home after doing double duty or an occasional 24-hour round when staffing was short. I had difficulty saying no when I realized nobody else could or would do it, especially when there were some very sick patients in the unit.

Once, when I was driving home after work, police officers stopped me because of my weaving pattern, driving when sleepy. The officers tested me on suspicion of drunkenness and interrogated me as to how much I had been drinking. When he could not detect alcohol on my breath, one officer had me get out of my car and made me walk. When they were able to verify that I was just tired, having just gotten off duty, I was counseled to drive carefully.

Some of my driving-while-tired experiences include ending up in a ditch, accidentally U-turning my car to face the traffic, and getting speeding tickets. I am thankful I didn't have any fatalities.

One day I decided to apply at a hospital within walking distance of my home. I prayed that I would be accepted, and God answered my prayer positively. This decision gave me double benefits. Now I have more time to walk daily and climb stairs regularly. The physical exercise provides me more relaxation and adds restful sleep for me at night. And no more risks on the road!

God's wonderful promise in the book of John is not a blanket promise. The important benefit of prayer is to receive directions through Christ for our lives. The monopoly of the Holy Spirit in our hearts is through our willingness to be directed. This adventure of seeking His direction has ministered to my body and soul.

Blessed Lord, use Your Word to work in me. Holy Spirit, I plead that You will do the same for my sisters all around the globe.

ESPERANZA AQUINO MOPERA

July 31

Barbara's Miracle

And the prayer of faith shall save the sick, and the Lord shall raise him up. James 5:15.

B ARBARA HAS BEEN A close friend of mine for many years. She had been recovering from the surgical removal of a brain tumor and was 18 months into recovery and doing remarkably well. While she and her mom were at the bank one Friday morning, Barbara suddenly developed a severe headache and passed out. The bank officials called 911 immediately, and Barbara was transported to the nearest hospital.

A quick workup was done. The elders of the church came to the hospital, and Barbara was anointed. Over the next few days things did not look good. We petitioned the Lord daily in prayer for her and with her.

The hospital stay stretched into a week. Tests continued to be performed, but no concrete answers were found. The doctors decided she needed an electroencephalogram (EEG) to monitor her brain activity for 24 hours.

My friend became extremely depressed, thinking of the unknown and what her tests might show. When I called her Sunday morning, she was hysterical. She felt that the results of her EEG would show that the tumor had returned. We talked at length about our blessed hope in Christ and claimed and held on to His promises. We prayed and prayed, speaking earnestly with the Lord. At the end of the call, Barbara expressed that she felt at peace.

Early the next morning the neurologist came to see Barbara and gave her the results of all of her tests. They had found no new tumor and no seizure activity in her brain.

"Your tests do show that you are anemic," the doctor stated. "That may have caused you to faint in the bank."

She was discharged from the hospital that same day. One week later she was able to travel to Chicago to attend the graduation exercises of her daughter and granddaughter.

What a mighty God we serve! The Lord not only healed Barbara; He raised her up to continue to serve Him and to witness to others. Her determination and faith brought her through this trial with shining colors.

SHARON MARSHALL

220

Bits and Bridles

"I will guide you along the best pathway for your life. I will advise you and watch over you. Do not be like a senseless horse or mule that needs a bit and bridle to keep it under control." Many sorrows come to the wicked, but unfailing love surrounds those who trust the Lord. Ps. 32:8-10, NLT.

I'VE RIDDEN A HORSE only a couple of times in my life, and I found the experiences fun but a little scary. I always felt as if the horse were going to take off on its own course with me, helpless and afraid, at its mercy. Maybe that's why horseback riding never particularly interested me.

As a kid I remember standing in line to ride a horse. Of course, there was a guide who stood with the horse as it slowly strutted and galloped through the small area designated for the ride. If the horse started to go too fast, the guide would say "Whoa," or yank the reins a little.

After I became an adult a friend and I went riding. We picked our horses from the riding stable, and after a few quick tips from the instructor, we mounted and were on our way. I was feeling carefree, excited—and cautious. If I pulled the reins one way, the horse obeyed and headed in that direction. If I pulled back and said "Whoa," the horse slowed. On occasion it went its own way, and I ended up with a few briers and thorns stuck to my jeans. My friend was enjoying the ride, too, and getting a bit cocky, he took off at a faster pace than I. I could hear him saying, "Slow down, fella," and "Whoa," as they disappeared. Before long he was stuck in quicksand and calling for help.

Carefully I attempted to guide my horse near the quicksand so I could rescue my friend. It was tricky. I had to get close enough to toss a rope to him yet remain on solid ground. My horse bucked and whinnied and slowly yielded to my leading (and pleading). Eventually, my friend's horse did, too. Every step in the right direction brought a quiet sigh of relief from both of us.

God says He will guide us in the best pathway, yet often, like wild horses or bucking broncos, we ignore His leading and travel our own paths laden with thorns and briers. Eventually we fall into quicksand and can only hope that somehow someone will rescue us. That Someone is Jesus. He gently, patiently leads and guides, without bits and bridles, till we are safe at last. Let's trust Him today and in the unfailing love of our heavenly Father live the best life ever.

IRIS L. STOVALL

August 2

Oh, to Be a VHP

Whatsoever things are true . . . honest . . . just . . . pure . . . lovely . . . of good report . . . think of these things. Phil. 4:8.

YESTERDAY I FELT ANYTHING but happiness. I was actually moved to tears for no apparent reason—I felt very sad and unhappy. I continued petitioning the Lord to reveal the reason and to help me feel better. There are always things that can make us feel sad and down—all the crime and hatred in the world; all the killing; all the illness; all the homeless and starving people. Yet none of these seemed to be it. I continued in prayer all day.

During worship at the office the speaker talked about VHPs—very happy people, people who internalize that which is good and holy and just and perfect. The two days before, she had zeroed in on VIPs—very important people—and VOPs, very ordinary people. Somehow I was especially moved and encouraged by the VHP topic. As she continued sharing, I began to feel a little better. Then my mind went back to Ohio, where I had visited my oldest brother only days before. We had had a nice time together.

As we prepared to leave, he invited my sister and me into the living room. "Mother is in here," he said, rather jokingly. I had no clue what he meant, for we had buried our mother more than a year earlier. He led us to a corner of the room where a small box sat on a table. I picked it up and read on the label our mother's name and date of death. Right then I felt nothing. But here, days later, it struck me. Here were the remains of the woman who had loved us so much that she had literally given her all for us six children, who went without so that we could have.

As I sat in worship that morning I realized this must be the reason for my unexplained sadness. I listened more intently to the speaker as we were admonished to think on the eternal, and that even in the face of imperfect situations in an imperfect world, dealing daily with imperfect people such as myself, we can still choose to be VHPs. I can choose to be a very happy person as I grow into a right relationship with God, my fellows, and myself. I can choose to be happy today in the thought that one day I will see my mother again, and that she and I, with our Father and our heavenly family, will be VHPs together throughout the ages of eternity.   GLORIA J. STELLA FELDER

The Value of a Bush

Thou shalt not covet. Ex. 20:17.

FOR MORE THAN A year I had noticed a large bushy tree covered with clusters of light-pink flowers. I considered asking my employer's permission to dig up one of the small shoots that was already showing signs of one day being a grand flowering tree.

I paused once more to take in the delicacy of the clusters that made up each flowering stem to form the perfect object of my envy. During the drive home, I drooled over my own thoughts: *I'm sure not very many people have one of those. I will be one of those lucky few.* And anyone who saw it would deem me so lucky to own it.

As I surveyed the progress of my vegetable garden the next day, out of the corner of my eye I caught a slightly familiar sight. Where had I seen these flowers on this small, disarrayed shrub before? But the bell-shaped flowers were not as clustered; the branches were a little droopy; its trunk not as stately erect. Surely this could not be a replica of the beautiful tree growing yonder!

My mind traced the years of its occupancy there. I had forgotten about its existence because of the majestic roses, the tulips, the intoxicating aroma of the lilacs, and my pride and joy: the mauve clematis. I bent down to retrieve the faded and wrinkled tag still attached. "Beauty Bush," it read. How could I have passed by this small object, struggling to be the best that it could be?

How could I overlook the beauty I possess while coveting the same in others? Do I envy others and not look at what God has given me? Do I envy another's talents or church position? Or do I grow the best I can where planted?

Satisfaction can be in your own backyard. But you will have to acknowledge it, water it with prayer, nurture it with His Word, and seek diligently for all the beauty from your Creator that you can.

My branches may droop, my gems of truth may not be clustered in perfect unison, my leaves may not be as polished in comparison to others. But in my yard I am my Master's "Beauty Bush." I value myself because God values me. He dug me up as a little shoot and planted me in my corner of this world. I need no other gods; I have Jesus my Lord.   VIDELLA MCCLELLAN

August 4

A Sense of Belonging

Fear not, for I have redeemed you; I have called you by name, you are mine.
Isa. 43:1, RSV.

MANY YEARS AGO, after my divorce, I felt rejected and very lonely. I returned to college to improve my qualifications, but it took a very long time to feel wanted again. I was searching for any group that would count me in. I joined church groups, singles clubs, and organizations of all kinds just to get mail that made me feel a sense of belonging to someone or something.

Everyone wants to belong. That's why our verse for today is so special to me. No matter what happens, I can feel as though I belong to God. He has called me by name! He says, "You are mine." And Isaiah 54:5 affirms, "Your Maker is your husband—the Lord Almighty is his name" (NIV). There are many promises for our comfort. When I feel downhearted I read these kinds of verses and remember I belong to Him.

I like the words Ellen White wrote: "Christ does not cast valueless stones into His furnace. It is precious ore that He tests. He sees that the refining process will bring out the reflection of His own image" (*That I May Know Him*, p. 277).

That is me—made in His own image. There have been many tests in my life, and I am still having them, but I feel a sense of belonging when I know that God is in charge of my life as I commit it to Him each day.

The worth of myself comes not in what I do or who I know on this earth, but in who I am, a child of God. Yes, I am a daughter of the King, an heir to the kingdom. And God knows my particular personality traits. He created them! I have "more value than many sparrows" (Matt. 10:31).

To become accepted and belong to God's family is the greatest blessing we can have from God. I can praise Him every day for that. I no longer need to join so many organizations to feel a sense of belonging. Praise God, I belong to His family!

Dear Lord, thank You for giving me such worth. I belong to Your kingdom! I pray that I will know You better as I read Your Word and pray each day.

BESSIE SIEMENS LOBSIEN

My Place

I go to prepare a place for you. John 14:2.

I ALWAYS CHOOSE TO SIT in the same place in church, worships, and committees. When I attend meetings I prefer to sit in the same place that I sat for the first meeting till the end of the meetings. In order to make sure I get the seat of my choice, I go for the meetings early. When someone else occupies "my" place, I feel I am robbed of my possession.

It was 4:00 p.m. My husband and I walked into the church to sit in "our" place to witness a wedding ceremony that was to begin at 4:30. To our surprise, the seats were rearranged and our place wasn't there. So we sat in the next choicest place, where another couple usually sat. What if they came? After a short discussion we concluded that since they usually do not attend weddings as we do, they might not come for this one. Even if they did, they could find other seats, because seats are not assigned to anyone. We were at liberty to sit anywhere we liked.

A few minutes later the man walked in. I pretended not to notice him. He sat down right in front of us, turned around and said, "I came early so that I could sit in my place before anyone else did. But you seem to have come before me."

We explained to him about our similar desire to sit in the same place and our discussion before we occupied those seats. We mutually exchanged the fact that we feel more secure when we get the same seats, no matter where. Finally, like good Christians, we moved to another place and offered him "his" seat, which he accepted graciously.

As I travel to different places conducting meetings, I find many people choosing to sit in the same place. It is a consolation that I am not alone in this. But this did make me think about Jesus' promise: "I go to prepare a place for you." This place is for anyone who chooses to live with Him. I wonder how big, beautiful, and convenient it will be? Will the place be assigned already before Jesus comes, or will it be my choice and yours? Can I go ahead of others and reserve a place of my choice?

It doesn't matter where "my" place is going to be because Jesus has planned everything perfectly. All that matters is I should be there. And you, too.

HEPZIBAH KORE

August 6

The Wonderful Lime Tree

For the jar of flour was not used up and the jug of oil did not dry, in keeping with the word of the Lord spoken by Elijah. 1 Kings 17:16, NIV.

THERE IS ONE LIME tree in the garden in our home that neighbors and church members think is special. This is because for the six years that we have lived in our house here in Gambia, there has not been a time when one could not find fruit on this tree. Most lime trees bear fruit in a particular season, then dry out for some time without further fruit. So why is it that our tree is perpetually bearing? If it's not a miracle, then what is it? Only God knows. One thing I know is that we share our fruit with everybody.

In Gambia the lime is an important fruit that is used in nearly every home by almost everybody. Some people do not enjoy their meals without lime juice. They hold the sliced lime in one hand and squeeze the juice, little by little, onto their rice, fish, meat, or soup as they eat. Lime juice is also used as medicine. Some women and children even add lime juice to fruits such as mangoes as a kind of flavor or appetizer. So limes are essential to the extent that at those times they become scarce and expensive on the market, people ask or beg from friends and neighbors.

Thus, our lime tree brings many friends and neighbors to our home. My husband and I often pick a lot of the fruit and take them to the different churches as we visit to worship together. Sometimes I squeeze the juice and keep it in jars to be given away later.

Like I said, we have realized that this particular lime tree is different. Some people have even asked how it is that the lime tree in the pastor's house bears fruit year-round. All I can say is that this is a miracle tree, and I think God has blessed it for His people. After all, did Jesus not curse the fig tree that didn't bear fruit? Why can't He richly bless a tree that is ready to bear fruit to His glory? That's how God works. He glorifies Himself among His people in simple situations just as He did for the widow at Zarephath, who shared her meager flour and oil with Elijah. I believe He will continue to keep a little lime tree bearing all the year round. Indeed, our God is a miracle-working God.

MABEL KWEI

Unexpected Guests

Be ye therefore ready also: for the Son of man cometh at an hour when ye think not. Luke 12:40.

ONE OF MOTHER'S FIRST cousins was celebrating his fiftieth wedding anniversary, the perfect opportunity for a reunion. What a joy and a privilege to escort my mother to Philadelphia! My son called earlier during the week, informing me that he might come home for the weekend. A few days later I called for a confirmation.

"Mom, I don't think I'm coming home. I have a few chores to do, and I'm still thinking about it," said Andre.

So I didn't prepare any of his favorite dishes.

I picked up my mother the evening before the occasion so we could leave from my house early the following morning. Around 2:00 a.m., while dozing, I heard a door close. With my bedroom window up, it was difficult to differentiate my door closing from my neighbor's at times, so I remained in bed. As I became more alert, I heard male voices downstairs. I ran into my mother's room to alert her that someone had broken into my home. We could still hear those voices as we raced back to my room to call the police.

I tried to telephone my neighbor but couldn't remember her telephone number. My heart felt as if it were going to jump right out of my chest. Any other morning my throat is full of frogs and cracks, but this morning I screamed loud and clear.

Suddenly my mom said in a quiet manner, "That's Andre. I recognize his voice."

"Andre?" I replied. I managed by the grace of God to go down the stairs. "I thought you weren't coming home," I said.

"I thought you were going to Philadelphia," Andre answered.

I had rehearsed a plan of escape in my mind in case of such an occurrence many times over. How could I have so easily fallen apart? I plan to see Jesus one day, and I don't want to fall apart then.

Dear Father in heaven, please help me not to fall apart but to implement my plan to be ready for Your Son's soon coming is my prayer in Jesus' name. Amen.

CORA A. WALKER

Project of Love

Honour thy father and thy mother: that thy days may be long. Ex. 20:12.

FOR MONTHS I HAD prayed that God would give me a missionary project I could fit into my already crowded day. I had a full-time job, a son still living at home, aging parents across town, and my share of extracurricular activities. However, I was confident He had something special for me that would fit my time and ability.

Early that year my father had broken his hip while visiting in Massachusetts and was taken to the hospital where 62 years earlier he had courted Mother. The memory of their love story had been written everywhere—on the walks, the buildings, in the shade of trees aging along with them. Now, back in their home, the constant care began. My sister and I, with our husbands, did what we could to lighten the load, but Mother's anxiety was taking its toll. As the weeks slipped by we knew some changes had to be made. We prayed often. Then the idea struck us: Why not invite them to live with us? Dad had always said he would never burden his children, and we wondered if we could convince him. Mother was eager but remained silent, waiting for his decision. Twenty-four hours later, Dad accepted our offer.

That next morning as I prayed I realized God had indeed answered my request. Tears ran down my cheeks as I thanked Him repeatedly for designing a project just for me. I recalled how Jesus had blessed John by giving him the care of His own dear mother.

I hoped my parents wouldn't miss their lovely apartment. I tried not to panic as we searched for space to accommodate their belongings and make them comfortable. But their happy, grateful spirit multiplied our joy. Consigned to apartment quarters? Not in our house! We shared it all. Dad's car sat in the carport, ready to take them where they wanted to go, with one thing added now—a chauffeur. Dad once more began taking his walks, and Mother returned to her contented, mischievous self. For nine happy years our togetherness lasted without ever a hint of contention.

Now my parents await the voice of Jesus, but the cherished memory of the project He designed just for me fills my heart with gratitude and love for a God who cares.

LORRAINE HUDGINS

Lost in the Supermarket

The Son of man is come to seek and to save that which was lost. Luke 19:10.

REMEMBER TO STAY close to Grandma," my daughter Esther cautioned her two lively daughters, 6-year-old Bethany and 8-year-old Rachel, as they set off with me to the store.

"OK," both girls agreed. And they kept their promise as we selected tomatoes, grapes, and oranges. They helped push the cart as we selected yogurt, milk, and fruit juice. Then becoming bored as I read labels, they wandered off in search of something more interesting.

So engrossed was I in my task that I didn't notice they were gone. Suddenly the intercom crackled on. "We have two little girls in pharmacy who are looking for their lost grandmother. Will Rachel and Bethany's grandma please come to pharmacy?"

I chuckled to think that they thought it was grandma who was lost! About 10 yards from where they had left me, I found them waiting at the pharmacy counter. "Here I am!" I waved to the girl behind the counter who had the intercom in her hand. "The lost grandma is found!"

"Where were you, Grandma?" Bethany asked. "We couldn't find you!"

"You did exactly the right thing!" I said. "Now I'll try not to get lost anymore!" I did notice that the girls stayed pretty close to me for the remainder of the time in the supermarket. They weren't about to let Grandma get lost again!

I was not lost in the supermarket. I knew exactly where I was, but engrossed in the task at hand, I had not noticed that we were separated. We could have gone around in circles for a long time. By going immediately to the intercom, Rachel and Bethany solved the problem.

How often this grandmother does get lost in life, separated from God because of my focus on the task at hand. When that happens, how often I grumble because God seems to be lost to me when it is I who has wandered. I hope when that happens I'll be as willing as my granddaughters to go to heaven's intercom for help, crying out in prayer, "God, I'm here. Please come and find me!"

Lord, help me to stay close to Your side today. But if I wander, please don't let me stay lost. Help me to call out to You so that I may be found.

DOROTHY EATON WATTS

August 10

A Room of One's Own

When you pray, go into your room, close the door and pray to your Father.
Matt. 6:6, NIV.

THE WORDS TUMBLED OUT pell-mell and chased each other through the air. Her family had just moved into temporary quarters—matchbox quarters, according to Melissa. "We're like sardines in a can!" she wailed. "I don't even have a room of my own!"

"A room of one's own is an absolute necessity," I began.

"I knew you'd agree with me," she interrupted excitedly. "Will you talk to my mom?"

"While a room of one's own is essential, it doesn't necessarily have to be a literal space," I continued. "Sometimes it's impossible. It can be a virtual room, however, a place to which you can retreat at any time."

"A virtual room?" Her eyebrows reached for the ceiling. "As in virtual reality?"

I nodded, as the new idea grabbed her attention.

"Do you have one?" Melissa asked.

"I've had one for decades," I replied with some nostalgia.

"Oh, tell me about it!" Her entire body resembled a tightly coiled spring.

"The builder had never intended mine to be a room," I began, "just a pause between the first and second stories of my childhood home. Jutting out over the back porch, with three walls made of glass, this landing pad provided a near-perfect retreat. Mornings, unless rain or snow pelted the east windows, the sun shot its warm rays through venetian blinds. From the north a great expanse of green velvet rolled down to the churning whirlpools that were the Red River. Beyond, wooded hills stretched away toward Hudson Bay." I paused, wrapped in memories. "Snuggled in a comforter, hot chocolate leaving its ring on the tiny glass-topped desk, I could watch a private showing of the sunset as it played itself out against the clouds, with the ballet dance of colorful autumn leaves, or travel south with Canada geese. I could pray and dream."

"I can do this," Melissa replied excitedly. "Only until I get a real one again, though."

Do you have a room of your own where you can pray and dream? It's a must!

ARLENE TAYLOR

Family Photograph

I am with you alway, even unto the end of the world. Matt. 28:20.

LOOKING THROUGH OUR photo albums was one of our favorite Sabbath afternoon pastimes. Our girls were elated to see themselves when they were small, and hear the stories that we had to tell them about each snapshot. One particular Sabbath, Keleen, our second child, was struck with horror.

"Where am I? I'm not in this picture! It's not fair. You didn't take me. Kadia is here, but I'm not."

"You weren't even born yet," we explained. "How could you have been in the picture?"

It took us quite some time to explain to a distressed 3-year-old that she was not yet born when we had taken that picture, and that was the only reason she was not in the picture.

"Well, then, why wasn't I born yet?" she demanded. She felt so disappointed. She felt that the fact that she was not yet born was not fair, either. "Kadia was having so much fun, and you made me miss out on it."

Her concern caused me to think of our relationship with God. He has promised always to be with us, but sometimes we leave Him out. Where does He fit into our spiritual picture or our daily routine? Do we include God in all the aspects of our lives? Can others see Him in our frame? Are they disappointed by not seeing Him in the picture of our lives? If we have not thought about it, there are several ways He can be included.

Find a quiet place and time to communicate with Him through His written words. We include Him when we talk with Him daily. We include Him in our picture by telling others of Him each day. Praising Him for His goodness and taking time out to count our blessings is an important way of including Him. We include Him by sharing His love with others.

Today, begin anew to include God in your daily activities. Pause right now and let Him know how you feel about Him. Ask Him to help you renew your relationship with Him. You will feel especially blessed when He is in the picture right with you.

GLORIA GREGORY

The Investment

Who gave himself for our sins, that he might deliver us from this present evil world, according to the will of God and our Father. Gal. 1:4.

A LARGE FARM LIES BETWEEN my house and that of my daughter. There are acres and acres of fields and forests. Without a doubt the people have occupied the land for decades, as so many do in Virginia. The farmhouse is an old style, probably inherited from ancestors who might have homesteaded the land. The cows graze in the pastureland down by the creek. The bluebirds flit happily. Life is peaceful and serene for those who live there. It is always with a sense of well-being and peace that I drive by this house and acreage on my way to visit my family seven miles away.

One day I noted with consternation that there were workers in the woods with chain saws and axes. As the days went by, acres and acres of the beautiful woods were stripped of their trees. The logs were loaded on trucks and carried away. I mentioned to Douglas, my son-in-law, that I thought it a shame that all those trees were being cut down. His wise answer surprised me. "They probably planted those trees years ago for an investment. Now it's time for the timber to be cut and sold."

An investment! The thought had never occurred to me. The land belonged to the people—they could do whatever they wanted to do with it. It was part of a long-range plan, a goal.

How like the long-range plan God has for our lives. His investment. Jesus came to plant the seeds and watch us grow spiritually, day by day, watered by His love and His perfect example. It is called sanctification. We must link our souls to Christ, lean upon Him, and cut loose from the world, its follies, and enchantments, if we would grow tall and straight and pure.

When the work of cutting the trees was completed on the farm, I could see a magnificent view of the Blue Ridge Mountains, no longer obstructed by the forest. I now stop my car from time to time to drink in the beauty of the land transformed.

God has a more glorious scene for His faithful followers. We work out the obstructions of this life with help from above, and they will be as nothing when the investment plan is harvested for eternity.

LAURIE DIXON-McCLANAHAN

Waiting for the Reunion

Therefore keep watch, because you do not know on what day your Lord will come. Matt. 24:42, NIV.

IT HAD BEEN AN incredibly stressful string of months, and the strain was beginning to show on my husband. I suggested he get away for a few days. He was able to schedule a six-day trip the following month.

On the second day of this trip he called and talked about how much he missed our young son and me and wished he were with us. By day three he was questioning why he had consented to be away for so long. The next morning when I called his hotel room, there was no answer. Shortly after, I received a phone call from him saying he had gone to another location to take pictures and that I would be unable to reach him that day. It was very suspicious. This, combined with some other behaviors, led me to believe that he had decided to leave early and was on his way home.

Oh, how I anticipated his coming! Every car that drove into the cul-de-sac was scrutinized. I occasionally would walk by the window or look through the door to see if anyone was approaching. Thoughts of his coming permeated my activity that day, and my ears were tuned to any sound that would announce his arrival. I dressed in an outfit I knew he liked. I spoke to my friends and expressed my belief that he was on his way. We shared joyous laughter over the thought that he loved me and missed me so much that he had left early to come and be with me.

There is Another in my life who went away a long time ago. He said He would be back soon; He even gave me signs that would signal His coming. He misses me and longs to be with me, even more than my husband did. But what is my attitude toward His coming? Am I eagerly awaiting His return? Are my ears tuned to the sounds that announce His coming? Do I share the news of His soon return with those around me? Do thoughts of His soon coming pervade my life?

After much delay the reunion with my husband was sweet. I had missed him and was very happy to have him home. One day soon I will have another reunion with One who loves me. It will be so much sweeter than any earthly reunion. I am looking forward to that day. Are you?   ANDREA C. HERBERT

August 14

A Father's Love

How great is the love the Father has lavished on us, that we should be called children of God! 1 John 3:1, NIV.

I HAVE A CONFESSION to make. Even though I'm an adult by every standard, I'm still a daddy's girl. There's no denying it. I really like my dad. Sure, I love him, but I like him. I think he's funny. He is my friend, and I enjoy spending time with him.

He was my very first hero. I deeply respect his opinion and seek his counsel on major decisions in my life. We like (and dislike!) many of the same kinds of food, share a lot of opinions, and have the same odd sense of humor. There are several inside jokes that only he and I laugh at. We joke about how similar our walks are, and people say we even look a lot alike. None of us is perfect, and we had our rough spots as I was growing up, but he was always there, always loving me. It is said that true love is freedom, and he and Mom never pushed or forced anything on me.

I knew that if anything went wrong—even if it was my fault—his arms were always there to run to. And if I wanted to laugh, he could usually help with that, too. Although I have a good relationship with all my family, Dad holds a special place in my heart.

Dad loves me, but the Bible says that our heavenly Father has loved us with an everlasting love. He knows my every thought before I even think it, and still loves me. Am I as quick to return that love? Yes, I may profess to love Him. I may go to church every week to worship Him, but do I really know Him well enough to *like* Him? Is He my friend? Do I like the things He likes, love the people He loves, and do the things He wants me to do? Do I want Him to be with me when I go somewhere?

At times I am childish and reject Him, but He is still there to love me. He will always forgive me when I sincerely ask, no matter what I have done. He lets me choose my own path, even though at times I don't choose wisely. Because He loves me so much, He will never force His ways on me. The choice is mine, but He is always there, always loving me. And His arms are even bigger than Dad's.

VICKI L. MACOMBER

Adopted Grandmothers

The end of a matter is better than its beginning, and patience is better than pride. Eccl. 7:8, NIV.

I AM A CARD-CARRYING, ever-stitching, fabric-buying, rabid quilt fanatic. When our family moved 700 miles south to San Diego, California, I missed my old quilting buddies. My experience has taken me to quilting guilds across the United States. Quilting has gone high-tech, and many do not use leftover fabrics or pass down well-worn patterns anymore. Quilts are designed, color analyzed, and precision sewn.

A coworker told me about the quilting ladies at the local church. Inside the double doors lay a forgotten world. White-haired women were already busily working. Nearest the door was Emma, celebrating nine decades, working with a once-square piece of cardboard, cutting with dull scissors. She knew nothing about fancy rotary cutters or acrylic rulers.

In the far corner two women sat working on a beautiful scrap quilt. As I gently touched the quilt top, I asked if I could help. All eyes fixed on me; no sound could be heard. Had I spoken out of turn? It began to dawn on me that most of these ladies were nearly double my age. Betsy quietly asked if I had ever quilted. Briefly I detailed my experience. She was skeptical, but cautiously willing. Her instructions were thorough: quilt only on the print fabric (to hide any bad stitching), and not on the solid white. This was difficult. In other places I had been recognized as an expert, but not here—I had to keep quiet. After several hours Betsy inspected my work, with and without her glasses, and eventually blessed it. As we worked, I learned about their families, personal struggles, and successes, and we shared the intimate secrets of our lives.

One day Betsy slid a small bag onto my lap. "Don't look until you get home," she demanded. Dutifully but impatiently, I waited until I got home to find a stack of beautiful 1930s quilt blocks. As the months passed, I realized I had been adopted as I inherited a large collection of blocks, quilt tops, and scraps, each delivered with a warm hug, sometimes tears, and always a comment that the giver was sure that I would know just what to do with the gift. Whenever I work on one of those blocks I think of what my grandmothers taught me. Although we do not share blood, we are kin because of our shared love for quilting. Shirley Kimbrough Grear

Elevator Experience

Give, and it will be given to you. A good measure, pressed down, shaken together and running over. Luke 6:38, NIV.

I CAME OUT OF THE surgeon's office with a light step. I had just been told that the results of my last exploratory procedure were good news. I stepped into the small elevator on the fourth floor, already occupied by three other people. At the third floor a man in a wheelchair and his attendant were waiting to get in, so I moved over to allow the wheelchair and its attendant to drive straight in.

As we approached ground floor, the man in the wheelchair looked at me and said, "You have shared something great with me today."

"Oh?" I laughed. "I only shared some elevator space with you."

"No," he replied. "I don't mean that. You shared your lovely smile with us, and thank you for that."

I was stunned! I hadn't even realized I had smiled at the man in the wheelchair. "Thank you for mentioning it—it makes my day even better," I told the man, and we were out of the elevator and going our separate ways.

I walked to my car as if walking on air. I had just received good news, and my happiness must have shown on my face as I gave that man a smile. But I received back far more than I had given. The man in the wheelchair will never know what a boost those few kind words gave to my morale that day.

I realized that God gave me a gift of a smile, and I prayed that I would use that gift not only when good things have just happened to me, but when the going is tough, too. I also understood that the verse in Luke 6:38, "Give, and it will be given unto you," doesn't refer only to money.

I thank God, too, for the good things He gives, "pressed down, shaken together and running over." May we always be willing to share—even a smile.

RUTH LENNOX

Watch the Signs

I have told you these things before they happen so that you will believe [in Me] when they do happen. John 14:29, NLT.

ONE OF THE DUBIOUS (gulp!) pleasures of having teenagers is the duty of teaching them to drive. Having survived the first one, I am in the process of teaching my second son to drive, and soon I'll have a third child of driving age.

Besides the physical act of adjusting the mirrors, snapping the seat belt, pushing the gas pedal or the brake, and watching the speedometer, I always stress that they need to watch the signs. Ignorance of the law won't play as an excuse if the law is broken. The police officer that stops you for speeding is not going to be sympathetic if you tell him you didn't see the signs or didn't know what the speed limit was.

Signs are an important part of our life. They tell us where we are going, how fast we can go to get there, and how far we may be from our destination. Some signs may be distracting from our journey, such as advertising diversions, alternate routes, or (even more disruptive) barriers and obstacles in the road. Then there is the all-important stop sign. Officers of the law get quite upset if you attempt to drive by these without paying attention.

Jesus also told His disciples to watch the signs. He knew there would be a lot of confusion and commotion and distraction right before His coming, and He wanted us to have our eyes on the goal. He was very clear in pointing out what the signs would be. We know what our destination is, and the road is well marked. Oh yes, there are distractions and complications and detours. Sometimes a bridge is out, and there seems to be no alternate routes. But God is guiding us on this journey and providing the signs. All we have to do is watch and journey on. And there are no stop signs!

Lord, help me today to recognize the signs of Your soon coming. Don't let me be fooled by false signs and signs that are put up in my path to distract me and lead me astray. Don't let me be detoured by an easier path. I know where I'm going, and I want to get there safely. FAUNA RANKIN DEAN

Face the Foe

So then, submit yourselves to God. Resist the Devil, and he will run away from you. James 4:7, TEV.

STAND LIKE THE BRAVE, with thy face to the foe." This paraphrase of the last line of the old hymn's chorus flashed through my mind as our little black sheep stopped running, backed itself into the fence, turned, and with head erect, eyes alert, stood bravely facing us, in spite of its sickness. To it, my husband and I were the foe. Being part of a flock of sheep and not a pet, it didn't realize that all we wanted to do was administer medicine that would make it well again.

In due course we completed the task and walked home across the paddock. I pondered the spiritual aspect of our evening's task. The words of the hymn continued to ring in my mind, and I still had the visual image of that brave little sheep facing human beings it thought were the foe.

As I walked I began to think of our spiritual lives. Satan is the foe, and just as we had relentlessly pursued our sheep, so he also pursues us, not to administer helpful things but bad things that will continue to chase us through life. It is only as we become like that little sheep, where we stop and turn and face the foe and remember Jesus, that we will be able to defeat Satan.

At first we run from Satan when he puts us into situations of perplexity, fear, disappointments, and discouragement. Unlike the sheep, we haven't learned to face the foe. When we run from these things, Satan has us where he wants us. But when we stop and remember Jesus, everything changes. Just as the sheep stopped, and turned to face the foe, so must we. When we do so, Jesus enables us to change our outlook. Instead of dwelling in perplexity, fear, disappointment, and discouragement, He gives us the courage to look back and retrace our steps to see why the perplexity, fear, disappointment, and discouragement began.

When we stop to think, and seek Jesus through prayer, it is no longer necessary to run. Through the strength of Jesus we are no longer fearful. Life takes on a stronger experience that enables us to help another through similar experiences.

Lord, help me today to stand, face, and address the fears in my life so that the devil will flee from me. MAY SANDY

I Miss You

The Lord hath appeared of old unto me, saying, Yea, I have loved thee with an everlasting love: therefore with lovingkindness have I drawn thee. Jer. 31:3.

MY HUSBAND IS GONE for several days on an international business trip. Usually he calls me every day while on a trip in the States, but the country he's in is a difficult and expensive one from which to initiate calls, so I didn't expect to hear from him until his scheduled return.

When my husband is home, I try to spend as much of my free time with him as possible. So now, while he's away, I busy myself with tasks that I've put off. Cleaning out some drawers and going through stacks of papers, I run across several cards he's given me—anniversary, birthday, Valentine's Day. The sentiments inside and the handwritten notes are a reflection of his character—open, honest, unashamed affection. No calculation of words or worn-out clichés. Instead, a genuine, almost naive, expression of his feelings for me. These love notes stir the feelings in the depths of my own heart. "I must talk to him," my heart tells me.

I make a call to find his number. Then begin the calls to get to the country and to the hotel where he's staying. By the time I finally reach him, he's already asleep. When he answers the phone, he's very surprised, but pleased to hear my voice.

"I miss you," I say.

His candid response assures me that the feeling is mutual. "Only two more days, and I'll be home," he tells me.

"I can hardly wait," I reply.

After replacing the receiver on the hook, I sit and muse. How similar to the love that Jesus has for us. Although He has gone away, He's left us love notes in His Word, sentiments that are pure and honest, written in His own blood. Getting those words out and reading them will cause us to love Him more and not only want to talk with Him, but be with Him.

Prayer is the easiest way to talk with Jesus; it's neither difficult nor expensive. He's delighted when we call on Him. We can't bother Him, because He loves us and is interested in the least thing that concerns us. He's looking forward to the time when we can be together and see each other, face to face. That time will be sooner than you think. *Come, Lord Jesus. I miss You.*

NANCY CACHERO VASQUEZ

August 20

Free at Last!

Behold, the Lord's hand is not shortened, that it cannot save; neither his ear heavy, that it cannot hear. Isa. 59:1.

WE WERE LIVING IN Virginia in a split-level house. The family room, on the ground level, had a fireplace and a door that opened out into the yard. One summer day my two older sons ran up the stairs, yelling excitedly, "Mom, come quick! There's a bird inside the house, and he's flying around the family room, running into the windows!"

When I followed them downstairs, I saw the purple martin sitting on top of one of the curtain rods. We decided that he must have flown down the chimney.

"How long do you suppose that poor bird has been trapped in our house?" I wondered.

We tried to catch him, but he flew to the next window, banging into it. We got a twin-size bedsheet and, using it like a net, tried to catch him, but he flew away from us time and again. Then we decided that if we opened the door, positioned ourselves around the room, and waited for him to fly again, maybe we could get him to fly out the door.

For more than two hours we tried unsuccessfully to coax the bird out the door. If only he could have understood what we were saying he would have known we wanted to set him free. Finally, when we were tired and the poor bird was tired and traumatized, we were able to catch him in the sheet and turn him loose outside. The instant we opened the sheet, he flew away into the trees, happy to be free.

If he could talk I'm sure he would tell of his nightmarish experience of being trapped in a house with crazy-acting people, waving their arms, yelling excitedly in some strange language, and throwing sheets at him!

How often we are just like the bird! God wants so much to set us free from Satan's traps, and we dodge Him as if He were the enemy.

Lord, help us today to listen as You speak to us, and help us to surrender our stubborn hearts to Your saving grace.   CELIA MEJIA CRUZ

Strength in Knowing He's Always There

Casting all your care upon him; for he cares for you. 1 Peter 5:7.

I HAD BEEN GOING through a very difficult and seemingly unbearable time in my life. My marriage was dissolving; I was jobless; bills piled up. God seemed to be nowhere in sight. All my hopes and dreams seemed to be fading, and despair began to take over. I wanted to give up.

One day I decided to take a walk to ease my mind. I thought that by telling God all of my problems and grievances my heavy load would be lightened. Despite the sunshine and the beautiful and peaceful path, I couldn't find comfort and began complaining to God about all my problems. I told Him my hurts, my pain, and my anger. I even questioned His plan for my life and His reason for allowing me to experience such anguish. I needed immediate answers to my problems. I needed evidence that God still loved me and pleaded with Him to prove to me that He was still there.

As I continued my walk I approached a cemetery and began to examine the various tombstones. I imagined how devastating it must have been for those who had to experience the loss of these loved ones. Then I thought about my own family. Realizing that I had been taking so many things in my life for granted, including a loving and supportive family, good health, having a roof over my head, and appropriate clothing, my frame of mind changed.

My complaints turned into praises and thanksgiving. The walk I intended for placing all my burdens on the Lord turned out to be a walk of gratitude.

As subtle as it was, God assured me that He had been with me all along and would never leave me desolate. He also encouraged me to trust that He knows best, and in His time He would make things right.

Now I look forward to seeing how God will bring me through these trying times. Knowing and believing that God will work things out for my good strengthens my faith in Him.

Lord, help me to be grateful for the life You have given me and to use it to the fullest. Help me to never give up, knowing You will never leave me nor allow me to experience anything You know I cannot handle. Amen.

LINDA ROCHELLE DUNCAN-JULIE

August 22

God's Wonderful Angels

He shall give his angels charge over thee, to keep thee in all thy ways. They shall bear thee up in their hands, lest thou dash thy foot against a stone. Ps. 91:11, 12.

TRAVELING ON INTERSTATE 10 in our new truck and camper, we were on our way from California to Florida to visit family. It was a lovely day, and I was driving while my husband was snacking on a can of peanuts he had just opened. It was Sunday morning, and the freeway was almost deserted.

Suddenly there was a loud bang, and I almost let go of the steering wheel. The truck traveled from one side of the freeway, across four lanes, to the other side, leaning precariously on two wheels to the left, then switching to the right side. Peanuts flew everywhere as the camper threatened to topple over.

Frantically I grasped the wheel in an effort to steady the truck. My husband sat frozen, unable to say anything. "Lord, save us," I breathed. Before the prayer was scarcely out of my mouth I felt something like gentle hands take control of the truck. I heard a voice say, "Take your foot off the brake." At first I thought it was my husband speaking, but later I found out that he was as frightened as I was.

Slowly the truck came to rest at the side of the road. We were shaking as we got out to inspect the damage. The left front tire had blown out and shredded along the road. We marveled that not a car had been near us, because we had crossed the freeway about three times before coming to rest on the shoulder.

We thanked the Lord for saving us. It was a miracle that the freeway was deserted and that we had not caused anyone to be hurt, or worse. Right after that, traffic picked up. We were close to an off ramp and a service station and were able to buy a new tire. Soon we were on our way. How thankful we were that the Lord had sent His angels to protect us.

I will never forget the feeling of having other hands on the wheel.

Thank You, Lord, for Your watchcare over Your children. Help us to never lose sight of the fact that You are ever watchful of every aspect of our lives.

MARGARET E. FISHER

I Think I Can, I Know I Can

But they that wait upon the Lord shall renew their strength. Isa. 40:31.

AN EARLY SPRING THAW played havoc with my lean-to kitchen roof one year. I knew I was in big trouble when I heard the splashing on the countertop. I gathered up pots and pans to try to catch some of the drips before the puddle got any larger.

That was only one of many "thorns in the flesh" for me that year. It all started when a family of chipmunks took up residence in my attic. After months of my using traps and other deterrents, they finally gave up and moved elsewhere. *Now I can relax,* I thought. Well, not quite.

I came home one day to the sound of rushing water—a broken water pipe in the basement. Sometime later I went from too much water to none at all when the screen in the well became plugged. Luckily, I have close neighbors who allowed me to get water from their outdoor faucet until I could get things repaired.

When I was in the bathroom one day I noticed a parade of tiny ants on the vanity. Before long they invaded the kitchen sink, the pantry, and the cupboards. After several weeks of frustration I was able to get rid of them with the help of a "magic" potion.

The list goes on. I accidentally threw out a new supply of medicine with the trash, and a unit in the water heater bit the dust. I decided, enough already.

A dear friend who had a similar experience in his family some time ago remarked, "I'll be glad when enough time goes by that we can laugh about this." Some time was to pass before I had the courage to ask him, "Are you laughing yet?"

Have I laughed about my thorns yet? Yes, many times.

Even though I get disheartened at times, trying to keep my 100-year-old house from falling apart, I have so much to be thankful for. But I almost threw in the towel recently when my washing machine started acting up, putting out only hot water. So I had to have a new mixer installed, which meant more repairs.

"But they that wait upon the Lord shall renew their strength." My strength is constantly being renewed, and that's good enough for me.

CLAREEN COLCLESSER

Power Surge

Forget the former things; do not dwell on the past. See, I am doing a new thing! Isa. 43:18, 19, NIV.

IT'S FUNNY HOW THE same words can bring very different images to mind. For instance, take the expression "power surge." On the one hand, it can be very positive. Power surge—the burst of energy needed to finish a task, that second wind to get things done! It can range from inspiration that propels, to the short-lived energy derived from a piece of forbidden but oh-so-sweet candy.

Unfortunately, there is also the negative. An electrical power surge can start fires and damage equipment. If you have anything even remotely to do with computers, the thought of a power surge brings nightmarish mental pictures of lost data that can never be recaptured.

I had decided that it was time to give P31's newsletter a new look and had worked on the new issue for a good three hours. I was about to save my work when, you guessed it, there was a flicker. Only two seconds—but it was all gone.

"Why hadn't I saved my work?" I chided myself. The system had prompted me periodically to do just that. I really had meant to. Now all the shoulda-coulda-woulda in the world didn't much matter. I literally lay on the floor and shed a few tears for the time and effort wasted, indulging in a bit of self-pity and giving myself a few figurative kicks. Then the words I had recently read while passing a nearby church's announcement board came back to mind. "No experience is a waste if we learn from it." What had I learned? Then came the positive power surge.

I had learned a few things: l. layout design. I had invested time with this new layout, so the ideas could be re-created more quickly this time. 2. The blank page in front of me gave me an opportunity to break with the ideas that I had gotten locked into. So this change was not inherently bad.

Change isn't easy, but God knows when it's necessary. Is it time for you to try something new? It doesn't have to be big. Join me today and do something new. Drive down a new road, try a different color, walk on the other side of the street, go out a different door. And when you're doing something on the computer, save your work periodically!   MAXINE WILLIAMS ALLEN

A Wrong Turn

Since thou wast precious in my sight, thou hast been honourable. . . . Fear not: for I am with thee. Isa. 43:4, 5.

LOOKING BACK, THE previous year was a very good one for my siblings and nuclear family. We experienced two beautiful weddings: those of my youngest son and my beloved great-niece. We celebrated the births of my grandson and a grandnephew. However, it was on the occasion of my son Eric's wedding that we experienced God's providential care.

The sacred wedding ceremony was carried out with the usual hush, smiles, and wonder. The reception was quite festive. The members and friends of First church in Washington, D.C., were most hospitable and gracious with an outpouring of gifts and good wishes.

Following the reception, we began our trip back to our hotel in Gaithersburg, which was several miles away in Maryland. We had been given directions; however, it's difficult to follow even the best directions in a strange town at night. Arthur was somewhat familiar with the route and drove the lead car, but he somehow made a wrong turn. One can only imagine the horror of being stranded at night on a busy highway. We were lost. Which way to go? The entourage of cars pulled over so that Arthur could get his bearings. As it happened, a gas station was right across the highway from where we stopped. Behind our car was my other son, Ron. Little did we know that Ron's gas gauge had been on empty. We proceeded to the gas station. Ron, decked out in his military dress uniform, had no money with him. Praise God for the $6 in my small purse.

After arriving at the hotel safely, we realized that the wrong turn near the gas station had been providential. God had protected us, and that wrong turn was truly a blessing in disguise. Even now, I remember this incident with gratitude to our God, who is always at the crossroads of our lives. How good God is to us!

How blessed we are to know, O Lord, that although we are sometimes lost on our Christian journey, You find us and gently guide us back to Your path. Thank You for loving us and taking care of us, even when we may not recognize it. Amen.   MARTHA J. WALKER

August 26

A Call to Halt

Anyone, then, who knows the good he ought to do and doesn't do it, sins.
James 4:17, NIV.

COMING HOME FROM A biking tour that last Friday afternoon of our at-home vacation, I thought about preparing some extra chicken for my dearly loved two cats. I have to admit that the older male, Harlekin, and the cute young female, Jody, helped fill that empty space deep in my heart from not having a child.

Usually chicken is very welcome for both cats; however, that Friday night Harlekin refused to take even a piece of it. Yes, I had noticed that he had not eaten too much food that week, but this happened at times. All of a sudden I knew this was something serious.

He had been our first cat and had already spent more than 10 years with us. We didn't know his real age, as we had gotten him from an animal home. The next day I took Harlekin to the veterinarian. It was not good news, and he died quietly the following Tuesday night.

It still hurts. I could not even go to work that day. Instead, again and again I recalled the past 10 days, feeling I was guilty of paying too little attention to my good old Harlekin. I went to the animal home to look for another companion for Jody that same afternoon. It was also to relieve my grief and guilt, but it didn't help because I had to work it out.

You may say, "This was only a pet, and everybody knows that cats would never reach a human age and, moreover, he certainly enjoyed his years in your household." I agree; however, Harlekin's sudden death reminds me how often I am not aware of the condition even of those I love most—my husband, my parents, brothers or sisters at home or at church. Too often I am too busy doing my own things—my job, my housework, my hobby—thinking I will spend some time with them tomorrow, that I may let them know that I love them next time, that I will give them a hug after I have done my work. Actually, we never know if there will be any other chance. How painful it is to recognize that we may not get a second chance.

I pray to God not to miss any chance to share my love, which is actually the love He has given to me.

HENRIKE POTTHAST

Blind?

The Lord gives sight to the blind. Ps. 146:8, NIV.

IT WAS LATE SUMMER, and I had been very busy for many weeks that included a four-week Spanish course, coming back home, going back to work, visitors, making visits myself. Although this was rather "positive" stress, I felt worn out.

Then one Friday morning when I arrived at work I couldn't see clearly anymore. This was the third time this had happened within the past few months. I lay down on one of the benches in our office kitchen, hoping that my sight would become normal again after a few minutes. A half hour passed, but nothing changed. I really got frightened and started to panic. What would it be like if I did not gain my normal sight again? Would I become blind? What would happen if I became blind? I would have to quit my job. I couldn't read, look at the beautiful nature, or see my friends anymore. I would be completely dependent on others. My whole life would change! *O God, please don't let this happen! What shall I do?* These were the thoughts that flashed through my mind.

I phoned the emergency eye clinic, but they refused to accept me without a referral from an eye specialist. I had none in whom I trusted. I started to cry, got a headache, and had to go home. I was in the depths of despair, not able to think logically. Completely exhausted, I slept for about an hour. When I woke up again, my sight was normal, but I still had a terrible headache. I was able to think clearly again, and I called my family doctor.

She received me immediately. After a thorough checking, she told me that nothing serious was wrong with me. An eye specialist to whom she referred me the same day confirmed what my family doctor had said. There was too much stress, which had caused a migraine in my eyes.

As I left the doctor's office my heart was filled with praise and gratefulness to the Lord. I remembered the Bible stories telling how Jesus healed blind people. I thought about the question What would be worse, to be born blind or to become blind? I came to the conclusion that the important thing was that the Lord opened my eyes that day. I appreciate now so much more the perfect gift that the Lord grants us in seeing. *Praise the Lord!*

HEIKE EULITZ

No Time to Stand and Stare

There is a time for everything, and a season for every activity under heaven.
Eccl. 3:1, NIV.

WE LIVE IN A society that demands instant gratification. We have fast food, fast cars, and fast communication services. We have become used to getting everything instantly.

I was reminded forcibly of this at a recent flower festival I organized. A woman was soaking a block of the water-retaining foam into which flowers are inserted. It takes only 30 seconds to completely soak a block, but this woman couldn't wait. As the block floated on the water, she reached over and pushed it under. Instantly, it looked full of water and she put it in her dish.

She seemed appalled when I told her that her flowers would die if she used that block of Oasis. You see, by pushing the block under the water, she had created air locks, and although the block looked full of water, when we cut it open it was apparent that parts of it were bone-dry. What's more, because of the composition of the block, it was impossible for the dry parts ever to take up water again. The block had to be discarded.

Conversely, if a block of Oasis is soaked correctly and is kept wet, it will keep flowers fresh for the span of their natural lives, and it can even be used again and again. Once it has been allowed to dry out it is useless.

We all live busy lives these days, and often it is tempting to rush our devotional time; to cut down on the time we spend with God. If we do, we are in danger of having dry spots in our lives, and the flower of God's love will die. Especially because we are so busy, we need to take time to be "soaked" by the Holy Spirit. Taking time with God at the beginning of the day will not only give us spiritual refreshing, it will give us the physical and mental vigor to accomplish all we have to do.

Lines from a well-known poem ask, "What is this life if, full of care/We have no time to stand and stare?" ("Leisure," W. H. Davies, 1871-1940). Today let us take time to soak up the water of God's Holy Spirit, to talk to our Father in an intimate way, to stand and stare at the wonders He has created for us. If we do, our lives will be fragrant with the love of Jesus and we will have time for the important things of life.   AUDREY BALDERSTONE

Simple and Insignificant?

For lo, the winter is past, the rain is over and gone. The flowers appear on the earth, the time of singing has come, and the voice of the turtledove is heard in our land. S. of Sol. 2:11, 12, RSV.

I TOOK AN EARLY-MORNING stroll to inhale some fresh air and to contemplate God's wonderful love to me. The cooing of the turtledove sounded like a special song to me, welcoming in the new day. Just a song of a gray bird, but peace flooded my soul. The honeysuckle hedge could not be ignored as I sniffed appreciatively at the fragrance from the sprays of such tiny white flowers.

I noticed tiny lemon-colored flowers with cushionlike centers between the pavers in the path. There were yellow flowers, too—as small as my fingernail. Further I noticed some tiny lilac and mauve flowers with very short stems. On the verge grew purple flowers in clusters with longer stems. I got absorbed in admiring the beauty of these simple and insignificant little flowers. How they got there, I do not know, but I know God made them. No one takes notice of these simple, insignificant flowers. They are trampled on, ridden over, and mowed down, but these little flowers keep growing and lifting their heads to the sun.

Some women are like these simple, insignificant flowers, shying away between the pavers or on the verge. Some are also trampled on, ridden over, or mowed down by being abused, ignored, insulted, maybe for lack of education or finances. But just as these simple flowers daily lift up their heads to the sun, so can women also lift their heads to the Sun of righteousness.

We may appear to be simple and insignificant to some, but we are of value in God's sight (Matt. 10:29-31). We have talents that may still be hidden between the pavers that need to be identified to bloom and grow.

There was an "insignificant" girl named Mary. God sent the angel Gabriel to her to say "O favored one, the Lord is with you! . . . You will . . . bear a son, and you shall call his name Jesus" (Luke 1:28-31, RSV). Mary was from poor and humble origin. Simple and insignificant? God chose her to bear the Holy Child!

Thank You, Lord, for using the simple and insignificant. You love me so incredibly! You make me feel that I am special and cared about. Help me to love You more. PRISCILLA ADONIS

Volunteers

But the Helper, the Holy Spirit, whom the Father will send in My name, He will teach you all things, and bring to your remembrance all things that I said to you. John 14:26, NKJV.

THE BIBLE SHOWS US that the early Christian church leaders were volunteers. With the help of the Holy Spirit, they not only worked for the Lord, they also worked in various occupations to pay for food and clothing. The first volunteer, of course, was Christ Himself, who volunteered to leave a sinless world for a sinful one so that we will be able to leave a sinful world for a sinless one.

I have always believed in volunteering, both in the church and out. As a retiree I find I am giving much of my time in volunteer work, both for my church and for other organizations. I am church clerk, communications leader, coeditor of the church newsletter, and Bible class teacher each week. I serve as the church school chairperson, and gym-building committee chair, write two articles each week for the local newspaper, serve as treasurer for our food co-op, and write two newsletters for my husband's antique car clubs. As some other retirees have been known to say, "How did I ever manage to work all week, too?"

Our church is having a booth at the local fair this year. Since I have been involved in fair booths in the past, I have volunteered to help. It will be simple, since we are a small church. I am glad we will have a presence there this year. I thank God for the opportunities He provides to share. We have many retirees who say, "We have worked in the past; let the younger generation do it now." I think we all have to do what we can.

Retirement is not really a biblical concept. When we are active in body and in mind, we will be healthier, live longer, and be mentally competent longer. Research shows that those who no longer keep their mind active are more likely to get Alzheimer's disease or senile dementia. We may not be able to avoid these problems, but with the Lord's help we can certainly try.

Dear Lord, help me each day to realize what a privilege it is to work for You. Help me to remember that I will gain a blessing when I help others, whether I am young, a student, a worker, or a retiree. But most of all, help me to want to do it as a gift to You. LORAINE F. SWEETLAND

Be Still, and Know That I Am God

The voice of thy thunder was in the heaven: the lightnings lightened the world: the earth trembled and shook. Ps. 77:18.

IT SOUNDED LIKE A train rushing with tremendous speed right through our backyard. I was awakened by this most unusual noise at 1:30 in the morning. I pulled myself out of bed to investigate the source of this pandemonium.

All the trees in our backyard were at a 90-degree angle. Large objects were being tossed around as if they were small toys—chairs, tables, garbage cans, and what appeared to be sheets of plywood. It was as if the skies had opened up with a gale-force strength and poured forth buckets of water.

I called to my husband, who by that time was sitting up, rubbing his eyes, and asking what was going on. He told me to get the baby and go down to the basement. By the time I turned around to run to our daughter's room, objects had started hitting the house.

As I headed out of our daughter's bedroom toward the stairs, there was a sudden crash. Something extremely large had hit our home, shaking the entire building to its foundation. My husband was directly behind us and with one push we all fell into an open closet to the only safety we could find. We then felt our way down to the basement through the darkness. We sat praying in the corner, listening as the wind picked up and died down and then picked up again for another hour. We prayed that the Lord would spare our lives and protect us from the unknown conditions outside.

It wasn't until the sun came up that we could see the full extent of damage that had been caused by four small tornadoes that had formed over Lake Michigan. Giant trees and telephone poles had been snapped off like matchsticks, and damaged houses and debris were everywhere we looked.

This extreme example of unleashed power of the elements of nature shows how helpless we are, as mere humans, and how much God loves and protects us every day.

God's power is greater than the mightiest wind, rain, or thunder. We are under His protection daily. We can live without fear of the elements. "Be still, and know that I am God" (Ps. 46:10). CATHY L. SANCHEZ

September 1

Unforgettable Translation

I can do all things through Christ who strengthens me. Phil 4:13, NKJV.

M Y CHURCH, IN MY hometown of Jakarta, Indonesia, was preparing a program to tell my country about Jesus Christ. They needed some help to translate materials from English into Indonesian, so I volunteered.

As I translated the first material, which talked about the devil and his evil kingdom, I felt so restless, weary, and reluctant to continue translating. It was as if a voice spoke in my ear. "Why do you have to burden yourself with this work? No one cares if you cannot finish this translation. Don't bother yourself with this project."

I decided to translate the second lesson before finishing the first. As I translated this material, which didn't touch on anything about the evil kingdom, I had no difficulty at all and finished it within a short time.

When I went back to translating the first material and once more had difficulty, I realized that the enemy doesn't like the idea of disturbing his work. Then I prayed, "God, please give me the strength and the wisdom to be able to continue this translation. I know the enemy doesn't like this idea, but Lord, help me to be able to finish Your work so that people will know the truth and only Your name will be glorified."

After that, I continued translating again. And praise the Lord, this time, with God's help and strength, I was able to translate the 23 single-spaced pages only two days before the deadline.

I asked my sister, Daicy, who also helped translate, if she had had an experience similar to mine. She told me she had no difficulty, but she had no lessons regarding the devil. Then I asked Mrs. Sumarauw, who also helped translate. She mentioned she also had the same experience as I had.

Thank You, Lord, that Your loving kindness never fails. Thank You that You are always there for me, and help me to do all things through Jesus Christ who strengthens me. Lord, please help me to be Your instrument for Your honor and glory. LANNY LYDIA PONGILATAN

The Pretty Box

God sees not as man sees, for man looks at the outward appearance, but the Lord looks at the heart. 1 Sam. 16:7, NASB.

BACK IN THE 1970S when I was in high school, girls took home economics and boys took shop. I loved home economics, creating and sewing a dress, planning a home, and especially advancing my cooking skills. I received good grades and especially enjoyed this class. One quarter the school decided to have the girls and boys switch classes, so I got to take shop.

The first day of shop we were told that we were going to do a woodworking project, and I knew just what I was going to make: a recipe box! I distinctly remember telling the shop instructor that I wanted to make a 3" x 5" box. He showed us how to measure and cut, glue and sand. I lovingly worked on my recipe box, imagining how nice it would be when I could put it to use. I completed the box with a nice finish, and even added brass hinges and a cute brass latch.

I was so excited; I couldn't wait to see what my recipe collection would look like in the box. Before I was able to take it home, I brought in a recipe card, just to see how it would look. I was horrified to find out that the 3" x 5" recipe card did not fit into my pretty 3" x 5" box. My box was too small—it did not serve its purpose! The only reason I had made the box was to hold my recipe collection, and now the box was worthless to me. I'm sure you figured out the mistake that was made. In my inexperience, I didn't compensate for the thickness of the wood.

How many times do we take off on our own, planning, working, and building something we think will be just wonderful. We plan, we organize, we phone, we get all excited about "our idea," only to find out that the plan is too small. God knows about all the ins and outs. He knows the beginning from the end. He knows the big picture. If we could simply learn to take our plans to Him, we wouldn't have the disappointment of a box or a plan that is beautiful on the outside, but doesn't serve its purpose.

Lord, help me remember to bring all my plans to You first!

JUDY MUSGRAVE SHEWMAKE

September 3

A Letter From a
Teenager to a Teenage Sister

Don't forget the excitement of being young cause you to forget about your Creator. Honor him in your youth before the evil years come—when you'll no longer enjoy living. Eccl. 12:1, TLB.

DEAR SIS,
Today is a really special day for two reasons: first, it celebrates the day you were born, the day I got a playmate, someone to share the punishment with, to make up songs with, to play Barbies with, to joke with, and to share with. Today is special because it is the anniversary of our "sisterhood," something that means the world to me. With you, all my guard and pretenses are put aside and I am free to be me. That's why I love being with you. Thank you for being such a great sister, one whom I love and need.

Today is also special because you're 13, a teenager! Now don't go dyeing your hair pink or anything like that! These years are going to be what you make them. To some the teen years are the most difficult, a time of being out of control. To others they are a time of growth, fun, memories, and enriching experiences. Already you have experienced feelings inside you that you don't exactly know what to do with—frustration at not being allowed to wear what you want, having a crush on someone, etc., but just always remember Jesus is there. He was a teen once too. He will help you sort out these feelings and relationships. Trust in Him—He'll always be there.

One essential during the next few years will be communication. Whenever something is on your mind, let someone know. Talking things out and letting people know how you feel, in a nice way, avoids a lot of mess that could be created if you keep it all in to explode later. If you feel uncomfortable, tell Mom and Dad. They will be understanding, no matter what. They love you so much! The same goes for me.

Because of the person you are and your love for Jesus, these years will be wonderful.

I thank the Lord for you and the joy and love you bring me, Beamy. Remember that the choices you make now may change your life forever. My baby sis is growing up! Whenever you feel angry or confused, I'll be here and I'll understand.
SUSAN JEDA ORILLOSA

Faith That Brought Back the Ship

I tell you the truth, unless you change and become like little children, you will never enter the kingdom of heaven. Matt. 18:3, NIV.

THE BUSLOAD OF 60 excited schoolchildren rounded the final bend toward the jetty. The ship that ferried people and vehicles across to Ovalau was in full view. The children, many of whom had never taken a boat trip before, stood up to get a better view of the sea and the big ferry. They all exclaimed, "There it is! It's coming; it's coming!"

The excitement and happy noise got even louder and louder as children chattered about this new experience and imagined what it would be like. The adults on board the bus, however, looked at their watches and wondered about the destination of the boat.

On closer observation they determined that the ship was already on its way to Levuka. They had missed the boat. In bewilderment, they wondered what had gone wrong, why the boat had left without them, and whether the Lord had other plans for the children for the weekend.

The boat was now well into the deep waters. In desperation, the teachers quickly got together to decide what to do. The children, on the other hand, kept up the excitement, sang songs of praise, munched peanuts and dried beans, and maintained their trust in their heavenly Father that they would be on Levuka that same day.

Suddenly the children shouted with joy, "Look! Look! The boat is coming. It's coming!"

Sure enough, the boat was coming back. The big ferry reberthed at the jetty, the busload of schoolchildren was driven on board, and the children were bound for Levuka.

God made the captain decide to return just to pick up a plank—but most of all to take on board children with great faith. Even the captain of the boat said, "You children must have something special that a big boat had to come back for you."

God reminds me that my faith and Christian experience has to be similar to that of little children. Why do I worry when this great God has a way out for me in all my circumstances?

Thank You, God, for the faith of children. May we, through the power of Your Spirit, have this faith strengthened each day. FULORI BOLA

September 5

We Shall Behold Him

The dead in Christ shall rise first. 1 Thess. 4:16.

SHE STOOD IN THE bedroom, folding her things into a suitcase. It was just a brief stop at home in the transfer from the local hospital to the university hospital for more tests. She called me in and said, "Lois, I know what I have. It's cancer."

"Oh no, Mama, the doctors don't know yet," I interrupted.

"I know I am dying," she continued relentlessly. "It's all right. I'm tired."

Well, and why shouldn't she be? If anyone had had a hard life despite a generous spirit, it was Alpha. After almost dying twice of malnutrition in her childhood, she, one of four girls in a family of 13, had virtually raised her younger brothers and sisters.

She and her husband had one major thing in common—their love of children. Yet out of the six they had, two had died in childhood, almost more than a parent can stand. Even then, with an inner stamina she had kept together the young remnants of her sister-in-law's family after the parents' tragic deaths and a threat that the five youngest would be split up. She continued loving them even after they grew up and left. She never uttered a word of regret. Nor would she hear a word against them when others thought they seemed lacking in gratitude.

At 14 I, who did not really remember the deaths of my sisters, watched her grieve when my oldest brother drowned, and again wondered how she endured. Then shortly after her own mother's death she was diagnosed with breast cancer and had a mastectomy at the age of 55. Finally her last three were almost grown—I had just graduated from college, my sister was almost finished, and my younger brother had joined the Army after his troubled teenage years. Now at 57 she was telling me, "I'm ready to go to sleep. I'm not afraid to die. I'll just fall asleep," she said calmly, "and the next voice I hear will be that of Jesus."

Two weeks later she was asleep, resting in the arms of the One who had been her comfort throughout life.

Despite my tears I remember her words: "The next voice I hear will be that of Jesus," and I also cry, "O death, where is thy sting? O grave, where is thy victory?"   LOIS K. BAILEY

What if You Couldn't Read a Story to Your Children or Grandchildren?

You are the light of the world. . . . No one after lighting a lamp puts it under the bushel basket, but on the lampstand. . . . In the same way, let your light shine before others, so that they may see your good works and give glory to your Father in heaven. Matt. 5:14-16, NRSV.

I WAS WORKING ON the cover story for *Women of Spirit* magazine. One of the topics to be covered was literacy. Although literacy needs in the developing countries are well known, I had a sneaking suspicion that in modern, computer-savvy North America there were literacy needs as well.

Surfing the Internet, I found Literacy Volunteers of America (www.literacyvolunteers.org) and was surprised to learn that there are many people in this country who can't fill out a job application, read food labels, or even read a simple story to their children. I was amazed.

Around the world there are 1 billion adults who can't read. Most are women who can't read a Bible, help their kids with homework, or read the instructions on their medicine bottle. Learning such startling statistics, I thought, *Wow, reading and comprehension skills are so basic to making it in life! What can I do to help?*

I discovered that the easiest way to find out how you can help in your community is to call your local library or county board of education. I was put in touch with reading teachers in the schools near me. And what a reception I got! After one teacher heard I wanted to volunteer with literacy she cried, "You're mine!" You can read to younger kids during your lunch break or help older kids with comprehension skills or tutor college students in the evening. The sky is the limit, and arms are open wide to welcome you to the rewarding joys of literacy volunteering.

And just think—when you help a woman learn to read, you unshackle her to dream beyond her low-paying job or welfare status. And more than that, her whole family is empowered to develop the talents God has given them.

And when you read to young children, you are bathing them in the light of love and compassion. You're letting them know they're important, significant, special. Only eternity will tell the lives you have touched with the light of God's love.

HEIDE FORD

Dove Bars?

*My mouth will tell of your righteousness, of your salvation all day long.
Ps. 71:15, NIV.*

TWO HOURS. IF I could just make it another two hours it would be Sabbath, and I could forget all the things that had stressed me out all week. I could relax in my 24 hours of freedom. Today had been a microcosm of the past week. Up well before dawn, by the time traffic was getting heavy on I-4 I was at the home of a forgetful, elderly diabetic patient, attempting to teach him how to check his blood sugar. Next came a lonely, elderly woman with not only an open sore on her leg that required a complicated dressing but also emotional pain that required simple listening. Then on to a young multiple sclerosis patient living by herself and attempting to cope with overwhelming needs. Another patient followed in a roach-infested tenement who required complicated procedures and instructions; and another in a huge, beautiful home who craved human companionship much more than the needed medical treatment.

Finally the last patient was cared for, but this day—and this week—had taken its toll on me. I was tired, my head was hurting, and I just wanted to be home with my family. All week I had not found time to grocery shop, and if we were to eat over the weekend I had to stop at Publix, the supermarket.

Finally the grocery shopping was done, the bags were loaded in the car, and in two hours it would be another wonderful Sabbath. But I couldn't make it anymore. It had been five hours since my brown-bag lunch. My head was pounding, and I was just so weary. I rested my head on the steering wheel and prayed for strength. With a deep breath I started up the car and backed out of the parking lot. And then I saw it. God performed a miracle for me! A Dove Ice Cream Bar van opened its little window in front of Publix and was giving away free Dove Bars! I am certain God really does like chocolate. I stopped right behind that van and received a delicious ice cream bar from those angels in Dove Bar uniforms.

As I drove home, between bites I praised God for His incredible thoughtfulness. Then I thought, *Is it chocolate God likes, or is it me? Either way, I'm ready to spread a few more Sonbeams!*   SUSAN WOOLEY

Make Your Day

Do not boast about tomorrow, for you do not know what a day may bring forth. Prov. 27:1, NIV.

THIS MORNING I SAW a very touching scene. As I approached a school bus picking up kids, I watched as two young boys walked down their driveway toward the bus. Both were looking backward and waving. As I came to a stop I could see their mother standing in the doorway of their farmhouse, waving back. Finally the driver turned off the flashing red lights, and we passed each other. On the other side of the bus I saw the mother still standing there waving as the bus disappeared from sight.

Wow! I thought, *such a loving send-off for the day.* My mind began to wander. First, I wondered what kind of goodbye started the day for a 5-year-old girl who somehow got run over by a school bus last year. Then my thoughts turned to a mother in our little village who just last week left her 14-month-old son in the tub for a minute while she answered the phone. He drowned, and she never had a chance to say goodbye. Then there is the mother who left her husband and little boy because they weren't willing to share her new beliefs. The cult she joined told her to consider them dead to her, so she did.

How many times was I glad just to get our daughter out the door on time when she was in school? Forget about the goodbye part. I wish I could relive some of those days and include a happy goodbye, but I can't change the past.

Every day we have choices. We can make the day or break the day for others and ourselves. And we will face the consequences or reap the rewards.

Someday it will be different, though, because we have the promise of a bright and beautiful tomorrow. Instead of goodbye, it will be hello forever, and it's with this hope that we face today. As the old hymn says, "Some golden daybreak, Jesus will come," and because we have chosen Him as Savior, all the battles will be won.

Somehow I just knew that those two little boys I saw were going to have a good day, whatever the day might bring. And I know that mother will have no regrets if by some evil turn of events something bad would happen during the course of the day.

DONNA MEYER VOTH

September 9

Leave It There

Casting all your care upon him; for he careth for you. 1 Peter 5:7.

IT WAS SABBATH MORNING. Bill and I had just returned to Tennessee
from a trip to Florida for avocados. We had made our scheduled deliveries
but still had avocados to sell. Avocados do not keep very long.

When I awakened, this burden automatically popped into my mind. Then
I remembered: *It is Sabbath; I don't have to worry about selling avocados today.*
Instead, I thought of this text: "If you stop trampling on the Sabbath by pursuing your own interests and pleasures on my holy day, and honor the Sabbath,
making it a delight—not doing your own work or talking about your own
business on that day but considering others—then you will find the joy that
comes from serving the Lord" (Isa. 58:13, 14, Clear Word).

But it's hard to control your mind.

I was reminded of the words of an old hymn: "Leave it there, leave it
there, take your burden to the Lord and leave it there. If you trust and
never doubt, He will surely bring you out; take your burden to the Lord
and leave it there."

When I got up for my prayertime, I talked to the Lord about my burden,
and I was reminded of one of the operations performed for me by that marvelous invention, the computer. After I have typed a letter on my C drive and
want to save it to a disk on my A drive, I punch the appropriate keys. And
behold, a little picture shows my file fluttering from a folder on the left to another on the right.

I thought, *Isn't it wonderful that I can say a prayer, and the Lord's computer
transfers my burden to His unlimited network that has all the solutions to all of
my problems?*

*How can I thank and praise You enough, Lord, for Your omnipotent power
and unconditional love!*

"Let me tell you of the kindness of the Lord and the other deeds for
which He should be praised. Just think of all the Lord has done for us, of the
many good things He has waiting for His people. He is not only just but full
of love and compassion" (Isa. 63:7, Clear Word).   RUBYE SUE

260

Wait on the Lord

Wait on the Lord: be of good courage, and he shall strengthen thine heart: wait, I say, on the Lord. Ps. 27:14.

IN 1997 I WROTE my Lo+2 ISC exam from Narasapur, Andhra Pradesh, India. I was living at my uncle's and was teaching children until I got my results. I was anxiously waiting to see my grade when it was announced about six weeks later. Unfortunately, I was still at my uncle's place, but my grades were sent to my mother's. So I kept praying, *Lord, help me to pass my exam.*

My mother opened the envelope and saw it was sad news. I had failed the ISC in two subjects and passed only in the division exam. It was difficult for Mother to tell me, since I had passed each class except for the second class.

Mother came to visit to tell me the results. When she first saw me she said, "Child, don't be discouraged. I will still be willing to support you the second time." You see, my mother is supporting me alone. I felt even more hurt that I hadn't succeeded. I cried bitterly and opened my Bible to find God's promise. I needed to be comforted and to decide how to reach my goal.

Soon I discovered a promise in Psalm 27:14, our text for today. That really encouraged me a lot. The second text I found was Philippians 4:13: "I can do all things through Christ which strengtheneth me." These two verses were the exact encouragement I needed, and I was able to decide what I should do. I wrote my ISC again and was successful this time!

It is not easy to feel we have failed, but I praise You for bringing me through the experience and for strengthening my faith. Please be with those today who may feel like they have failed and do not know which way to turn. Help them to find the courage they need to face the future with You.

Now I am taking nursing as a profession and being trained to be the Lord's ambassador to serve humanity. The Lord is blessing me abundantly. So if we wait on the Lord, He will strengthen us and help us in our troubles and difficult times. Wait on the Lord!   SUSHMA EKKA

In the Dark

Fear not: for I am with thee. Isa. 43:5.

IT WAS SHORTLY AFTER the terrorist attacks on the World Trade Center and the Pentagon, and everyone was edgy. The FBI and the Justice Department had put everyone on high alert for another attack. Early in the evening a friend called to say that an acquaintance in the intelligence service had told him to be especially careful that weekend. Because we live in the Washington, D.C., area, we all felt very vulnerable. And I was alone.

My husband was out of the country, so I settled down in the family room for a quiet Friday evening of reading. Soft music played, and all was peaceful. Suddenly the lights went out—all of them, everywhere. Not for long, but long enough for the answering machine to click off and on, the compact disc player to restart, and all the clocks in the house to begin blinking. Not for long, but long enough for every conceivable sort of scary scenario to go through my mind.

I prowled through the house, trying to decide what had happened and what to do. Everything seemed to be in order, so I finally returned to my chair and my reading. But I couldn't get the event out of my mind. Was it a fluke, or had something more sinister happened?

Fear. Fear of the unknown. Not because there is danger, necessarily, but just because it is unknown. It fascinates me how often the first thing angels said when they appeared to people in the Bible was "Don't be afraid." The angel told Zechariah, "Do not be afraid, Zechariah; your prayer has been heard" (Luke 1:13, NIV). The young Mary was told the same thing: "Do not be afraid, Mary, you have found favor with God" (Luke 1:30, NIV). And, of course, we all remember that the angel told the shepherds, "Do not be afraid. I bring you good news of great joy that will be for all people" (Luke 2:10, NIV). From fear to joy in Jesus Christ.

This world is filled with fear. Fear of the unknown. Fear of the known. Thank God, however, whether the lights are on or off, whether terrible things are happening or we are enjoying peace and quiet in our own homes, He is there. The angels told the shepherds, "Glory to God in the highest heaven, and on earth peace among those whom he favors!" (Luke 2:14, NRSV). That is our hope and peace today. Fear not. He is with us.

ARDIS DICK STENBAKKEN

Tested With a Test

Behold, I will do a new thing; now it shall spring forth; shall ye not know it? I will even make a way in the wilderness, and rivers in the desert. Isa. 43:19.

THREE O'CLOCK. WHERE HAD the time gone? My schedule had been juggled and squeezed to fit everything into an increasingly crowded day, and there were still two things I needed to do. There was no time for both.

I knew when I decided to return to college at 32 that it wouldn't be an easy task. I was by no means in shape to run mental races with young minds, fresh out of high school. It seemed my brain was sluggish from nonacademic use. It needed a jump start to shake away the cobwebs. Beside that, I didn't feel comfortable attending classes in the North after growing up in a segregated South in the 1940s, even though it was now 1974. But I was determined. I would get my associate's degree, no matter what. I'd sacrifice. I'd get up a couple hours earlier than my four young daughters. I'd prepare for my classes and be a good student, wife, and mom. But today the routine didn't work. Somewhere I had tripped up. Fallen short on the thing I needed most: time.

The clock stared back at me, proof of my dilemma: 3:09. The minutes quickly ticked away. It seemed that I had just put the girls down for their afternoon naps. Somehow, between laundry, dinner, picking up after the girls, and settling squabbles, I had gotten off track. The hours had whizzed by, and when I finally sat down to study for my class test I discovered it was late afternoon and I hadn't even had my daily Bible study. There wasn't any way I could do both—It had to be one or the other.

I picked up my textbook and put it down. "If I flunk, I flunk," I told myself. My time with God is one thing I wouldn't sacrifice.

That evening when the professor entered the room, I waited for him to give instructions for the exam. He looked around the class, then without any explanation announced, "The test has been canceled."

I was shocked. I hadn't asked God for special favors. I left the situation to Him; however, He chose to work it out. I had sought God and His righteousness—and He had handled the rest. ETHEL FOOTMAN SMOTHERS

September 13

What If...?

The Lord knows what we think. He knows how irrational and futile man's thoughts can be. Ps. 94:11, Clear Word.

OUR PLANE MAKES A near-smooth landing at the Lahore International Airport in Pakistan. As we descend the ramp to the shuttle bus, I instantly feel the hot and humid air. The setting September sun does not bring any relief.

Evelyn eases her way out of the parking area onto the highway, skillfully dodging bicycles and pedestrians. The air hangs heavy around us. We exchange pleasantries, but with the van's windows open, coupled with the honks and beeps of cars, trucks, motorbikes, and rickshas, conversation is quite impossible.

Some thoughts come whirling into my mind. "What ifs" tumble one after the other, somersaulting in disarray. *What if our decision to come to Pakistan is a mistake? What if this incessant noise becomes unbearable? What if the heat gives me the dreaded rash again? What if we can't make it here? What if...*

My face is hot and red. My shirt is wet with perspiration. My head throbs. Then I hear Evelyn say that the temperature has actually gone down, that July and August are the hottest months. But when the cooler months arrive, they forget how hot the summer is.

Inwardly, I feel embarrassed. Why all these unpleasant thoughts? Where is my faith that this call was from the Lord? Didn't we pray for guidance as we made our decision? I send a quick petition to God to change my thoughts into more grateful ones.

I focus on what Evelyn is saying. I look around. I see tall eucalyptus and shady juniper trees that line the highway. We pass by mango groves along the canal road that leads to the compound. I catch sight of carts filled with bananas, cantaloupes, watermelons, grapes, guavas, and pomegranates arranged in an appealing display. I see possibilities of a better life ahead.

I thank God for giving me thoughts that are more satisfying. I thank Him that in spite of my doubts and weaknesses, He tells me that I am a possibility—a possibility for His kingdom. What an awesome thought!

MERCY M. FERRER

264

Airline Tickets and Love

Love covereth all sins. Prov. 10:12.

THE FEUD HAD STARTED with a mix-up of airlines and airline tickets, and there had been terrible confusion just before a long-awaited trip. My husband and I were going overseas to visit our son, who lived on the other side of the world. Because Laudia was the travel consultant, I blamed her entirely. None of it was her fault, not one thing, but I was really angry.

The anger stayed bottled up within me, and on my return Laudia and I had an enormous argument. I have no doubt that half the company heard us as we shouted at each other. I blamed Laudia, she defended herself, and neither of us would back down. So if there was one person at work I hated, it was Laudia. We would glare at each other if we passed—and if looks could kill? To avoid her, I would go into the staff lunchroom or someone's office or the ladies' restrooms, or anywhere handy. If I could avoid Laudia, I would.

Months came and went, a year passed, and gradually Laudia and I learned to be civil to each other. (After all, we were both grown women.) We could now pass each other in the passageway and exchange a "good morning."

Then Jesus came into our lives. Different places, different ways, but at the same time, and oh, what a change! The former hatred was replaced with love. We would work side by side in the office in complete harmony. Going to work was extraspecial now. I had Laudia to share my faith with. We could talk about experiences; we could laugh together. Nobody has such a beautiful laugh as Laudia. You simply have to laugh with her. A beautiful laugh, an infectious laugh.

Years have come and gone, and our love for each other and, more important, our love for God have grown. Situations do change, though, and sadly, today was Laudia's last day at work. She starts at a new place of employment soon. How I will miss her; miss her smile; miss that wonderful laugh.

Tears filled our eyes as we hugged goodbye, but the tears were replaced with smiles as we talked of the soon coming of Christ when separation will be no more. What a day that will be!   LEONIE DONALD

September 15

To Have Eternal Life

And eternal life means to know you, the only true God, and to know Jesus Christ, whom you sent. John 17:3, TEV.

I WAS BORN AND brought up in a non-Christian, idol-worshiping family. I memorized all the slogans of that religion one should know. I used to go to the temples at 5:00 a.m. every day to worship, five days a week. I used to fast for the idols.

After my graduation I found a job as a teacher in a nursery school in a remote village that didn't even have regular bus service. One day at work I heard someone teaching about a vegetarian diet and about temperance. I started asking questions regarding the Bible and its teaching. For three long years I studied the Bible with the pastor and finally accepted Jesus as my personal Savior. I respected God's Word and obeyed. I stopped my idol worship and started to read my Bible and pray to the true God only.

My parents gave me lots of trouble. They asked me not to read the Bible and pray to Jesus, so I had to go to church on Sabbath without anyone in my family knowing. I read my Bible in the bathroom and prayed in secret. I even fasted and prayed without anyone knowing. I was baptized after much fasting and prayer. When I came home after my baptism, my family members beat me and told me that I was an untouchable. They threatened me and ordered me to leave our home. I left my home without anything. I explained all this to the pastor who had given me the Bible studies. He discussed the matter with the church leaders. Finally, by the mercy of our Lord Jesus Christ, the pastor married me because of my steadfastness to Jesus.

Today I am very strong in the Lord. Nothing can shake my firmness or the love of my Lord Jesus Christ. My Lord has blessed abundantly. He is my everything. I visit many villages with other people and preach the gospel where the illiterate villagers are perishing because there is no one to share Jesus Christ or the love of God with them.

Lord, many people have accepted Jesus Christ, been blessed, and have given their lives to You so that they can have eternal life. I thank You for Your love that has guided and blessed my life too. GIRIJA DANIEL

September 16

Wait and Be Blessed

And so after waiting patiently, Abraham received what was promised.
Heb. 6:15, NIV.

IN THE CHRISTIAN WALK, waiting plays a very important role. One should know that God has His own time. It is only when we are in tune with Him that we can derive the most benefit from the waiting period. In Hebrews 6:15 it is written, "and so after waiting patiently, Abraham received what was promised."

For 12 years I have taught in a nonsectarian, private high school. Life at home was difficult. Many of us, though we worked hard, still lived in poverty. Thus, almost everyone, including myself, dreamed of migrating to other countries to look for greener pastures. Friends told me to leave my job and work abroad.

Some of my friends left home to work outside the country and even promised to send for me when they got settled. But the promises were broken. None of those who made those promises sent for me, and my hopes vanished. Finally a friend came home for a holiday in South Africa, and I told her of my desire. Through her help I got a job in another country, and my dream was realized.

It took long years for such a dream to come true—I almost gave up on it. But now I realize that it was during that waiting period that God was teaching me how to be patient and to put my trust in Him. I do believe that it was God's plan for me to be where I am today. Though I waited so long for the realization of my dream, I received blessings far beyond my expectations. Not only did He provide me with material blessings but, most important of all, He helped me grow spiritually.

We should not get ahead of God and go beyond His divine leading. We should not expect Him to respond immediately to our prayers if that is not best for us. We cannot hurry God, because He knows better than we. He has a purpose for everything that comes into our lives. In His time things will be made beautiful.

Are you losing hope in waiting for an answer to your prayer? Don't! Though it tarry, wait for it, because it will surely come.

MINERVA M. ALINAYA

September 17

Renewed Vision

Now we see through a glass, darkly; but then face to face. 1 Cor. 13:12.

SUDDENLY THE WORLD WAS light and bright as the doctor removed the patch from my right eye. Brilliant sky blue and verdant spring green came into focus, along with a crystal-clear white. I was excited! For six years I had lived in a graying world as the cataract slowly clouded my vision. Road signs had now become unreadable from a distance. Frequent changes of eyeglass prescriptions had not helped. At the annual checkup the doctor had stated, "It is now time for your cataract to be removed."

It was not without qualms that I submitted to the surgeon's scalpel. Now it was done, and what a contrast. Brightness, light, and vivid colors! It had all started so imperceptibly, this gradual graying process that had seemingly become normal to me. My world had become grayed, and I knew it not. But now in a matter of moments all was changed.

How like my life! Compromises, grayed perceptions, half-truths, creep in and imperceptibly cloud my world. When I cry to the Lord for the cleansing of my heart and life, He brings the surgeon's scalpel and shows me wherein my sight was imperfect.

In another way the apostle Paul wrote, "Now we see through a glass, darkly; but then face to face." I can't wait for the day when my spiritual eyes will be perfect, and I will see the beauties and wonders of the heavenly home He has prepared for me. The grayed perceptions of my earthly life will forever be gone. My spiritual discernment will be sharp and bright with clear contrasts. I will look into my Savior's face and see Him in all His glory. For as it is written, "Eye hath not seen, nor ear heard, neither have entered into the heart of man, the things which God hath prepared for them that love him" (1 Cor. 2:9).

Lord, help me today to trust You as my spiritual surgeon and know that the trials You allow to cross my pathway can be the very scalpel needed to remove film from my vision. Allow me to see You in Your beauty and holiness and to keep my gaze fixed on the heavenly home You have prepared for me. Amen.

JOAN MINCHIN NEALL

God Wanted a Girl

For you created my inmost being; you knit me together in my mother's womb. I praise you because I am fearfully and wonderfully made; your works are wonderful, I know that full well. Ps. 139:13, 14, NIV.

SARAH WAS CRYING. SHE was beautiful, extremely talented, with a wonderful family. She was married to a minister, and together they made a very effective team. She was a talented musician, famous across her whole country. But Sarah was crying because all her life she had tried to please her dad, and she had never quite made it.

For years she couldn't understand why he didn't accept her. Then, in her 40s, she began to realize that it was because she was a girl, and not a boy. She was the youngest of four daughters. That last pregnancy was his last chance to have the son he longed for, but he had yet another daughter. Out of his own pain and loneliness he had found it so hard to accept Sarah.

Discovering the problem was a mixed blessing. She could never meet his need for a son—that took pressure off. But neither could she ever be the son her dad longed for.

Sarah shared her story in our prayer group one day. We prayed for her and her father as the tears rolled down her cheeks. As we were saying our goodbyes, I felt strongly impressed to go to Sarah and say something. I didn't know what I was going to say. I was shy and clumsy, and knew I would probably say the wrong thing. But it was as if God picked me up and led me over to Sarah. I gave her a hug and whispered something in her ear. To me, it seemed a very simple sentence, but it moved Sarah's heart. To my astonishment, she hugged me and laughed and cried, and said, "That is the most beautiful thing anyone has ever said to me!" What I had said was "Sarah, your dad wanted a boy, but God wanted a girl. God wanted you just the way you are." That simple sentence transformed Sarah's picture of herself, her dad, and God.

Sarah's story is not unique. Many women are hurting because their fathers wanted a son, or because of other unmet expectations and hopes. But God says to each of us, "No matter what anyone else wanted, I wanted you— just the way you are. You are special to Me as a daughter, and I'll love you and accept you forever!"

KAREN HOLFORD

The Made-up Bed

I meditate on the works of your hands. I stretch out my hands to you; my soul thirsts for you like a parched land. Ps. 143:5, 6, NRSV.

IN A FLURRY OF preparation, I cooked, cleaned, and did the laundry. My brother and his family were bringing our parents to welcome in the new year with me. I was excited, but fatigue seeped through my pores. *Just for three minutes,* I promised myself as I sank into my favorite armchair and closed my eyes. I had not yet made up the bed in the room where my brother's family would be staying, but there would be time enough I promised myself.

The doorbell awakened me a half hour later. I rushed to the door to greet the family. As we sat around the supper table a little later, my youngest niece whispered excitedly, "Auntie, I have something to show you."

"Not now, darling. I have some things I have to do right now. But later, I promise."

Huge tears welled up in Briana's dark brown eyes, but she said nothing more. Clearly there was something important I had to see, and I had to do it right then. As the others continued eating, I slipped out of my chair, telegraphed a message to my sister-in-law, and took Briana's hands.

Smiling, the child ushered me into a bedroom. The king-size bed was as perfectly made up as a 5-year-old could manage it, comforter and all! I was amazed. When the bed was new, making it by myself was a gargantuan task. Now a little girl had done it all by herself.

"I had to stand on the bed in my socks sometimes, but I did it, auntie; I did it!" My niece was ecstatic.

It was my turn to swallow tears. Where were my priorities? I had almost missed her special gift. And I had said I had other important things to do just then! How could I have said that, knowing that her visit was brief?

God showers gifts upon us daily. He sends them, but we often miss them. Sometimes, lost in the bustle of our daily living, we do not even notice His handprints on each blessing we receive. What are our priorities?

Forgive us, dear Lord. Help us trace Your hand in everything we see, everything You do.   GLENDA-MAE GREENE

September 20

Doves Versus Jays

As soon as Jesus was baptized, he went up out of the water. At that moment heaven was opened, and he saw the Spirit of God descending like a dove and lighting on him. Matt. 3:16, NIV.

FOUR FEEDERS AND THREE birdbaths are visible through our sliding-glass doors. My husband and I never tire of the entertainment provided by our feathered friends as we sit down to eat. During the winter hordes of goldfinches in their brown winter garb gorge on thistle and sunflower seeds from the tubular feeders. House finches pick through the wild birdseed on the platform feeder. Much of the food drops to the ground, where the golden and white-crowned sparrows, juncos, and mourning doves gobble it up.

There is a constant phenomenon that never ceases to amaze us. A host of feathered creatures may be animatedly feeding and bathing, when suddenly the sky fills with fleeing birds. In the blink of an eye everyone clears out. Why?

It's only a few more seconds before the culprits come into view. The scrub jays have moved in for their lonely feast. Some uncanny sense of selfishness pervades the atmosphere when they arrive. Their raucous, aggressive personality drives almost everyone else away.

On the other hand, when the large, sleek mourning doves descend into the crowd and mingle with the ground-feeding goldfinches, sparrows, and juncos, nobody is even slightly disturbed. In fact, they seem to enjoy their camaraderie.

Occasionally we witness a confrontation. The jays try to grab some ground feed, and the doves ruffle up their feathers and stand their ground. The jays always beat a hasty retreat.

As I contemplate the scene at the Jordan River and the scenes in our backyard, they are intertwined. The dovelike Holy Spirit prepared Jesus to meet and confront Satan in the wilderness and throughout His life. This Holy Spirit power also made it possible for Jesus to "draw all men to [Himself]" (John 12:32).

Jesus, I want more than anything to confront my self-centered thoughts in order to reach out to every person who crosses my path, whether my family, my church, or my community. Give me a joy, a radiance, that will be possible only through the dovelike power of the Holy Spirit. DONNA LEE SHARP

A Well to Be Desired

If ye shall ask any thing in my name, I will do it. John 14:14.

MY HUSBAND AND I knew this would be the last house we would build. Over the years of our marriage we had built several homes to accommodate the changing needs of our family. For the past two years we had been looking for some acreage on which to build our dream home. My husband, Norman, was raised on a large farm in Canada; his love of the earth and growing things are still very much a part of his life.

One sunny fall afternoon we were out for a ride. He had picked up a real estate magazine on his way home from work. One listing took us to a winding dirt road through the countryside. We were unable to find a For Sale sign, so we used the cellular phone to call the real estate company. The property had been listed that day, and the agent had not had time to put the sign up yet. When we met her at the property the next morning, she quoted us a reasonable price and told us that the road was to be paved in early spring. We made an offer and purchased the land before the For Sale sign was ever put up. The agent remarked that she thought the Lord intended for us to have it, since six other people were waiting to see it. We felt the Lord had blessed our purchase.

We had great fun poring over house plans, finally selecting a builder we had used previously and trusted to do a good job. Both of us were at the land the afternoon the well drillers arrived. We excitedly watched them set up the equipment and wondered what kind of well we would get. I leaned over to Norman and said, "Let's ask Jesus for a good well."

We bowed our heads right there and prayed that we would get a well full of good water suitable for household use and outside watering. A vein had been hit at 90 feet yielding 10 gallons per minute. We were delighted, but my husband asked them to drill a little deeper. Soon one of the men came to us, smiling, and informed us that they had struck another vein yielding 30 gallons per minute. He said we had enough water for several houses. We were ecstatic.

After the casing had been put down and a cement pad had been poured around the well, I took a nail and wrote, "Thank You, Jesus." I was not ashamed to tell anyone that Jesus had given us an outstanding well full of pure, cool water!

ROSE NEFF SIKORA

Love and Obey

When he was made perfect, he became the source of eternal salvation for all those who obey him. Heb. 5:9, TEV.

IT'S EASY ENOUGH TO get a pet to obey you when you offer it a treat. Likewise, if you scream at your dog every time it does something wrong, it will soon figure out what it is that makes you so angry. Rewards and punishments are something even a small child can understand. But there's another way to get your dog to obey you—get it to love you.

One of the things I learned when I took my dog to obedience classes was that the words or signals you use to train your dog aren't all that important. What is important is the relationship you have with your animal. Once your dog trusts you and understands that you're in charge, that you're the leader of the pack, all you have to worry about is telling it what you want it to do.

My grandma had two dogs, strays left by cousins, and they were perfectly behaved. She never took them to an obedience class or even cracked open a book on dog training. She simply decided that she was the one in charge, and her animals obeyed her—and loved her. Though not an animal lover by nature, any pet left in her care thrived. They were confident and secure, always knowing what was expected of them.

Modern secular society tends to view Christians as legalistic because they choose to obey the Bible. Spirituality, defined as a vague feeling that there is some sort of power running the universe, is considered acceptable. Religion—the hard-core kind where you actually go to church regularly and spend time in Bible study and prayer—is considered, if not a bad thing, at least old-fashioned and hopelessly out of date.

Those who embrace "spirituality" without embracing God just don't get the point of obedience. You don't obey Him so that you can get on God's good side. You obey Him because you're already there. It's not a question of obeying a list of "thou shalt nots" to win a ticket to heaven; it's simply cause and effect. The cause is a loving God; the effect is obedience. Being a better person doesn't make you a Christian, but being a Christian makes you a better person. And you don't even have to go to obedience school to learn how to obey God. GINA LEE

September 23

A "Hot" Retreat

But the day of the Lord will come like a thief. The heavens will disappear with a roar; the elements will be destroyed by fire, and the earth and everything in it will be laid bare. 2 Peter 3:10, NIV.

THE WOMEN'S RETREAT HAD been a blessing so far. The messages had been challenging, especially the last one Sabbath evening regarding the end of time. Now it was time to go to bed and be ready for the Sunday morning activities.

A noise I could not identify immediately woke me up. After a few seconds of trying to organize my thoughts, I looked at the clock—it was 2:00 a.m., and the noise was the hotel fire alarm. I woke up my roommate.

"It is the alarm of a car. Go back to sleep," she said.

"Norma, we are on the twelfth floor. No alarm from the parking lot could be heard up here," I insisted. To be sure, I opened the door and saw the emergency lights going on and off in the hallway and other sleepy faces emerging from rooms, wondering, like I, if it were a real fire.

My roommate was hard to wake up and even harder to convince to leave. We put on our shoes and coats on top of our nightgowns, grabbed our purses, and went down the stairs.

What a spectacle that was! Some young girls were outside in the cold, wearing only oversize T-shirts. A few more mature ladies had had time to dress completely. Many had dragged all their luggage down the stairs. Quite a few had rollers in their hair; others displayed their beautiful hats. You could hear conversation and laughter and complaints and prayers.

I never found out exactly what happened in the hotel that night. Some said it was a small fire in the penthouse. Others said it was a fire drill. What I know is that the Sunday message got a new meaning. What if, instead of a fire alarm, the noise had been the trumpets of the angels announcing the second coming of the Lord?

Had we been ready? What was important to each of us at that moment? My roommate was grateful I had insisted she go outside. The other women traveling with us were in a sober mood during our return trip—both had slept through the whole thing!

ALICIA MARQUEZ

274

Beware of the Dog

They helped every one his neighbour; and every one said to his brother, Be of good courage. Isa. 41:6.

THERE ARE MANY WALKING trails where I live, and on occasion I discipline myself to walk 30 minutes to my volunteer job and home again. On one of my not-so-rushed days, I walked to work. The day was calm and refreshing as I walked home at a brisk pace, absorbed in thought, until I noticed a big dog coming toward me in a suspicious manner.

I'm not a lover of dogs to the extent that I'd like to own one, but neither am I afraid of them. However, there was something about this dog that made my heart beat faster. My mind raced to decide how to handle the situation. My first instinct was to not change my pace or show fear.

A busy street ran beside the trail, but no cars were in sight. Even if one did come, would I be able to get the driver to stop? I had to come up with an alternative, and fast! I glanced on both sides of the trail, hoping to see a big stick—a very big stick. There was no weapon on the freshly mowed grass. I didn't even have an umbrella in my satchel, only my sweater. Even the satchel wouldn't inflict much injury, no matter how hard I might fling the bag. Time was running out as the distance between us shortened.

Suddenly a red sports car appeared. Without any signal from me, the car stopped opposite the dog. The driver rolled down his window and whistled. The dog stopped. The driver made more shrill sounds. The dog stared in his direction several seconds, and then turned around and loped off into the woods.

When I came abreast of the car, the driver asked if that was my dog. When I told him it wasn't, he said he didn't like the dog's demeanor so thought he better stop in case there was trouble. I thanked him graciously, but words couldn't convey the extent of my relief.

We all appreciate a kindness shown, especially when least expected. This experience has taught me to be more alert. Should an opportunity arise, I hope I will not hesitate to lend a hand to one in potential danger.

EDITH FITCH

The Race of Our Lives

Remember that in a race everyone runs, but only one person gets the prize. You also must run in such a way that you will win. 1 Cor. 9:24, NLT.

IN SEPTEMBER 2000 THE Olympic Games came to Sydney, my home city. What an exciting time it was as Sydneysiders mingled with the thousands of athletes and overseas visitors in a partylike atmosphere. The spectacle of the opening ceremony was thrilling: the symbolic flame hovering high over the stadium, the Olympic rings glowing in lights from the Sydney Harbour Bridge, and the elation when a local athlete claimed gold in front of a roaring home crowd. All made for indelible memories. One of the most poignant images to come from the 2000 Olympics was the distressed face of a young race walker disqualified from the 20-kilometer walk just 200 meters short of the finish line.

Race walking is a difficult sport with complex rules governing the required leg action. Several other top athletes had already been disqualified, a disappointing and frustrating end to months of training and hard work. But for the Australian girl, it was a particularly bitter blow. She had a clear lead and was on the very point of entering the stadium to complete the race. She could hear the crowd inside cheering for her in anticipation. She could almost smell and taste victory; the gold medal was hers! Then an official holding up a red card stepped into her path. The television cameras captured the moment as her face registered horror, disbelief, then anguish. It was the race of her life, and she had lost. The prize was wrenched from her grasp.

No doubt the apostle Paul, a first-century games spectator, would have sympathized with her predicament. While encouraging fellow Christian "athletes" he certainly didn't want to miss the prize himself. "So I run straight to the goal with purpose in every step," he said. "I discipline my body like an athlete, training it to do what it should. Otherwise, I fear that after preaching to others I myself might be disqualified" (1 Cor. 9:26, 27, NLT). However, winning the race of our lives is not so much about what our limbs are doing as where our eyes are focused. "Let us run with endurance the race that God has set before us. We do this by keeping our eyes on Jesus, on whom our faith depends from start to finish" (Heb. 12:1, 2, NLT).

JENNIFER M. BALDWIN

God Cares—and Acts

Before they call I will answer; while they are still speaking I will hear.
Isa. 65:24, NIV.

I WILL NEVER FORGET that Friday afternoon. On my way home I usually pick up Rene, my part-time schoolteacher daughter, at her home. That Friday she phoned to tell me not to pick her up, as she was meeting a former colleague who had taught with her at high school. I had no idea where they were meeting, so I decided to do my Friday shopping at a mall near my home.

After the usual drift from shop to shop, I was about to take the escalator down to the ground level when, to my utter amazement, I saw my 6-year-old grandson, Ivan, coming up the escalator toward me. The Alberton Shopping Center was the last place I expected to find him, as Rene did not tell me where she was going. And he was alone!

I asked why he was alone and where his mother was. He said he didn't know where she was. He had gone to the men's room while Rene had gone to the mothers' room to change his baby brother's diaper. When he came out, he claimed that the door was locked, so he concluded that his mother was not there anymore. He had searched all around the first floor, gone to the ground floor, and was now coming back upstairs because he couldn't find her anywhere.

Hand in hand, we went to look for Rene. We found her still in the mothers' room, still busy with little Eric, unaware that for some time Ivan had been wandering on his own around a very large, very busy and, for unaccompanied children, potentially dangerous place. The potential for trouble and panic staggers the imagination when I think of how Rene would have reacted when she found Ivan missing.

That evening I marveled at what a wonderful God we serve. Only a watchful and loving God could have placed me at the right place at exactly the right time to see my grandson coming up an escalator all by himself. In the life of the Christian divine care goes far beyond coincidence!

Thank You, Lord, for Your infinite love toward Your children!

Denise Newton

While I Was Speaking

I love the Lord, because he hath heard my voice and my supplications. Ps. 116:1.

SQUINTING IN THE AFTERNOON sun, I walked the four blocks from the bus stop to my parents' home to wait for my husband. We had been married for a little more than a year, and inevitable financial obligations seemed to be overwhelming us.

"You know what I need, God? An evening job," I said out loud. I had taught English as a second language in the evenings for a time, but had had to quit because of schedule conflicts when I enrolled in a master's program. Shortly after that there was another schedule change, and I wondered if I'd reacted too hastily by giving up my evening job.

There were a number of language centers where I could find part-time evening employment with attractive compensation. I had sent out many résumés but had not received any answers.

"That would take care of a lot of bills," I continued as I opened the gate and petted Rook, the too-energetic golden retriever doing his crazy little welcome dance.

The phone was ringing—there was nobody home. I dashed up the stairs, followed closely by Rook, who thought it was a new game. "Dinorah Blackman?" a pleasant male voice asked. "I have in my hands the résumé you sent us last year. Are you still interested in teaching evening courses? And could you begin tomorrow?"

Surprised and almost speechless, I wrote down directions and instructions.

With a lot of enthusiasm, he told me how much I would be remunerated per hour and asked if I would be available for 10 hours a week. Making quick mental calculations, I realized that not only would we be able to pay the bills, there would be enough left over for fun things!

An instant answer to prayer! What a wonderful God who supplies all our needs and some of our wants, according to His own timing!

I hung up the phone in awe. As I bribed Rook into leaving his spot on Mom's sofa, I whispered, "Thank You for hearing my prayer and for answering while I was yet speaking."

DINORAH BLACKMAN

GPS

And thine ears shall hear a word behind thee, saying, This is the way, walk ye in it, when ye turn to the right hand, and when ye turn to the left. Isa. 30:21.

IT WAS TIME FOR a new minivan, and I was so excited with the one we had chosen. It came equipped with a global positioning system (GPS). This new feature intrigued me. "If you put in any physical address, with city and state," the salesman had assured us, "it will give you directions on how to reach your destination." *Wow! I'll never be lost again,* I thought smugly.

Soon I was off to visit a friend who had recently moved. "Just give me your address," I said confidently when she began to provide me with directions, "and I'll see you soon." I typed in the information.

"Proceed to the highlighted route," a pleasant voice invited, and off we went.

I had had a general idea on how to go, but the GPS had promised to get me there. The positioning arrow showed our progression. *This doesn't look right,* I thought after driving a bit, so I pressed the button again.

"Continue for six miles," the same pleasant voice encouraged.

"I'm counting on you," I quipped. "I've got only 10 minutes to make it on time."

"Slight left turn ahead." After following several more instructions I was beside myself. Where was I going? But still I proceeded.

"Destination ahead on your right," the voice announced triumphantly. I couldn't believe it. Just as it said, the destination was just ahead. It had brought me a different way to my destination. And shorter, too, I would later learn.

The spiritual application hit me loud and clear. If I could place such confidence in a computer system, proceeding even when the way did not appear to be correct, why do I doubt God's ability to bring me to the place that is best for me?

Lord, help me to trust in Your GPS, (God's perfect solution) for all the challenges in my life. Help me to have faith, though at times I cannot see or understand Your overall plan. And as I greet this new day with You at my side, help me to once again realize that together we can accomplish what I haven't dared to dream.   MAXINE WILLIAMS ALLEN

September 29

Scars

Those whom I love I rebuke and discipline. So be earnest, and repent.
Rev. 3:19, NIV.

IN RETROSPECT IT SEEMS to me that while I was growing up, my family expected much and was very strict with me. Thus, I grew up trying to please everyone, and I became a workaholic, never taking time for rest, relaxation, or restoration.

I've been ill and have had to have multiple major surgeries. The scars are constant reminders of the pain and emotional distress I endured and of the many prayers for me and the healing I have received. I'm the only grandchild in the family, who has had to interrupt my daily routines for major medical reasons. I've tried to live a healthful lifestyle, more than others in my family have. I asked God why they got only minor illnesses, while I got the major ones. God revealed to me that He has been there all the time, taking care of all my needs, but He needed to get my attention and time. I am now better for it.

The scars of sin committed in my youth are ugly. God in His mercy relieved me of some excess baggage, and the scars I will carry on this earth are reminders. There is no earthly process to remove these scars.

Those whom God loves, He chastens. Like good parents who see imperfections in their children, it is a duty to chasten them so they can grow up honorably. Sometimes it will take physical illness to help perfect Christian character. It takes chastising to get one ready to do His will on earth and go to heaven. I pray daily that the Lord will continually work on my character. When He is finished with me I will be able to see His face in peace when He returns; I will not try to run to the rocks or mountains for shelter from His brightness. I will put off mortality and put on immortality and become a new person; the scars of this life will not be an issue ever again.

Nail scars. Jesus endured the cross, and His blood washes me whiter than snow. His shedding of blood and His death on the cross was for me because He loves me. I want to see the nail scars He suffered. If He had not suffered, there would be no heaven to look forward to.

Father, I have sinned and come short of Your glory. I love You and thank You for being my Lord and Savior. Whatever it takes to prepare me for Your kingdom will be worth it. Amen.

BETTY G. PERRY

I Know He Cares

Lo, I am with you alway, even unto the end of the world. Matt. 28:20.

A S I WAS LYING in the hospital bed, my world was falling apart right before me. I was in pain; I had just had a surgery that I never expected. Yet God was with me; the doctor said that the Lord had saved my life. There was nothing he could have done unless the Lord helped him to diagnose my problem.

This had all happened on the Sinhala and Tamil New Year's Day, a holiday time in Sri Lanka. The shops were closed, the city was dead, and the doctors were on holiday. It was then that I got stomach pain and had to be rushed to the nearest hospital. The doctor examined me and advised me that I had to undergo surgery immediately. The Lord knew what was going to happen, and He was ready, preparing a particular surgeon to be on duty that day. I was taken into surgery immediately.

As soon as the doctor started the surgery he knew what my problem was. I had conceived a baby in my fallopian tube, and the tube had burst. I had lost four pints of blood, infecting my appendix. So the doctor first opened and removed my appendix. Then he had to clean up my womb, making two incisions, one with six stitches and the other with 10 stitches. The fallopian tube was removed, leaving me with only one. The pain was hard to bear; after the surgery even a cough was painful.

I cried, *Why did this happen to me, Lord? Why me?* At the same time I realized He knows and wants the best for me. I knew in the midst of darkness that His gentle hands had carried me through.

Today I am not crying anymore, because I have been taught to wait upon Him. He says, "Lo, I am with you alway, even unto the end of the world."

I have forgotten my pain and faced the reality that my chances of having children are only 75 percent. When I go home with Him I am sure He will have many children for me so that I will be able to hold them in my arms. I love Him so much. God is good. Always. ESTHER AMBIKAPALAN

October 1

Waiting Patiently

Wait for the Lord; be strong and take heart and wait for the Lord.
Ps. 27:14, NIV.

WAITING PATIENTLY HAS NEVER been one of my strong points. As a matter of fact, I cannot stand waiting. Patience is required in so many areas of my life. Most of my friends have told me how they enjoyed being pregnant, waiting for their babies to arrive. Not me! Being pregnant has been one of the most frustrating times of my life. Too many unanswered questions. Is it a boy or a girl (you have to wait four months before you can find out!)? What color will the eyes and hair be? Will the baby be healthy? The days of my three pregnancies felt years long; by the fifth month I had everything ready for the new arrival.

It seems to me that God has paid special attention to this weakness. Even though He started His training gently, it has gotten tougher, year by year. Eleven years ago I remember wondering impatiently whom I would eventually marry. *Please God, just tell me who it is!* To my great delight, God answered this prayer. Soon after that one of my good friends and I realized that we were actually in love. Two years later we were married.

That's when the training really started. To be married to a pastor involves a lot of waiting. Every week after church I wait for my husband to greet and chat with the church members. I'm starving, and the kids are tired, but we wait. During the week nights I wait and wonder, *Are the meetings going well? When is he finally coming home?*

You would think after almost nine years I would have finally learned patience. I have not. It is especially difficult waiting for God to answer me. Sometimes I get upset at Him. Does He really care for me? Maybe my prayers aren't reaching Him. Then, when I am almost ready to give up, the answer comes.

Lately I've learned that waiting patiently for God has to do with our faith in Him. When He lets us wait for His response, He is asking us to trust Him. As long as we try to fix things up ourselves and do not trust God to do so in His own time we don't know Him well. To really know Jesus is to trust Him.

Do you know Jesus well enough to trust that He can, and will, take care of you? I certainly want to get to know Him better today; what about you?

KERTTULI GIANTZAKLIDIS

Wonderfully Made!

Thank you for making me so wonderfully complex! Your workmanship is marvelous—and how well I know it. Ps. 139:14, NLT.

IT IS FAR BEYOND my comprehension just how complex and how marvelous we are, and how remarkably we are put together. Each one of us is a masterpiece, designed by the Master Creator Himself.

It's easy to see how intricately our bodies are put together when we think about how diligently a crafter works, and how beautiful is the finished product. A great deal of patience, lots of time, and a genuine desire to complete the work, are invested in handiwork. An example is the quilt in the Women's Ministries Department where I work. It is a gorgeous quilt of painting, appliqué, and embroidery. Women from 10 countries worked on this quilt that shows women in various ministries, women around the world joined together under the banner of the cross. This quilt sat in a box in a closet for years, its magnificent work unappreciated and unknown to many.

Quilting, like many other crafts, is painstaking and laborious. Every minute detail must be planned—thread by thread, color by color, stitch by stitch, piece by piece. Custom-designed.

And so it is with us. Sometimes it looks as though we are unfinished, uninteresting, and cut from the same cloth as everyone else, or that we are something to be scoffed at, ignored, or discarded. But as the Master continues working on His creation, we become unique, special, custom-designed! The loving touch of the Master Creator makes all things beautiful. As the quilt that is patiently yet persistently worked on, we are His very own handiwork! "And we, out of all creation, became his choice possession!" (James 1:18, NLT).

We can never fully know what this gift of love cost, but we do know that He gave all He had to make us all that we can be. We weren't discarded or discolored remnants. We weren't thrown together carelessly or thoughtlessly. We weren't the product of many authors or creators. We were, and are, a special work in progress—new and renewed each day through Him.

The Lord says, "Be glad; rejoice forever in my creation!" (Isa. 65:18, NLT). Be happy today with who God has made you to be!   IRIS L. STOVALL

October 3

Our Down-to-Earth God

Delight thyself also in the Lord; and he shall give thee the desires of thine heart. Ps. 37:4.

WITHIN ONE WEEK GOD not only answered my prayer, He also showed me that He loves and cares for me, even in the minutest aspect of my life.

My 17-year-old son was getting ready for his high school banquet and wanted to get a new shirt. He went shopping with his friends and found a brand-name shirt that he liked in a very expensive store—for $80! Since he has been brought up to spend his money wisely, he didn't buy it.

The day before the banquet he asked me to go shopping and help him get a shirt. Habitually, we always pray before starting the car. That day we prayed that God would help us find a less expensive shirt. A nice salesman at the very first store we went into helped us find a shirt that was on sale. When we went to the counter to pay for the things we had selected, we were pleasantly surprised to see the clerk deduct an extra 15 percent off on each of the items. My son was overjoyed to see that for $78 he had gotten two shirts and two matching ties. This incident strengthened our faith. When we trust in God, He blesses us much more than we can ever expect.

A few days later I was in a store where I had paid for my purchases by credit card. I picked up my two bags and was about to leave when the woman standing next to me reminded me that I had left my credit card wallet on the candy rack. If I had forgotten it, anyone could have easily walked away with that wallet that contained all my credit cards and my bank card. I would have been devastated if this had happened—it would have been very difficult to cancel all those credit cards that night. It makes me shudder even now to think of such a loss.

My God made sure that an honest person was standing right next to me, and He impressed that lady to remind me to take my wallet. I came home rejoicing with a grateful heart. I praise God every day for the many ways in which He shows His love for me. Truly, "delight thyself also in the Lord; and he shall give thee the desires of thine heart."   STELLA THOMAS

Consolation and Blessings

The Lord has given me the tongue of a teacher and skill to console the weary with a word in the morning. Isa. 50:4, NEB.

AFTER MY HUSBAND DIED I started writing in a spiritual journal early every morning to ease my pain and to pray for God's help and comfort. My writing skills have developed from using it as a therapy. I drew great strength from telling the Lord how wretched I felt. Gradually, I began to realize that this was a way I could help others. I was better writing about the comfort this journal has given me, and I wanted to console people who were going through similar experiences of bereavement and loss. I was able to say, "I do understand."

I attended several writing classes; it was good to meet writers and gain from their experiences. I had many opportunities to tell the good news of the gospel. Great blessings came from making friends and learning skills.

This gave me the confidence to volunteer for the rehabilitation of young people suffering from emotional and mental disorders. My previous nursing training and relaxation teaching were a valuable asset. I started a creative writing class in 1997 and have four young men with different abilities and interests. I enjoy teaching them and observing their progress.

Recently I had the privilege of being selected to attend a wonderful retreat in England's Lake District with 25 other Christians to concentrate and focus especially on devotional genre writing. This was a great blessing, as my writing instruction for the past five years never dealt with Christian writing.

I am seeing more of the beauty of God's creation than ever before. My eyes are open to appreciate the countryside and to tell others in poetry how wonderful and glorious is the Lord's handiwork. There is so much sorrow and suffering; it is a very welcome blessing to see the positive side and great beauty of our world. Numerous Bible texts have encouraged me to express these positive thoughts in writing and to tell others what the Lord has done for me.

Dear heavenly Father, thank You for the comfort and strength You have given me. Please continue to guide me and increase my talents so I can witness for You.   PHILIPPA MARSHALL

October 5

The Big Picture

Great is our Lord, and of great power: his understanding is infinite. Ps. 147:5.

A CHRISTIAN WRITER OBSERVED a small boy on a tricycle, racing pell-mell down a hill right into the path of an oncoming truck. Fortunately, a rock caused the child's tricycle to overturn, and he fell before he entered the street and mortal danger. Bruised and crying, the little boy ran home to be consoled and bandaged. Writing later about the experience, the author imagined that the boy and his mother might have wondered, Where was God's protection? Why wasn't he kept from injury? From the author's point of view, the child's life was spared by the providence of a rock.

In 1986 I lost my bid to become director of pastoral care to a man with less education and experience in chaplaincy. I was angry, hurt, and tearful. Here was another case of gender discrimination, and I cried before the Lord about the unfairness of the situation. Then I found out that I was also three months pregnant and saw the wisdom of God as He delayed my appointment to management. It was obvious that God's no to this promotion was for my best good. As an additional perk, my new boss, who is still a dear friend and an invaluable colleague, gave me the opportunity to develop my management skills while working with him. He also gave me the raises that were comparable to what I would have received as a director.

God sees the big picture. Our past, present, and future are a continuous present to Him. It is so hard to conceive, but He already knows. The exciting part of the mystery is that He has promised that what He has worked out will be for a glorious end for me. "For surely I know the plans I have for you, says the Lord, plans for your welfare and not for harm, to give you a future with hope (Jer. 29:11, NRSV).

Yet like the little boy, the daily scrapes and bruises of this life sadden me. They are easily misinterpreted to be the result of something that others wished upon me, a mess of my own making, or just an unfortunate accident. Yet God's Word says He orders my steps, and none of my steps will slide (Ps. 37). He governs even the missteps in my life. When I do fall, I can run tearfully to the One who can console and bandage me up. He who knows the big picture says, "All things work together for good."   WANDA DAVIS

286

Minced Oaths

Set an example for the believers in speech, in life, in love, in faith and in purity. 1 Tim. 4:12, NIV.

A S A TEENAGER I read an article titled, "Minced Oaths." The writer pointed out that as Christians we do not use vulgar words in our conversation, nor do we blaspheme God's holy name by using it in senseless fashion or as an oath. Nevertheless, unless we are extremely careful, we take God's name in vain by using "minced oaths."

That's about all I recall of the article. I remember more clearly that Mother had taught us as children that we must not say "gee" or "jeez," because they were an abbreviated form of Jesus' holy name. Nor should we say "golly" or "gosh," because those words referred to the Holy Ghost.

In our area English immigrants were something of a novelty, and their patently English exclamation of "gorblimey" or "corblimey" was, Mother said, a corruption of "God bless me." She also told us that our hearty friend, who closely resembled John Bull himself and began most of his conversation with "bai jove," was unwittingly blaspheming God by saying, "By Jehovah."

All this led to my growing up to be extremely sensitive about the name of any member of the Trinity being used lightly. Nowadays I shudder at the way "gawd" and "good lord" are used in every sentence some people speak.

When I visited a new neighbor some months ago, I noticed that she was a prime offender. She is a lonely person, so I dropped in every week. Occasionally I tried to talk about God's love, but she reacted so harshly that I gave up and simply paid friendly visits.

I don't remember how much later it was that I noticed her catching herself each time she said "gawd." Now, at least when I am visiting, it has dropped out of her vocabulary. Perhaps teaching by example is useful for unbelievers also.

We often use words and expressions without knowing or thinking about their purpose or meaning. It might be good to do a vocabulary inventory. We also need to immerse ourselves in God's Word each day, focusing on God's power and grace. Then our words and lives will be a witness of beauty, with nothing minced.

GOLDIE DOWN

October 7

The Lesson of the Leaves

Search me, O God, and know my heart: try me, and know my thoughts: and see if there be any wicked way in me, and lead me in the way everlasting. Ps. 139:23, 24.

ONE COLORFUL, CRISP DAY I was walking in the woods. I began to pick up colorful leaves that had fallen from the trees that surrounded me. Again and again, I would stoop down, pick up a leaf that had caught my eye, and, if it was perfect enough, add it to my growing collection. But if the leaf was obviously flawed, as happened more often than not, I threw it away. Many leaves were brown and dead and had been trampled underfoot. I didn't even look at those leaves. And then I felt the Lord speaking to my heart.

"Why do you reject the imperfect? Are they not My creations? They serve a purpose other than to fill your eyes with beauty. I have created them all."

I knew, of course, that the Lord was not talking about leaves. I realized that I often deal with people in the same way that I was dealing with less-than-beautiful autumn leaves. My heart pricked me. How many times have I rejected a potential friend because of some real, or imagined, inner flaw? How many times have I judged someone because I didn't understand their behavior or circumstances? How many people—broken, trampled under-foot, chewed up and spit back out by life, as I have been—have looked to me to understand them and love them, but I was so afraid to get too close and left them there in their pain? How many people have I hurt through my rejection? How badly have I hurt myself by not allowing these people to enrich my life?

I looked up at the trees, then back down at the leaves the forest floor was wearing. Up high, the leaves formed a canopy of color—no two exactly the same shade of color—painting a tapestry of intricate beauty. Down below, the leaves formed a fading carpet, turning into a mulch that would nourish the very trees that had cast them down. I noticed a leaf, full of spots where an insect had eaten on it. I stooped down, picked it up, and carefully added it to my collection.

Father, please forgive me for practicing rejection. Help me to be more sensitive to the needs of my brothers and sisters—whether they are part of the beautiful canopy of color above, or part of the nourishing carpet below.

LYNDA MAE RICHARDSON

Cure for Leprosy

If we confess our sins, he is faithful and just and will forgive us our sins and purify us. 1 John 1:9, NIV.

I NEEDED TO TAKE BUJO, our flat-nosed Pekingese dog, with me to the bazaar to buy fruit and vegetables for the hospital.

One morning as Bujo and I approached the entrance to the open-air market, the usual cluster of chattering men was squatting at one side. Among them was a leper—disfigured face, flat nose, stubs for fingers and toes. A man standing in the forefront of the group looked at my dog, then at the leper, and then turned to me with a smirky grin. I made no response. He repeated the procedure several times. Finally he pointed to the leper, then to the dog, and explained to me: "Madam, leper like dog!" Chills ran up and down my spine. How disrespectful!

I straightened my shoulders and responded, "Sir, I enjoy my little dog, but he is still only a dog. This leper is a man." The idle talk ceased. I continued, "God said, 'Let us make man in our image' [Gen. 1:26]. Can we compare a man made in God's image with a dog?"

There was no more smirking or chatting. Eyes were downcast. With moisture-filled eyes the leper looked at me, and through his disfigured lips said very simply, "Thank you, madam. Thank you." The flat-nosed Pekingese and I went into the market to shop.

Throughout the day visions of lepers and leprosy invaded my thoughts. I recalled that centuries before Jesus—and for centuries after—leprosy had been considered the result of and punishment for sin. I remembered, too, that Scripture says, "All have sinned" (Rom 3:23). I didn't have to remind myself that I have sinned—many times. *I have leprosy?* What a horrible thought! Physically, mentally, spiritually disfigured by sin! My already somber mood plummeted.

But Scripture always has a solution for every human concern, including mine. The Bible story says Jesus healed a leper completely and immediately (Matt. 8:2-4). Jesus will do the same for me. If I confess my sins, He will forgive me and purify me (1 John 1:9). Jesus is faithful. He is just. Restoration is immediate and complete. No longer a leper? My mood soared upward. Indeed, no longer a leper. I am forgiven and restored by the unbounded love and mercy of God!

LOIS E. JOHANNES

October 9

Adopted

Some friends play at friendship but a true friend sticks closer than one's nearest kin. Prov. 18:24, NRSV.

A FTER SEVERAL YEARS OF being the top dog in our house, our Australian shepherd, Molly, got a "sister" in late 1998.

Alix, as we renamed her, was a 10-month-old Rhodesian Ridgeback who came to us from a breeder. Her original owner had become terminally ill and was unable to keep her and her mother. Because we had been wanting a Rhodesian Ridgeback for several months, we drove the hour to the coast to see her and immediately fell in love. She came home with us that same day.

Sweet and easygoing, at 65 pounds she was about twice 2-year-old Molly's size. We were a little concerned about how high-strung, jittery Molly would accept this tall, lanky stranger, so we took great pains in introducing them to each other. When both were finally allowed to run loose, Alix came right up to Molly in an attempt to get acquainted. Molly tucked her behind (she doesn't have a tail) and slunk behind a chair. Not to be deterred, Alix followed her. Around the coffee table, around the couch, down the hall, under the table they went. The only place Molly could find refuge was under the bed—Al was too big to follow her there! Molly could not understand that Alix wasn't trying to hurt her, and that they were part of the same family now.

Later, when they were a little better acquainted, Alix would pat at Molly in an attempt to get her to play. The problem was, Alix is so much bigger that her "pats" knocked over diminutive Molly and did nothing for her opinion of her new housemate. Over time they became like old, inseparable friends, but initially the relationship was more than a little strained.

The parallels to my life have really jumped out at me. I sometimes tend to avoid the friendly advances of those who are different from me or new to the family of God. I am uncomfortable around them or afraid of them—afraid of the possibility of rejection or hurt. And sometimes things are said or done in an attempt at "play" that may emotionally bowl me over, but I need to keep in mind that we are really adopted sisters in the family of Christ. The relationship for now may be a bit strained, but hopefully, with time, we can become old friends.   VICKI L. MACOMBER

The Wise and Peaceful Way

But the wisdom that is from above is first pure, then peaceable, gentle, willing to yield, full of mercy and good fruits. James 3:17, NKJV.

ONCE WHEN MY HUSBAND was away a family problem came up that required a quick decision, but I felt unable to make the decision. I waited a week until he came home. I was so troubled that the week was the longest in my life. As soon as I opened the door for him you can guess what I did. Yes, I blurted out everything. My husband quickly said, "Wait; wait; I am not prepared to hear anything." So I shut my mouth, realizing I needed to give him time to wash up, eat, and rest before we sat down to talk about the problem.

I thought, *What if I were in Abigail's place?* She was told that David was on his way with his men to take revenge on her husband—not just her husband but every one of her household. There was no time to lose, yet she acted in a wise and peaceable way. She made her own decision, in spite of the attitude of her husband. She loaded her donkeys with plenty of food for David and his men. She humbled herself before David, prostrating herself at his feet. She took the blame for all the misdeeds of her husband. She advised David to refrain from shedding blood which he would later regret. She also expressed her faith that one day he would be the king.

I thought of Queen Esther, who made her own decision, and through wisdom and patience saved the whole nation of Jews from death. The law was that no one should go and see the king without being called. Those who did so risked death. Yet Esther was willing to go. She moved with tact and discretion. She called for fasting for three days. Only then did she approach the king. Instead of falling at his feet and blurting out everything, she remained calm and sweet and invited him to a banquet. And not just one banquet, but another one the next day, entertaining the king—and her worst enemy. What was the result? A great victory for God's people.

Yes, I still have many things to learn. I pray that God will help me make the decisions I need to make and to be more gentle and wise as I wait on Him—the wisdom that is from above.

BIRDIE PODDAR

Be Prepared!

Be ye also ready. Matt. 24:44.

WITH JUST AN HOUR to pack for a long weekend at a camp, I hastily gathered my things up and tossed them in the suitcase. At the last minute the principal had decided that I should go to the Bible conference to chaperon the teenage girls. My husband was doing double duty, driving the bus and supervising the boys during the conference.

All went well until time to prepare for bed that night. I had failed to put in a toothbrush. With town and stores miles away and no transportation except the bus, there was no feasible way to buy one. With gallantry above and beyond the call of duty, my husband offered to share his with me—even letting me use it first each time!

Since then I have kept a toothbrush and other necessities in my small train case, ready to go at a moment's notice. Even though I've never had to pack so quickly again, it's nice to have a head start when we are getting ready for a trip. Although I don't particularly enjoy packing, I have to confess that unpacking is a more dreaded chore when we get home. The excitement of the vacation is over, there is laundry to be done, and all the "stuff" to put away.

Remembering the missing toothbrush episode, I wondered what I might be forgetting to "pack" for the grandest trip of all time—the one when our Lord and Savior comes to take us home with Him, not for a weekend but for all eternity. I have often heard it said that the only thing we can take with us to heaven is our character, so the "packing" consists of how we live our lives day by day. With the guidance of the Holy Spirit and the example of Jesus, we can be prepared for that wonderful journey. When we get there, we'll have no unpacking to do, just settling in to stay and to enjoy the glories and wonders of heaven! "As it is written, Eye hath not seen, nor ear heard, neither have entered into the heart of man [or woman], the things which God hath prepared for them that love him" (1 Cor. 2:9). With love and sacrifice above and beyond the call of duty, Jesus has made it possible for us to live with Him forever.

Don't you want to be there? I do!

MARY JANE GRAVES

Tornado

Call to me, and I will answer you; I will tell you wonderful and marvelous things that you know nothing about. Jer. 33:3, TEV.

IT WAS 1:30 A.M. on a warm, stormy night in October 1966. I was just getting off work at a hospital in south Miami. Since I was the only single person in the department, I had to cover until the night clerk arrived. We had heard warnings on the news of possible tornadoes, and I was concerned as I left for home after a long day, tired and sleepy as I entered the expressway to drive the 20 miles home. I asked God to send His angels to keep me safe and alert as I drove.

Traffic was light, but it was raining quite hard. As I drove along cautiously, trying to see out of the windshield between the swipes of the windshield wipers, I saw an 18-wheeler go past in the opposite direction. I went on for several more miles, not seeing any other cars or trucks. The only sounds were the rain, my car engine, the wheels on the wet pavement, and the whistling wind. It was all I could do to keep the car on the road because of the strong wind pushing me toward the shoulder.

Suddenly, before I knew what happened, I felt my car being lifted and spun around. In a few seconds I was back down on the pavement. I could hear my heart pounding even louder than the rain, wind, or car engine. My hands were shaking as the reality set in that I had been picked up by a small tornado and gently put back down!

I was still the only one on the expressway, but I was no longer sleepy! I noticed an information sign and realized I was heading back toward the hospital. I quickly took the next exit and reentered the expressway, going home again. When I finally arrived home at 2:30, I was physically and emotionally drained but very thankful to be alive. Once again I thanked God for sending His angels to keep me safe. What an awesome God we serve!

CELIA MEJIA CRUZ

October 13

Damascus Road

Now as he journeyed he approached Damascus, and suddenly a light from heaven flashed about him. Acts 9:3, RSV.

I WAS HANDED A BLACK robe, and the attendant indicated that I should pull the hood up over my head. My baggy brown pants and loose shirt were not appropriate attire to wear into the mosque in Damascus.

I had never entered a mosque before and was impressed by the columns, the calligraphy spelling out the names of God, the absence of seats, the open spaces. There were not many other tourists like our family; but there were several Arab men sitting in a group, talking and eating.

I couldn't understand their use of the mosque for these activities. Their behavior didn't fit in with my compartmentalization of work and worship. I had thought that a person worshiped at certain times—family devotions, church service once a week—and that other times were for secular activities. This wasn't time for a service; perhaps there would be one soon. But why were they eating? That's not what we did back at home in church—except during Communion.

And then my eyes grew even bigger. A man was lying on the floor. He wasn't trying to be inconspicuous by lying in a corner. He was sleeping by a column near the middle of the mosque. The tourists openly stared as they walked around him. The men continued talking and eating. His presence in the mosque was accepted and natural to them.

It suddenly dawned on me that in this part of the world worship was not something that happened occasionally; it was something that surrounded people, something they embraced at all times. Worship permeated all their lives.

Paul was blinded on his way to Damascus; I had my eyes opened in Damascus and decided that I wanted to integrate worship into all aspects of my life. I didn't want a spiritual life that was lived apart from daily life. Rather, I longed for one that was a part of everything I did.

Now as I grade papers, make applesauce, or wait for X-ray results with my son, I endeavor to have every aspect of my life filled with worship.

DENISE DICK HERR

294

No Need to Fear

And he said unto them, Why are ye so fearful? how is it that ye have no faith? Mark 4:40.

I WAS NOT FAMILIAR WITH the expression "white coat syndrome" until my doctor told me about it one day during my routine physical. I couldn't understand the terrible fear and panic I experienced each time I had to go for a checkup. I tried for years to analyze my feelings, but always came up against a stone wall. There was no apparent logic for the fear I felt as soon as I neared the parking lot of the clinic. I could feel the palpitations escalate and my blood pressure soar. By the time I found a seat in the waiting room, I was almost a basket case.

Several days before my appointment, preparations would begin for the ordeal. I would meditate and try to think only happy thoughts and do anything that would have a calming effect. I tried breathing exercises while sitting quietly in my chair. I looked up Bible texts on fear and faith and typed them on small cards I could refer to as needed.

On appointment day I spent much time in prayer, pleading with the Lord to perform a miracle and give me peace of mind. When it was time to leave for the office, I found the eight-mile drive went by much too rapidly. I wish I could say my visit was totally stress-free, but I did survive, and I thank my heavenly Father for giving me the strength to get through it.

I felt so guilty about my fears and lack of faith. As a child of God I should be stronger. I was up and down with my emotions so much I felt like a yo-yo. I experienced great strength one minute, and then the fear would raise its ugly head and I was back in the pits again. I told the doctor I felt as though I could go through the floods and fires, but spare me the visit to his office.

My problem with white coat syndrome started several years ago when an illness involving my blood sugar left in its wake varied phobias and fears I hadn't experienced previously. A change in diet was the prescribed treatment.

I find comfort in these words: "All things, whatsoever ye shall ask in prayer, believing, ye shall receive" (Matt. 21:22). I may not be there yet, but with God's help I'm going to make it.

Lord, help my unbelief.   CLAREEN COLCLESSER

October 15

The Peace He Promised

The mind controlled by the Spirit is life and peace. Rom. 8:6, NIV.

WHILE MY MORNINGS DURING the week are pretty routine, this particular Friday morning was different. I left for the store at 6:45 to grab some items I needed for Saturday's meal while my husband completed the dishes from supper the previous night. The clock struck 7:40, and we still weren't ready. I knew then that we would be late dropping the boys off at school, and I would be late to work. And if you've ever lived in Maryland, you know that as soon as it drizzles, traffic backs up. Except this morning it wasn't drizzling, it was raining!

Like many working, multitasked mothers, I gobbled down my breakfast and asked my older boy, Gabriel, 10, if he knew his spelling. I quizzed Joshua, 6, on his memory verse and hollered at my husband to hurry up. My stress level had increased again. I was off my schedule, and my nerves began to frazzle.

Life got more complicated as I headed out into the already congested traffic. Impatient drivers honked, my windows fogged up, a utility truck blocked my way, and I was upset. At the rate I was going, I knew the boys would get to school after 8:20. When I apologized to the boys for getting them to school late, Joshua said, "It's OK, Mommy. The teacher won't punish us." With loving kisses and goodbyes, they were out the door, and I missed them already.

Joshua's words put me in a reflective mood. Am I punishing myself by getting stressed out when my day doesn't go the way I want it to? Why am I always rushing? Did God intend for me to live my life this way? All the way to work I took a few deep breaths, decreased the speed at which I was driving, and turned on the radio. As beautiful music flooded the car, I considered the words of the song and felt at peace. As I went about my duties I caught myself a couple of times humming the song. The peace I felt remained with me that whole day. What a precious reminder my Father gave me that morning.

In the rush of the day I really do need to be controlled by Your Spirit, which is life and peace. Oh, how I need that peace! Thank You, Lord.

VIOLA POEY HUGHES

Who Is Watching Me?

You are the light of the world. A city that is set on a hill cannot be hidden. Matt. 5:14, NKJV.

IT WAS ON A HOT and humid day when I entered the Manila Domestic Airport to board a plane for the southern part of the Philippines. As I looked around the one-room airport, I saw a huge room with several gates and many seats in rows. In one corner was an air-conditioning unit that was trying in vain to cool the immense room that was full of people.

The room reeked with tobacco smoke, so I glanced around to see if I could find a corner where there were fewer people and less smoke. Finally I saw four empty chairs at one side that were facing a statue of the virgin Mary. It didn't take me long to decide that might be my answer, so I walked toward the statue and sat in one of the empty seats.

I noticed a small written prayer hanging from the statue. As I read the prayer, I thought it was quite interesting. Why not copy it down? So I brought out a piece of paper and began writing down the prayer. I hadn't written very many words when a lovely Filipino woman came and sat beside me. She also took out a paper and pencil and started copying down the prayer. I was even more amazed when a young Filipino man followed and sat down on the other side of me. He also got out a paper and pencil and began copying down the prayer.

By this time I had finished copying the prayer, and I watched my two new friends continue their writing. Then they left. I thought about how widespread my influence had been, and I had been totally unconscious of my effect upon others. There had been probably more than 100 people in the room with me. I thought no one was even watching me; and then two of them decided to do exactly what I was doing.

How little we know who is watching us. Our children are watching us. Our friends are watching us. Complete strangers are watching us. It is my prayer that my actions will always be as a light to those around me, so they will not stumble but will walk in the right path. ROWENA R. RICK

October 17

Face-lift

In a moment, in the twinkling of an eye . . . we shall be changed. 1 Cor. 15:52.

FROM THE YELLOW PAGES I found an optometrist whose ads stated he had what I needed to be able to see far and near, and read small letters as well. I had been squinting.

After the vision tests, I was fitted with more powerful lenses. Now I could see well. The optometrist also tested my peripheral vision. If my eyelids were more open, he said, I could see better. With the new lenses, I could wear the same pair of glasses for reading, viewing the computer screen, and reading road signs without squinting. I was thankful for the difference.

"But your peripheral vision is impaired," Dr. T explained. "You would be able to see better than you can now. I will refer you to an ophthalmologist. It may mean an eyelid lift."

When I made the appointment, I found that Dr. M is a cosmetic surgeon. He also explained that I needed an eyebrow lift. "If that is what it takes, I'll go for it" was my reluctant reply. However, since my insurance wouldn't cover the additional procedure, we agreed on one procedure only, and he set the date.

An hour before the operation, a nurse asked me to sign a paper that included the other procedure, too. I reminded the doctor about the uninsured portion in the surgery and that we had agreed to do only one procedure.

Two days later, after he removed my head bandage and eyelid dressing, he handed me a mirror. He had done both procedures. I again reminded him of the lack of coverage. He said, "I hear you."

One year later I am still in pain, and my eyelids and eyebrows are still asymmetrical.

Someday when Jesus returns for the second time, I will claim today's promise in 1 Corinthians 15:52. We are also promised that "we look for the Saviour . . . who shall change our vile body, that it may be fashioned like unto his glorious body" (Phil. 3:20, 21).

I pray that the Lord will help me to wait patiently until He performs a painless surgery at the snap of a finger. I shall be renewed.

ESPERANZA AQUINO MOPERA

Penetrating the Fog

I will lead the blind by ways they have not known, along unfamiliar paths I will guide them; I will turn the darkness into light before them and make the rough places smooth. Isa. 42:16, NIV.

WHEN I FIRST BEGAN my drive to work this morning, the sun was shining brightly. However, as I approached the lake area, the entire world around me became engulfed in dense fog. It surrounded me from all sides, blocking the view front to back, as well as side to side. Only scraggly twists of trees and dim silhouettes penetrated the dense fog. Traffic ahead slowed to a snail's pace as I struggled to keep in line behind the small flickers of the taillight in front. The total focus of each driver was to watch the white line, keeping us straight on the otherwise invisible pavement.

I suddenly thought, *This is what blind faith is all about.* Many times in our lives we stumble along blindly, groping our way through our own difficulties. Unable to see which way we should go, we become confused and unable to see the answers. That is where our blind faith has to take over. If we fail to follow those illuminated lines of instruction, we swerve aside and disastrous crashes result. Just as I knew the sun was still up above the clouds and fog, even though not visible to me, our faith reassures us that the Son of God is still there, ever present.

I received another lesson from that drive in the fog. How very dependent we really are on each other. It is so easy to become lost when you travel alone. Without the light from other cars we could not have followed one another down the road. The Bible tells us that now we see through a glass, darkly, but then we shall see face to face. With the light of God's love in our hearts our faith will take over in the foggy times of our lives.

Faith is a gift of God. It is not a material that can be seen, heard, tasted, smelled, or touched. Still, it is as real as anything that can be perceived with these senses. For faith is as certain as the sky we see, the sound of thunder we hear, or the taste of fresh-picked fruit. It is also as certain as the fragrance of the rose we smell, and as real as the warmth of the sun, or the feel of a loving touch. Hope is a wish, a longing for something not now possessed; but faith is what adds surety to the expectations of our hope. By trusting in our Savior and focusing our eyes on Him, we will stay on that straight pathway that leads to His kingdom.

BARBARA SMITH MORRIS

October 19

The Great Day

So you also must be ready, because the Son of Man will come at an hour when you do not expect him. Matt. 24:44, NIV.

IT'S NOT EASY TO get up every day at 5:45 a.m. to send your children off to school and get ready to leave for work yourself. However, staying in bed a few more minutes can bring many problems to the daily routine. So that I do not run the risk of being late, I set the alarm to ring 10 to 15 minutes before the time I really need to get up. But one day I was so tired that I turned off the alarm and continued sleeping. I do not remember doing this, but since the clock is on the night table beside my bed, I was the only one who could have turned off the alarm.

What despair and fright when we woke up to the honking of the school bus that picks our daughter up at 6:30. We were sleeping! We all jumped from our beds without knowing what to do. The school where our children study is not close to our home, and we work the whole day very far from our home and the school. People who use school transportation must be ready on time, because if only one child is late, all the others will be late. There was not much that we could do. We apologized that we were late and told the driver to go on without our child.

This simple delay changed the entire routine of our day. My husband needed to change his route to work so he could leave our daughter at school—not to mention the explanations that he had to present to the school monitor.

This situation made me meditate on the return of our Lord. Are we ready, waiting for Jesus to come and get us? Or are we sleeping just a little longer, and when Jesus calls will we be in despair, able to do nothing more, and thus miss the opportunity for eternal life?

I knew that the school bus would arrive every day at 6:30. Jesus has not told us when He will return, but He said that we must always be prepared!

Thank You, Jesus, for the lesson that You taught me today! Help me to be prepared to meet You every day.   MARINÊS AP. DA SILVA OLIVEIRA

A Child-taught Lesson

And whoso shall receive one such little child in my name receiveth me. But whoso shall offend one of these little ones which believe in me, it were better for him that a millstone were hanged about his neck, and that he were drowned in the depth of the sea. Matt. 18:5, 6.

COME TALK TO ME, Nat," Samantha, our 4-year-old neighbor, shouted from behind our backyard chain-link fence. She's an only child and appreciates attention.

"When I've finished watering my garden I'll come, Samantha," I replied.

"Come now!" she persisted.

Just then her father called her and talked to her about interrupting my work. I felt sorry that my morning demands were so overwhelming that I neglected my little neighbor's call. I thought, *Now, I've offended not only Samantha but also her father. I wonder if she'll ever return to our back fence to visit with me again?*

Later I heard her call, "Nat, come talk to me. I want to give you something."

I must not disappoint her this time, I told myself. A gentle breeze tousled her wispy, long, blond curls. Her pale blue eyes met mine. Her soft little hand reached toward me with a tiny white stemless flower. "I picked this for you, Nat."

"Thank you, Samantha! I'll have to put it in water so it will last," I said, and turned to go.

"You forgot something, Nat. You forgot to give me some pansies."

"Oh, yes, I did! Just wait here and I'll get some for you."

Exchanging flowers had become our summer ritual. After I'd explained the pansy's face to her, she grew to love the smiling blossoms as much as I do. I returned to the fence with a few pansies and said, "Remember, they are smiling just for you!"

"I'll put them in water right away," she told me, and darted toward her home.

This sweet child taught me loving forgiveness and forgetting. Obviously, she had forgiven me for putting her off previously. Is that why Jesus said "except ye be converted, and become as little children, ye shall not enter into the kingdom of heaven" (Matt. 18:3)?

Dear Lord, please help me become as accepting and forgiving as Samantha.

NATHALIE LADNER-BISCHOFF

October 21

The Humble and Simple

*Let all those who seek You rejoice and be glad in You; and let those who love
Your salvation say continually, "Let God be magnified!" Ps. 70:4, NKJV.*

A YOUNG GIRL WHO works in one of our parochial schools had cancer
in her womb. Though she had taken many tablets and injections for her
cancer, the pain was not reduced, and she was not healed. She suffered a lot.
She often called me for prayer, so I went regularly and prayed for her. As the
leader of the women's ministries, I met with other women and prayed for her
earnestly every Sabbath afternoon. Her stomach bulged as though she were
eight months pregnant, but her body, hands, and legs were so thin. She could
neither sit nor walk for some time and couldn't eat properly or even sleep. In
spite of this, she went to school and work.

But God answered our prayers, one by one. Since she couldn't sleep
down on the floor, she needed a cot. We prayed for a cot. God spoke to one
of our church members, and a cot was purchased. Then she needed a mattress. We prayed for a mattress, and God helped us get a mattress for her.
Each week she needed 250 to 300 rupees for medicine and injections. The
women's ministries helped her buy them. The doctors warned that she
should be operated on within two months or she would die. The operation
would cost 25,000 rupees.

After the operation she would need to be in bed for six months and was to
be given a good diet along with the medicines. It all seemed so very costly. She
was an orphan—she didn't have anyone: father, mother, brother, or sister. All
the expenses were to be met by either the school or the church, but neither
could give that much money. So we started praying very earnestly.

Our prayer was answered again. Our mission gave Rs.10,000, and someone else gave Rs.15,000. She was operated on successfully. For six months she
was in bed, and again volunteers took care of her. God led us wonderfully
and miraculously. Now she is so happy and active and comes along with us
for ministry. God is the refuge for the humble and the simple.

*Praise be to the Lord; even a mother can forget her sucking child, but You,
our Lord, never forget us.*
GIRIJA DANIEL

Help From the Lord

I will lift up mine eyes unto the hills, from whence cometh my help. My help cometh from the Lord, which made heaven and earth. Ps. 121:1, 2.

THE LONE WINDOW AT the end of the long hospital corridor on the third floor of the pediatric wing of the Puerto Rico Medical Center opened to a view of that part of the island where no hills could be seen. I desperately wanted to see a hill, a symbol of the source of help I sorely needed at that time.

It started with a persistent cough, accompanied by flulike symptoms that gradually progressed to double lobar pneumonia. Soon my 7-year-old son had to be airlifted from our home island of St. Thomas, in the United States Virgin Islands, to the Commonwealth of Puerto Rico for medical care. He was suffering from an illness that had reduced him from a happy, normal child to an invalid who could not walk unassisted, control his bowel movements, or swallow his saliva without choking. He had also lost eye coordination and spoke with slurred speech.

The physicians held many consultations, ran numerous tests, took several X-rays, and finally a CAT scan before they concluded he was suffering from viral encephalomyelitis, a condition in which the brain stem is stripped of its covering, affecting the functions that it controls.

As I looked at the emaciated form of my child, I realized he was dying and cheerfully began to speak with him about falling asleep in Jesus. That is, I tried to be cheerful for his sake, but my own heart was breaking, and I needed to see a hill. Through tear-filled eyes I could see only fluffy white clouds in a blue sky. During his 15-day stay in the hospital I found relief in that corridor as I paraphrased the text to meet my need: "I will lift up mine eyes unto the [cloud] from whence cometh my help. My help cometh from the Lord, which made heaven and earth."

Help suddenly came one morning when my son sat up in his hospital bed unassisted. I had received a miracle! Not from the hills or from the clouds, but from the Lord, who made heaven and earth!   CANDACE SPRAUVE

Heavenly Kisses

Those who fear the Lord are secure; he will be a place of refuge for their children. Prov. 14:26, NLT.

I RECEIVED A SPECIAL e-mail from my sister, Jan. She has given me permission to share what happened. We believe that our sense of humor helps keep us sane. *Jesus, thank You for the gift of laughter.*

Jan, her husband, and her 17-year-old son, Kory, were driving home. It had been a special day for Kory, so they were discussing what a great day the Lord had given them. Everything had been going well, but then a little discord started to creep in among them because of something that was said. Later, no one could remember what was said or who said it, but tension began to mount. At that moment they noticed something speeding up behind them. Then it zoomed past as they looked on in amazement. There beside them, bigger than life, towered three large tin-foil-wrapped Hershey's Kisses. They appeared to be sitting on a flatbed trailer, complete with headlights and taillights, but it wasn't being pulled by any rig that they could detect. They couldn't see a windshield or a driver, just three giant kisses flying down the highway. Across the back was written, "Love Mobile" or "Kiss Mobile." (Jan couldn't remember which it was, but at the time they all just started laughing.) They tried to catch up with the Hershey's Kisses, but the Kisses were going much too fast, and Jan and her family were nearing their exit.

She wrote, "We laughed just thinking about such a funny sight. The discord was gone. This thought popped into my brain. *The three of us had just been kissed by our loving Father, who was not going to let the enemy come in and steal the praises we were giving Him on that night!* "Draw nigh to God, and he will draw nigh to you" (James 4:8).

Kory is 3 years older than his cousin, Sonny, who is my son, and who is severely mentally challenged. For years Kory has taken Sonny on the kiddy rides at the county fair. Kory delights in making Sonny feel special. To me, Kory is special. With love I tease him that his freckles are "angel's kisses."

Our heavenly Father loves to kiss us with special love, coming at just the right moments, and delights when we share that love with those around us.

JANET TERRY AND DEBORAH SANDERS

In Relation to the Mall

Therefore thus saith the Lord God, Behold, I lay in Zion for a foundation a stone, a tried stone, a precious corner stone, a sure foundation: he that believeth shall not make haste. Isa. 28:16.

AFTER MOVING TO TENNESSEE I had a hard time figuring out where I was going. Not only were there more streets to deal with, many streets didn't have visible street signs, and many were curvy, which added to the mystery. The streets and cities seemed to never connect in my mind for quite some time. It didn't help my sense of direction that my husband would vary his route to a location every time we went somewhere. I soon discovered that environment played a part in my directional dilemma. I found that the bounty of beautiful trees not only provided shade but served as the edges for the maze I was in.

One day my husband asked me to run an errand for him. I could feel my stress level begin to rise. He didn't sense my fear as he began telling me how to get where he needed me to go. (He sometimes forgets I am geographically challenged.)

"Please, just give me directions in relation to the mall. That will give me a reference point," I said to my husband. The location of the mall was one place I knew. I could get there and back with ease by taking a familiar route. He gave me the directions, and I was off on my adventure.

My life is like traveling. Many times I've traveled along, not really knowing where I was going. At times I've relied on instinct to get me to various destinations in life. This usually proved to be very dangerous, and I found myself on unstable soil. In order to put my life in perspective, I need a cornerstone as a guide on my map. I need something to relate to so I don't become lost. The Lord puts me on sure and stable ground when I ask the question "In relation to Christ, where is that in my life?"

Lord, thank You for helping me travel this far with few bumps and bruises. I pray that daily I will ask for and accept Your guidance in my life. I know You are with me when I deviate or become lost. I love You, Lord.

MARY WAGONER ANGELIN

October 25

Can We Ever Outgive the Lord?

Give, and it will be given to you. A good measure, pressed down, shaken together and running over, will be poured into your lap. Luke 6:38, NIV.

A S I OPENED MY e-mail one morning I was delighted to see a letter from a dear friend who had lived in the same town as we did years ago when our children were small. We had exchanged Christmas cards and letters over the years, but until the year before when we attended a church reunion, we had not had a personal conversation, nor did I know that she had e-mail. I was really looking forward to reading what she had to say.

She opened with some news about her and her husband, then went on to describe the little church elementary school in their hometown. She told of the lovely facility, the excellent teachers, and wonderful students; then she mentioned the financial problems they were having in meeting the expenses of the school. The majority of their members were elderly and on fixed incomes; the young families were struggling to put food on the table and pay the rent. Then she boldly asked if we would be able to give some financial help.

My first response was "No way!" We were having some financial difficulties of our own at the time, and I couldn't see any way we could send them anything. I looked at the checkbook, and it confirmed my feelings. Then it hit me: If the Lord had impressed her to ask us for financial help, He would provide a way for us to send that help. My next action was to write a check for a sizable amount and place it in the mail. I encouraged my mother to send a check as well, which she was happy to do.

That afternoon when I went out to get our mail, there was a check for some old furniture we had sold on consignment. It had been a while since we had sent the furniture to be sold, and we'd almost forgotten about it. The amount not only covered the amount of the check I had written to the school, but was half again as much.

What timing! We know the children in the school were blessed, but I think we were blessed even more. God is so good to keep His promises.

ANNA MAY RADKE WATERS

306

Jesus Never Fails

Casting all your care upon him; for he careth for you. 1 Peter 5:7.

IT HAD BEEN JUST one week since my husband, Ed, had been rebaptized, and my two sons, Sanjeev, 14, and David, 12, had been baptized. This was a time of rejoicing for my family as we walked with Jesus, preparing for His kingdom. However, Satan didn't like this and had to intervene.

I dropped my older son off at school, did some grocery shopping, came home, and started to unload my groceries from the car trunk. I was so surprised when I was confronted by two teenagers standing near our townhouse. The younger of the two came close to me and asked where house number 2001 was. I wasn't sure where it was located, so I tried to divert their attention in another direction. They hesitated for a while. Then the older boy turned to me and said, "Ma'am, what nationality are you? Are you an Indian?"

I responded, "Yes, I am an Indian." I closed my trunk and went inside. That's when I saw a note David had written and left for me: "Mommy, please close the back door." I went toward the back to check the door. From there I could see that the two teens were still standing around by the fence. I quickly bolted the door. Almost immediately the doorbell rang. I peeped through the hole and realized it was the same youngsters.

Gently I opened the door just a little, and immediately the taller, older boy pointed a gun at my face. "Open the door and let us in, or else I will kill you!"

By God's grace, I was able to force the door shut with all my might, while I shouted, "Police! Police! Help!"

Jesus answered my feeble cry immediately. The boys fled. I regained my courage and wits enough to call the police. They came shortly and took a detailed report, spending two hours questioning me, as well as giving emotional comfort.

Praise God, He delivered me when I most needed Him. Surely the angels of the Lord do camp around us and deliver us (Ps. 34:7).   QUTIE DEWAR

October 27

Catch Those Falling Leaves

I press toward the goal for the prize of the upward call of God in Christ Jesus. Phil. 3:14, NKJV.

O N A COLD, WINDY Sabbath afternoon three young girls and a mother dared the gusty wind to celebrate Beamy's sixteenth birthday. Her birthday wish was simple: a picnic in a park with her best friends. So still in the our church dresses, we headed for the park.

We happily spread the food on the table, sang a birthday song for Beamy, took some pictures, and sat down to enjoy the scrumptious picnic lunch. The breeze loosened the amber leaves that floated down, sailing in the air before dropping to the ground.

"Oh, I want to catch some leaves for each of us. I've been told it's good luck when you catch one." Carey left her lunch to catch the falling leaves.

"It's superstition, Carey," one of the girls pointed out.

"I know, but I just enjoy catching fluttering leaves," she answered.

We watched her dart here and there, trying to catch the falling leaves. She looked very naive and trusting. She finally caught one leaf and held it close to her heart.

"Carey, I saw several leaves right close to you, but you were aiming for the ones that seemed far beyond your reach," I commented.

Aren't we sometimes like that, aiming for what we cannot reach, something that's beyond our means, or for someone who is not with us? Perhaps we tell ourselves that if we can go to a faraway land to be a missionary, then we will be happy. Or maybe we try to live in the past—if only Mom were still alive, I would visit or call her often. Pause and look around. We are surrounded with a vast mission field. Our family, friends, coworkers, neighbors—they need us to give them the love of Jesus.

Often we take our family members—husband, children, sisters, brothers, parents—for granted. How about our office mates in the next cubicle? They're right there, very close to us; they are within our reach. We can touch them and hold them close to our hearts. The joy will be mutual.

Help me, Lord, to share Your love with everyone I come in contact with today.

JEMIMA D. ORILLOSA

Lost Things, Broken Things

*I will seek that which was lost . . . and will bind up that which was broken.
Eze. 34:16.*

OUR WEDDING PICTURES WERE missing! We were married at Fort
Francis E. Warren in Cheyenne, Wyoming, where my husband was stationed during World War II. The Army Signal Corps took our pictures and
posted them on the bulletin board, but a few days later they were gone. Now
only the precious memory of it is all that remains.

Years later I realized our wedding book was missing, too. I don't know
when it was lost. I just didn't come across it anymore. The same thing happened to my husband's Army service pins. Still missing is the beautiful walking cane that Parkin Christian of Pitcairn Island carved and gave to us when
he was a guest in our home. And information I had not backed up was lost
the day my computer crashed.

I shed a few tears when my beautiful crystal basket was broken. A few
more were shed when I discovered my prized porcelain Lipizzaner horse
from Vienna had been broken. And a broken arm certainly didn't brighten
my day. Broken promises, broken hearts, and broken lives—all seem too
painful to endure.

But we're not alone. I remember that God has experienced lost and broken things also. One sad day He endured the loss of one third of His beloved,
magnificent angels. And their loss resulted in lost children created in His
image. He has felt the pain of broken things as well, greater by far than I can
comprehend. Once a beautiful sapphire gem of great magnitude on which 10
messages were engraved with His own finger came crashing down a moun-
tainside. It was a transcript of His character. Sadly, it has been broken many
times since by His children.

But somehow I think there can be no grief greater than that of losing a
child. God must have felt that way, too, because even though it broke His
great heart of love, He accepted the offer of His beloved Son to pay the price
to redeem us, His children in a world gone wrong.

Someday our loved ones, missing in death, will be restored. There will be
no more broken promises or broken hearts, no more broken lives or broken
dreams. I look forward to residing in that happy place where all is happiness
forever. I can hardly wait!   LORRAINE HUDGINS

Blessed Rice

And He took the five loaves and the two fish, and looking up to heaven, He blessed and broke and gave the loaves to the disciples; and the disciples gave to the multitudes. Matt. 14:19, NKJV.

THE BINTARO CHURCH IN Indonesia wanted to have evangelistic meetings every night for two weeks. Because the church could be used only on Wednesday and Saturday nights, they had to find another place to conduct the meeting. My parents offered our house.

Those in charge estimated there would be about 30 people attending every night. We planned to serve them a meal each evening before the meeting. However, the first night there were 75 people! My mom was in a panic and instantly decided to cook more rice. When she took the rice from the rice box, she discovered there was only a small amount left. She asked me to remind her to buy more before the next meeting.

The following day we were so busy preparing foods for the evening meeting we forgot to buy more rice. When my mom checked the rice in the rice box, I heard her scream, "Lanny, please come here." She was standing in front of the rice box. "Lanny, look. I can't believe this. Yesterday I asked you to remind me to get some more rice, remember? But look—the rice is still here!"

I came closer and saw that the rice was still there, exactly at the same level it had been before we had used it.

In our surprise, we thanked and praised the Lord for the miracle. Seventy-five people attended the meetings every night for two weeks, and we never bought more rice. When the meetings ended, our rice supply also ended. To add to our family's happiness, seven souls were baptized as the result of the meetings. Praise the Lord!

God, You are so good. Thank You for being our best provider and helper. I want my testimony to help others to know that You are real and can be present in their lives as well.
LANNY LYDIA PONGILATAN

Rooted in the Lord

Continue in the faith grounded and settled, and be not moved. Col.1:23.

FIERCE RAIN AND WINDS the strength of a tornado howled around our
log cabin like a roaring freight train, rushing at demonic speed to inevitable destruction. The force was terrifying. We frantically endeavored to
secure windows, doors, and breezeways. Debris of all kinds whirled in the atmosphere. Neighbors living in less secure buildings rushed to take refuge in
our den. We weathered the night together. The storm abated as quickly as it
had come, but darkness hid the destruction around us.

At the first rays of morning light, we stepped outside to view the carnage.
Hundreds of giant oak trees lay like fallen generals on a battlefield. They
crisscrossed roads, making them impassable to traffic. Shingles were missing
from rooftops. Barns and outbuildings were demolished, and their splintered
frames scattered over the ground. Power lines lay tangled, and communication lines were broken. Electric power was out. We were in a disaster area
caused by a number of small tornadoes.

We were aghast at the destruction of hundreds of trees around our home.
We noticed with great interest that these giants of the forest lay uprooted
from the base. These particular trees had no taproot, no anchor root pene-
trating deep into the sod. They had only a very shallow root system, spreading out just below the ground surface. This caused them to topple when the
big storm came.

What a lesson for my life! If my roots are shallow, if I do not dig deep
into the Word of God and be nourished by the waters and nutrients far down
in the earth, like these oak trees I will have no foundation to withstand the
winds and storms of life. If my relationship with God is shallow, the surface
roots will not provide a secure foundation, and I will be toppled when the big
storm comes.

*Dear God, help me today to dig deep into the well of salvation that I may be
"rooted and grounded in love" and righteousness and be able to stand against the
winds and storms of life* (Eph. 3:17). JOAN MINCHIN NEALL

October 31

Conduit of His Love

A word fitly spoken is like apples of gold in settings of silver. Prov. 25:11, NKJV.

IT WAS THE LAST DAY of our stay on the island where my husband and I had conducted some evangelistic crusades. Before I could relax, though, someone asked me to speak to the ministers' wives that evening. As thanks for the hard work we had just finished, we were on our way to enjoy some relaxation and see the longest underground river. I refused the invitation, giving all kinds of reasons, because I didn't have any resources with me. I didn't have enough time, either. Besides, we'd be on the trip for the whole day.

But for every excuse I gave, the woman gave a more convincing reason that I should speak that evening. Finally she said, "I've read your articles in the women's devotionals, and I know you're capable of leading the group tonight." Then, of all things, my husband said, "Honey, God can use you tonight."

My mind raced. What should I talk about? I closed my eyes and lifted my heart heavenward right there in the van. "Lord, please impress me as to what I should say to the ministers' wives." I thought of how those wives could be the best support of their husbands' ministry. I thought of how a well-ordered home could be one of the best arguments in favor of Christianity, as a favorite author of mine had said. Ideas flooded my mind as the Lord impressed me. Late that afternoon, after we came back from the trip, I jotted down a few Bible texts, and then scribbled out a short outline. I asked God to help me be an instrument in His hand and prayed that the Holy Spirit would attend that evening meeting.

As soon as I finished my presentation, many wives asked questions. God was so gracious to help me during that question-and-answer forum. Several women asked if it was possible for me to give the same talk to their husbands the following morning. I told them that my husband was scheduled to speak prior to our leaving the following morning.

I praised the Lord for using me that evening. Yes, as a humble instrument in His hand, God made me a conduit of His love.   OFELIA A. PANGAN

Help! I've Fallen, and I Can't Get Up

The Lord upholds all those who fall and lifts up all who are bowed down.
Ps. 145:14, NIV.

HELP! I'VE FALLEN, and I can't get up." Remember that commercial from a few years ago? A lot of people laughed at it, but I didn't, because that has been one of my fears for years—that I would fall, probably down the steps, and there would be no one there to help. When my children were small and my husband was away on temporary duty with the Army, I worried about this. Not obsessively, but enough to make me very careful as I went up and down stairs.

In later years when the children were away at boarding school or college and my husband was traveling, I wondered who would miss me if I should fall and not be able to get up.

My cousin Dottie fell and couldn't get up. She lived in a senior housing unit but couldn't reach her call button. Fortunately, someone soon came to her rescue. Others are not so blessed.

We worried about my father-in-law living by himself and ordered a call button for him to wear around his neck. Often, when we visited, we found that he was not wearing his button. "I've never fallen or needed it before, so why should I need it now?" he would argue. One day we received a call. He had fallen and had been unable to get up; however, he was wearing his call button! In a few minutes his neighbor was there to help him and to call an ambulance. His hip was broken. We don't know, as is often the case, whether his hip broke and he fell, or if he fell and broke his hip. Either way, he was down and couldn't get up without help.

Help, Lord—I've fallen, and I can't get up. In fact, there's nothing I can do to help myself. There is no way to lift myself out of this bog of transgression and iniquity.

There are so many ways to fall, almost all of which I have tried at one time or another. We've also all sinned. Paul called himself the chief of sinners, but I'm quite sure he was no worse than the rest of us. I'm so glad that I have found the way to get back up again when I fall; by the grace of God I can have help immediately. Lifted up, brushed off, cleaned up, and set on my feet again. *Help! I've fallen, but help is already on the way. Thank You, Jesus.*

ARDIS DICK STENBAKKEN

The Holy Spirit Leads Me

As for God, his way is perfect: the word of the Lord is tried: he is a buckler to all those that trust in him. Ps. 18:30.

WHILE I WAS VISITING my daughter and her fiancé, the topic turned to spiritual things. David said that if he had a Bible he would look up the topics. I thought little more of it for three months. Then I asked them over for an engagement supper and thought about giving them something as a memento gift. I was thinking about what David had said about wanting a Bible and knew that I had some new ones on my bookshelf.

"Lord," I prayed, "if You want me to give a Bible, as I am shopping for a gift today, don't let me find that gift. Then I'll know You want me to give the Bible." I didn't find a present, though I looked for hours. When I got home, I took a Bible down and wrapped it up.

When I had gone out to buy the engagement present, I had also wanted to give my daughter a special gift that would reflect a spiritual theme. I had an angel in mind, and while I was shopping I had a prayer in my heart that the Lord would lead me to the right one. A merchant in the mall told me of a gift boutique around the corner that carried angels. Sure enough, there were lots of them, but they were either not what I wanted, or they were too expensive.

As I was walking out the door, disappointed, something told me to go back. There, in the rear corner on a shelf, was the perfect thing. I picked it up and held it ever so reverently in my hand. As I cradled it, it molded gently into my palm, and tears came into my eyes. Not only was it an angel, but a praying angel with a most delicate tiny candle attached to it. *Perfect. I want my daughter to know that prayers are answered, and one day she may need to come to God. Thank You so much, Lord,* was my silent prayer.

When I gave David his gift, my husband frowned and said, "He doesn't want a Bible!"

David said, "Oh, yes I do."

After my daughter read the note attached to her gift, she got up and flung her arms around me and cried, thanking me for the touching words. David had his nose stuck in his Bible all the rest of the evening, and the conversation was on spiritual things.

VIDELLA MCCLELLAN

Lord, Hear My Cry!

My soul finds rest in God alone; my salvation comes from him. He alone is my rock and my salvation. Ps. 62:1, 2, NIV.

MY FATHER HAD FALLEN and broken his hip. He was very weak, and the operation was too much for him; he was not recovering. My parents live in Sweden, my sister in Canada, and my brother in California. Living in southern Germany, I was the closest. None of us was able to be with my parents at this time, but we were in constant contact by telephone.

I was restless and wandered around. But then my piano pulled me like a magnet, as it always does when I'm under emotional stress. I sat down and started to play and sing the song by Bertold Engel that happened to be open on the music stand: " 'Lord, hear my cry, I need You so! Lord, hear my cry! I need some rock on which to stand. I know, You will carry me home.' "

"Yes, I need You, and my father needs You, Lord," I prayed as I played.

My sister and brother-in-law had been to see Dad a few weeks earlier, and I had asked them to pray with him on behalf of all of us. My sister prayed with him, holding his hands. He pressed her hands very hard in confirmation of her words. Then she said, "We are waiting for the day when the Lord will come again so that we can all be together once more."

Dad simply said, "I am waiting, too."

"I know, You'll carry me home. I know You will carry me home." *Yes, Lord, carry him home, and not only him but all who have longed for His appearing. Lord, guide us through the darkness of this world to that heavenly place where we all want to feel at home. We want to be with him in Your kingdom.*

When Mom called a little later to tell me that Dad had passed away at 8:35, I realized that just at the moment when he found rest, I was singing this song. When we compared notes later, we realized that my sister and brother-in-law had been in prayer for him at approximately the same time. So although we were not able to be physically at his bedside, all of us had been with him in spirit. "Yes, Lord," I pray once more, "carry us all home, and give us the crown of righteousness You have promised."

HANNELE OTTSCHOFSKI

Election Deadlock Broken

The Lord will be king over the whole earth. On that day there will be one Lord, and his name the only name. Zech. 14:9, NIV.

A S I WATCHED THE news Tuesday evening, November 7, 2000, the presidential election day in the United States, it was surprising to see that no decision could be made because of a gridlock in the "razor-thin" race. The two candidates had a nearly equal number of electoral votes, which determines the winner. Long into that night the race continued. At one moment it was thought that one candidate had won, but in a few moments it was the other candidate. Presses were halted while printing the new headlines. History was on hold. Until a recount could be made, no one would know for sure who would become the new president of the United States.

The next morning the news was still the same. Throughout the night it had been back and forth from one candidate to the other; the race was so close. No one could say for sure how it would turn out. It all depended on the recount.

For many days I listened for the results of the election. Would the candidate I had voted for win? The votes of three counties in Florida were to be recounted. No one knew who was ahead—it was so confusing. Some of the voters in one county claimed the ballots were wrong. Campaign leaders tried to secure lawyers to file a lawsuit. The opposing candidates protested the resulting numbers. Many days of frustration followed.

The count went on. Weeks later the final winner was announced. Now my country finally could get on with its business of preparing for its transfer of power to a new president.

I thought of the long controversy between Christ and Satan, a power struggle that's been "on hold" for centuries. However, I know the ending. I've read the last of the book, Revelation. I voted for Christ, and I know He will win in this race. Even though Satan will make a last desperate attempt to overturn the vote, Jesus will win! Yes, I like the ending of that story, and I want to be with my choice of candidate, Jesus Christ, forever.

Dear Lord, I want to be with You, the certain winner of that great election. I want to be among the saved and be forever with You! BESSIE SIEMENS LOBSIEN

The Straight Road

Strait is the gate, and narrow is the way, which leadeth unto life. Matt. 7:14.

A FEW YEARS AGO my husband and I were asked to accompany a friend of our family and her aunt to a small village in a location neither of them knew. We had a name; that was all. After traveling for what seemed a long time, the women in the car became concerned.

"Let's ask if we are on the right road," I suggested.

"That's not necessary. We'll find it," my husband replied.

Once again the male ego showed its full colors, and my husband continued, in spite of the concerns of the women in the car.

"I really think we should ask someone." My friend sounded anxious, and so was I.

We approached an elderly gentleman. "Here is an adult; it will not hurt to ask him."

"Are we on the right road to Campbell's Castle?"

"You are on the right road, but about a mile from here you will come upon two roads. One is narrow and rocky, and the other is wide and straight. Do not be fooled into thinking that the straight road is the right one. Keep on the narrow road. Follow it, even if you feel that it is the wrong one. It will take you straight into Campbell's Castle."

Sure enough, the narrow roller-coaster road took us to the place. The road was so bad in some places that we really thought of going back to the other road, but the old man's voice echoed in our heads, *Keep on the narrow road.*

Our Christian experience seems like a rocky, narrow, difficult road at times. We are doubtful if the path that we are following is indeed the one that God would have us follow. The Written Word will come to our rescue in these times of doubt. The assurances are always clear and straightforward.

Dear God, when life gets complicated and the road seems narrow and I cannot see where You are leading me, help me to sense Your presence and follow, in spite of my confused feelings.

GLORIA GREGORY

November 6

Come Home

But in keeping with his promise we are looking forward to a new heaven and a new earth, the home of righteousness. 2 Peter 3:13, NIV.

GROWING UP IN A rural community, my siblings and I were able to roam the countryside exploring caves, building tree houses, climbing large rocks, splashing in the creek, and searching for Native American artifacts such as obsidian arrowheads. We were able to wander freely for several hours at a time, playing with neighbors and pets. I have many fond memories of times spent with my brother and sisters, enjoying the outdoors. When it was time to come home, my mother had a special signal: three honks of her car horn—*honk, honk, honk!* This was the signal to come home from wherever we had wandered and from whatever we were doing.

"Come home!" said my mother's call. "I'm going into town. Do you want to come with me?" "Come home! I need to talk to you." "Come home! The dress I'm sewing for you is ready for you to try on so we can pin the hem." "Come home! Supper is ready, and the family is gathering to eat." I remember pausing from whatever we were doing and saying, "Hey, that sounded like a car horn. Yes, it's Mom honking. Let's head home." And home we would dash to see why Mother was calling us.

Since my childhood I have known about God's promises to prepare a heavenly home for His people and to someday call us home to live in heaven with Him. In fact, I've read and heard those words so many times over the years that I sometimes take these promises for granted. It is always uplifting to me to talk to new Christians who are filled with enthusiasm as they discover the wonderful promises of God. How excited they are to discover that Jesus is calling—calling them to come to Him, to get to know Him, to get their lives ready so that they will be able to respond when He calls them to come home to live with Him forever.

Lord, help me today to rediscover the joy of knowing that You are preparing a place just for me and that someday soon You will call me home. With the enthusiasm and excitement of a child hurrying home when mother calls, let me be ready to respond to Your call to come home with You forever! SANDRA SIMANTON

The Price of Discipline

The Lord disciplines those he loves. Heb. 12:6, NIV.

WHAT FUN IT WAS that November day to accompany my friends to the chrysanthemum gardens in a nearby town. The rain was pouring down, and other flowers had long since finished blooming, but the mums were in their prime. It seemed that each plant we saw was more beautiful than the others, and it was difficult to decide which to purchase for our own.

I finally chose three plants to keep indoors since winter was almost upon us. Even though I tried to give them good care, only one plant survived. In the spring I set that plant out in my garden and hoped for the best. It survived, even multiplied and had a few blooms. The second season, when summer came, my plants were growing really well. But the instructions said that I was to cut them back severely in July. That was hard for me to do, because I didn't want to lose my remaining chrysanthemum plants.

They looked rather sad after their pruning, especially since my other flowers were now in full bloom. The summer passed quickly, and I had almost forgotten about my mums, which were obscured by a tall rosebush.

One day in the fall I looked behind the rosebush, and what a surprise met my eyes! The chrysanthemums had not only survived, they were loaded with the most exquisite blooms. I quickly shared the news with my husband, and the next day when a friend came I had to show her my treasure.

"Oh, may I have some of them? They are just what I need for my presentation tomorrow, and all my flowers are gone."

I was so happy to share them with her, as she had shared plants with me many times.

Sometimes in my life trials and hard times come, and I feel beaten down. I feel that I have nothing to share with anyone. Then I remember that the Lord disciplines those He loves, and if I accept that discipline I will become a stronger Christian and will be able to help others through my experiences.

Thank You, Lord, for Your love and Your discipline today. BETTY J. ADAMS

Cindy

We should behave like God's very own children, adopted into the bosom of his family, and calling to him, "Father, Father." For his Holy Spirit speaks to us deep in our hearts, and tells us that we really are God's children. And since we are his children, we will share his treasures—for all God gives to his Son Jesus is now ours too. Rom. 8:15-17, TLB.

CINDY WAS 6 YEARS OLD when I met her. I was a rookie social worker just out of college, and she had already spent three years in a foster home. Cindy had been born to parents who had no parenting skills and who lived in poverty. She had an older brother and sister, and the three of them were frequently left to fend for themselves. When Cindy was 3, the circumstances in the home had deteriorated to the point where there was no food or supervision. One day, out of desperation, they stole some money from their mother's purse to get something to eat. When the parents discovered the "theft," they took turns beating each child unmercifully with a pool cue. That is when Cindy and her siblings were moved into foster care.

Now, three years later, I was given the assignment of finding an adoptive home for Cindy. I read adoptive home studies and interviewed families until I found the family that seemed just right for her. The family included a mother, a dad, and four brothers—and they wanted a girl! I described Cindy to them, and they were interested. A visit was arranged. Cindy worried during the entire four-hour trip. Several times she asked if I thought they would like her, or if they would beat her like her parents had.

They had a wonderful visit—and another one a week later. It was during the second visit that we had a family conference. Mom, dad, and the four boys asked Cindy to join their family. Cindy considered the proposal quietly, and then asked them if they would always love her. They assured her that they would, and with tears in her eyes she went to each family member in turn and said, "You are my mom. You are my dad. You are my brother."

Whenever I remember Cindy, I think of the verses in Romans 8 that tell us that because of Jesus' sacrifice of His human life, God offers adoption to us. We can be joint heirs with Jesus and permanent members of God's family. The choice is ours.   CLARICE B. TURNER

Soup Sisters

The wise are known for their understanding, and instruction is appreciated if it's well presented. Prov. 16:21, NLT. Get all the advice and instruction you can, and be wise the rest of your life. Prov. 19:20, NLT.

GREEN SPLIT-PEA SOUP! How could this hot liquid that is loathed by some and loved by others provide quality time between a mother and her six daughters?

Maude, my mother, never attended college to take family psychology, but she knew her girls liked green split-pea soup. She knew if we disagreed on everything else, she could catch up with our joys and sorrows, give sound counsel, and help mend our relationships around that pot of soup.

Mom confided in me that when her girls were entering puberty she had to find some way to talk to them, away from their brothers. She knew her sons weren't going to rush home for dinner when green split-pea soup was on the menu. Now that we were all grown up, she confessed that she missed knowing how we were doing. Therefore, this female slurping retreat was revived. Annually, on a Saturday afternoon, the matriarch of our family convened her court.

At first just her daughters gathered around her kitchen table. Mom thought the dining room was too formal. Then the granddaughters and, later, the great-granddaughters joined the sisterhood of Soup Sisters. Each generation brought their challenges with parenting, dating, marriages, decisions, and testimonies of God's miracles. Mom listened as we sipped and slurped. She served up the soup, the rolls, the crackers, and, most of all, her wisdom and love. By talking to each other we found our own silent answers and responses to life.

When I became a vegetarian, Mom made me a separate pot of green split-pea soup, so I had no excuse for missing what her tribe calls "Soup Sisters Meetings."

Our blessed mother fell asleep in Jesus, and she awaits His voice. Yet her annual tradition lives on with a very important twist. Now the males of the family join in making it a family reunion. This gathering is just a foretaste of that great table set for us in heaven where Jesus will sup with His daughters, sons—and Mom, too. Will you meet us there?   JUDY M. KERR

Set Your House in Order

*So always be ready, because you don't know the day your Lord will come.
Matt. 24:42, NCV. Set thine house in order. 2 Kings 20:1.*

MY IN-LAWS LIVED in the South, about 1,000 miles away from us. We would visit about twice a year, making the trip by car, traveling day and night.

Before leaving we'd have the car serviced to make sure everything was working properly and that the tires were in good shape. We washed the car. We packed our suitcases. A day before leaving, we'd buy a gallon of Swiss chocolate ice cream, my mother-in-law's favorite flavor, from a certain ice-cream shop and pack it in dry ice to take to Mother. Knowing how pleased she would be and the anticipation of seeing loved ones made our adrenaline rise.

Mother was an immaculate housekeeper, but when she knew we were coming, she'd do something extra: she would cook our favorite foods and bake our favorite desserts. Sabbath dinners were always special. She didn't want us to tell her what time we would arrive—she just wanted us to arrive safely. However, when we drove in the driveway, she wanted everything ready and in order. The greetings, the hugs, and the smiles made the long trip worthwhile.

I thought about another trip that I will soon take. This time it will not be in a car, and it will take seven days to reach the final destination. I will not be tired. Nevertheless, before I close my eyes to await that time, I must be certain that my house is in order. Since I don't know the day or the hour when Christ is coming, I must be ready. I must ask Jesus to clean up my spiritual house. All cobwebs in the recesses of my heart must be swept away. My words and thoughts must be acceptable in His sight. I must make eternal preparations.

The Lord is making preparations for me also. He is building a mansion just for me. I enjoy good food, but there is no food here on earth that will compare with the bread of heaven. Christ will have everything ready and in order for me. I have to be certain that I tell Jesus that I want to be with Him so that my spiritual house is in order.

What a reunion that will be when we meet our loved ones once more, never to say goodbye again!   MARIE H. SEARD

I Am Missing You

I will come again, and receive you unto myself; that where I am, there ye may be also. John 14:3.

ANOTHER SNOWSTORM SWIRLED OUTSIDE in the dark night. We were gathered around the fireplace watching the flames and listening to the roaring of the fire. My daughter was visiting from England, and we had no concern for the snow depth or what it was doing.

The sharp ring of the telephone broke our peaceful reveries. My daughter said, "Mom, you answer it. It's always for you."

"I am missing you." It was Mei, my former student. These were the usual words that came across the many miles from China.

I replied, "I am missing you, too." We had a pleasant chat about our lives in two different countries so many miles apart, after having lived so close together for so many months in China.

This brings to my mind our friend Jesus. We have accepted Him into our hearts and claimed Him as our best friend. But sometimes we get busy, and our Bibles are left untouched. I think as we walk past our Bible that Jesus is saying, "I am missing you."

God and Jesus at Creation made the most beautiful world there ever could be for us to enjoy—the majestic hills; the roaring, endless oceans; the luscious green grass; the intricate, beautiful, multicolored flowers; and the peaceful blue dome of sky filled with clouds. Wherever we live, some of this is visible to us. It is God's second book. Are we thankful for the beauty? Do we see it? Remember the saying, "Stop to smell the roses along the way."

Last year my New Year's resolution was to take an art class—I don't have any great talent, but it helped to open my eyes even more to the beauty around me, to God's nature, and even to man's handicrafts. Is God saying "I am missing you" as we hurry along and do not read or enjoy His second book, nature, that is all around us in its wonderful beauty?

Mei writes me, e-mails me, and then spends her yuan to telephone me; she wants to hear my voice. I become more real to her. And God is waiting for our voices in prayer. He has accepted our commitment to Him; He wants to be part of our life for the day. We must take time to invite Him. Mei is missing me; I miss Mei. God misses us even more.　　　　DESSA WEISZ HARDIN

November 12

The Soda Surprise

Listen, my dear friends! God chose the poor people of this world to be rich in faith and to possess the kingdom which he promised to those who love him. James 2:5, TEV.

I KNOW A LOT ABOUT being poor because I've been there. When I was little most of my friends were poor, too, so I didn't feel sorry for myself very often. People were always giving us things, such as outgrown clothes, used toys, and home-grown produce.

Of course, it's wonderful to donate to charity clothes you've outgrown. When I have an item I no longer need, I always try to find it a good home instead of simply tossing it in the garbage. But giving up something you don't want doesn't require much thought and isn't particularly generous.

When you're poor, you accept any gift with a smile and a thank-you. But your true gratitude for the donation depends a lot on the attitude of the giver. Some people embarrass you by making a big production about giving you cast-off clothing. They make you feel as if they are better than you in some way just because they have more money.

My father was once on disability. A sweet church lady brought us a big box of groceries. If you've never gotten a box from a food drive let me tell you what's usually in them. People donate practical, cheap food that won't spoil. That means things such as spaghetti, peanut butter, crackers, and canned vegetables. After all, if you're truly hungry you don't worry about whether something actually tastes good, right? All those foods were in the box, but there was something else, too—a large bottle of soda. Apparently some kind soul had realized that the poor like to have a party as much as everyone else.

Whenever I donate something to a food drive, I remember that soda and try to give something a little extra and impractical, like snack foods and candy. Giving away that dented can of pea soup or that sweatshirt with the big stain on the front is fine, but a generous person is willing to spend a little money to give someone a gift they will really enjoy. The poor like the same things other people do, only they don't have the means to get them.

God gave the most expensive gift of all. I want to be like Him.   GINA LEE

Out in a Fog

Let the words of my mouth . . . be acceptable in thy sight, O Lord. Ps. 19:14.

WE WERE OUT IN a boat along the Florida Keys with some visitors, enjoying the beauties of nature. This was a region Merlin and I had never ventured into before, but the man at the helm had been in this backwater several times. Suddenly a fog rolled in unexpectedly—a rarity in this area. (We later learned that it had been in the forecast.) There was no way to tell where we were, since the fog had closed about us so quickly. It was already late afternoon. We were having evening worship, singing and expressing thanks, but with children in our group there was reason for a certain amount of uneasiness. Our experienced boatman couldn't tell where we were located or what direction to head to find our way home. We bowed in prayer.

I don't know why, but the thought came to my mind to ask God to send us two angels in a boat to lead us home. In fact, I said those words aloud, adding that it would be OK with us if they were His human angel helpers.

Moments later a boat headed toward us in the fog. Two fishermen appeared out there in the middle of nowhere. We signaled to them, telling them we were lost, and asking if they knew where they were and how to get us home. They asked us where we wanted to go, and we told them Big Pine Key. They said, "Follow us; we know the way. We're going there also."

Oh, how close we followed them that dark, foggy evening. We were a long way out. Big Pine Key is a large island with a number of entrance channels. Since we didn't know where our channel was in the fog, we decided to follow exactly, going into whichever entrance our guides led us.

The answer-to-prayer fishermen led us directly into the very channel we needed. They stopped their boat after we were well inside, asked if we could find our way home, and after we had thanked them profusely, turned, and went their own direction.

We marveled. We knew we had been led home in direct answer to prayer. And we can all know, just as surely, that God will lead us to our heavenly home no matter how deep the fog is around us. He won't leave us to be lost if we're willing to keep Him in sight all the way. We can trust God to help us know what words to use, even when we pray. Great, isn't He?

JUANITA KRETSCHMAR

God's Way, Not Mine!

Let your light shine before men. Matt. 5:16, NIV.

"MAKE ME A BLESSING to someone today." The tune and words of the song wouldn't stop ringing in my head. "Yes, Lord, I do want to be a blessing to someone, but how?" I prayed as I walked.

Living on a Christian school campus with an international student body, you hear so many stories of remarkable instances of blessings. Many students have had personal experiences of God's leading and protection, and they can testify of extraordinary circumstances and sometimes fearful occasions when their lives have been in danger and God has remarkably intervened and saved or delivered them.

I felt a little covetous of their experiences, but knew in my heart that God loved me and watched over me just as much. Their stories did touch my heart, and I felt blessed by them as I was drawn to God. He is such a great and mighty being, yet so loving and approachable to one and all.

A colleague passed me while I was thinking about all this, and I smiled at her and commented on how vibrant the different colors of green of the leaves and grass were after the rain. Then we went our separate ways, she to her appointment and I to mine, again humming the tune "Make Me a Blessing."

A few days later, as I entered my office I picked up an envelope that had been pushed under my door. It was a letter from the friend I had passed the day I had been musing about being a blessing. She told me that she had been very depressed that day, and after meeting me she had felt lifted by my smile. I had smiled at her, and she had been forced to return it and had felt better for it. She said my words had encouraged her to look for the beauty around her, and she had been led to search for God. "You were a blessing to me," she wrote.

I was touched. I had been a blessing and had not known it. God had used me! I felt humbled. I learned something that day that I will never forget: We are all useful and usable in God's sight if we seek Him and are willing to be used in His way.

ANNE BISSELL

A Distress Call

Be merciful to me, O Lord. . . . I come to you for safety. In the shadow of your wings I will find refuge. . . . I cry out to the most High God, who fulfills His purpose in me. Ps. 57:1, 2, Clear Word.

HE CAME OUT OF nowhere. I really don't know who he was or where he came from.

The distress call had come from Fe about 9:00 p.m. She could hardly be understood; her voice was shrill and hoarse. She had been sick in bed for the past couple days, and this day she had worked 12 hours. So she was awfully tired, and she still had to drive for Jesse. Her stress escalated. After two hours they finished their business and were on their way home. They started onto the highway when they discovered the right rear tire was down. They returned to the parking lot to check the problem. The tire was flat. The car was disabled.

Out there in the parking lot in ordinary clothes in subzero temperatures, she called me. Right away I called someone for help, but nobody could come and I wouldn't know what to do. I have always depended on someone else for my car trouble. Finally, I got Ed and we hurried to Fe. Ed and Jesse tried to fix the tire, but they had so much trouble finding the right tools and fitting the spare tire. Fe and I were in the car, trying to keep warm and praying that the car could be fixed soon.

Ed and Jesse were now shivering and their noses were running. They were about to give up when a new sports car with two young men in it stopped behind our car. One of the young men got out. He brought out a wrench and a jack that fit, and in only a few minutes fixed the trouble. We all thanked him repeatedly. He just smiled and drove away.

We praised God and thanked Him for sending help in time of trouble. God is only a prayer away. He cannot be overburdened, for He knows His children's every need. He knows exactly when to send help. He also sends the right person at the right moment and in the right circumstance. He has never failed.

O Lord, help us to continue trusting in You, and thank You for supplying our every need and for fixing our faith in You. ESPERANZA AQUINO MOPERA

Winter Blast

For I will restore health to you and heal you of your wounds. Jer. 30:17, NKJV.

I ARRIVED IN MARYLAND in the fall of 1995. The autumn leaves were stunning. Then came my first winter—soft, dazzling snow. Later, a big snowstorm came. Although my family was out West, I wasn't lonesome. I moved into my bare place, with not even a bed, yet there was joy and peace in me. Then came the "winter blast."

January 31, 1996: I sat in Dr. Marter's office. He pulled up a chair and gently held my hands. "The laboratory results of the biopsy show malignant cells." He spoke almost inaudibly.

"You mean it's cancer?" I asked limply.

"With breast cancer you have a better chance of recovery from chemo and radiation," he consoled.

I let my family know. Like me, my sisters and brother tried to keep their fears at bay by being matter-of-fact about it. But I felt their deepest pain and concern. My youngest sister, who is a doctor, couldn't hide her fears. She sobbed on the phone.

"Lord, for my family's sake, please heal me," I cried. The heartbreak this was causing my family was harder to take than the cancer.

The pathology report after surgery was grim: 12 lymph nodes were positive—breast cancer, stage 2. Chemotherapy was strongly suggested. A specialist explained the procedure. I dreaded its side effects. "What are my chances if I don't take the treatment?" I asked.

"Two years," the doctor said.

More than the healing of the body, I begged the Lord for the healing of my soul. An anointing service was held in my living room. I knew that whatever happened, the Lord would see me through.

The Lord has carried me through those difficult times. I barely missed work. I often ask Him, "Why am I so special to You?" It's been eight years now. Every day is a precious gift from God, an expression of His eternal love for me. Each day gives me an opportunity to return praise and thanks to my loving Father.   LINDA ALINSOD

The Promise Fulfilled

You may ask for anything in my name, and I will do it. John 14:14, NIV.

WE HAD JUST FINISHED breakfast and immediately began planning a schedule for the remaining days of my visit out West with my daughters. The shrill ringing of the telephone brought all conversation to an abrupt halt. The voice on the other end of the line was that of my daughter, Trich, back home in Newfoundland, relaying a message to me from the Social Services Department; she stressed the importance of a return call from me.

My heart skipped a beat; I could think of only one explanation for a call such as this and what it must mean. My adopted 22-year-old granddaughter had been endeavoring to find her birth family; she was finally looking for us, just as we were looking for her.

My prayers during the past nine years had finally been answered. It seemed that at last God had seen fit to fulfill the greatest desire of my heart. Oh, how many times I'd knelt before Him, pleading with Him to help me find her. How my heart ached as I longed for that void to be filled, that empty spot in the family circle. In one moment of desperation as I cried out to God I actually accused Him of not keeping His promise. I did not, at that time, understand that His ways are not our ways, nor is His time our time. But being calmed by His Spirit and assured of His forgiveness, I continued in prayer.

Words could never adequately express the joy that was mine as I embraced not only my granddaughter, but also a precious little 4-month-old great-granddaughter—an extra blessing of which I had no knowledge. Next to Jesus' sacrifice on the cross for me, this was the most wonderful act of love for His hurting child. My God never ceases to amaze me as I continue to witness promises fulfilled. Truly He is a most kind, caring, and loving Father, always looking out for our best interests, even forgiving us when our faith wavers.

Oh, my Father, how could I have doubted Your word? You have told me again and again how very much You love and care for me. You have guarded my steps. And most assuredly You will lead me in ways everlasting. I resolve today, Father, to trust You completely and without question all the remaining days of my life. I do love You, Lord. I can do no other! VIRGINIA CASEY

November 18

That Long Table

Blessed are they that do his commandments, that they may have right to the tree of life, and may enter in through the gates into the city. Rev. 22:14.

DURING THE DEPRESSION YEARS of the 1930s it was often difficult for me as a young wife to keep my family supplied with good food. To provide three meals a day, school lunches, and my husband's lunch, I had a large garden and canned many quarts of fruits and vegetables and baked many loaves of bread.

Sometimes I failed to keep the bread box filled. If I didn't get the new baking done in time for the next meal, I'd break off blobs of bread dough and fry it for a hurried meal. I wasn't satisfied that this was good food, but what else could I do? I never felt that I was a good cook, as were my mother, my four daughters, or my mother-in-law.

Years later my daughter, Vivian, wrote that she was hungry for my fried bread dough. She missed the foods that I used to make. My other children said the same. It surprised me that they remembered and that they missed them. They liked to come home and gather around my table.

Now I think of the supper table we will gather around in heaven some-day. That food will be so delicious, nutritious, and healthful. I read a description of that supper that I like:

Jesus called His children, saying, "Come, My people, you have come out of great tribulation, and done My will, suffered for Me; come to supper, for I will gird Myself, and serve you." We will shout, "Alleluia! glory!" and enter the city. We will see a table of pure silver, many miles in length, yet our eyes will be able to extend over it. We will see "the fruit of the tree of life, the manna, almonds, figs, pomegranates, grapes, and many other kinds of fruit." If we are faithful, in a little while we will "eat of the fruit of the tree of life and drink of the water of the fountain" (*Early Writings*, pp. 19, 20).

Oh, let us strive to be there, with our families, to gather around that long table in heaven and forever enjoy its bounties, and to be at home with Jesus.

GLADYS FOWLER MARSH

Kosheela, Come Back; Come and Eat

Come, all of you . . . , come, buy and eat! . . . Buy wine and milk without money and without cost. Isa. 55:1, NIV.

WE WERE LIVING AT the mission station at Karmatar, Bihar, India, a little sleepy town far from the maddening crowds and noise of modern civilization. The district where the mission was located had been declared a famine area. The poor were starving. Cattle were being led to slaughterhouses. Fruit trees had been stripped bare of leaves. A woman with a heart problem came daily with her two children, one 4, and the other, Kosheela, a babe in arms, for the meal I provided. When we were away on a mission itinerary, the watchmen had turned her away, saying we were out. Returning after a few days for medicine and food, she again received the same message.

One morning after we returned I heard a loud wailing near our gate. I was surprised to see Kosheela's mother, followed by her husband, who was holding her dead baby in his arms. Pointing to the child, she cried, "If you had been here, my baby would not have died."

As the woman left, tears filled my eyes, and I told her that I would visit her home. That afternoon a colleague and I walked to her house with a basket of food. The house was full of women who had gathered to comfort and help in preparations for the burial. Those who can afford fuel cremate their dead. The poor dig a pit and place the body in the pit after carefully wrapping it in a shroud. It costs them nothing.

The woman looked at the basket and wailed loudly again, "Kosheela, food has come; come and eat. You asked for food before you left me."

The child wanted food, and there was nothing to feed her. Now there was plenty of food, but it would do Kosheela no good. What a tragedy! The mother's words kept ringing in my ears as we silently wended our way back to the mission campus. The years have gone by, but the scene of the dead child has not been erased from my mind. I cannot forget.

There are millions starving for food that can make their sinsick souls whole. Jesus is counting on us to be His voice, inviting men and women to the feast He has prepared. "Come, all of you, . . . come, buy and eat! . . . Buy wine and milk without money and without cost."   BIROL C. CHRISTO

November 20

A Conversation With God

In all their affliction He was afflicted, and the Angel of His Presence saved them; in His love and in His pity He redeemed them. Isa. 63:9, NKJV.

MY BURDENS ARE REALLY heavy today, Lord. I do my best to treat everyone kindly and to be honest, but there are people who criticize me and tell things about me that aren't true. This really hurts, Lord.

No. They've not beat me, mocked me, or spat in my face as the crowds did to You. Neither does a multitude rise up against me and accuse me of subverting our nation as they did You. I'm just upset that no one seems to appreciate me, no matter how hard I try. Even my family neglects me. But no, Lord, I have never been disowned by any of them as having never known me.

I am really sick, though, Lord. I used to have good health and could walk and be so active, but now my arthritis keeps me confined. I suffer such pain. Why must my life be filled with taking medicine and going to the doctor?

But no, Lord, I didn't have to stumble and crawl up a dusty road with a heavy cross upon my back. Nor have I ever had nails driven through my hands—such ultimate pain!

I am really having a difficult time right now. You see, my bills keep piling up, and it seems I will never get ahead. I worry about cold weather coming, and I really need a new coat. These financial problems are really getting me down. After the house payment, I hardly have enough to buy milk to drink.

But no, Lord, no one has ever stripped me of my clothes and fought over who would get them. And I have never had to drink vinegar to quench my thirst. And yes, I remember, You did not have a home to call Your own.

No, Lord, I have not given my life for someone else, even when many did not care. You died on that cross just for me and rose again from the tomb just to give me hope. You bore it all to give me a chance. You took my place so that I might break free from the shackles of sin in my life. Forgive me for being so ungrateful. I am really quite blessed. Thank You, Lord, for bearing my burdens and carrying my cross.

BARBARA SMITH MORRIS

332

One Bite at a Time

She sets about her work vigorously; her arms are strong for her tasks.
Prov. 31:17, NIV.

FIVE DAYS UNTIL THANKSGIVING, and so much to accomplish: odds and ends from the last three seminar trips to put away, grape harvest dust to wipe off every visible surface, newly washed sheets and fluffy towels to replenish the guest room, garbage to take out, groceries to purchase, mail to sort, e-mail to read, voice mail to hear, tempting traditional fare to prepare. Talk about overwhelming!

Melissa found me sprawled across the chaise lounge, uncharacteristically immobile. Hands on her early-adolescent hips, she surveyed the scene, her head cocked to one side.

"No, I'm not sick," I answered in response to her unspoken question. "There's simply too much to do and too little time in which to do it." Waving my hand hopelessly, I felt neither vigorous nor strong at the moment. "If only I had a housekeeper—"

"A housekeeper would invade your space," Melissa retorted. A saucy grin split her face. She knew me very well. "So," she continued a moment later, "how do you eat an elephant?"

"Oh, Melissa," I sighed. "This is no time for humor!"

"It's always time for humor," she replied. "And you need to remember how to eat an elephant!" She threw the last phrase over her shoulder as she exited the room.

I groaned. She had my voice inflection down to a fare-thee-well.

Was that the sound of vacuuming? Melissa was vacuuming? Without being asked? Suddenly the punch line popped into my mind—one bite at a time. She was right! I'd been concentrating on the whole elephant. The more manageable approach was to break up what needed to be accomplished into smaller tasks without losing sight of the big picture.

Picking up a stack of mail, I headed for my office. I met Melissa in the hall. "You remembered!" she exclaimed, her eyes shining, the vacuum smoothly caressing the carpet. "I'm taking the first bite for you."

I shook my head. How quickly we tend to forget. Once again God had used Melissa to teach me a lesson.

ARLENE TAYLOR

November 22

Tenderly He Watches Over Me

The angel of the Lord encamps all around those who fear Him, and delivers them. Oh, taste and see that the Lord is good; blessed is the man who trusts in Him! Ps. 34:7, 8, NKJV.

MY MEETING ASSIGNMENTS AT the university in the snow belt of Michigan were over, and I planned to leave early the next morning for the South Bend airport 20 minutes away. In the morning I awakened early and began packing my bags. Then I happened to glance outside. Even though it was still dark, I could see by the motel lights that it was snowing. Six inches on the ground, and more was coming fast. I would be snowed in unless I left immediately for the airport.

Out the door I flew with my suitcase and purse and into my compact rental car. I turned on the radio, which was already set for the university radio station, and was happy to hear a devotional in progress. After a quick prayer for God's protection, I pulled onto the road. There were no tracks of other cars on the road and no sign of any snowplow. I slowly drove down the middle of the road, not sure where the edge of the road was.

When I was about halfway to the airport I saw in my mirror that a vehicle was coming up very fast behind me. I gradually pulled to the right to leave as much room for the passing vehicle as possible. As the much larger vehicle flew by me at probably twice my speed, I suddenly lost control of my car. No doubt the wind of the passing vehicle somehow affected my car. I applied the brake (the wrong thing to do), which only made my spin worse. In horror I noticed that my car was now headed for the ditch—about a six-foot drop and no guardrail. "O God, help!" I cried. Just as the front tires reached the edge of the ditch, my car stopped.

As I sat there catching my breath and realizing how close I came to landing in the ditch, I heard a beautiful tenor voice from the radio singing these words: "Tenderly He watches over me—every step, every mile of the way." The timing of that song still amazes me. I shall never forget how in this experience God spoke in a human voice to tell me He is the one who saved me from disaster that day.

ROWENA R. RICK

Rejoice Always

Rejoice in the Lord alway. Phil. 4:4.

IT BEGAN AS A frustrating November day, bitter cold, but since I needed the exercise I walked to my office where I worked as a part-time secretary. As soon as I arrived I realized I had forgotten a very important item—my glasses. I had left them where I had had my devotions earlier. Because we were going to Florida the next day for the winter, we had already put our phone on "vacation" mode. I could not call to ask my husband to bring me my glasses.

I turned the computer on anyway, thinking I could at least see the screen and send a letter to the printer. The printer did its usual noisy routine of squealing and beeping but refused to print. Then someone requested I type some letters for her—handwritten letters. Now I was really in trouble without my glasses. I finally appealed to my dear friend across the street from our house to bring my glasses.

Now I was ready to type the letters—but the computer refused to cooperate. Our pastor's wife had donated a lovely, almost new IBM typewriter, so I decided to write her a thank-you letter on it before I attempted the other letters. When I endeavored to do that, however, the erase feature would not work. Has anyone written a whole letter without a single mistake?

Frustrated, I decided to walk home and type the letters on my old computer. Typing the letters went fine, but the printer insisted on having its own way with the margins.

As I drove back to the office I decided Satan was trying to ruin my day and it was time to call on the One who had defeated him at Calvary. I started to sing "Praise God from whom all blessings flow" and recited Paul's admonition to "Rejoice in the Lord alway"—even in trials.

By this time my boss had come in. When I told him of my woes with the computer and printer, he asked the treasurer to take a look. The treasurer reached over and restarted the computer. No problems. The printer worked, too. I was able to do the letters and other necessary work. Christ had triumphed over Satan again—this time on a November day in my life.

RUBYE SUE

November 24

The Mystery Bible

O taste and see that the Lord is good: blessed is the man that trusteth in him. Ps. 34:8.

I WONDERED WHAT GIFT I should get for my younger brother. A friend of mine showed me a Bible, a Life Application Bible, and I was impressed to get this Bible for my brother's birthday. I immediately went to the Christian bookstore and bought one for him, and one for my daughter. I had my brother's name engraved in gold lettering on his Bible.

I went to the counter and paid for both Bibles, then saw something else I wanted to get. When I finished my shopping, I looked in the shopping cart for the bag that had the two Bibles in it. To my utter shock, the Bibles were gone. I immediately went to the counter where I had checked them out and asked the cashier if I had by mistake left them there. They looked everywhere and couldn't find the bag. They even checked to see if one of the store clerks had taken it to the storage area at the back of the store.

After much searching and checking around, the store finally was very kind to refund my money. I told God how much I wanted to give that Bible to my brother for his birthday, only a month away, so I was hoping either the store would find it, or if someone took the bag by mistake they would be honest enough to return it. I called weekly to check, but it still hadn't shown up by his birthday. I had to buy another Bible, but the cover wasn't as nice as the first one, so I didn't have it engraved. However, my brother was very happy to receive the Bible.

Five months later I received a phone call from the bookstore asking if I had bought a Bible that had my brother's name engraved on it. When I asked them how they got the Bible back, no one knew. My brother was pleased to exchange the plain Bible for the engraved one.

I thank God for His care and concern in making me happy even in such a small matter. This experience has greatly strengthened my faith and brought me closer to my heavenly Father, who is even more real to me.

STELLA THOMAS

Leaving Our Comfort Zone

He . . . knelt down and prayed, "Father, if you are willing, take this cup from me; yet not my will, but yours be done." Luke 22:41, 42, NIV.

"MOM, DEBBIE THREW A heavy bottle at me and hit me. She almost hit the baby." Her son's voice quavered a bit. "I can't take it anymore. I went to the police and filled out a report."

"Where are you now?" Amy asked, her heart aching.

"I'm driving around with the kids. It'll be several hours before they send someone out to arrest her." This was the latest in a series of emotionally and physically abusive episodes caused by Debbie's methamphetamine addiction. Amy was thankful Alex had finally decided to act, because Debbie would never be motivated to seek help otherwise.

A week later Alex called again. "The house is a mess; I don't have time to clean it, take care of the children, run my business, get a restraining order, and apply for custody of the kids."

"I'll see if I can get tickets and come for a week," his mom promised.

The look of relief on his weary face when Amy arrived was reward enough. But when she walked into the house, she found heaps of unwashed laundry, stacks of dirty dishes, toys everywhere, and a sticky kitchen floor. *Can I stand a week in this environment?* she wondered, thinking of her peaceful, orderly home. "I was glad to help, but it was almost more than I could handle," she reported. Every night I prayed for courage to get through another day."

Then one day a thought struck me: *Is this how Jesus felt when He left heaven to come live with us? Is that why He spent so many nights in prayer with His Father? Was He asking for strength to get through the days and years until He could go home again?*

As dearly as Amy loves her son and grandchildren, she confessed that as she boarded her flight home, she did so with a feeling of relief. Yet Jesus, after suffering rejection by most of those He came to save and after dying a terrible death, lingered another 40 days with His earthly friends. She felt humbled by Jesus' love.

Dear Jesus, thank You for leaving Your comfort zone and coming to our chaotic, disordered world to bring us comfort and help and salvation.

CARROL GRADY

Not Me, Lord

So teach us to number our days, that we may gain a heart of wisdom.
Ps. 90:12, NKJV.

"IS IT CANCER?" I asked as I spoke to the doctor, who was still clad in his surgery apparel that Sunday morning.

As gently as possible he answered me. "It always is. I hope I got it all."

My husband had left work and driven himself to Urgent Care on Friday because he had what he thought was a severe case of the flu. They examined him, then sent him to X-ray where a mass was discovered in his colon. He was admitted to the hospital and underwent emergency surgery two days later.

Our two adult daughters and I listened in shock to the doctor's words. Why did this happen to our loved one? How could this happen to someone who enjoyed exercise, the outdoors, had a marvelous sense of humor, and loved God and the church?

Our pastor came and prayed with us. We stayed at the hospital until Art was awake and able to talk to us. After my daughters went to their own cars, I got into mine, feeling the need to be alone with my thoughts and my prayers of anguish. As I drove into the nearby hills, I asked myself what it was going to be like to be a widow—something that happened to other women, not me. I clung to the doctor's words, "I hope I got it all," and I prayed, "Lord, please let him be all right."

Art returned to work while undergoing a year of chemotherapy. We were pleased about how well he did. Two years later he was back in the hospital. The cancer had reappeared; however, after more surgery he bounced back. Three years went by, and the symptoms were back again, this time more severe. A third surgery gave us five months of time with him; then he was gone.

Sooner or later disappointment, sadness, and heartache come to each of us. How grateful we can be we serve a God who understands our tears and gives us the ability, by faith, to accept His will for our lives.

Dear Lord, You have promised You will make all things plain when You come again. Meanwhile, please hold our hands when we are too weak to hold Yours. Amen.

MILDRED C. WILLIAMS

Stray Cat?

The Lord our God is merciful and forgiving, even though we have rebelled against him. Dan. 9:9, NIV.

FINDLAY, ONE OF MY tuxedo-colored cats, mirrored our human nature one afternoon while I was treating myself to a healthy snack of warm zucchini bread. When she hopped up on my chair and curled up on my lap, I quickly finished off the last few bites of bread so I could pet her. She seemed to purr louder with each stroke of her silky coat.

Curiosity got the cat, however, when I placed my plate on the table. Findlay "giraffed" her neck just high enough to see what goodies she could devour. The remaining few crumbs were enticing enough to cause a dilemma: Should she give up the comfort of a warm lap for a potentially yummy snack? She looked down at my lap, then glanced back at the tempting plate several times. The poor little thing was really torn. I could feel her fluffy body stiffen with the tension of such an important decision.

Finally, when she seemed to rationalize that a few morsels of food weren't worth sacrificing her cozy position, she rested her head on my belly and resumed purring. I thought the struggle was over and was quite impressed with her willpower.

A few minutes later, however, my tabby tomcat, Sidney, jumped up on my lap, disturbing the peace. He fled the scene, leaving a startled Findlay to contemplate the plate once again. This time it was as if she were thinking, *Oh well, now that I'm up . . .* Sure enough, she hopped onto the table, sniffed the plate, and took a nibble. "What's this?" she seemed to ask. "This is health food, isn't it!" She walked away. My lap no longer appealed to her, either.

Cats aren't the only creatures who do such things. Often we humans successfully resist temptation, only to succumb to it moments later. Satan tries to disturb our peace and knock us off balance. Have we ever felt there's no regaining our position with God after we've made a bad choice?

Thank You, God, for Your unfailing kindness and forgiveness. Please continue to give us strength to resist all forms of temptation and to rest in Your loving arms. Amen.
CLARISSA MARSHALL

November 28

About Right and Wrong Directions

But small is the gate and narrow the road that leads to life, and only a few find it. Matt. 7:14, NIV.

MAYBE YOU REMEMBER THE train accident that happened in the tunnel from Kaprun up to the Kitzsteinhorn in Austria in 2000. At the beginning of a ski season 155 passengers met their death in the burning train that was taking them to the mountaintop. It's still not clear how this tragedy happened.

Twelve people survived because they ran in the right direction. They followed the advice of somebody who told them to go downward. All others who were able to climb out of the small hole that somebody had broken in a window didn't pay attention to the counsel. They ran upward and died. The tunnel had become like a huge chimney, created by the air drawn through the open entrance below.

Many people run the wrong direction while living here on earth. It is the broad way that most people follow. The Bible tells us that the way to heaven is narrow. People who follow Jesus are swimming against the tide. They choose to fight against evil because of the reward waiting for them at the end—eternal life. Let's ask God to help us to be faithful even in difficulties.

There are many personal destinies to mourn from this accident. Families became separated—some members were already at the top; others had stayed in the valley to wait for the next train or took a cable car. Children became orphans, men and women lost their spouses. What a tragedy!

There are probably people from our own families who are going the wrong direction. Let's encourage them to make the right choice and follow Jesus. The fire and the toxic smoke in the tunnel spread within seconds. We have no time to lose in warning others. The message is urgent.

Thank You, Lord, for having reminded me today of this important truth. Often, I am apprehensive about sharing the gospel with others for fear of refusal or opposition. Please give me the opportunity and the courage to be a witness for You today.
HEIKE EULITZ

Please, Can I Have an Extra Day, God?

Let them give thanks to the Lord for his unfailing love and his wonderful deeds. Ps. 107:31, NIV.

IT WAS ONE OF those days—too much work, too little time, an in tray that threatened to collapse under its load of things to do, and a lengthy counseling situation on the telephone.

"Dear God, please help me. There is too much work to be done. I know if I had even one day to catch up that I could meet these deadlines. But the phone keeps ringing, and sometimes the people really need to talk, and I can't turn them away."

It was hard trying to juggle the needs of a family and a demanding job. To fit work around the school run, I worked a short day at the office, making it hard to keep on top of the work. With all the faith in the world, I still found it hard to believe that God could create an extra day just for me!

I decided to let my husband pick up the children and look after them for the evening while I worked until I had caught up with my paperwork. But I still had a huge writing assignment to complete. Whenever would I fit it in?

I worked hard all evening and managed to clear my in tray and get ahead on a couple things, so I began to feel a little more in control.

Then the phone rang. It was my husband, reporting that our youngest son was quite ill with the flu. I wouldn't be able to go in to work the next day. As I gathered all the papers and books I needed for the assignment, I thanked God for working everything out for me. If I hadn't been busy, I would have gone home at the usual time without all the papers I needed. God had kept me at the office long enough to find out that my son was ill and that I would need to bring home all my work.

My son was so ill the next day that he slept on the floor by my feet as I typed. I was able to finish the entire project. All the time my heart praised God for untangling the situation and meeting all of my needs in such an incredible way. So there I sat, thanking God for overwork and sick children, secure that He was aware of my every need, caring for me as His child, and working things out in creative and surprising ways!   KAREN HOLFORD

November 30

Guidance Assured

For the Holy Spirit will teach you in that very hour what you ought to say. Luke 12:12, NKJV.

RECENTLY OUR SECOND daughter and her two girls, ages 9 and 6, moved in with us. She works as a nurse to support them. Sometimes, besides her regular eight-hour schedule, she's on call on weekends. One particular Friday she called from the hospital to say that she would be two hours late because of two emergency surgeries. That evening the girls wanted to wait up for their mother. Unfortunately, they fell asleep before my daughter arrived.

The following morning, before 7:00, my daughter was called to the hospital again. She quietly tiptoed so that the girls wouldn't wake up. Caitlin, the older girl, heard her car leaving and ran after her mother crying, "I want my mommy; I want my mommy!" Before I could comfort her, Courtney, the younger one, woke up, too, and cried for her mother. My daughter had already gone, leaving my two granddaughters crying for their mother.

What am I going to do? I wondered. *Here we're getting ready to go to church, and I don't want to be late. If I censure the girls, what good will that do?* The girls felt betrayed that their mother had left without saying goodbye.

I bowed my head. *Lord, please help me to say comforting words that won't antagonize my granddaughters.* Like a flash of lightning, the thought of Jesus healing the sick came clearly as if the Lord was putting in my mouth what to tell the girls. I called Caitlin and Courtney to the kitchen while I was preparing our breakfast and said tenderly, "Caitlin and Courtney, do you remember the stories about Jesus' taking care of the sick? Remember how He healed the sick; how He made the lame walk; how He opened the eyes of the blind?"

No response. They just stared at me.

I continued, "Well, Mommy is doing what Jesus did. Your mommy is helping the sick at the hospital. And you are helping Jesus also because you're making it easy for your mommy and for me. The Bible says that if we help people, we are doing it for Jesus."

Amazingly, both girls stopped crying, ate their breakfast, and dressed themselves for church. Truly the Lord helped me say the right words at the right time to the girls.

OFELIA A. PANGAN

342

Modern Miracle

Our help comes from the Lord, who made heaven and earth. Ps. 124:8, TEV.

I STARED AT THE ATM screen in disbelief. "Out of Service." This could not be happening to me! I discarded the idea of walking home—it was too far away. And there didn't seem to be any other ATMs around. What was I going to do?

But let me start at the beginning. My fiancé had taken me out to lunch. Since there were a couple of last-minute wedding errands I needed to run, and I knew he'd be bored to death, I decided to stay downtown while he went on his way. Big mistake!

By the time I finished, it was pretty late and traffic was beginning to thicken. I thought, *The buses will be full, and I'll probably not find a seat, which means I will have to stand for most of the 15 minutes or so it takes to get to my stop.* So I searched in my coin purse for the exact fare, as it's not a good idea to be fishing around in your handbag while trying to balance yourself in a moving vehicle. Imagine my surprise when I found my purse had no money. I almost tore the lining out trying to find 15 cents, but came up with only two pennies.

Looking around desperately, I noticed an ATM machine across the street. As much as I hated the idea of crossing four lanes of traffic, there was no other choice. With a quick prayer I stepped out into the busy street, dodging cars and irritated drivers who honked instead of stopping.

I made it across and stepped into the booth. That's when the screen politely informed me that this particular machine was not working. "God, I have no money to get home or to call anyone to pick me up, and it will be dark soon. Please perform a miracle right now. Thank You."

I pushed my card into the slot. The wait seemed endless. Then the machine started to groan, and it happened—money! I grabbed it, rejoicing in God's compassion.

Just in case anyone who reads this story might be tempted to doubt, the receipt slip that popped out said "Out of Service."

No bus for me that day. I took a taxi!   DINORAH BLACKMAN

It Amazes Me

But my God shall supply all your need according to his riches in glory by Christ Jesus. Phil. 4:19.

DID YOU EVER HEAR your mom or dad say that finances were low, so low that expenses had to be cut? Then the next thing you saw was your mom and dad sending money to missions, or maybe having guests come over to have meals, or even stay with you? I didn't understand this when I was a little girl.

Times were rough, and we struggled financially. But I distinctly remember early Friday mornings: Mom went to the market to buy food with the little money we had. She cooked rice, meat, and vegetables in what I thought then were the biggest pots in the world. When the church service ended, she stood at the door and invited not only the visitors who came to church that day, but anybody who needed a meal. She believed that when you share with others, the things that you have not only double, they multiply significantly.

As an adult, when my family were missionaries in Africa and the Middle East, our house was like a motel all the time—with three meals included! Although our salary was only $250-$300 per month, we never experienced a lack of food. The Lord always made sure that there was food in the pantry. Often, after guests left, I'd find that I didn't have to buy my groceries just yet. The Lord kept the fruits and vegetables fresh and always plentiful.

During our first year in Maryland, many missionary friends from Africa came, and we invited them to stay with us. When they left, our bank account was almost zero, and payday was not until the following week, but guess what? God came in, as He always does. Friends had had to leave town on an emergency. The day before, they had stocked their refrigerator with food. To my amazement, they brought it all over to us—a large box filled with more than two weeks' supply of food. I thanked the Lord again for supplying our needs.

God has proved to be our best business partner. He never runs out of bonuses, and you don't have to wait to get your profit—it comes exactly when you need it. If you are a wise investor, invest all you have in the Lord. Support His work, and help others. He will faithfully multiply what you have invested in Him.

JEMIMA D. ORILLOSA

My Little Tree

That they might be called trees of righteousness, the planting of the Lord, that he might be glorified. Isa. 61:3.

ABOUT 10 YEARS AGO my mother gave me a pretty little tree. I planted it opposite my front door and cared for it daily. Unfortunately, Mother didn't know its name, and so far I've been unsuccessful in finding out, but it yielded a tiny yellow berry and very tiny lilac flowers. It grew to about three feet (90 centimeters) tall.

Winter came, and the cold winds howled and the storm blew. The rain fell in torrents. In August 1999 a tornado hit our neighborhood and our home, causing so much disaster and damage. Our hedge fell over onto the little tree. There were so many other more important matters to attend to, such as repairing the roof, replacing gutters, and fitting in new windowpanes, that it took nine months before my husband and I lifted the hedge and freed the tree. Our hands were scratched and bleeding from lifting and tying up the dry, cracked twigs and branches of the hedge. So you can imagine how the little tree looked—leafless and lifeless. My husband said, "It is dead; I'll pull it out and throw it away."

I begged, "Please give it a chance."

He would agree to only a month. I trimmed off some of the damaged and cracked branches. I watered it, and watched it carefully. The sun smiled on it, too, and soon I saw tiny green shoots appearing. By the end of the month, most of the branches yielded pretty new leaves. New life had come!

As I stand back and admire my little tree, I think of my loving Lord, the Master Gardener. He never gives up on me. He sees me beset with sin. I get loaded down with various problems and trials. I cannot relieve myself of these burdens, this hedge of troubles that has fallen upon me. In desperation I call to God; He hears my pleas and comes to my aid. As He lifts the hedge of briers off my back, He scars His hands for me and His precious blood is shed. Now I am free!

My loving Master Gardener stands back to admire me. He did not leave me to die but gave me new life! Victory. Another chance. I am now free to bloom where I am and blossom for His glory. *Thank You, Lord, for another opportunity to glorify You.*

PRISCILLA E. ADONIS

December 4

Creating a Family Heirloom

Teacher, we saw a man using your name to cast out demons, but we told him to stop because he isn't one of our group. "Don't stop him!" Jesus said. . . . "Anyone who is not against us is for us." Mark 9:38-40, NLT.

WHAT A PERFECT BOOK *cover,* I thought to myself as I opened my gift copy of *Fabric of Faith,* the women's ministries latest devotional book. *It reminds me of our family quilt.* Several years before my grandma passed away our family presented her with a special quilt. We were each given a square, all the same size. We could embroidery whatever we desired on that square to represent each family, including names, marriage, and birth dates. I chose to copy and enlarge the maple leaf from the Canadian penny.

Because Sonny, my special-needs child, consumes all my time, I came up with a plan. "Mom, can you please embroidery my square?"

Lovingly, Mom did so, and Aunt Betty took all the individual pieces and made the quilt "with all our love." Grandma cherished her quilt, but treasured even more the loved ones it represented.

I felt heaven's smile when I looked more carefully at the book cover. Beside the quilt is a journal. Jesus has indeed blessed my efforts to witness via my personal journal, which I call *Dimensions of Love.* Over the years, through these precious books, Jesus has helped me create a family heirloom not only for my immediate family, but for the church family as well.

God leads my mind to explore further thoughts: The individual squares in the quilt can represent each person witnessing for Jesus. But unless the squares are sewn together, a quilt is not made. A single square can cover a limited amount of space, but squares connected to each other can reach beyond to the unreached. Not one person, or even one denomination, can do all the work that needs to be done.

Lord, please unite us so that together we'll spread the quilt, Your Word, to every nation, kindred, and tongue. We, the Christian church, are the family heirloom that Jesus will soon present to His Father. Amen. DEBORAH SANDERS

Runaway Shopping Carts

We should no longer be children, tossed to and fro and carried about with every wind. Eph. 4:14, NKJV.

IT WAS A COLD, brisk, and gusty morning as I drove the usual roads on my way to work. The wind blew fiercely, scattering leaves, papers, and debris all about. A few brave people walked along, huddled into the warmth of their winter coats, as the rush of the wind quickly helped them down the street. Even my car was jostled as I traveled along.

Nearing a shopping center, I saw two shopping carts in front of some small stores zipping along at top speed through the parking lot. Not a person or car was in sight in the parking lot as the runaway carts picked up more speed, driven by the increasing force of the wind.

I thought, *What if a car pulls around the corner? That would be disastrous!*

As I waited at the red light I continued to watch the carts, praying that no one would drive through the parking lot at that moment, unaware of the situation. One cart soon hit a curb and was immediately stopped in its tracks. The other one passed through one intersection of the parking lot and continued on its course. I knew it was inevitable that there would be a crash, either with a parked car or a moving one, and its crash course would instantly end. The light changed and I continued to check my rearview mirror, watching as the shopping cart was tossed to and fro.

Often we allow ourselves to wander away from the safety and security of our Lord and foolishly vacillate here and there in our thinking, tossed and blown, driven by foolish ideas, unrealistic desires, or erroneous doctrine. Like those unrestrained shopping carts, we breeze through life, oblivious to the harm we could do as we continue on our collision course. At some point we will be stopped, and then there will be damage assessment and restoration to the injured. Thank God, when we remain in His territory we will be grounded in Him forever.

Lord, help me not to be swept up in Satan's windstorms and carried away from Your safety and security. Amen. IRIS L. STOVALL

December 6

Brokenness and Healing

Be ye transformed by the renewing of your mind. Rom. 12:2.

WHEN I BECAME A Christian, I heard all the love and forgiveness sermons, but I couldn't apply them to my family from whom I had been
estranged for many years.

My first attempts were superficial. Love on both sides seemed to be
awakening, but inside I was filled with resentment. By my actions I felt I was
saying that the hurts in the past didn't matter, that I had to deny them in
order to have reconciliation with my sisters and mother. That premise
seemed true by human reasoning, but it is like what sometimes happens
when people first come to church. They don't participate, yet seemingly by
osmosis, they're still getting something. Seemingly the hurt child of the past
wasn't getting anything out of the present relationship, but if memories have
cells—those hurt emotions stuck in time—they were absorbing those friendships in the making.

Under acute stress, I was aware of my fractured self—a large baby that
was too heavy to carry around anymore. A few years later, during an almost
fatal automobile accident, I could almost feel a scared 6-year-old in the car
with me. Now, in the intense stress of a third move in two years, the hurt
child reemerges, a ragged and barefoot, broken and needy child, older now,
around 11.

You're coming too, I instinctively say in my mind.

The miracle is I now have compassion for myself instead of hate. While I
was trying to obey the love and forgive parts but not understanding how it
was helping, God was healing my emotions. He could have healed me instantly, but I'm thankful to catch a glimpse of His wonderful scientific laws of
the human mind. My emotional self will catch up to my biological age, and I
will be whole. For some this is the work of a lifetime.

I am reminded how immigrants to this country feel incomplete until they
are reunited with the ones they left behind. Yet even the family left behind re-
ceives hope and help. Our Savior wants to be one with us. To the broken and
hurting He says in effect, "You're coming too. I go to prepare a place for you
. . . that where I am, there you'll be also."   ALEAH IQBAL

The Night the Angel Came

And the angel said unto them, Fear not: for, behold, I bring you good tidings of great joy. Luke 2:10.

MY DAUGHTER'S THIRD BABY was due the early part of December, about the same time the First Baptist Church in our town has their annual presentation of the *Messiah*. There is an orchestra, a large choir in authentic costume, and numerous actors. Our family feels the Christmas season has not started until we attend this production. It is a very moving experience that helps us remember what the season is truly about.

The whole family decided to attend on Friday night. The second scene had just been presented in which the heavenly angel tells Mary, "Fear not, Mary: for thou hast found favour with God. And, behold, thou shalt conceive . . . and bring forth a son, and shalt call his name Jesus." I noticed a woman walking down the aisle, looking as though she was searching for someone. I recognized her as a relative of my girlfriend, Betty. She motioned for me to follow her.

When we entered the narthex, there stood the same beautiful angel who had just given the wonderful news to Mary. His white satin robe shimmered in the dim light. He raised his glittering wings and said to me, "Your daughter, Julie, is in labor at the hospital and wants her mama to come right now!"

My heart leaped, for I, too, had just been given wonderful news by the angel! As I entered the hospital elevator, I met my son-in-law, who was on his way to the admitting office. He called over his shoulder, "She's about to have the baby; she's six centimeters dilated." Within two hours little Grant Mitchell was born and was making his presence known by screaming loudly. His father was back in plenty of time to cut the umbilical cord.

Meanwhile, the *Messiah* was over, and numerous cousins, aunts, uncles, and my husband had migrated to the hospital. When mother and baby were suitably cleaned up, the entire family was allowed to see the newest family member. After the oohs and aahs were over, we all held hands as my pastor brother prayed a prayer of dedication for the baby and his family.

Each year when December arrives I start thinking about gifts. Try as I might, I cannot think of a more wonderful gift than little Grant, whose birthday was announced by an angel.

ROSE NEFF SIKORA

December 8

God's Covenant

When the rainbow appears in the clouds, I will see it and remember the everlasting covenant between me and all living beings on earth. Gen. 9:16, TEV.

THE WEATHER WAS GETTING colder in New England. I had so many errands to run—many of which weren't even mine to do, but were for those who depended on me. I was a little bogged down as I went from the bank to the post office to complete my mission.

As I came out of the post office a strange thing happened. The sky in the west was sunny, but it began to rain and hail while the sun still shone brightly. Weird! On my left the eastern sky was an eerie black, blacker than I had ever seen the sky in all my 76 years.

I looked to the west again, and the sun was still shining brightly. The sky to the east remained black. I stood there in awe. Suddenly there appeared the most perfect rainbow I had ever seen. From one end to the other the rainbow was perfect—a perfect arch of colors.

"O Lord, thank You," I said aloud, and my spirits rose.

I had been feeling abandoned and weighed down, all alone, all morning. Now, looking at the beautiful sight against the eerie black sky, I knew that no matter how stressful life can get, our loving heavenly Father is always there.

Life for me is not about to change. I have to keep on doing for those who cannot. But now whenever I am weighed down with the cares of this world, I always remember that black sky that seemed so treacherous. The beautiful rainbow assured me that God is in His heaven, and though the earth seems dark and dreary, I remember to look up and keep my eyes on Him. God is in heaven, and all is right with my world.

Heavenly Father, often I am weighed down with the cares of life and feel stressed out, overwhelmed, frustrated, or inadequate. Even then, Lord, I am assured that You are watching over me. Help me to keep my eyes on You and trust that everything will turn out perfectly, according to Your will. Amen.

PAM CARUSO

Angel Tree Gift

And we know that all things work together for good to them that love God, to them who are the called according to his purpose. Rom. 8:28.

THE WOMEN'S MINISTRIES DEPARTMENT of our church was sponsoring 50 children for Project Angel Tree, a program that gives gifts to children whose parents are incarcerated. We give the gift to the child in the name of the parent. Our budget was very small, so we were depending on help from our church family to fulfill these wishes.

I had been shopping for gifts and had been able to purchase something to meet most of the children's wishes, but now the fund was almost totally exhausted. Two days prior to the deadline, I was driving down the road, praying, petitioning the Lord, pouring out my heart, asking Him to supply my need to find and be able to purchase these gifts. I arrived at Toys-R-Us with my "angels" in hand, looking for a Barbie Volkswagen Beetle.

The sales assistant was surprised to see me coming into the store again, asking for the same toy again. She was emphatic: "I told you yesterday that we don't have any of the toys you are looking for."

I had a handful of paper angels on which was written the children's names and their requests. I explained the program again to the sales assistant. She was very receptive but negative in response. I walked away to look for another toy. All of sudden I was impressed to go back to the same area where I had looked earlier for the Barbie Volkswagens.

A woman standing next to me said, "Look at the Barbie Volkswagen Beetles."

On the shelf sat six beetles. The woman hurriedly picked up two for her children, and I picked up one for my Angel Tree child.

The sales assistant ran over to the area, and exclaimed, "How did those toys get there?"

The woman said, "This woman is walking around with angels in her hands, and angels supplied her need. I'm happy to be here with her because I was blessed also."

No one could explain how the toys appeared on the shelf. The Lord allowed me to see one of His promises in action. He will do the same for you.

Sharon Marshall

December 10

Trouble

God is our refuge and strength, a very present help in trouble. Ps. 46:1.

IT WAS A COLD December night, and a blizzard warning had been issued by our local TV station. I thought I was prepared for emergencies: I had food, bottled water, matches, candles, batteries, and a lantern on hand. I felt confident that I had done all that I could to be ready. So I settled into my favorite tilt-back chair in my living room to read the evening paper.

About 8:00 I began to notice that my home seemed to be chilly. Checking the registers, I found only cold air coming out. I went to the basement to look at the furnace and discovered that the fan was working, but no heat. I had trouble!

I phoned the emergency number of the heating company and was told that the repairman would be there in about an hour. At 9:00 the repairman arrived. He inspected the furnace and said it needed a new igniter switch, as the present one wasn't receiving enough electricity to allow it to work properly. Then he added that he didn't have a new replacement part in his truck for my furnace model—he would have to order one. What was to be done in the meantime? He decided to see if he could find something in his truck to use as a substitute part, and he went outside.

I went upstairs and turned on the TV for the latest weather report. A bulletin flashed across the screen, warning that the snowstorm would arrive around 10:30 and that people should be prepared for it.

After praying for God's help, I returned to the basement. The repairman came back, wearing a smile. He held up a small box in his hand and said, "Mrs. Baker, good news. I just found this under a pile of boxes in my truck. It's just the part I need for your furnace. I never knew it was there. Now I'll have your furnace fixed in no time at all."

The furnace was repaired and working by 10:00, and the repairman had left for his home only a few miles away. Thirty minutes later the blizzard arrived.

With a very grateful heart, I thanked God for His wonderful help and miracle!   ROSEMARY BAKER

Blessings Amid Chaos

Our help is in the name of the Lord, who made heaven and earth. Ps. 124:8.

I WORK IN AN INNER-CITY intensive-care unit that is routinely fast-paced and somewhat chaotic. But during the few weeks before Christmas the workload and stresses had reached such a fevered pitch that even we seasoned "pillar" nurses were beginning to crumble. Although we knew that Christ was the greatest gift, amid the blood and beeps of a multitude of alarms it was easy to forget. Patients, families, and staff all longed for a blessing to reassure us that we were not forgotten, that this messy and dangerous work had meaning.

I was in charge of the unit that night. Tempers were short, alarms mounted, and as I raced to reconnect another detached vent, I ran into Katey, one of my other pillar nurses. She was red-eyed and mopping at the tears running down her cheeks. "I can't take much more of this," she cried.

I reached out and grabbed her hand, pulling her into room 287 where Mr. Cooper, a comatose patient, slept the sleep of the dying. "We need to pray right now!" I said, and my tears mingled with hers as we pleaded with God to lay a shield over our unit, to protect our patients, to give us strength to do the task, and to let the families of these patients have some hope and peace, and that we would be permitted to see the goodness of God. We raced back to our duties and rarely had opportunity to speak the rest of our 12-hour shift. I would like to tell you that the unit grew calm and manageable, but that didn't happen. The frenzied pace rolled on, but God did have a miracle for us.

About 30 hours after our prayer session in room 287, Mr. Cooper experienced a dramatic turnaround. This man had been in ICU for 33 days. He lay comatose, fevered, dying. But late that evening his lung pressure dropped, his temperature normalized, and by morning he was awakening from the coma. When Mr. Cooper could speak again, the staff gathered in his room briefly to welcome him "back." The intensivist gave him a gentle high five and said, "You're our 'miracle man.'"

To this Mr Cooper responded, "Well, I opened my eyes and see'd nurses prayin'."

We were reassured that Immanuel was with us. We were not forgotten.

JOANN ASHWORTH

December 12

Patches of Love

She is not afraid of the snow for her household: for all her household are clothed with scarlet. Prov. 31:21.

A S MY THREE CHILDREN were growing up, I loved to sew for them. Many nights the old Singer sewing machine hummed into action long after they were tucked into their cozy and warm beds, and I stitched away on their clothing while Daddy worked long hours at his engineering job. (My son was the only boy in school who had marble bags to match his shirt.) And then the children outgrew my efforts as they entered their teens.

I wonder if my children ever wondered why the fragments from their homemade dresses and shirts were never sewn into quilt tops. There were always pieces when I finished cutting and sewing. Did they wonder what had happened to those leftover scraps?

When we moved many years ago we packed up boxes of everything in preparation for the move. In several boxes were all those pieces of material, each piece carefully pressed, folded, and preserved. Quilts should have been on my mind at that point in my life, but quilting was some distance up the road and wouldn't take shape until much later. If I had only known to keep those swatches. Instead, I gave them away to a special woman who did a lot of sewing. She took them with thanksgiving.

If I had only known that quiltmaking was to be a favorite and welcome project in the years ahead, what fun it would have been to incorporate swatches of familiar material into quilt tops for my children and grandchildren to pick out and reminisce about. Quilting is almost a lost art today—few are interested in the necessary stitches anymore. But old-time quilts have a story all their own to tell. The bright colors were happy times in the life of the quilts; the dark colors depicted the depths of despair.

Life was not easy for our ancestors, and even today life has its joyous times as well as its dark days. Perhaps my children will remember as they snuggle down in one of my quilts made in later years that a great deal of love, stitching, patience, and heart went into each one. That is how God works with each one of us with His love, patience, and heart.

LAURIE DIXON-McCLANAHAN

What a Little Light Can Do

But if we walk in the light as he himself is in the light, we have fellowship with one another, and the blood of Jesus his Son cleanses us from all sin.
1 John 1:7, NRSV.

OUR HOUSE WAS BUILT 40 years ago. It is small by today's standards and is probably quite typical of tract homes from the early 1960s. "Barely adequate" is an accurate description. In 1972 we moved our family of two boys and a girl into it. What our abode lacks in elegance has been more than compensated for by an abundance of love. It is the place our children call home, and we have many happy memories of our years here. Now it is the place our grandchildren come for Thanksgiving and Christmas. They call it Grandma's house. We have laughed together in the warmth of those familiar rooms and wept together when we have suffered loss.

We certainly have not done much to update our house other than a coat of paint now and then. The kitchen is small, with tiny windows, so it has always seemed a bit dark. Recently we bought a new ceiling light in hopes of brightening it up.

My husband, Rich, installed the new fixture. When he flipped the switch it seemed like the sun on a clear summer day. I never expected to see sunrise in my kitchen, but that is the best way to describe the change.

All the illumination did something else. It glinted off the splatters and nicked finish on the cupboards and glared from a cobweb in the corner. The extra brightness highlighted the dog's muddy pawprints on the floor. It became apparent that fresh paint was in order. It is truly amazing what a little light can do.

I have noticed a similar situation when the Light of the World comes into my heart. He chases the shadows of sin out of the darkest corners, highlights cobwebs of selfishness, and brings unlovely attitudes and actions into the clear light of day. He doesn't wait for me to clean up the mess but goes right to work with His Spirit and disposes of all the ugly stuff. He doesn't just cover the dirt with a coat of paint, He creates a whole new me.

I want the sunshine of God's love in my heart. Jesus is ready to throw the switch, and it is truly amazing what a little Light will do.

BARBARA ROBERTS

My Neighbor

Thou shalt love thy neighbour as thyself. Matt. 22:39.

I LOVE PEOPLE. THAT is, I love people who are easy to love. On my long walk through life there have been those who are not easy to love. Robert was one of those people. He lived in my apartment building and was a lonely, bitter, cantankerous old man. This bitterness came out in his relationship with the other residents. He would talk to them so mean that they would avoid him, if at all possible. Somewhere, down deep, I remembered that even Robert is one of God's creatures, so I would always say hello when I saw him.

But even I would reach my limit with him. We lived in a secured building with a code for residents to enter and a call box for residents to admit their visitors. Robert liked to sit in the lobby and admit anyone who walked up to the door. This seemed to give him some satisfaction. Even after being told many times that he must not do this, he continued to do so. This bothered me. I liked living in a secure building, so if I saw him doing this I would remind him that this was not the thing to do. He would get very angry and really give me a tongue-lashing. But the next time we met, it was as if it had never happened.

One day I heard that Robert was very ill and had been taken to the hospital next door. My first thought was, *Ann, if you don't go visit him, he will have no visitors.* Even then I put it off until the next day. This was not a visit that I especially looked forward to.

When I reached Robert's room, a nurse was with him. As soon as he recognized me, he turned to his nurse and said, "This is my buddy. I knew she would come to see me."

Wow! He was so sure that at least I would come to see him.

Shortly after that Robert died, but I have never forgotten his words. I keep asking myself, "What if I had not gone?"

Lord, please help me to love my neighbor, especially the unlovely.

ANN VANARSDELL HAYWARD

December 15

Life on One Foot

Do not worry about tomorrow, for tomorrow will worry about itself. Each day has enough trouble of its own. Matt. 6:34, NIV.

TEN DAYS BEFORE CHRISTMAS I broke my ankle. How? It was easy. As I neared the bottom of our steps with a load of laundry, I leaned forward to look into the living room. My fall cracked my fibula and broke three bones in my foot. The orthopedic specialist put my foot in a splint to my knee and scheduled surgery. Afterward, I was given crutches and told not to put any weight on my left leg.

I spent seven l-o-n-g weeks on crutches. I couldn't even rise from a chair without grasping on to something. I couldn't lift myself up a four-inch step. To get me into the car was as much trouble as handling a toddler, diaper bag, and stroller. Because of the ice, I used a walker outside. Someone else carried my crutches, purse, and anything else I needed.

You're supposed to learn something from these inconveniences. I learned that a break in your ankle weakens your whole body. I learned that I can slow down. I can ask people to fetch and carry for me. Contrary to my nature, it's not necessary to do everything for myself. I learned to stop rolling around our downstairs (on a small desk chair) trying to rule the world, and to rest when I got tired. My family would pitch in and take care of me.

I also learned that virtually everyone will hold open a door for someone on crutches. From elegantly dressed professional women to scruffy, scary-looking men, they all opened a door with a smile and held it while I hobbled through.

And I learned greater respect for so-called disabled people. It takes strength and coordination to use crutches. My unmuscled arms quickly wearied of working the wheelchair. But without crutches, I'd have sat! Period. A wheelchair made it possible to do shopping.

When you see someone in a wheelchair, don't think, _Oh, dear, poor thing,_ and look away, embarrassed. Instead, say, "Hey, that woman has wheels. She can go!" And be glad for her. Offer help, but don't insist. Treat her like the normal person that she is.

Lord, thank You for this time to slow down. Help me to remember the lessons I learned. PENNY ESTES WHEELER

JOSH &
1ST W.fe

Be Hopeful—God Works
in His Own Time

Ask, and it shall be given you; seek, and ye shall find; knock, and it shall be opened unto you. Matt. 7:7.

OUR FAMILY HAD LIVED here in Texas for many years. Finally we planned to move back to our native Jamaica, West Indies. We made several trips back and forth, trying to decide. We sold our house and relocated in Florida with the intention of selling our family dental practice and then moving to Jamaica. In spite of many efforts to sell the practice, we failed. Finally the traveling back and forth produced so much strain that we decided to move back to Texas and settle down. Obviously, God's timing and plan was different than ours. Temporarily, we rented a townhouse.

Two and a half years passed by quickly, and we finally decided it was time to go house hunting. In the meantime I had bought a floral crystal water fountain that needed fixing. I kept asking my husband to take me to have it done, but he kept putting it off. One day I got very firm with him and insisted that he get it fixed. While doing this errand, my husband was led into a new subdivision where he was able to look at the new houses for sale. He saw one that he liked, and took us that very afternoon to see it. We all fell in love with the house. The next day I called the broker and bargained on the price with him. Each offer I made, he honored. I had never done this type of business before. Everything happened so quickly and smoothly that I really felt God was leading.

On the job, I asked a woman for some boxes. She directed me to a room full of boxes, more than I needed. The loan was approved immediately, and the paperwork was quickly finished. The final touches to the house were moving faster than we could imagine. Certainly we could say, "God moves in a mysterious way His wonders to perform."

Lord, I am ready to move again—home with You in that beautiful home of Paradise. I don't want to do any more packing and moving here on earth. Thank You for answered prayers and for allowing us to wait on You in Your time and way. Praise God for His blessings. QUTIE DEWAR

I Love My Grandpa

For God so loved the world, that he gave his only begotten Son, that whosoever believeth in him should not perish, but have everlasting life. John 3:16.

EVERY DECEMBER THE CHURCH school in my community holds a special Christmas program in the gymnasium for grandparents and seniors. The 30-minute program begins at 11:00 in the morning and culminates with a luncheon of soup, sandwiches, and assorted cookies served by the students.

Proud grandparents beam as their precious little ones sing, recite, and giggle. The younger children crane their necks to spy Grandma and Grandpa somewhere in the audience. When they find their favorite people some give shy smiles, while others wave excitedly.

For their part in the program, the fourth-grade students told what they liked about their grandparents. One by one the long line of students spoke into the microphone. Some clutched a card on which they had written their comments. The nervous ones read their notes, while the confident ones spoke from the heart. A few had difficulty being specific, so it was amusing to hear them using the meaningless noun *stuff*.

"I like my grandpa because he helps me build and make stuff."

"I like my grandpa because he takes me fishing."

"I like my grandparents because they buy me candy and toys and all the stuff I want."

"I like my grandma because she takes me places where my mom won't."

"I like my grandma because she lets me eat the food I like."

Each of their comments brought a chuckle from the audience. Most of them emphasized the material things grandparents did to please them. But there was one young lad, Mason Pedersen, who struck a chord in my heart. He turned the tables. He said, "I give stuff to my grandpa and he keeps it forever. I love my grandpa."

This made me think of God, who gave us His Son. Are we keeping Him forever, or do we accept God's Gift and then cast Him aside? May each one of us determine to keep Him forever in our heart. It would make Him as happy as Mason.   EDITH FITCH

My Knight

I love you, God—you make me strong. God is bedrock under my feet, the castle in which I live, my rescuing knight. My God—the high crag where I run for dear life. Ps. 18:1, 2, Message.

BATTLES IN LIFE ARE inevitable. Change usually causes a fierce struggle. Right now I'm in a battle between the forces of good and evil. It comes down to who I'm going to allow to control my life. For a long time I've let a negative attitude envelop me. I see the bad instead of the good in life. I am sick of my life in the pits. My attitude of gloom is subconscious. I brush away the good that comes my way and rip myself up over the things that don't go perfectly. Right now I feel totally helpless, but that's where my Knight comes in.

Yes, my Knight. Maybe fairy tales are true. He rides over the fields on a beautiful horse, hair streaming behind Him, eyes shining with love, a peaceful smile on His kind face, with a Bible in His outstretched hand. He calls through the gloom, darkness, and despair: "Fear not, I will conquer. Do not doubt, I will save. Though the night is dark and the storm fierce, though it seems impossible, though it seems all hope is fading and your dreams are in pieces, I will rescue you, for you called. I will strengthen you; I will restore all that was taken and make it better than before. Hold on, and you will see the sun again. Never fear; I am here."

You see, my knight is Jesus. He has promised me in His lifeline to fallen humans: "Never will I leave thee, never will I forsake thee." "I will complete the good work I began in you." "I have loved you with an everlasting love. I have drawn you with lovingkindness." His precious promises give me hope, hope that better things will come if I trust Him to do His work of restoring me to what He knows will be best for me.

I still fight the impossible and run up against walls, but He always comes when I call, riding into my heart, breaking my gloom and giving me hope. It's a battle, I know, but if I keep trusting my Knight, the sun will shine again, and I will conquer through Him.

O Lord, be our knight this day. Come rescue us from our human-made hell. Free us from the negative pall that controls our thoughts. Bring us deliverance so we may see the sun of joy instead of the night of darkness that we too easily let envelop us. Amen.   RISA STORLIE

Tangiwai Disaster

For he shall give his angels charge over thee, to keep thee in all thy ways. Ps. 91:11.

AUSTIN, AUSTIN! THERE HAS been a terrible accident. I've just heard on the wireless. A train disaster. Your mother and daughter!"

It was Christmas Eve 1953. Our neighbor left his cowshed in the middle of the early morning milking and came running down the country road to my father's New Zealand farm. Dad was also busy milking his cows.

My grandmother and an older sister were coming home for Christmas and the annual Christian camp meeting soon after. This meant an overnight train trip from Wellington to Auckland. Halfway between these two cities is a large national park, a popular skiing destination during winter. But winter that year had been very severe, and there was a lot of snow lasting longer than usual.

Suddenly the weather warmed (remember that December is summer in the Southern Hemisphere), and the sudden thaw turned the Whangaehu River into a swiftly flowing torrent. With this water came sand, silt, boulders, and debris. On the night of the twenty-fifth this turbulent deluge, called a lahar, smashed into a railway bridge downstream at a little settlement called Tangiwai, and some bridge pylons were washed away.

Just after 10:00 on that dark night a very brave postal worker on his way home saw the collapsed bridge and ran down the railway track toward the oncoming train for as long as he dared, waving his torch. The engineer failed to see the warning light, and the train sped past and onto the bridge, taking more than 150 people to their death.

My father quickly, and thankfully, told our neighbor farmer friend that my grandmother and sister were safe. They had come home the day before.

Like the postal worker, our Lord holds out a lamp to warn us of the danger of sin: "I am the light of the world" (John 8:12). Just as tragically as the train engineer, we can rush heedlessly on, ignoring the dangers. I pray that we see the lantern in time and stop to listen to Jesus' voice.   LEONIE DONALD

December 20

His Perfect Love

Herein is love, not that we loved God, but that he loved us. 1 John 4:10.

I AM BLESSED WITH two amazing little boys who are so different in every way, and I love them both dearly.

When my first son was a baby, he did not cry at all—not when he was hungry, and not when he needed changing. He was a perfect, happy baby. At times he would lie awake in his bed, enjoying his surroundings or playing by himself. Except when he was sick. Then he would cry, and I knew then something was really wrong with him and he needed extra care.

With my second baby, I was excited as I anticipated his arrival. A new addition to the family! I couldn't wait! I was thinking he would be just like his brother, having the same temperament, even though my friends told me that every baby is different. I realized how true that was when my second son arrived. I was in for the surprise of my life—he kept me guessing all the time. He always wanted to be held and would let me and the entire neighborhood know when he was awake or when it was feeding time. He constantly cried, even if he was fed and dry. Sometimes I wondered, "Where is the manual for this one? He's nothing like his brother. I'm even a little afraid to think of how much care he will need if one day he is not feeling well."

Taking care of my first son, I thought I had it together as a new mother. With my second son I realized that it was not so. Every child is truly different. As a wise friend told me, each is special and unique in his or her own way. Even though my sons are different in many ways, I love them both dearly; one not more or not less than the other. In my eyes they are both precious individuals, and I love them unconditionally.

God loves us very much, no matter how different we are as individuals. To Him we are special and unique sons and daughters, made in His image. He made us special, and He loves our uniqueness. Despite our differences, He loves us unconditionally. We were bound by sin and He freed us and took us in—His love is perfect. The love of God is greater far than ever I can tell. *Thank You, God, for Your Love.*   VELNA WRIGHT

I'll Be Home for Christmas

Instead, they were longing for a better country—a heavenly one. Therefore
God is not ashamed to be called their God, for he has prepared a city for them.
Heb. 11:16, NIV.

HAVE YOU WITNESSED THE drama of life portrayed in airports and bus stations? There you will observe both sorrow and joyous excitement in the eyes of the traveler.

I am a people watcher who loves to watch as planes land and their travelers disembark, or as they load and pull away. You see tears, welcome hugs, squeals of delight, and parting kisses. Best of all, I love to see families reunited: a daughter returning from college for the holidays, a son from the military, a dad home from a business trip, or a grandma and grandpa coming in for an extended visit. The joy radiates out from the family circle and touches all those standing nearby. Even though they are strangers, you feel a part of their happiness or sorrow.

One scene etched forever in my mind is that of a large family. They were waiting to welcome a son back from the Gulf War. They held a large, hand-lettered banner in bright red saying "Welcome Home, Brad!" Suddenly, the family erupted in a loud cheer as they caught sight of the homecoming son. There was a welcome that can only be described as chaos. I don't know if they cried, but I know that I and many others had tears in our eyes.

I am a softy when it comes to reunions. I get a lump in my throat each time I read the story of the prodigal son. I can just see that aging dad out there beside the road as the last rays of evening begin to fade. His pulse quickens as he squints into the evening sun and recognizes the familiar silhouette coming toward him. Then he leaves his dignity behind and runs to meet his boy. They embrace in the middle of the road, neither daring at first to speak. Imagine the expression on the father's weathered face as he holds his son to his heart, unwilling to let him go. No questions asked, no conditions given, just welcome home!

Everyone of us is, after all, a prodigal, at times straying away from the Father's love. But whatever our journey, the important thing is that during the holidays all of us can sing, "I'll be home for Christmas." Nothing would bring greater joy to the heart of the Father.   BARBARA SMITH MORRIS

December 22

The Gift of Ourselves

Mary hath chosen that good part. Luke 10:42.

CHRISTMAS! MY FAVORITE TIME of year. Too busy, too stressful, yes, but my favorite time anyway! I love last-minute shopping—colorful lights, happy faces, bright music, crisp air. People are a little friendlier. The world smiles a little more.

Last Christmas my shopping included buying a bag of gifts for Syd, my high school chum in a rehabilitation center, who will never walk again. She can't even sit up. I often called her on the phone and visited her. She was my prayer partner, and I tried to cheer her long, weary days.

One Christmas I planned to visit friends in another town, but Syd had no family close by and would be spending Christmas alone. I delighted in finding little gifts for her: a big black gorilla with smirky eyes, holding a red chocolate rose; a little jewel box with something inside I knew she'd like; a bag of pretzels; and an angel basket filled with candy. I packaged them all— one to open the day before Christmas, one to open Christmas Eve, and one to open Christmas morning. And I told her that if she were very, very good she could open the chocolate rose the smirky gorilla held in his hands.

I was so happy to give Syd the gifts; however, she didn't appear as delighted to receive them. She was quieter than usual when she said "Thank you."

As I turned to leave I noticed a couple of tears roll down her cheek. I turned back. "What's wrong, Syd?" I asked.

She didn't want to tell me. Another tear rolled down. Finally she said, "I don't want to spend Christmas alone."

Then I realized that all the pretty gifts scattered across her bed could not replace the gift of myself, a friend to be with on Christmas.

And I thought how often we spend time and money and stress ourselves out buying gifts for those we love, when the gift they want most of all is the gift of time spent with them, a gift of our love—ourselves.

EDNA MAYE GALLINGTON

Locked in the Restroom

And Jesus came and touched them, and said, Arise, and be not afraid.
Matt. 17:7.

IT WAS A FREEZING cold morning, –30°F (–34°C), when I left home to drive 50 miles to teach a skin-care class. It was two days before Christmas and so cold I doubted anyone would come, but I was paid to do this, so I went anyway. Class was to be held upstairs in a café bowling alley. I hauled the boxes and setups upstairs to be ready for the noon class, but I kept hearing the loud bowling balls and wondered if the noise would interfere with my class. I didn't wonder long, because it was soon apparent that no one was coming. Disgusted that I'd gone through all the trouble, I decided to wait a few more minutes and use the restroom before leaving.

When I tried to leave the restroom, the door locked. I was frantic, up there alone. With the huge racket downstairs, I knew no one would hear me. Even worse, I'm asthmatic, and my inhalers were in the next room. Noticing a small vent at the bottom of the door, I got down on the floor and shouted through the vent as loudly as I could. *Strange,* I thought as I peered through the vent holes, *I never noticed all these shelves with restaurant supplies when I came in.* Everything looked different. The loud laughing and bowling sounds continued from downstairs. I panicked, and my mind began working overtime. Here I was, alone, the day before Christmas Eve; it was 30° F below; maybe no one would open tomorrow. Worse, maybe they'd turn the heat way down, and I'd be stuck up here over Christmas, and my family wouldn't know where I was.

Imagining the worst, I hollered again, this time louder. Soon I heard a man calling, "Lady, I'm comin'! Should I call an ambulance?"

In the next moment he came through the door—right behind me! I was still lying on the floor, now in shock. Because I was so frightened, I had failed to notice the other door, the one through which I had entered the restroom. The poor man howled with laughter but was relieved I was OK. I was so embarrassed and, even worse, I was upset with myself because I hadn't prayed. If I had, surely the Lord would have spoken to me about the door.

O Lord, when I am afraid, help me to remember You first.

DARLENE YTREDAL BURGESON

December 24

Importance of Christmas

And she shall bring forth a son, and thou shalt call his name Jesus. Matt. 1:21.

THE SUN SHONE BRIGHTLY; the temperature was well up in the 40s (7-10 ° C). This would be another Christmas without the longed-for white snowflakes, and without any of our loved children at home. Our son was in California, and our daughters in their homes in Europe. My husband and I would be alone. We slept in late, then made the cheerful long-distance phone calls across the miles, exchanging our greetings.

At last we were out the door in the gray-black wonderland of Christmas Day on our way into Boston. We drove to the Italian North End, which was gaily decorated for the holiday. We knew of one restaurant, purported to have superb food, that was open on this important day, but we weren't sure of the street. At last we stopped to ask for information from a woman who was out walking her dog. Yes, she knew where Mama Cantina was.

We finally found Mama Cantina, a small unpretentious café, and joined the others who were celebrating Christmas. Our delicious pasta was served in big bowls, and we enjoyed the interesting new food and the coziness of the place. Somehow we felt a kinship with the other diners on this special day. I whispered to my husband, "It's Christmas; let's give the waitress a big tip."

We stepped out into the cold air where darkness had descended and the Christmas lights and decorations shimmered in even brighter colors against the blackness of the sky. We joyfully walked the streets to the plaza, where the 52-foot (16-meter) Christmas tree with its 17,000 lights had been knocked completely over by the storm of the past weekend. We looked at the destruction and were sorry to see this magnificent tree in such a heap.

We thought about the whole Christmas day. We didn't need snow to make it truly white. We didn't need the big tree to stand tall or to see 17,000 lights burning. We didn't need the children to be at home on December 25. None of these things were important to this special day. It was the time to remember the birth of the baby Jesus in the manger in Bethlehem so long ago that you and I might have eternal life. DESSA WEISZ HARDIN

My Son!

Blessed is she who has believed that what the Lord has said to her will be accomplished! Luke 1:45, NIV.

AS I LOOKED INTO His laughing eyes, it was an unbelievable feeling knowing that my son—my firstborn—would be the One chosen to save mankind. How could all this have happened within the last nine months?

Holding Jesus against my suckling breast, I recalled the last unimaginable months. I had been so excited about my perfect-planned, romantic wedding day. I remembered the words of the angel as if it were yesterday: "Do not be afraid, Mary, you have found favor with God."

"How will this be," I had asked the angel, "since I am a virgin?"

"The Holy Spirit will come upon you. . . . So the holy one to be born will be called the Son of God," the angel said to me.

"I am the Lord's servant," I answered. "May it be to me as you have said." Then the angel left me (Luke 1:30-38, NIV).

This was a horrible time for me. I was numb with the thought of being the mother of Immanuel. I was frightened, not knowing when I would feel the first stone thrown at me. I was lonely for Joseph's comforting embrace. How could I be a mother before becoming a wife? I couldn't make sense out of this.

My son—the Savior of the world? Would He face pain? Could He face rejection? I was forced back to reality when Jesus began wiggling and crying in the straw-made bed Joseph had fixed for Him. The smell of the cattle, sheep, and the camels wasn't what I had envisioned for my precious Son's nursery.

As I ran my fingers over His soft, tiny fingers, I imagined how many people those hands would touch. Counting His 10 toes, I could hear His footsteps along the rough and rugged pathways He would walk. Ah, His heart beating so rapidly—how often my heart would be broken, realizing that His heart was the one that would be broken for all sinners, including me. My son! My one and only Son! I loved Him with a mother's love. I accepted Him. My Son! My Savior! Have you accepted His love this Christmas season?

MARY MAXSON

Free Gift

Now may the God of hope fill you with all joy and peace in believing, that you may abound in hope by the power of the Holy Spirit. Rom.15:13, NKJV.

IT WAS THE 1998 church Christmas program. Everybody was happy— friends trying to catch up with each other, others just visiting. Snatches of conversation could be heard from all directions. Then the program leader called for attention; the program was starting.

After the welcome and prayer, the program leader brought in a box with a few papers in it. She asked, "How many of you have written your name and dropped it in this box?" There was silence. "If you were keen enough," she continued, "you noticed the sign on the entrance table that read 'A free gift. Just write your name and drop it here!'"

Honestly, the moment I entered the room I had busied myself visiting with friends. I think I saw some signs but was too busy to read them.

The names were called and gifts were given, mostly to children. They had taken the time to write down their names. I was a little disappointed with myself; I should have taken time to write down my name, too. It would have been fun to receive a free gift. Well, it was too late.

As I contemplated this during the program, I realized that the same thing is happening in our Christian lives. We're all so busy visiting, making money, hoarding educational qualifications, showing off the little we have, being proud of our accomplishments, doing God's work (or so we think!) that we forget the free gift that the Lord is offering to us every day. All we have to do is sign our name and give it to the Master.

We have to take time, though, just as the children took time to write their names and drop them in the box. I'm happy it's not yet too late for us; we can still give our names to the Master. The gifts are ready to be given; let's hurry and call to the Savior. Let's give our names to Him today.

"Now may the God of hope fill you with all joy and peace in believing, that you may abound in hope by the power of the Holy Spirit" (Rom. 15:13, NKJV).

JEMIMA D. ORILLOSA

Patches

We love him, because he first loved us. 1 John 4:19.

WE WERE RENTING AN old farmhouse on a 200-acre farm. The owner had moved to town and rented the house to us while he decided what to do with the aging farm. The scenery was beautiful, with rolling hills, 100 head of cattle, and five horses. A picturesque setting indeed. My sons enjoyed playing in the fields, petting the calves, and helping the owner feed them and the horses. Occasionally he would allow them to ride the horses.

The farm was complete with a cat named Patches, who lived in the barn and ate whatever she could catch. Of course, my five children insisted on buying her cat food so she would have a better diet. So we bought her a dish and food, and she got used to coming up on the porch to eat. She was a bit wild, but over time, as she got used to us, she would let us pet her. After several months of being around us, she finally got to the point of jumping up in our laps when we sat on the porch.

One winter evening my husband got home and parked the car in the driveway. Later that night we got in the car to go out. As the engine started, we heard the cat shriek from under the hood. Patches had climbed up under the hood of the car to take advantage of the warmth from the engine and had fallen asleep there. She had done this many times before but had always jumped out as soon as she heard the car doors open and shut. This time she must have been in a very deep sleep. I still don't understand how it happened, but the fan blades caught Patches' hip and ripped a four-inch-long section of fur and skin off her right back leg.

We all tried consoling the poor cat. I held her legs down while my husband sprayed a first-aid anesthetic on the injury so she would allow him to dress her wound. Every day we washed her wound and put more ointment on it. Eventually it healed and new fur grew in.

Patches learned to trust us and love us because we loved her first.

Thank You, Lord, for loving us before we even knew who You were!

CELIA MEJIA CRUZ

No Waters Too Deep

When you pass through the waters, I will be with you; and when you pass through the rivers, they will not sweep over you. Isa. 43:2, NIV.

L IKE THE REST OF the world, I had always wondered what the year 2000 would hold. I could never have foreseen all that did happen to me. From the start I felt as if someone out there was determined to destroy me.

In April I acquired a fairly new Toyota car. When inquiring about insurance, the AAA was very impressed by my accident-free record since 1974. Two weeks later I was parked when a bus slammed into my car from the side. That night many cars on our street were vandalized, and radios and valuables stolen. Mine went in for repairs and panel beating.

In June I was in an intersection when a car rammed me from behind and slammed me into the car in front. My car had to be towed; for months I suffered extreme back and neck pain.

In August I stopped at a traffic light on my way home from work. A street beggar came up to my passenger window. The next moment the window was smashed and my handbag grabbed. I tried to pull it back, but it went flying through the window. I was devastated! My whole life was in that bag—checkbook, credit cards, bank cards, and lots of money. My driver's license, identity document, diary, address book containing irreplaceable information, and attendance and payment records from our women's retreat were in there, too. Every time I looked for something, I remembered it was gone. Here I was, a victim of crime once again.

I sank into an uncharacteristic depression that lasted a long time. My family was baffled. How could they understand how I felt about the loss, especially of photographs. I was angry at God and at myself. Then I began to ask myself some questions: What does a woman's life consist of? In my present state of mind, how could I be of use to God, self, or family? Had I become nobody just because I'd lost all my identification?

What was I to learn from all this? The Lord offered no explanation, but He told me that I am important to Him and that He loved me enough to die for me. He told me that He was with me all the way. In the end, that was all I knew, or needed to know.

DENISE NEWTON

White as Snow

Though your sins be as scarlet, they shall be as white as snow. Isa. 1:18.

IN DESPAIR I LOOKED at my clothes as I removed them from the washer. My white sheets had orange streaks, my white pants and shirts were in varied shades of orange. Socks, underclothes, everything was ruined, I complained to my husband.

And then I related my troubles to my always-understanding and sympathetic neighbor, who advised me to buy some Iron-Out on our next trip to town. I added Iron-Out to my shopping list. My husband was patient as I toured the whole department store without success. My neighbor assured me that I could find it at any grocery store. But alas, they must have been just out.

Finally I decided to try our local hardware and, yes, the obliging salesman not only agreed that it was there but showed me exactly where it was on the shelf.

After reading the directions carefully, I immersed the discolored garments and linen in the proper mixture of water and Iron-Out for the prescribed five minutes, then washed them as usual. And behold, they were again pristine white! I called for my husband to come see the miracle.

A familiar song came to my mind: "Lord Jesus, I long to be perfectly whole; I want Thee forever to live in my soul; break down every idol, cast out every foe; now wash me, and I shall be whiter than snow. Whiter than snow, yes, whiter than snow; now wash me, and I shall be whiter than snow."

I am steeped in sin, discolored by my tendency to have my own way. "We shall often have to bow down and weep at the feet of Jesus because of our shortcomings and mistakes, but we are not to be discouraged. Even if we are overcome by the enemy, we are not cast off, not forsaken and rejected of God. No; Christ is at the right hand of God, who also maketh intercession for us" (*Steps to Christ*, p. 64). Jesus' blood has washed me whiter than snow. What cause for rejoicing!

RUBYE SUE

Leaving Things Behind

Let us throw off everything that hinders and the sin that so easily entangles, and let us run with perseverance the race marked out for us. Heb. 12:1, NIV.

MOST OF US HAVE little habits that we cherish. Some are habits from early childhood or developed as we grew. I'm one of those people. I really like eating something sweetish or salty at bedtime. I cannot fall asleep without a little treat. Unfortunately, I know that it isn't good for my health or my teeth.

I've tried many times to break this habit, but it is so entangled around me. Sometimes I force myself to sleep without the little treat, but in the middle of the night I wake up to have something. It's only recently that I gave this little habit over to the Lord, and I thank Him for helping me to be an overcomer. All along I thought I could overcome by my own strength and power, because I thought it was just a "little habit." I was wrong.

You might be like me, possessed by little habits that we think don't matter. It's time to give them up to the Lord—leave them behind, throw them off, and get blessings. When I think that my Lord Jesus Christ left some things behind (not little habits, of course), it gives me courage. He left heaven to come and die for our sins, to give us the blessing of eternal life.

Joseph left his cloak behind to flee from sin when Potiphar's wife wanted to sleep with him. It gives me courage that he didn't go back to fetch his cloak—he simply left it for a good reason. While fishing, the disciples also left their nets to follow Jesus, and they became fishers of men. Yes, the woman at the well left her jar behind to proclaim good news to the city after she met the Savior, the man who told her everything about her life. She didn't hesitate to throw off her shame and pride. What an example!

We, too, can leave things behind that are a hindrance to our relationship with the Lord and with others, things that are a hindrance to our salvation. Those things might be little things, little habits, but dangerous; beware of them.

Lord, I give my cherished little habits to You. Give me the courage to leave these things behind and do Your will, for it is perfect. Amen.

NTOMBIZODWA ZIPHORA KUNENE

His Way Is Better

Shout for joy, O heavens; rejoice, O earth; burst into song, O mountains! For the Lord comforts his people and will have compassion on his afflicted ones. Isa. 49:13, NIV.

THE YEAR 2000 WAS going to be very special for me, but it wasn't what I had expected.

It was not the turning of the century, the end of the millennium, or any of the dreadful things people were afraid of that was going to make it special. There were going to be even more important events that year: I was going to turn 50 years old, it was going to be my thirtieth wedding anniversary, and my older son had informed me that I was going to become a grandmother!

I couldn't understand how the big 5-0 was upon me so soon. I felt energetic, with many plans for the future, lots of activities at work and in church, even looking into going back to school. And of course, I was too young to become a grandmother.

The year 2000 came and went. And it was all wrong! One month before our anniversary my husband and I separated. My plans for a big bash for my half a century turned into a very quiet dinner with one of my sons and his girlfriend and then going back to the empty apartment I could barely afford. That was the year in which the beginning of menopause gave me the biggest health problems of my life, sending me to the hospital on two occasions and making me see more doctors in 12 months than I had seen in my whole existence.

But the event I was most afraid of, becoming a grandmother, was the best thing that ever happened to me. The Lord knew I was going to need to hold that little baby in my arms.

I knew the promises of comfort, the promises of peace, the promises of love. God transformed the biblical promises into something I could touch, smell, kiss, talk to, sing to, tell all my problems. I would speak, and she would listen, her big eyes wide open, and smile back to me. Problems? What problems?

The promise is that things are made new in the Lord. Don't cry for what you have lost—looks, youth, spouse, whatever. There is hope; there are new beginnings. Don't despair. There is a future filled with smiles and giggles.

ALICIA MARQUEZ

BIOGRAPHICAL SKETCHES

Betty J. Adams is a retired teacher with three grown children and five grandchildren. She is active in Community Services and prayer ministry in her church. She has had articles published in *Guide,* and enjoys writing, quilting, mission trips, and her grandchildren. **Apr. 13, July 27, Nov. 7.**

Priscilla E. Adonis is a women's ministries coordinator in South Africa. She enjoys Bible studies, crocheting, collecting things for a children's convalescent home, writing letters, arranging flowers, and attending women's retreats. She has had recipes published in *Seasoned With Love.* She has two married daughters. **Jan. 15, Mar. 21, May 1, Aug. 29, Dec. 3.**

Maxine Williams Allen resides in Orlando, Florida, with her husband and two small sons. An entrepreneur with her own business, she loves to travel, meet people, and experience different cultures. Her hobbies include writing, reading, and computers. She has special interest in family, children's, and women's ministries. **Jan. 1, May 15, Aug. 24, Sept. 28.**

Minerva M. Alinaya is a lecturer in biology and music at Bethel College. Her hobbies are reading, playing the piano and the recorder, and needlework. She is a first-time author. **Mar. 9, June 22, Sept. 16.**

Linda Alinsod enjoys life in Maryland. **July 5, Nov. 16.**

Esther Ambikapalan works in the Sri Lanka mission office as a secretary. A children's Sabbath school teacher and women's ministries leader at her church, Esther loves to sing. She and her husband, a convert from Hinduism, have been married more than seven years. **Sept. 30.**

Mary Wagoner Angelin lives in Chattanooga, Tennessee, with her husband, Randy, and their daughters, Barbara and Rachel. Mary works at a large psychiatric hospital as a social worker and admissions counselor. She is a member and advocate for the LaLeche League and does volunteering, writing, keeping up with health information, working out, and finding vegan recipes. **Jan. 19, June 28, Oct. 24.**

Joann Ashworth has been a certified critical care registered nurse for more than 28 years. Married for 28 wonderful years to Richard, they are the frazzled parents of two teenagers, a daughter who graduated from Highland View Academy, and a son they are home schooling. Joann says it's an honor to serve Christ through nursing. **Dec. 11.**

Lois K. Bailey teaches English, drama, and art at Bermuda Institute of Seventh-day Adventists. As a single parent, she has one grown daughter, whom she adopted when she was an infant. She is thankful that God has certainly fulfilled His promises to us. **Mar. 8, June 12, Sept. 5.**

Rosemary Baker, a freelance writer living in Iowa, is author of *What Am I?* (a children's book), and has had contributions in other magazines. She is a member of the Iowa Poetry Association and the Quint City Poetry Guild, is active in church and volunteer work, and enjoys working with children. Arts, crafts, poetry, music, and painting are hobbies. **Dec. 10.**

Audrey Balderstone is a director in her husband's company. As well as being active in her local church, she raises large sums of money for charities through church flower festivals. She is also assistant editor and chairman of the board of *The Flower Arranger,* a magazine with a readership of 80,000. **Jan. 6, Aug. 28.**

Jennifer M. Baldwin writes from Australia, where she is clinical risk management co-ordinator at Sydney Adventist Hospital. She enjoys church involvement, travel, and writing and has contributed to a number of church publications. **July 17, Sept. 25.**

Dawna Beausoleil, a former teacher, is living in northern Ontario. She loves to sing, write, and to do jigsaw puzzles during the long winters and enjoys the outdoors during the glorious summers. **Jan. 27, Mar. 27.**

Priscilla Handia Ben is women's ministries director of the Eastern Africa Division. After teaching home economics in Zambia, Africa, for 12 years, she decided to become a full-time literature evangelist. She was conference and union publishing director in Zambia. Married to Pastor Strike Ben, from Botswana, she is the stepmother of one daughter. Her hobbies are jogging, traveling, cake decorating, and reading. **Feb. 17.**

Annie B. Best is a retired schoolteacher. She and her husband of more than 50 years have two grown children. She enjoys being with her three grandchildren, reading, and listening to music. She has worked as leader in the cradle roll and kindergarten departments of her church, a job she enjoys and finds rewarding. **Feb. 23, Apr. 6, June 9.**

Anne Bissell lives in the Philippines, where she serves as an editor. She is a Canadian, the mother of four, and grandmother to six grandchildren with twins due shortly. She enjoys traveling, swimming, reading, sewing, knitting, and most needle work. **Nov. 14.**

Dinorah Blackman is a high school chemistry teacher, actively involved in her church as Sabbath school superintendent, adult class teacher, and assistant choir director. She has been married since 1997, loves to read, write, and do public speaking. **Sept. 27, Dec. 1.**

Fulori Bola, a schoolteacher by profession, works in the Education Department at Fiji Mission, South Pacific Division of Seventh-day Adventists, where she is also Sabbath school director. Widowed, she has a daughter, 9, and a son, 7. She enjoys being with women who love the Lord, praying with and for prayer partners, being involved with women's ministries, and reading. **Jan. 29, June 6, Sept. 4.**

Evelyn Greenwade Boltwood is the mother of one young adult and one teenager. She is working toward an A.S. business degree in pursuit of a B.S. degree. She is the western New York area Pathfinder coordinator and a member of Akoma, a women's gospel community choir. **June 8.**

Darlene Ytredal Burgeson is a retired sales manager. Her hobbies include sending notes and cards to shut-ins, writing, photography, and raising prize irises. **May 16,**

July 4, Dec. 23.

Pam Caruso is the mother of 10 grown children and the grandmother of 10. She plays the piano in the cradle roll Sabbath school of her church and is active in women's ministries. She works out on the treadmill every day. **Jan. 30, July 10, Dec. 8.**

Virginia Casey is a retired municipal collections clerk and resides with her husband in Conception Bay South, Newfoundland. She enjoys immensely her involvement in church-related duties. She is a volunteer with the Discover Bible School in her area. Her hobbies include cross-country skiing, walking, reading, writing, and spending time with friends. **Nov. 17.**

Frances Charles is a retired school principal. She is the women's ministries director for the Kwazulu Natal-Free State Conference in South Africa. She is a bereavement counselor and a caregiver at a hospice. Her book, *My Tears, My Rainbow,* has been published. Her hobbies include reading, writing, and making pretty things. **Feb. 8.**

Birol C. Christo, a schoolteacher by profession, also worked as a secretary and division statistician. She was the first director of Shepherdess International for the Southern Asia Division. She lives with her husband in Hosur, India, has five children and 10 grandchildren, and enjoys gardening, sewing, and making crafts to finance her project for homeless children. **July 8, Nov. 19.**

Marsha Claus taught elementary school for two years. After having a child six years ago, she chose to be a stay-at-home mom. Her husband is the manager of the Wisconsin and Illinois Adventist Book Centers; they enjoy traveling around the state on the bookmobile. Her hobbies include traveling, writing, and crafts. **June 25.**

Clareen Colclesser, a retired L.P.N. and widow since 1994, has two children, six grandchildren, and five great-grandchildren. She enjoys her family, homemaking, and quiet times with a good book. Clareen stays active in her church. Hobbies include writing letters and short stories, and her collection of interior decorating magazines. **Apr. 14, June 18, July 11, Aug. 23, Oct. 14.**

Celia Mejia Cruz is a pastor's wife, mother of five adult children, and grandmother of four toddlers. A church elder and women's ministries leader, Celia enjoys entertaining, reading, playing with her dog, and collecting Siamese cats. **Feb. 16, May 13, Aug. 20, Oct. 12, Dec. 27.**

Yvonne Leonard Curry is a scientist who works as a director for diversity programs in science for underserved populations. As a single mom of two teenagers, she enjoys running, crocheting, reading, and writing. **Mar. 17.**

Marinês Ap. Da Silva Oliveira works as a secretary in an international bank. She is married and the mother of two children: Caroline and Henrique. She lives in São Paulo, Brazil, where she is active in the church. This year she coordinates the women's ministries activities in her church. She likes to travel, listen to music, write, and shop for her children. **Oct. 19.**

Girija Daniel and husband, Ahab, live in Tamil Nadu, India, where they both work for a small mission school, she as headmistress. A former Hindu Brahman, she says, "By the grace and mercy of our Lord, I was converted and now work for the Lord." Girija is women's ministries director at her church. She has a son studying theology, and a daughter in ninth grade. **July 14, Sept. 15, Oct. 21.**

Arielle Davis was 11 years old and attended the Portland Adventist Elementary School at the time of this writing. She enjoys music, reading, Barbie dolls, and church. She wants to be a psychologist and a concert pianist. **July 2.**

Wanda Davis is staff chaplain at Adventist Medical Center in Portland, Oregon. She is an elder at her church. Married and the mother of three, she enjoys preaching, teaching, facilitating small groups, and gardening. **Mar. 20, June 14, Oct. 5.**

Fauna Rankin Dean lives in rural Kansas with her husband. They have one grown son and two teenagers, as well as eight dogs, two cats, and two horses. She likes writing, photography, baking, needle crafts, gardening, and traveling. **Mar. 15, Aug. 17.**

Graciela Noemi Hellvig de Hein is a licensed nurse and director of women's ministries in the Northwest Argentine Mission. She is the wife of Carlos Hein, president of the mission. They have three children. Her interests include nature, riding bicycles, walking on the beach, crafts, and gardening. **Apr. 4.**

Qutie Dewar is a registered nurse. She worked one year at University Hospital of the West Indies. After marriage she migrated to the United States. Wife of a dentist and mother of Sanjeev and David, she stays busy with house chores, running errands, shopping, family trips, crocheting, gardening, reading, and writing. **Apr. 11, Oct. 26, Dec. 16.**

Laurie Dixon-McClanahan, now retired, was a Bible instructor for the Michigan Conference of Seventh-day Adventists. She keeps busy with gardening, quilting, reading, genealogical research, letter writing, culinary arts, and e-mail. **Feb. 9, May 5, Aug. 12, Dec. 12.**

Leonie Donald has lived in Brisbane, Australia, since 1987 and enjoys the warm climate. Her hobbies are reading and exercise and spending hours in her garden that tells her of God's love. She has held many church positions over the years, but really enjoys being with and teaching the little ones. **Jan. 13, Mar. 13, June 23, Sept. 14, Dec. 19.**

Goldie Down is an Australian evangelist's wife, missionary in India for 20 years, writer, teacher, and mother of six adult children. She has 25 books to her credit and numerous stories and articles in magazines and newspapers. Now retired, the Downs work harder than ever producing two Bible-based archaeological magazines. **Feb. 6, Apr. 22, Oct. 6.**

Louise Driver lives in Beltsville, Maryland, with her pastor-husband, Don. They have three grown sons and four grandchildren. At church she is involved with music and women's ministries. She also works in women's ministries at the General Conference of Seventh-day Adventists. Her hobbies are singing, music, skiing, reading, crafts, gardening, and traveling to historical places. **Jan. 4, Apr. 26, July 23.**

Linda Rochelle Duncan-Julie is a registered nurse who is pursuing a second profession in digital communications and design. She enjoys helping and encouraging others. A freelance writer with published articles, she hopes to one day write an article that may be used as God's tool to save someone who may find herself at the crossroads of hopelessness. **Aug. 21.**

Joy Dustow writes from Australia. She is a retired teacher and takes an active part in the spiritual and social activities of the retirement village where she lives with her husband. **Jan. 7**

Sushma Ekka was a nursing student at Ranchi Adventist Hospital in Bihar, India, when this devotional was written. **Sept. 10.**

Heike Eulitz comes originally from Germany. She left her home country when she was 19 and became a secretary in Switzerland. She is active in the prayer ministry of her local church. Her hobbies include all kinds of crafts, baking, nature, and swimming. **Aug. 27, Nov. 28.**

Gloria J. Stella Felder, born in Louisiana, currently works in the Northeastern Conference of Seventh-day Adventists. She and her pastor-husband have a merged family of four grown children and five grandchildren. Gloria enjoys music, writing, public speaking, and practicing the guitar. She has written articles for several magazines and is currently working on her second book. **Feb. 27, Aug. 2.**

Mercy M. Ferrer writes from Pakistan, where her husband is the treasurer of the Pakistan Union Section of Seventh-day Adventists. They have been missionaries to Egypt, Cyprus, and Russia. They have a daughter and son in college. Mercy enjoys traveling, cooking, entertaining, word games, photography, and gardening. She loves e-mailing family and friends. **Feb. 1, Apr. 18, Sept. 13.**

Margaret E. Fisher is retired after 40 years in nursing. She spends time writing poetry and short stories. She and her husband travel in the winter, giving out Christian books and literature. They belong to the Dayton Seventh-day Adventist Church in Dayton, Tennessee, and work with their Communication Department. **Aug. 22.**

Edith Fitch is a retired teacher living in Lacombe, Alberta, Canada. She volunteers in the Archives at Canadian University College and is a member of the Lacombe Historical Society. She enjoys doing research for schools, churches, and individual histories. Her hobbies include writing, traveling, needle work, and cryptograms. **Jan. 25, Apr. 2, Sept. 24, Dec. 17.**

Heide Ford, the associate editor of *Women of Spirit,* lives with her husband, Zell. She holds a master's degree in counseling and loves reading, flowers, and whale watching. **Jan. 2, Sept. 6.**

Josephine T. Francis has worked for 20 years as a schoolteacher in India and has worked as a nurse in the United States. She has served as a church deaconess, church clerk, Sabbath school superintendent, and Investment secretary. Her hobbies include knitting, crocheting, quilting, and sewing. All proceeds from projects are for Global Mission. **July 15.**

Edna Maye Gallington is part of the communication team at Southeastern California Conference of Seventh-day Adventists and is a graduate of La Sierra University, with courses from University of California, Riverside. She is a member of Toastmasters International and the Loma Linda Writing Guild. She enjoys freelance writing, music, gourmet cooking-entertaining, hiking, and racquet ball. **Mar. 16, June 26, Dec. 22.**

Kerttuli Giantzaklidis, from Finland, is married to Yiannis, from Greece, who is currently pastoring the Nicosia church on the island of Cyprus. They have three sons. Kerttuli is responsible for the English language section of the Middle East Centre for Correspondence Studies and is actively involved in the local church with Bible studies for the juniors and teens. **Oct. 1.**

Evelyn Glass enjoys her family and loves having her grandchildren live next door. She and her husband, Darrell, live in northern Minnesota on the farm where Darrell was born. Evelyn is active in her local church and in her community. She writes a weekly column for the local paper and serves as women's ministries-family life director for the Mid-America Union Conference of Seventh-day Adventists. **June 10.**

Carrol Grady is a minister's wife who is enjoying retirement in the beautiful Pacific Northwest. She is a mother of three and grandmother of six, whose spare-time delights include quilts, music, writing, and reading. Much of her time is devoted to her ministry for families of gays and lesbians. **Nov. 25.**

Mary Jane Graves and her husband enjoy retirement in beautiful western North Carolina. They have two adult sons and two granddaughters, who are growing up too fast. Among other things, Mary Jane enjoys reading, gardening, family, and friends. **Apr. 20, July 20, Oct. 11.**

Shirley Kimbrough Grear writes from New Jersey, where she lives with her husband, Carl. She is a speaker and seminar and workshop leader throughout the United States. She is a master quilter. Her articles and quilts have been widely published and exhibited. **Mar. 26, Aug. 15.**

Carol Joy Greene writes from Florida, where she delights in being able to taxi her young granddaughters around after school. She is an active member of her church's women's prayer circle. **May 7.**

Glenda-mae Greene was formerly the assistant vice president of student services at Andrews University in Michigan. She is now retired and living in Florida. She finds pleasure in writing, teaching, and preaching. What she enjoys most is the company of her God, her three nieces, and her nephew. **Jan. 14, Mar. 1, Apr. 28, June 2, Sept. 19.**

Gloria Gregory is a minister's wife, mother of two girls, and an associate professor of nursing at Northern Caribbean University (formerly West Indies College), Mandeville, Jamaica. A graduate of Andrews University's Extension Program with a Masters in Education, her hobbies include hand craft, playing word games, sewing, and gardening. **Apr. 9, Aug. 11, Nov. 5.**

Dessa Weisz Hardin and her physician-husband spent five months of volunteer teaching in China, a wonderful experience with eager students and of making great friends. Now she is at home in Maine sharing her knowledge of China and artifacts with the enthusiastic first graders in her hometown. **Apr. 3, Nov. 11, Dec. 24.**

Ann VanArsdell Hayward is retired after 30 years in the healthcare industry and lives in a small town north of Nashville, Tennessee. She has three children and five grandchildren, of which she is very proud. She is active in her church and enjoys reading, bird watching, sightseeing, and writing devotionals. **Dec. 14.**

LaVerne Henderson is the assistant communication director for the Columbia Union Conference in Columbia, Maryland. As the news and information coordinator for the *Visitor* magazine, she's most grateful to serve the Lord in this capacity. LaVerne attends the Emmanuel Seventh-day Adventist Church in Brinklow, Maryland. **Jan. 9.**

Iris Henry is director of women's and children's ministries for the West Indies Union in Jamaica, coordinator for the union office/University Shepherdess Club, and general secretary of the United Nations Association of Jamaica local chapter. She has four grown married children and five grandchildren. Hobbies are gardening and listening to good music. **June 16.**

Andrea C. Herbert, originally from Jamaica, lives with her husband and son in Virginia. She is the communications leader for her church and enjoys mothering, photography, reading, writing, travel, and entertaining family and friends. **Aug. 13.**

Denise Dick Herr teaches English at Canadian University College in Alberta, Canada. She participates in archaeological excavations in Jordan with her family and is interested in connections between biblical narratives and the contemporary world. She has written *Men Are From Judah, Women Are From Bethlehem: How a Modern Bestseller Illuminates the Book of Ruth.* **Feb. 15, July 16, Oct. 13.**

Judy Holbrook is married to Bob and lives in Maryland. A former missionary to South America, she daily utilizes her Portuguese and Spanish, and continues to learn Japanese and German. A published poet, she writes lyrics and music for her autoharp. Her hobbies are antique pastel glassware, her garden, bird watching, walking, rock climbing, collecting shells, traveling, and beautiful note cards and stationery. **May 11.**

Karen Holford is married to Bernie Holford, and they have three children. Karen has authored several books and works alongside Bernie in family ministries. She also works part-time as an occupational therapist in a brain injury rehabilitation unit. If there is any spare time, she enjoys walking, crafts, and writing. **Feb. 13, Apr. 12, July 28, Sept. 18, Nov. 29.**

Lorraine Hudgins is retired with her minister-husband in Loma Linda, California. Her working career includes Faith for Today, the Voice of Prophecy, and the General Conference of Seventh-day Adventists. She has authored two books, and her poems and articles appear frequently in various publications. Her favorite hour is her early-morning quiet time with her heavenly Friend. **Feb. 22, May 4, Aug. 8, Oct. 28.**

Barbara Huff is the wife of a retired church administrator, a mother, and grandmother. She is a freelance writer and a serious amateur photographer. Her hobbies include bird watching and shell collecting. **June 15.**

Viola Poey Hughes, originally from Malaysia, lives with her husband, Chris, and two boys in Silver Spring, Maryland. She works at the United Nations Liaison Office of the General Conference of Seventh-day Adventists. When she's not working on her graduate work, Viola leads out in family life activities for her local church and teaches the juniors with her husband. **Oct. 15.**

Christine Hwang is a family physician working in Toronto, Ontario, Canada. Her hobby is food—from eating it to cooking and baking it. Recently, she had an article on vegetarian eating in Toronto published. **May 20.**

Aleah Iqbal is a freelance writer who lives with her family in Willimantic, Connecticut. She home-schooled her children for 10 years. Her publishing credits include a book of poetry, original recipes, and health store newsletters. In the past she hosted her own local cable television show. She is currently writing a children's book. **Mar. 25, June 7, Dec. 6.**

Consuelo Roda Jackson, now retired, enjoys her husband and family. She taught at a community college and a university, and worked in medical records and quality assurance. Active in her local church, her interests include music, bird watching, and writing. She is a perpetual student who hopes to study under the great Teacher and Author of all life. **Mar. 29, May 28.**

Lois E. Johannes is retired from overseas service in southern and eastern Asia and lives near a daughter in Portland, Oregon. She enjoys knitting, community service work, patio gardening, her four grandchildren, and two great-grandchildren. **Jan. 16, May 31, Oct. 8.**

Marla Johnson lives in Maryland with her husband and two young daughters. She is a registered nurse, but at present is a full-time mom and home-schooler. She enjoys traveling, gardening, sewing, windsurfing, running, and cooking. **July 21.**

Pauletta Cox Johnson and husband, Mike, live in Michigan, where she grew up. She is an interior designer, a freelance writer of children's books, and does gardening, sewing, and crafts. Active in her home church, she is the proud mother of three grown sons, one daughter-in-law, and has two young grandsons. **Jan. 12, Mar. 28, May 27.**

Judy M. Kerr is married with five children and five grandchildren. She is a teacher, holding both a B.S. and an master's degree in education. Judy has served as a women's ministries leader in the Bermuda Conference, Atlantic Union Conference, and Northeastern Conference of Seventh-day Adventists. She thanks God she has a rainbow of thousands of sisters! **Nov. 9.**

Marjorie Kinkead, a schoolteacher, enjoys reading, walking, water aerobics, and playing with her grandson and granddaughter. She believed in the imminent return of Jesus when she first learned of it as a teenager, and still does. **Feb. 26**

Toya Marie Koch is married, has two tabby cats, and Lucie, her cocker spaniel. Toya leads a praise and worship team at her church in Maryland and is church bulletin secretary. Hobbies include writing, music, reading, photography, and sewing. She sings and plays the guitar and lap dulcimer. **May 17.**

Hepzibah Kore is the director for women's ministries, Shepherdess International, and special ministries of pastors' wives of the Southern Asia Division of Seventh-day Adventists. She and her husband, Gnanaraj, have one daughter, a son-in-law, a son, and two grandsons. Her hobbies are gardening, reading, and listening to music. She enjoys meeting with women of various cultures. **Mar. 19, Aug. 5.**

Betty Kossick worked as an independent journalist for more than 30 years. She delights in "discovering" people through interviews. She and her husband, John, moved to Battle Creek, Michigan, in 2000. She writes that her husband declares "the women's devotional books are the very best of any, because women are the most practical Christians." **Jan. 5.**

Patricia Mulraney Kovalski retired after teaching 38 years. She now spends her time doing crafts, giving teas, substitute teaching, and traveling with her husband—especially to visit their children and grandchildren. **Mar. 7.**

Juanita Kretschmar lives with her husband in the Florida Keys, where in "retirement" (after mission service in Brazil, northwestern United States, and Greater New York) they have established (through prayer) a Creation-centered tourist attraction called "A Key Encounter." A mother of three, grandmother to seven, Juanita enjoys writing, video production, and sharing God's power in prayer. **Nov. 13.**

Ntombizodwa Ziphora Kunene is from Mafikeng, South Africa, where she lives with her pastor-husband and son Tebogo. Operating a feeding program called Because U Care for Kids, for the underpriviledged children, she serves breakfast daily. She enjoys training new officers at her church, cooking, gardening, intercessory prayer, sharing the Word, encouraging others, reading, and writing. **July 18, Dec. 30.**

Mabel Kwei is the wife of the Gambia Mission president, director of Gambia women's ministries, lecturer at Gambia College in English language, art history, and appreciation and educational studies. She works side by side with her husband in pastoral work and loves reading. **Feb. 4, Aug. 6.**

Nathalie Ladner-Bischoff, a retired nurse, lives with her husband in Walla Walla, Washington. Besides homemaking, gardening, and volunteering at the Walla Walla General Hospital gift shop, she reads, writes, knits, and crochets. She's published several magazine stories and a book, *An Angels Touch.* **Apr. 1, June 21, Oct. 20.**

Gina Lee is the author of more than 600 stories, articles, and poems. She enjoys working part-time at the public library and caring for her four cats. **Jan. 3, Mar. 18, June 29, Sept. 22, Nov. 12.**

Ruth Lennox is women's ministries director for the British Columbia Conference of Seventh-day Adventists in Canada. She writes and produces monologues of first-person stories of Bible women. She is a retired family physician, and she and her husband have three married children and four granddaughters. **Mar. 11, Aug. 16.**

Bessie Siemens Lobsien, a retired professional librarian, worked as a missionary librarian in foreign countries and in the United States. She likes to write and has been published in church papers. She helps her local church as the communication secretary, and sews small quilts for Seventh-day Adventist orphanages. **Jan. 21, Mar. 3, May 10, Aug. 4, Nov. 4.**

Betty Lyngdoh is the women's ministries director of Khasi Jaintia Conference of Seventh-day Adventists in India. She and her husband, who is president for this conference, have three sons: Julius, Shem, and Stefan. Betty enjoys this new work and is looking forward to helping women to be more active for the Lord. **Apr. 29.**

Vicki L. Macomber is a secretary in the Book Division at the Review and Herald Publishing Association in Hagerstown, Maryland. She enjoys reading, writing, scrapbooking, and spending time outdoors. **Feb. 21, May 18, Aug. 14, Oct. 9.**

Alicia Marquez has been the accountant of the Greater New York Conference of Seventh-day Adventists for 10 years, having previously worked for the Spanish telecast *Ayer . . . Hoy . . . Manana* for 11 years. She is chair and treasurer of conference women's ministries activities and an elder at Far Rockaway Spanish Adventist Church. Born in Uruguay, South America, she came to the United States 29 years ago. **Sept. 23, Dec. 31.**

Gladys Fowler Marsh, a homemaker, lives in an old stone house on a Michigan farm, where she and her husband, now deceased, raised their six children. She enjoys reading, writing, memorizing poetry, and quilt-making. She has been active in children's programs in her church. **Nov. 18.**

Clarissa Marshall works in radio and television production at Three Angels Broadcasting Network in southern Illinois. Formerly a missionary on the island of Guam, she is extremely grateful for the opportunity to reach the world in these last days with a global media ministry. **Nov. 27.**

Philippa Marshall is involved with her local church and volunteer work. She enjoys writers' holidays and meeting other writers. She attends women's ministries retreats and visits friends and family. **Apr. 7, Oct. 4.**

Sharon Marshall, nurse-counselor, mother of two grown daughters, and grandmother of five, is also the codirector of her church's Sunday soup kitchen. She is currently the women's ministries director of her church and is active in the counseling of young women. Interests include singing in the church choir, reading, and writing, and she is a certified CPR Instructor. **Mar. 10, July 31, Dec. 9.**

Peggy Mason, living in Wales with her husband and one of her two adult sons, is a teacher of English and a writer whose hobbies include dried-flower growing and arranging, cooking, sewing, gardening, and reading. She is a pianist-composer and enjoys working for her church and community. **July 26.**

Soosanna Mathew lives in India and is an office secretary in the Publishing Department of the Southern Asia Division of Seventh-day Adventists. An elementary education graduate of Spicer Memorial College, her hobbies are writing poems, articles, and stories. She and her pastor-husband have two grown children, David and

Hannah. Soosanna taught school for more than 20 years. **Mar. 12, June 24.**

Debra Matshaya is a single elementary school teacher at Bethel Primary School, Butterworth, South Africa, where she also teaches sports. She is studying for a B.A. in communications from the University of South Africa, enjoys gym, and loves gospel music. **Jan. 26, Apr. 17.**

Mary Maxson is women's ministries director for the North American Division of Seventh-day Adventists. She and pastor-husband, Ben, served in team ministry in the United States and in Argentina and Uruguay. She is certified in marriage enrichment and as a hospital chaplain associate. Mary has been Shepherdess coordinator, an editorial secretary, and administrative assistant. **Feb. 12, Dec. 25.**

Ellen E. Mayr, for the past 10 years, has worked as department director at the union level for women's ministries, children's ministries, and family life in West Africa. She and her husband have two grown children, Siegward and Hearly. She enjoys reading, preparing materials, writing, and singing along with the piano. **Jan. 23, Mar. 23.**

Vidella McClellan is a home-care provider and newspaper distributor for her local paper. A wife and a grandmother of seven, she enjoys her children and grandchildren, loves country life, travel, and cats. She is involved with personal ministries at her church. Her hobbies are gardening, crafts, writing, reading, scrapbooking, poetry, and growing flowers. She hopes to get back to painting soon. **Feb. 24, Apr. 8, May 23, Aug. 3, Nov. 2.**

Patsy Murdoch Meeker of Virginia is a writer, reader, occasional photographer, and avid listener. Visiting her scattered family brings her joy. **July 25.**

Quilvie Mills, a retired college professor, lives with her pastor-husband, Herman, in Port St. Lucie, Florida. Actively involved in her small church, she has a deep interest in young people and does what she can to assist them in achieving their goals. She enjoys traveling, reading, music, gardening, and word games. **May 29.**

Marcia Mollenkopf, a retired schoolteacher, lives in Klamath Falls, Oregon. She is involved in local church activities and has served as a school board member. Marcia enjoys reading, bird watching, hiking, and crafts. **Feb. 11, June 17.**

Esperanza Aquino Mopera is the mother of four adults, grandmother of five, a school nurse, and director of women's ministries at her Tidewater Adventist Church. She likes gardening and watching birds and fish in the backyard lake. **Mar. 6, July 30, Oct. 17, Nov. 15.**

June E. Morgan is a single mother of two who lives in Lithonia, Georgia, and attends the Lithonia Seventh-day Adventist Church. She loves the Lord and is praying that when the trumpet sounds, she and her children will meet Jesus in the air and live with Him eternally. **Jan. 17.**

Barbara Smith Morris is executive director of a nonprofit retirement center. Each day she has a daily devotional over the speaker system. She served seven years as a Tennessee delegate, representing housing and service needs of low-income elderly. Barbara is women's ministries leader for her church and presents seminars on elder life issues. She is the mother of four grown children and grandmother of six grandsons. **May 12, July 6, Oct. 18, Nov. 20, Dec. 21.**

Bonnie Moyers lives with her husband and two cats in Staunton, Virginia. She is a certified nursing assistant, musician for two Methodist churches, and does painting and papering, and freelance writing, whenever she can fit it in. She is the mother of two adult children and has one granddaughter to enjoy. Her writings have been published in many magazines and books. **June 3.**

Jean S. Murphy is a retired music teacher living in Fletcher, North Carolina. She directs two handbell choirs and rings in one. She likes to spend time with her three children, four grandchildren, and two cats. Her hobbies are traveling, growing flowers, reading, e-mailing friends, and church work. **July 24.**

Lillian Musgrave and her family have enjoyed the unique qualities of northern California for more than 40 years. She enjoys having time for family and church activities and responsibilities. Her interests include but are not limited to writing, poetry, and music. She has been active in the HIV spiritual support group in her area and has established a Parents Support Group. **June 20.**

Joan Minchin Neall was born in Australia, lived in England, and now makes her home in Tennessee. She is a registered nurse, and she and her retired pastor-husband have four adult children and nine grandchildren. She is the women's ministries leader for her church and enjoys journaling, young women's Bible study groups, and spending time with her family. **Sept. 17, Oct. 30.**

Denise Newton is the director of women's ministries at the Transvaal Conference within the Southern Africa Union. She is a mother, grandmother, and independent business owner. **Sept. 26, Dec. 28.**

Jemima D. Orillosa works as an administrative assistant at the General Conference of Seventh-day Adventist world headquarters in Silver Spring, Maryland. She loves visiting elderly people and talking to them about Christ. She is active in her local church and lives in Maryland with her husband and two teenage daughters. She enjoys gardening and making friends. **May 8, June 11, Oct. 27, Dec. 2, Dec. 26.**

Susan Jeda Orillosa was 15 when she wrote for this devotional. A graduate of Highland View Academy in Hagerstown, Maryland, she is now a college student at Pacific Union College in California. She enjoys reading, singing, public speaking, mountain climbing, swimming, basketball, and other sports. **Jan. 11, Mar. 31, Sept. 3.**

Hannele Ottschofski lives in Germany with her family. She is editor of the local Shepherdess newsletter and loves to read and write. From time to time she presents seminars at women's ministries retreats. She is a piano teacher and directs a choir in her local church. Sewing is one of her favorite hobbies. **Jan. 8, Apr. 24, Nov. 3.**

Ofelia A. Pangan is married to a minister who pastors in the Central California Conference of Seventh-day Adventists. She enjoys visiting and playing with seven grandchildren, reading, walking for exercise, gardening, traveling, and playing Scrabble. **Jan. 20, Mar. 24, May 2, Oct. 31, Nov. 30.**

Revel Papaioannou is the mother of four sons, grandmother of seven, a pastor's wife, and an English teacher in the biblical town of Berea. Her hobbies include reading, hiking, and collecting stamps, coins, and phone cards. **July 29.**

Betty G. Perry lives in Fayetteville, North Carolina, with her pastor-husband. They have three adult children and three grandchildren. An anesthetist for 29 years, she's now semiretired. Her hobbies are piano, organ, needlework, and making new recipes. **Sept. 29.**

Birdie Poddar is from northeastern India. She and her husband enjoy retirement but keep busy. She enjoys gardening, cooking, baking, sewing, reading, writing, and hand crafts. They have a daughter, a son, and four grandsons. **Apr. 19, June 30, Oct. 10.**

Lanny Lydia Pongilatan, from Jakarta, Indonesia, works in the Sabbath School and Personal Ministries Department at the General Conference of Seventh-day Adventists in Silver Spring, Maryland. A professional secretary, she was an English instructor in Indonesia. She enjoys playing the piano, listening to Christian gospel songs, reading, tennis, and swimming. **Mar. 4, Apr. 23, May 25, Sept. 1, Oct. 29.**

Henrike Potthast is a pharmacist working in the research field in a German institute. She has been married since 1980. She attends an American military Adventist church group in Frankfurt, Germany, where she has been a pianist for several years. Her hobbies are animals, sports, music, reading, and gardening. **Aug. 26.**

Darlenejoan McKibbin Rhine, born in Omaha, Nebraska, raised in California, and schooled in Madison, Tennessee, is a widow with one adult son. She holds a B.A. in journalism and has for many years been public relations secretary for her church, Los Angeles Central City, in California. **Mar. 14, July 19.**

Lynda Mae Richardson is an administrative assistant for an architectural-engineering firm in Southfield, Michigan. She is active in her church's music ministry and is a Competent Toastmaster. Lynda has had two short stories published: "The Music Box" and "The Gift." Her hobbies include writing, singing, baking, hiking, and bicycling. **May 21, Oct. 7.**

Rowena R. Rick served the Seventh-day Adventist Church for 41 years, 21 of those years overseas in the South American Division and the Far Eastern Division. Her last position was as an associate treasurer of the General Conference. **Apr. 21, July 12, Oct. 16, Nov. 22.**

Gladys Rios lives in Maryland, is married to "the best man in the world" and is the mother of two wonderful daughters. After being a home mom for 20 years, she now works for the Ministerial Association at the General Conference of Seventh-day Adventists in Silver Spring, Maryland. She is a nurse and teacher and enjoys telling other women how much God loves them. **May 6.**

Barbara Roberts is a homemaker who enjoys her grandchildren. She serves her church as elder and Sabbath school superintendent and is an author of poetry and numerous articles of a devotional nature. She grows orchids, reads, sews, and writes for fun and relaxation. **Dec. 13.**

Hilkka Rouhe now lives in Sweden. Although her children live far away and she is very much by herself, she has a constant Friend she can depend on in all life's situations—Jesus. She has skilled hands for all kinds of handicrafts and has knitted many baby jackets for an orphanage in Romania. **Feb. 5.**

Cathy L. Sanchez writes from southern Illinois. She and her husband have a 10-year-old daughter, Emily. Cathy has served her local church through women's ministries, health ministries, vegetarian cooking schools, and women's retreats. Interests include gardening, vocal music, writing, small group goal setting, and, most of all, her family. **Aug. 31.**

Deborah Sanders enjoys sharing from her personal journal, *Dimensions of Love.* She goes by the pen name "Sonny's Mommy." She lives in Canada with Ron, her husband of 32 years. They have been blessed with Andrea, a son-in-law, and Sonny, who is severely challenged with autism. Deborah is also a deaconess in her church. **Feb. 20, Mar. 30, May 24, Oct. 23, Dec. 4.**

May Sandy grew up on a mixed farm in the Murray mallee of South Australia. It was from this background that she developed an interest in farming and sheep. Today, as a hobby, she farms black sheep for the craft industry. Currently she is learning to spin and prepare the wool for knitting into garments. **Aug 18.**

Marie H. Seard enjoys reading and writing. She participates in women's ministries in her church and organized the Say-It-Now-With-Flowers Committee that pays tribute to faithful, dedicated members. She is active in her community civic association and was elected chaplain of the Washington, D.C., Inter Alumni Association of the United College Fund. **July 9, Nov. 10.**

Packialeela Sam Selvaraj is a pastor's wife in South Tamil, India. She received a degree in elementary education, works in the Seventh-day Adventist school in Madurai, India, and loves teaching. She has taught primary Sabbath school, and loves to read, garden, and basket weave. She and her husband have a son and a married daughter. **Feb. 28, May 9.**

Donna Lee Sharp is on her church's worship committee, and also carries organ and piano responsibilities and involvement with two community organizations. Traveling to various parts of the globe to be near family members, hiking, birding, and interacting with college-age grandchildren are some of her favorite retirement pastimes. **Sept. 20.**

Carrol Johnson Shewmake is a retired pastor's wife, mother of four adult children, and a grandmother of eight. She has authored five books about developing an intimate relationship with God and given many seminars on the same subject. Her current hobbies include house planning and nature walking. **Feb. 2.**

Judy Musgrave Shewmake and her husband, Tom, live in northern California. They have a married daughter, a son studying for the ministry, and a son and daughter still at home. Judy has always home-schooled her children and is editor of the *Adventist Home Educator.* Her favorite hobby is writing, but she also enjoys reading, genealogy, and making memory scrapbooks. **Sept 2.**

Rose Neff Sikora and her husband, Norman, live in the beautiful mountains of western North Carolina. A nurse at Park Ridge Hospital for the past 20 years, her interests include camping in the travel trailer, writing, spending time with her three grandchildren, and helping others. Rose has had articles and stories published in magazines and books. **Sept. 21, Dec.7.**

Sandra Simanton is a licensed clinical social worker and works as a family therapist in Grand Forks, North Dakota. She lives with her husband and two children in nearby Buxton. She works with children's ministries in her church and enjoys reading and sewing. **July 3, Nov. 6.**

Dolores Smith is a retired registered nurse and certified midwife. She worked as a nurse practitioner in obstetrics for many years. She lives in Florida, enjoys traveling, and has traveled extensively. She obtains great satisfaction helping people. **Feb. 3.**

Christine May Smith-Shand is an accountant in the banking sector in Jamaica. She is married, an active Master Guide, and works in the Sabbath school, youth, and lay activities departments at her local church. Reading and Bible work are her favorite pastimes. **Mar. 22.**

Ethel Footman Smothers writes from Grand Rapids, Michigan. She is a published poet and children's author. Ethel and her husband, Lee, have four daughters and seven grandchildren. **Apr. 10, Sept. 12.**

Candace Sprauve is a reading teacher and the parent of three adult sons and a daughter. She also has two delightful grandchildren. Candace serves her church as an elder and the general Sabbath school superintendent. She is a Literacy Link of America volunteer, and her hobbies are reading, gardening, and sewing. **Oct. 22.**

Ardis Dick Stenbakken edits the submissions to this book as she travels the world, leading out in women's ministries for the Seventh-day Adventist Church. She and her husband, Dick, have two married adult children. Ardis lived in China and the Philippines as a girl, so travel is not new, but she especially enjoys helping women discover their full potential in the Lord. **Jan. 24, Mar. 2, July 1, Sept. 11, Nov. 1.**

Risa Storlie is a busy college student who loves coming home to see her cats and dog. In her spare time she enjoys reading, crocheting, writing, cooking, and hiking in nature. **Feb. 19, Dec. 18.**

Iris L. Stovall, originally from New Rochelle, New York, is married and has two sons and a daughter. She is administrative secretary and assistant editor of the General Conference women's ministries monthly newsletter. The head elder at her church, Iris enjoys singing, videography, reading, creative writing, and spending time with her granddaughter. **Apr. 30, June 5, Aug. 1, Oct. 2, Dec. 5.**

Grace Streifling is the proud mother of four adult children and is a retired nurse. She taught school part-time for four years and has had children's stories published. Her hobby is quilting, and she enjoys Bible study, visiting neighbors, and watching someone else mow her lawn. **June 4.**

Rubye Sue is a retired secretary who still enjoys her work, her family, her church family, and witnessing to others. **Apr. 27, Sept. 9, Nov. 23, Dec. 29.**

Loraine F. Sweetland, a retiree living in Tennessee, is a newsletter editor, school board chairperson, school building committee chair, and Sabbath school teacher. She writes weekly for the local newspaper in her hometown. Hobbies are teaching computers to retirees and surfing the Internet. She also has four young dogs. **Jan. 18, Feb. 18, Apr. 25, July 22, Aug. 30.**

Arlene Taylor is risk manager for three Adventist health hospitals in northern California and founder-president of a nonprofit corporation pledged to promoting brain function research and related educational seminars. She has recently ventured into the world of Internet radio, creating programs to help individuals learn how to be more successful, personally and spiritually. **Feb. 25, Apr. 5, Aug. 10, Nov. 21.**

Audre B. Taylor, a published writer, is a retired administrative assistant for Adventist Development and Relief Agency International. One of her hobbies is choral conducting, and she won an Angel Award in national media competition for one of her choral performances. She is a psychotherapist in the Washington, D.C., Metropolitan area. **Jan. 28, July 13.**

Janet Terry and Jess, her husband of 23 years, are blessed with the gift of hospitality. They have two children, Jessica and Kory. Janet was a United States Post Office rural mail carrier for 24 years. They own and operate their own business. **Oct. 23.**

Stella Thomas is the administrative secretary for the Global Mission Office at the General Conference of Seventh-day Adventists in Silver Spring, Maryland. She is very happy to be involved in God's work and would like to see Jesus come soon. **July 7, Oct. 3, Nov. 24.**

Anne Tinworth is a first-time contributor who lives with her husband in Australia. She enjoys taking part in the spiritual and social welfare of her church and the retirement village where she works. **Feb. 7.**

Nancy Ann Neuharth Troyer and her husband are directors of the Adventist Servicemen's Center in Frankfurt, Germany. She and Don have one daughter, Stephanie. Nancy spent the past 24 years traveling around the world with her United States Army chaplain-husband. To keep awake in church, Nancy, "the notetaker," takes sermon notes in calligraphy and line-drawing illustrations. **May 26.**

Phulmah Tudu was a second-year student at Ranchi Adventist Hospital in Bihar, India, at the time of this writing. **Jan. 10.**

Clarice B. Turner is a social worker by profession. She is currently the CEO for a hospice in western North Carolina. Clarice has one grown son. **Nov. 8.**

Nancy Cachero Vasquez is volunteer coordinator for the North American Division of Seventh-day Adventists. She is a wife and the mother of three adult daughters. She coauthored *God's 800-Number: P-R-A-Y-E-R*, and is a former missionary who enjoys reading, writing, shopping, and spending time with her husband. **Apr. 15, Aug. 19.**

Donna Meyer Voth is a substitute teacher and volunteer for the American Cancer Society. She enjoys giving Bible studies, watercolor painting, traveling, and camping.

She and her husband live in Vicksburg, Michigan, and have a daughter in college. **May 19, Sept. 8.**

Cora A. Walker lives in Queens, New York. She is a retired nurse and an active member in a local Seventh-day Adventist church in Queens. Reading, writing, sewing, classical music, singing, and traveling fill her leisure time. She has one son. **Jan. 22, June 1, Aug. 7.**

Martha J. Walker, a retired educator and mother of two adult sons, lives in Huntsville, Alabama, with her husband of 47 years. She has served in several church offices: church clerk, treasury assistant, women's ministries, and Sabbath school. She still enjoys contact with young people, in and out of the classroom. **May 30, Aug. 25.**

Anna May Radke Waters is a retired administrative secretary from Columbia Adventist Academy in Washington. She is an ordained elder in the Meadow Glade church, serves as a greeter, and has too many hobbies to list. But at the top of her list are her seven grandchildren and her husband, with whom she likes to travel and make memories. **Feb. 10, Apr. 16, June 13, Oct. 25.**

Dorothy Eaton Watts is associate secretary of the Southern Asia Division of Seventh-day Adventists. Dorothy is a freelance writer, editor, and speaker. A missionary in India for 16 years, she founded an orphanage, taught elementary school, and has written more than 20 books. Her hobbies include gardening, hiking, and birding (with more than 1,000 in her world total). **Jan. 31, Mar. 5, May 3, Aug. 9.**

Penny Estes Wheeler, editor of *Women of Spirit,* enjoys friendships with authors and others around the world. Her loves include the ocean and travel. She has walked the Great Wall and seen the colorful walls of the Ishtar Gate of ancient Babylon in the Pergamom Museum in Berlin, Germany. Penny is a new grandmother. (Ask to see her pictures!) **June 27, Dec. 15.**

Mildred C. Williams lives in southern California and works a few hours a week as a physical therapist. She enjoys Bible study and teaching, writing, public speaking, and gardening, as well as sewing for daughters and granddaughters. **Nov. 26.**

Patrice Williams-Gordon lectures in the Natural Science Department at Northern Caribbean University in Jamaica. She enjoys speaking, writing, planning events, and anything family-related. Married to Pastor Danhugh Gordon, they enjoy team ministry. They have two daughters. **May 22.**

Susan Wooley works part-time as a home-health nurse. She edits her church's newsletter, *Sonbeams.* Susan has been married for more than 23 years and has two teenage boys. **Feb. 14, June 19, Sept. 7.**

Velna Wright is a stay-at-home mom of two boys. Married, she is a deaconess, a bulletin editor, and is active in her church's cradle roll department, Vacation Bible School, and women's ministries. She enjoys home-schooling her older son, floral arranging, crafts, sewing, and cooking. **May 14, Dec. 20.**

Prayer Requests

_____

_____

_____

_____

_____

_____

_____

_____

_____

_____

_____

Being confident of this very thing, that he which hath begun a good work in you will perform it until the day of Jesus Christ:
—Phil. 1:6.

Prayer Requests

_____

_____

_____

_____

_____

_____

_____

_____

_____

_____

Thou wilt keep him in perfect peace,
whose mind is stayed on thee: because he trusteth in thee.
—Isa. 26:3.

Prayer Requests

_____

_____

_____

_____

_____

_____

_____

_____

_____

_____

Consecrate yourself to God in the morning;
make this your very first work.
—SC 70.

Prayer Requests

_____

_____

_____

_____

_____

_____

_____

_____

_____

_____

Cast thy burden upon the Lord, and he shall sustain thee:
he shall never suffer the righteous to be moved.
—Ps. 55:22.

Prayer Requests

_____

_____

_____

_____

_____

_____

_____

_____

_____

_____

_____

If I take wings of the morning, and dwell in the uttermost parts of the sea;
Even there shall thy hand lead me, and thy right hand shall hold me.
—Ps. 139: 9, 10.

Prayer Requests

_____

_____

_____

_____

_____

_____

_____

_____

_____

_____

Trust in him at all times; ye people, pour out your heart before him:
God is a refuge for us. Selah.
—Ps. 62:8.

Prayer Requests

_____

_____

_____

_____

_____

_____

_____

_____

_____

And be ye kind one to another, tenderhearted, forgiving one another,
even as God for Christ's sake hath forgiven you.
—Eph. 4:32.

Prayer Requests

_____

_____

_____

_____

_____

_____

_____

_____

_____

_____

Let us therefore come boldly unto the throne of grace,
that we may obtain mercy, and find grace to help in time of need.
—Heb. 4:16

Prayer Requests

_____

_____

_____

_____

_____

_____

_____

_____

_____

_____

Delight thyself also in the Lord;
and he shall give thee the desires of thine heart.
—Ps. 37:4

Prayer Requests

_____

_____

_____

_____

_____

_____

_____

_____

_____

Thou wilt shew me the path of life: in thy presence is fulness of joy;
at thy right hand there are pleasures for evermore.
—Ps. 16:11.